Alternative Contact

Alternative Contact
Indigeneity, Globalism, and American Studies

Edited by Paul Lai and Lindsey Claire Smith

The Johns Hopkins University Press, Baltimore

Printed in the United States of America on acid-free paper
9 8 7 6 5 4 3 2 1

The Johns Hopkins University Press
2715 North Charles Street
Baltimore, Maryland 21218-4363
www.press.jhu.edu

ISBN 13: 978-1-4214-0060-0
ISBN 10: 1-4214-0060-X

Library of Congress Control Number: 2010940270

A catalog record for this book is available from the British Library.

These articles were originally published in the September 2010 issue of *American Quarterly.*

Front cover: *Manufactured Savages* (2008). Image and Siapo courtesy of De Young Museum. Digital manipulation by Elizabeth Clare. Back cover: *Vaster Empire* (2007), by Andrea Carlson. Courtesy of the artist.

Contents

Preface

The recent history of *American Quarterly* suggests that the field of American studies is in the midst of being transformed by research in Indigenous studies. Over the last few years the journal has published important work at the intersection of those two fields, including Michael A. Elliot's "Indian Patriots on Last Stand Hill" (58.4), Michelle Raheja's "Reading Nanook's Smile: Visual Sovereignty, Indigenous Revisions of Ethnography, and *Atanarjuat* (*The Fast Runner*)" (59.4), Tiya Miles's " 'Circular Reasoning': Recentering Cherokee Women in the Antiremoval Campaigns" (61.2), Shari M. Huhndorf's "Picture Revolution: Transnationalism, American Studies, and the Politics of Contemporary Native Culture" (61.2), and Matthew Sakiestewa Gilbert's "Hopi Footraces and American Marathons, 1912–1930" (62.1). Particularly significant in this regard is the forum "Native Feminisms without Apology: Native Feminisms Engage American Studies" (60.2), guest edited by J. Kēhaulani Kauanui and Andrea Smith. In their introduction, Kauanui and Smith argue that, because settler colonial states (as well as certain tribal governments) are "built on the logics of heteropatriarchy," an Indigenous feminist project is devoted to articulating "alternative forms of governance beyond the United States in particular, and the nation-state in general" (244–45). The "Native Feminisms" forum was preceded in the issue by Thomas A. Bass's think piece, "Counterinsurgency and Torture," which suggests that the contemporary war on terror is mediated by histories of Indian warfare. In the wake of 9/11, the settler colonial U.S. state remains alive and (un)well, and in such a context scholars in American studies can ignore Indigenous studies only at great intellectual and political peril.

This book, *Alternative Contact: Indigeneity, Globalism, and American Studies*, builds upon and contributes to the Indigenous turn in American studies. More precisely, the following essays help us think about Indigeneity, race, gender, modernity, nation, state power, and globalization in interdisciplinary and broadly comparative global ways. Organized into three thematic sections—"Spaces of the Pacific," " 'Unexpected' Indigenous Modernity," and "Nation and Nation-State"—this volume attempts to shift the analysis of settler colonialism from an exclusive focus on "first contacts" between Europeans and Indigenous peoples in order to clear space for other kinds of critical, comparative narratives about relations among Indigenous peoples and other kinds of colonial subjects, migrants, refugees, and racialized groups. And among other kinds of contact, the contributors to this special issue also imagine alternative connections between Indigenous and American studies.

Producing this ambitious special issue required the work of many hands, starting with the guest editors, Paul Lai and Lindsey Claire Smith. The members of the *AQ* Managing Editorial Board were immediately struck by the power and significance of their vision for the issue, and Paul and Lindsey have helped guide it to a brilliant completion. Additionally, I thank board members who served as readers, including Macarena Gomez-Barris, J. Jack Halberstam, Dylan Rodríguez, John Carlos Rowe, Shelley Streeby, and Clyde Woods. I am particularly grateful to our managing editor, Jeb Middlebrook, for his excellent work on this issue and for the last three years. Thanks are also due to the incoming managing editor, Jih-Fei Cheng, and editorial interns Stacey Moultry and Heather Agnew from California State University, Fullerton. The issue was copyedited with great care and grace by Stacey Lynn, and the striking cover was designed by William Longhauser.

Though currently headquartered at a private university, *American Quarterly* significantly depends upon the labor of California State University and University of California graduate students and professors, many of whom serve on the journal's editorial board. In this current moment of neoliberalization and crisis in public education, it is especially important to recognize this labor.

Curtis Marez
Editor
American Quarterly

Alternative Contact

Introduction

Paul Lai and Lindsey Claire Smith

This volume arose from informal conversations between the coeditors at the New Directions for American Indian Research conferences in 2004 and 2005 at the University of North Carolina in Chapel Hill about our respective fields, Asian American and Native American studies.[1] Even though the two fields are often linked as versions of "ethnic studies" and share connections to 1960s third world decolonization politics and antiwar protests, in our discussions of concepts such as "race," "nation," "America," and "citizenship," we discovered that the guiding assumptions and critical questions of the fields are drastically different; in fact, they often directly contradict each other. For example, while Asian American studies explores how the U.S. racial state has excluded Asians in its immigration policies and withheld citizenship, Native American studies argues for the sovereignty of Indigenous tribes such that they might negotiate with the United States as independent and separate nations. Asian American studies seeks recognition within the United States—even if it is critical of the nation-state as a neoliberal, imperialist entity—while Native American studies attempts to establish more self-determination for Native Americans in distancing them from U.S. rule and the U.S. settler state. What is social justice for one group is sometimes diametrically opposed to the justice sought by the other. Though such characterizations are necessarily broad generalizations, we contend that thinking across the boundaries of our fields clarifies the stakes of a more critical ethnic studies enterprise that challenges the feel-good liberal multiculturalism suffusing popular discourses of ethnic and cultural difference. In turn, such thinking and theorizing can only infuse activist and political work with more sophisticated understandings of our contemporary world.

Curious about these contradictions as well as resonances in our fields, we organized a series of panels at conferences for the Association for Asian American Studies in New York City in 2007 and the American Studies Association in Albuquerque, New Mexico, in 2008. Drawing together scholars from several areas, our panels emphasized "alternative contact"—contact apart from narratives of "first contact" between Native Americans and Europeans (including

Euro-Americans)—among Indigenous Americans and other populations in the United States and around the world. Additionally, we sought presentations that explored current theoretical trends in American studies, such as transnational flows and regionalisms in the context of Indigenous peoples and ideas. Our sense from our participation in these intellectual forums was that new and unconventional work, which unsettles more traditional approaches to American, ethnic, Indigenous, and postcolonial studies, was already well under way.[2] The preceding recapitulation of the intellectual journey that has led to this collection of essays in this journal also demonstrates the collaborative work that we believe is crucial to all scholarly endeavors, but especially to the kind of cross-field project envisioned in "alternative contact."

This book emerges out of our desire to provide further space for the generative possibilities of cross-disciplinary and cross-national discussion of Indigeneity.[3] Within the intellectual space created here, these essays challenge our various fields to approach research concerning the Americas in promising new ways that highlight historical and contemporary exchanges between Indigenous peoples and others. Such research offers alternative theorizations of links among U.S. imperial projects, sovereignty, and racial formation that supplement and challenge recent American studies work on imperialism, globalization, and hemispheric frameworks. It also expands on work in Indigenous studies that has both centered and cautioned against discourses of postcolonialism, hybridity, and tribal nationalisms. By taking up these strands of thought, the essays push against the idea that Indigenous peoples of North America and the Pacific are invested only in concerns of their lands while remaining blind to connections with Indigenous peoples of other continents and the struggles of migrant and minority communities more broadly. This research puts Indigenous peoples in the role of active, mobile, and even cosmopolitan actors on the world stage in ways that complicate static or incomplete definitions of Indigenous identity. Whereas much recent work has focused on problematizing essentialisms through discourses of mixed blood, the alternative contact discussed here foregrounds encounters as discrete sites of critical exchange that raise questions of ethical relations.[4] The rest of this introductory essay traces some of the critical thought underlying our interest in Indigeneity and contact, offers a case study of Arizona's recent anti-immigration law to show how this project might spur new insights into contemporary politics, draws a genealogy of theoretical concerns in Indigenous studies up to this moment, and ends with an overview of the essays in the volume.

Indigeneity and Alternative Contact

Although our interest is in setting aside discussions of Indigenous contact with mainstream white America, we are not suggesting that an analysis of the United States as a settler state is unimportant. Philip J. Deloria argues in *Indians in Unexpected Places* that Indians have long functioned as foils for narratives of white American progress and modernity, and to see Indians engaged in the trappings of modern civilization (such as in photographs of Geronimo sitting in a Cadillac) is jarring and unexpected in a way that points to alternative histories of Indians and modernity.[5] Similarly, we suggest that encouraging ourselves to see Indians in contact with other non-Euro-Americans, to bracket for a moment the world-shattering consequences of "first contact," provides an unexpected quality that might shake loose new possibilities for critical, interpretive, and activist interventions. These moments of alternative contact might then be turned back to deconstruct anew those narratives of first contact.

We might also argue that grappling with the United States as an entity and an idea is inevitable. In considering the reach of U.S. imperialism, we draw from postcolonial theorist Dipesh Chakrabarty's discussion of "provincializing Europe." Chakrabarty writes, "European thought is at once both indispensable and inadequate in helping us think through the experiences of political modernity in non-Western nations, and provincializing Europe becomes the task of exploring how this thought—which is now everybody's heritage and which affect us all—may be renewed from and for the margins."[6] That is, in this project, Indigenous peoples and nations in the Americas are irrevocably enmeshed within discourses of American modernity and civilization. The task is not to reject American modernity wholesale but to explore how American thought, full of contradictions and ambivalences, structures the very means of arguing for sovereignty and Indigenous self-determination. And it is to recognize that Indigenous thought is an important, distinctive, and viable force that ultimately exceeds American modernity's attempts to tame it. The act of provincializing America historicizes the terms and values of American modernity, wresting it from universalist claims of freedom, progress, and civilization. Furthermore, by decentering Indigenous contact with Anglo-America, this volume searches for that renewal of thought "from and for the margins" of Indigenous spaces.

Even with an acknowledgment of such overwhelming American influence, it is possible and in fact necessary to dismantle notions of an all-powerful United States in Indigenous struggles. In her essay "American Studies without America:

Native Feminisms and the Nation-State," Andrea Smith challenges ethnic studies and feminist scholars to think of the United States as something other than a given, unchangeable entity in order to create a model of sovereignty that is not predicated on genocide and exploitation: "Native women activists have begun articulating spiritually based visions of nation and sovereignty that are separate from nation-states. Whereas nation-states are governed through domination and coercion, indigenous sovereignty and nationhood are predicated on interrelatedness and responsibility. In opposition to nation-states, which are based on control over territory, these visions of indigenous nationhood are based on care and responsibility for land that all can share."[7] By disarticulating nations from nation-states, she emphasizes the possibility of Indigenous liberation struggles that do not seek the establishment of a "statelike form of governance."[8] In searching for a different form of nationhood, such activists refuse the logic that liberal democracies and their settler-states are the pinnacles of modern governments and societies.

In another vein, Kevin Bruyneel argues that the multipronged and self-contradictory ways in which the U.S. government has related to Indians over the centuries necessitates a response that is flexible enough to confront such relations: "A postcolonial politics on the boundaries generates its power by moving back and forth across the institutional and discursive boundaries of settler-states. This is done by challenging colonial impositions and provoking colonial ambivalence to open up discursive and institutional space in the settler-society's political system through which claims for indigenous liberation can be expressed and gain a clearer hearing."[9] His interest in American boundaries in time and space is geared toward revealing the fissures in a system of U.S. colonial domination. This system changes its relationship to Indigenous nations whenever necessary to maintain control. By exploiting gaps in the ambivalence of colonialism, Indigenous nations can carve out a "third space of sovereignty" that refuses the binary logic of "domestic dependent nations."[10] It is this reaching for multiple forms of sovereignty that lie outside yet engage with the politics of the United States that ultimately enables self-determination.

The spaces of comparative Indigeneity, especially evident in this volume's cluster of articles on Indigenous Pacific Islander encounters, offer different sites of cultural and political exchange and make visible other moments of contact that highlight opportunities for activism. In this regard, both Gloria Anzaldúa's transformative conception of "borderlands" and Mary Louise Pratt's influential phrase "contact zones" help to emphasize how contact occurs in particular sites that accrue histories of cultural negotiation. As Anzaldúa demonstrates, too, these borderlands need not be limited to geographical spaces; they also characterize the subjectivity of and relations between groups of people.[11] Pratt writes of contact zones, "I use this term to refer to social spaces where cultures meet, clash, and grapple with each other, often in contexts of highly asymmetrical relations of power, such as colonialism, slavery, or their aftermaths as they are lived out in many parts of the world today."[12] The alternative contact sought in the essays of this volume highlights such borderlands and contact zones with particular attention to the "asymmetrical relations of power" in them. They offer a way to sidestep the "spectres of comparison" that often haunt Indigenous knowledge, replacing Euro-American modernity with other modernities that might open up radical decolonial strategies rather than relegate Indigenous peoples to the not-quite-modern.[13]

The work of Stuart Hall is useful for analyzing the historicity and specificity of particular political issues. Hall develops Antonio Gramsci's thoughts on hegemony, arguing for the importance of exploring "conjunctures," discrete moments in culture and politics that are always contingent and shifting. In these conjunctures, the critical questions we ask take on meanings that may change in other moments. He writes of such questions, "They have their historical specificity; and although they always exhibit similarities and continuities with the other moments in which we pose a question like this, they are never the same moment. And the combination of what is similar and what is different defines not only the specificity of the moment, but the specificity of the question, and therefore the strategies of cultural politics with which we attempt to intervene in popular culture, and the form and style of cultural theory and criticizing that has to go along with such an intermatch."[14] These moments are dependent upon a number of historical, social, economic, and political forces that create hegemonic truth or common sense. This focus on conjunctures allows Hall to open up each issue and moment to possibilities that may initially seem irrelevant or impossible. The question posed by this volume—what insights might we gain in exploring Indigenous contact with other people and places outside the dominant narrative of first contact with Europeans?—thus arises in a unique conjuncture of world history and academic study that each essay addresses through concrete examples of contact. The historical conjunctures that each essay examines, in turn, define distinct problematics for the study of Indigeneity, nation, and imperialism by way of contemporaneous connections among different peoples.

Our interest in contact and conjunctural analysis calls for conversations and dialogue between fields of study. Following the example of *Fresh Talk / Daring Gazes*, a volume of short essays on Asian American artists by artists from different backgrounds, we hope others will open up spaces where cross-field conversations occur.[15] In that volume, Flathead Indian artist Jaune Quick-to-See Smith reflects on Japanese American painter Roger Shimomura's work on Asian dislocation in the Midwest, for instance, and Diné-Seminole-Muscogee photographer Hulleah J. Tsinhnahjinnie examines Vietnamese American artist Hanh Thi Pham's work on refugee and expatriate experiences. Margo Machida explains in the preface of these "new lines of communication and cross-identification": "It provides the grounds for direct engagement with members of other groups in acts of meaning-making, and thus extends the discourse arising from contemporary Asian American experience to broader publics."[16] This thinking across racial identities and histories of American presence generates novel commentary on issues of assimilation, resistance, and aesthetics. Such interactions encourage scholars, artists, and activists to think more concertedly about their methodological and political investments. Additionally, foregrounding Indigeneity and Indigenous peoples within and across other ethnic, cultural, and American studies fields returns us to the centrality yet invisibility of Native histories and bodies to all studies of the Americas. The continual disappearing of the Indigenous, even in fields that are critical of U.S. hegemony, suggests the incompleteness of many anti-imperialist and antiracist accounts of the United States.

Arizona's Anti-Immigration Law and Alternative Contact

The critical purchase of this project might be demonstrated by considering a contemporary political issue. In addressing discourses of immigration rights and laws differently, "alternative contact" shifts the problematics of the issue at hand, which is about the presence of non-Anglo peoples in the Southwest and the question of belonging for different groups in the region. Rather than acceding to the logic that nonwhite means "immigrant" and "alien" (to the U.S. nation-state), Indigenous perspectives upend these binaries of citizen and alien but also suggest the power and possibility of coalitions between Indigenous and Mexican groups.

On April 23, 2010, Governor Jan Brewer of Arizona signed into state law Senate Bill 1070, reauthorizing local and state officials not only to act on behalf of the federal Department of Homeland Security in detaining suspected "illegal immigrants" but to declare in no uncertain language that such detention is necessary and must be pursued even in the absence of suspected major criminal activity.[17] As reported in the *New York Times*, "the law would require the police 'when practicable' to detain people they reasonably suspected were in the country without authorization. It would also allow the police to charge immigrants with a state crime for not carrying immigration documents. And it allows residents to sue cities if they believe the law is not being enforced."[18] This state legislation reinstates some federal policies that President Barack Obama's administration had scaled back in 2009. That earlier change was spurred precisely by concerns that the existing federal immigration-policing program had led local officials to overzealous questioning of people about their immigration status, regardless of suspected serious criminal activity. The Arizona legislature, in refusing this change, authorizes racial profiling, enabling the continued persecutions of people who purportedly look like immigrants. As in federal immigration policies, this law creates a state of immigrant paranoia, erases distinctions between different levels of law enforcement, and transforms every local and state officer into "La Migra," with an added charge to actively ferret out "illegal immigrants."

News of this legislation hit the national scene even before Brewer signed it, and many public figures voiced disagreement with and concerns about the bill's enshrining of racial profiling in the law. Obama spoke out against the law before it was signed, and afterward, he commented on the bill in a joint statement he issued with President Felipe Calderón of Mexico about U.S.-Mexico relations. Though the statement primarily emphasized the presidents' views on trade and labor issues between the two countries, Obama noted of S.B. 1070: "We also discussed the new law in Arizona, which is a misdirected effort—a misdirected expression of frustration over our broken immigration system, and which has raised concerns in both our countries." His response to these immigration debates is to recognize that there are problems in the existing system and, rather generously, to suggest that S.B. 1070 is a good-faith effort at dealing with undocumented migration. His comments also reveal that his administration and the Department of Justice are examining the law to see if it violates any civil rights protections. But, ultimately, his attempts were to appease those Americans afraid of hordes of "illegal immigrants" when he declared, "Today, I want every American to know my administration has devoted unprecedented resources in personnel and technology to securing our border."[19] Obama's administration, though supportive of programs that put undocumented migrants on the path to legal immigrant status, therefore reinforces a need to police the border and people who might cross it without federal authorization. In fact, a week after this joint statement, Obama promised an increase in the National Guard presence at the Texas border with Mexico to deal with drug trafficking violence.[20]

In the joint statement, President Calderón more directly addressed the stakes of anti-immigration legislation: "In Mexico, we are and will continue being respectful of the internal policies of the United States and its legitimate right to establish in accordance to its Constitution whatever laws it approves. But we will retain our firm rejection to criminalize migration so that people that work and provide things to this nation will be treated as criminals. And we oppose firmly the S.B. 1070 Arizona law given in fair principles that are partial and discriminatory."[21] Careful to reinforce U.S. sovereignty, Calderón nevertheless underscores how S.B. 1070 effectively casts all migrants as suspected criminals by virtue of their movement across borders and calls for a "firm rejection [objection] to criminalize migration." Unlike Obama's comments that call for more impermeable borders, Calderón's insistence that this law criminalizes migration suggests the need to understand and accept the permeable nature of national borders. Both presidents ultimately condemned the way the bill casts suspicion of criminality on all "Mexican-looking" people and effectively authorizes racial profiling by law enforcement officers.

Following the passage of S.B. 1070, a number of municipalities, states, and civil organizations began calling for boycotts of Arizona.[22] For example, issuing an order to prohibit city employees from traveling to Arizona, Mayor Chris Coleman of St. Paul, Minnesota, noted, "It would be immoral to not stand up in the face of a piece of legislation that is rooted in hate and fear. We are a country of immigrants—and S.B. 1070 is an affront to our Constitution and the values we hold dear as Americans."[23] The Los Angeles County Board of Supervisors approved a motion, 3–2, to boycott the state, noting that the bill "simply goes too far and should be strongly condemned and universally rejected. It sends a strong message to all immigrants to avoid contact with any law enforcement officer, aggressively discouraging witnesses and victims from reporting crimes, and making the entire community less safe."[24] The National Council of La Raza, in coalition with worker unions and other racial justice groups, declared explicitly: "The rhetoric of hate groups, nativists, and vigilantes—once limited to the fringe of American politics—has gained a strong foothold in the public debate. Their policy positions frame the country's political discourse, and their members have penetrated the mainstream media. In short, extremists are defining the debate on immigration, and the portrayal of Hispanic Americans, at every level."[25] The range of voices calling for a boycott of Arizona touches on differing aspects of the anti-immigration legislation; Chicano advocacy groups, labor unions, and Asian American organizations, for example, decry the discriminatory legislation for reasons such as state-sponsored racism, workers' rights, and immigration reform (which are not mutually exclusive). Most of the proclamations emphasize that the bill violates the civil rights guaranteed by the Constitution and that the undefined "reasonable suspicion" the bill references as justification for asking persons for documentation leads to racial profiling. Despite much public outcry against the immigration law, the news media report that a majority of Americans support more stringent immigration laws of this kind.[26] Furthermore, Arizona's example has spurred other states to consider immigration legislation, pointing to a shift in balance between state and federal government control over immigration.[27]

The language of the bill importantly constructs not just undocumented persons but all suspects as subjects requiring proof of identification and legal residence. Section 2 of S.B. 1070 states, "A person is presumed to not be an alien who is unlawfully present in the United States if the person provides to the law enforcement officer or agency any of the following: 1. A valid Arizona driver license. 2. A valid Arizona nonoperating identification license. 3. A valid tribal enrollment card or other form of tribal identification. 4. If the entity requires proof of legal presence in the United States before issuance, any valid United States federal, state or local government issued identification."[28] The odd wording of the first sentence refuses full citizenship status even to those who have the requisite papers. The negative construction of the subject allows persons to be only either the suspected "illegal" or not. There is no possibility of being lawfully present or anything but an "alien" to the nation.

The anti-immigrant sentiments of the bill specifically target Mexican peoples, and Chicano organizations, along with many other groups, have rallied to protest the law. Because the law makes it a crime for immigrants to go about in public without immigration documents, it effectively remakes all people who appear to be Mexican into potential criminals. Such a policy, of course, denies the history of a Chicano borderlands that spans the current U.S.-Mexico border. Mexican and Mexican American peoples have long lived in and around the geographical region of Arizona, with families reaching back earlier than the incorporation of the state. These families have not always moved; instead, the borders of the Spanish Empire, then the Mexican Republic, followed by the independent Republic of Texas further east, and finally the United States proper have shifted in ways that designate them as denizens of a succession of different nations. S.B. 1070 refuses to acknowledge the prior residence of these peoples, instead insisting that they raise "reasonable suspicion" that they are "illegal aliens." A clearer example of Althusserian interpellation is hardly possible, with the hailing of a whole range of people into the category of possible "illegals" who must demonstrate with identification papers that they are *not* who they appear to be. In this context, as Mexicans and Mexican Americans are cast out of the American body politic, any histories and cultures they might share with the Indigenous peoples of Arizona are also made invisible and irrelevant to the issue of belonging. This strategic separation of the two groups is especially disingenuous since Mexicans have long understood their identities as mestizos—mixed-race Spanish/European and Indigenous Americans. The law inadvertently reminds us that the border is a fiction that divides people with shared histories more than it divides distinct groups of people from each other.

Up to this point, we have looked at the discussion about S.B. 1070 in the terms that most news sources use. The bill is about immigration and racialization; it is about violations of the U.S. Constitution's guarantees of civil rights. Yet, given the bill's a priori assumption that all suspects are already outside the realm of the proper U.S. citizen, we might ask what else is at stake in this moment besides the intrusion on the privacy and civil rights of Arizona residents. For example, which persons residing in the region fall under the reach of the U.S. nation-state and are beholden to its laws in the first place? What sense is there in the label of "illegals" and what ways can we imagine undocumented persons otherwise? Which peoples have sovereignty over the lands of the area? What role do Indigenous peoples of the region play in this move to exclude particular outsiders? How might Chicanos and American Indians in the region learn from each others' experiences of racialization to jointly contest the law's force? Opponents of S.B. 1070 who decry the law on the grounds that it justifies uneven treatment of nonwhite persons do not necessarily question the legitimacy of the United States or of the state of Arizona in asserting laws in the first place. The claim to equality under the eyes of the law implicitly endorses the legitimacy of the government, even as it acknowledges the contradictions of the racial state. Discourses of sovereignty help open up this relationship to U.S. governance, questioning the way that the government does or can assert control.

Indigenous perspectives on nationhood and sovereignty, in addition to civil rights claims, undermine the bill's attempts to cast the suspicion of alien status on people who "look Indigenous" rather than white. Ironically, the bill itself ruptures an anti-immigration perspective's binary logic of citizen-alien, the expectation that every person is either a legal resident of the United States or a foreigner. Returning to the language of the bill, we note that one of the documents that serve as proof that one is "not . . . an alien who is unlawfully present" is a "valid tribal enrollment card or other form of tribal identification." This statement marks the different status that Indigenous peoples residing within the boundaries of Arizona have to local, state, and federal governments. Within the logic of the bill, Indians are neither U.S. citizens nor aliens, regardless of actual U.S. citizenship status, but they also disrupt a sense of homogenous white American identity since they reside within the geographical boundaries of the United States. Yet S.B. 1070 effectively likens Indians to Mexican immigrants; both are persons who are suspect, assumed not to belong lawfully to the area by virtue of their appearance and speech. Indigenous persons might cause "reasonable suspicion" that they are in the United States illegally. This site of alternative contact between Indians and Mexicans, then, suggests different strategies for dismantling the xenophobic logic of the bill. The bill's conflation of Indians and Mexicans reminds us of Mexican-mestizo identifications with Indigenous pasts and the fact that Mexicans are much more like American Indians in their long-standing presence in the region than they are the more recent Anglo-American settlers.

Recognizing the impact S.B. 1070 will have on Indigenous people, the twenty Indigenous tribes of the Inter Tribal Council of Arizona voiced their official opposition to the new law. Despite living on their own lands under their own system of governance, these Indigenous peoples are subject to this Arizona law that enjoins all persons to carry official identification at all times in order to prove legal residence. The Tohono O'odham Nation, in particular, issued a press release opposing the new immigration law.[29] The O'odham Nation's lands cross the U.S.-Mexico border, and their attempts to assert homelands on both sides of that border resonate with Mexican and Mexican American families who do the same. Yet their legislative council's statement opposing the bill notes that "the Tohono O'odham Nation has been actively concerned with the negative impacts from illegal immigration and drug trafficking across the international border, including damage to the Nation's cultural resources, increased demands on tribal law enforcement, violence and crime, illegal dumping, and environmental degradation."[30] The O'odham Nation has long patrolled the seventy-five-mile U.S.-Mexico border within its lands in the interests of the United States and themselves. Their acceptance of the militarization of the border stems in part from a perception that criminals constantly lie in wait on the Mexican side of the border to enter the United States. Ironically, the O'odham council reinforces the U.S.-Mexico border as a strategy of aligning themselves on the side of the "legal" residents of Arizona. Here, then, is a missed opportunity for identification with others who are native to the region, but it is also important to remember the relative lack of sovereign power that the O'odham council wields in the face of U.S. and Arizona power.

What the O'odham Nation opposes in the bill is the reach of Arizona law enforcement into the lives and lands of its people. In their statement, they note that "S.B. 1070 provides that a tribal member who can show a tribal enrollment card or other tribal identification will be 'presumed' not to be an illegal alien, but the Nation opposes any state law requirement that members carry proof, under threat of arrest, that they are lawfully present within their aboriginal homelands."[31] The O'odham point out the absurdity of Indigenous peoples having to prove to an outside government that they belong in their own lands. They also pick up on the language of the bill that allows for only two kinds of suspicious persons—"illegals" or those "presumed" not to be "illegal aliens." The implication is that O'odham people will fall into that category of suspicious persons and thus be required to prove their tribal enrollment.

The O'odham Nation's council thus presents some moments of connection with, as well as disjuncture from, the plight of Mexican and Mexican American people under this law. Perhaps more interestingly, though, is the way some O'odham youth have mobilized their Indigenous identity and presence to combat the anti-immigration law and to claim stronger connections with migrant communities. Following passage of the bill, the O'odham Solidarity Across Borders Collective tirelessly organized protests and occupation of border patrol headquarters.[32] The collective of O'odham youth strives for self-determination and sovereignty as well as the right to live in their traditional way of life. Their press releases about their protest actions enumerate their demands that "the Border Patrol (BP), Immigration Customs Enforcement (ICE), their parent entity, the Department of Homeland Security (DHS), and the Obama administration end militarization of the border, end the criminalization of immigrant communities, and end their campaign of terror which tear families apart through increasing numbers of raids and deportations."[33]

In their analysis of S.B. 1070 and Arizona's broad claims to police the U.S.-Mexico border, the collective notes, "The state's power to waive pre-existing laws (such as NEPA, NAGPRA) in the name of security, directly attacks Indigenous autonomy/sovereignty. The 'political' solution will bring forced removal and relocation of the many Indigenous nations that span 'their' borders by means of a reinforced physical barrier."[34] Dissatisfied with the rhetoric of the security state, the collective instead puts "Indigenous autonomy/sovereignty" at the center of its concerns rather than an expectation that the United States government will act disinterestedly to protect Indigenous people's lands and civil rights. They reference the way that laws purportedly offering Indigenous people some federal and state protection from American intrusion are often cast aside when they get in the way of security concerns. These concerns, in turn, are driven primarily by the needs of transnational corporations rather than what is best for the environment or for Indigenous people's self-determination.

Finally, the passage and signing into law of S.B. 1070 has also affected Indigenous studies organizations and scholars. For example, the newly formed

O'odham Solidarity Across Borders Collective standing in solidarity with Migrant communities against SB1070 outside of AZ State Capitol. Courtesy of OSABC.

Native American and Indigenous Studies Association (NAISA) had planned to hold its fourth annual conference in Tucson, Arizona, May 20–22, 2010. On the eve of Governor Brewer's signing of the bill, NAISA member Margo Tamez posted a blog entry on the organization's Web site about Arizona congressman Raul Grijalva's call for a boycott of the state until the repeal of S.B. 1070. Identifying Congressman Grijalva as a Mexican American with origins in Sonora, the Mexican state bordering Arizona, Tamez then proceeded to call on NAISA leaders and members to turn their attention to this issue: "I sincerely wish to see the elected leaders of NAISA and the membership examine the unfolding events in Arizona, with ripples across the U.S-Mexico borderlands . . . NAISA's role in speaking directly to the centrality of white supremacy and specifically—anti-Indigenous—in Arizona's turn to a brutal site of human rights violations begs for a serious NAISA engagement."[35] By pitching the law as something other than an immigration bill—instead as an instantiation of white supremacy and anti-Indigenous policy—Tamez argued that Mexican and Mexican American issues have resonance for all Indigenous peoples. Indeed, Mexicans are Indigenous peoples of the Americas, and the fact that they are treated differently from American Indians within the United States yet perceived (visually seen) as similar should guide us to examine the contradictory logics of U.S. immigration laws and relations with Indian tribes. It is worth noting, however, that Indigenous groups within Mexico also form autonomous communities that are differentiated from the mestizo population, and these groups in turn maintain contested relations to and within the Mexican nation-state. The discourse of mestizo Indigenismo, in fact, often erases this other Indigenous presence and politics.[36]

Over the next month, NAISA leadership and members engaged in fervent debate about the response the organization should take, both publicly, on the organization's blog site and other Indigenous studies online spaces, as well as privately, through e-mails and in-person conversations. Many called for a boycott of the state and thus absence from the conference. Others suggested that the conference presentations and forums should be transformed into venues to develop political actions to protest the bill. The NAISA council drafted and sent a letter of protest to Governor Brewer, stating, "in response to your actions the NAISA council is working toward using our upcoming meeting as a forum for addressing how we as an organization and as individuals of conscience can bear witness against the racial profiling you are now set to unleash."[37] The NAISA council decided to move forward with the conference as an organization, noting that an economic boycott would be ineffective at such an early date—the bill not taking effect for three more months—and that using the conference space as protest against the bill might create more of an impact with the concentration of Native bodies and radical Indigenous perspectives.[38] This decision generated heated debate in the comments of various posts, leading the council to post a follow-up statement detailing the council's decision-making process and plans for the conference. The statement noted that NAISA as a young organization would not survive financially if it pulled out of its contract with the conference hotel.[39] This point about the financial factors in staging a boycott would become a sore point for many members.

The Southern California Native Feminist Reading Group posted an open letter to the NAISA council, acknowledging the importance of continuing with the conference while calling for more concrete options to make the event felt, economically and politically, as a protest of the bill.[40] The Native Feminist Reading Group noted that NAISA's suggestions to transform the conference into protest were all insular actions, geared to the participants of the conference, who were understood, by and large, to be opposed to the bill already. Subsequently and in concert with the O'odham Solidarity Across Borders Collective, Mishuana Goeman of the Native Feminist Reading Group issued an announcement of a planned protest at the Tucson Immigration Court on Friday, May 21, during the conference proceedings.[41] Many individual NAISA members weighed in to state their own intentions—to attend the conference or not, and to do so either as protest against the bill or to NAISA's stance on the issue. The NAISA council decision not to join the boycott called for by Congressman Grijalva and many other civil rights organizations touched a nerve among Indigenous academics, with many decrying the leadership of the organization as sell-outs and as unresponsive to the will and concerns of the members at large. If nothing else, S.B. 1070 has mobilized NAISA leadership and members to engage in conversations about the nature of activism, scholarship, and ethical relationships to Indigenous and other peoples.

Just a week after signing S.B. 1070, Governor Brewer also signed House Bill 2281, legislation that bans ethnic studies in the state's primary and secondary level public schools. The bill calls for elimination of any programs that "promote the overthrow of the United States government. 2. Promote resentment towards a race or class of people. 3. Are designed primarily for pupils of a particular ethnic group. 4. Advocate ethnic solidarity instead of the treatment of pupils as individuals."[42] As with the anti-immigration law, though the language of the legislation never explicitly names Mexicans and Mexican Americans, the bill targets education for and about them. The call to treat "pupils as individuals" over and above "ethnic solidarity" aligns the bill with the language of American individualism and color-blind ideology that refuses to acknowledge the complexities of racial differences.

Curiously, the bill specifically mentions caveats to the prohibited curricula; courses prescribed by federal law to cater to Native American pupils must be respected, as must teaching about the Holocaust.[43] Here, it would be worth pushing on this reference to the peculiar relationship between Native Americans and the United States. Tracing the long history of assimilationist programs and institutions that have attempted to stamp out Indigenous identity could shed light on the way this bill hopes to eliminate the distinctiveness of Mexican peoples and cultures. The troubled history of Indian boarding schools, in particular, might explain why federal law specifies that particular classes be geared toward Native American pupils' needs at all. Noting this moment of contact between Indigenous peoples across several national boundaries by way of their shared yet differently manifested subjugation under Anglo-American rule makes clear the need for alternative methodologies that account for these conditions.

We offer an analysis of the Arizona bills here as a case study of alternative contact, a moment in which—in one critical conjuncture—multiple complications emerge and explode an assumed colonial-colonized binary. As is the case in each of the situations that the authors of this collection describe, the two bills link overlapping communities in debate about the implications of such concerns as sovereignty, racial and national identities, and the potential for activism. By including Indigenous peoples among those who may be assumed to be "illegal" and by requiring them to produce documentation to U.S. authorities within their very homelands, S.B. 1070 enshrines suspicion of Native peoples. However, the unexpected presence of Indigenous people in the immigration bill disrupts the binary national terms (U.S.-Mexico) that usually erase Indigenous concerns and alliances.

Our analysis pushes against how the bill makes invisible the kinship of Indigenous peoples of the Americas across nation-state borders and how it relegates brown peoples to one of only two possible categories: "Mexican immigrant" or "U.S. Citizen" (with a caveat for legal but suspicious American Indian tribal citizens). We also suggest that the complete absence of Indigenous peoples of Mexico and Central America in these discussions of U.S.-Mexico migration is a problem that our project seeks to uncover. Finally, H.B. 2281 shows, in its explicit concern with school curricula and in its role in initiating conflict among academics, that our work as scholars and teachers has important stakes. It is our hope that with this special issue's release, more light will have been shed on these bills and the ideologies underlying them, and that opportunities for coalition that the current terms of this debate make unimaginable will have been realized.

Theoretical Currents in Indigenous Studies

Each essay here reconsiders the usefulness of terms associated with theoretical movements that are in conversation with and within Indigenous studies. The authors' efforts to offer specific explanations of words such as "Indigenous," "sovereignty," "nation," "nation-state," "transnational," "globalism," "diaspora," "comparative indigeneity," and "citizenship" indicate the slippage inherent in discussing difference from discourses historically centered on U.S. and European imperial projects with academic language constructed around those very discourses. Indeed, it seems that our respective conversations about these concepts have at times employed them almost interchangeably without having thought through their theoretical implications. Our title for the collection is suggestive rather than prescriptive, crafted to provoke critique, when necessary, of the above concepts. The care with which several of the authors in conversation here, such as Judy Rohrer and Hokulani K. Aikau, employ alternative, more culturally appropriate words for framing their scholarship is testament to their commitment to constructing sound and consistent theoretical positions.

Our emphasis on Indigeneity as an organizing focus of this issue connotes intellectual engagement with Indigenous peoples' experiences, including active resistance to empire, in multiple sites. It is important to note, however, that Indigeneity as a concept has involved continual renegotiation and has served varying, sometimes contradictory purposes. As Jeff Corntassel explains in his "Who Is Indigenous? 'Peoplehood' and Ethnonationalist Approaches to Rearticulating Indigenous Identity," appropriate application of the term must strike a balance between the rights of peoples for self-identification and the demands of international law.[44] In this collection, James H. Cox points toward these shifting linguistic dynamics by placing Todd Downing's detective novels within the framework of Mexican *indigenismo*, exposing ways in which Indigeneity has at times been appropriated to legitimate imperialism. And as JoAnna Poblete-Cross explains, Indigeneity has been invoked within anti-immigrant rhetoric, which, in her estimation, colludes with imperial purposes. Our sense of "alternative contact," therefore, recognizes that colonizer and colonized are not locked into an easy binary. Those who are active in Native American studies are already familiar with ways in which Indigenous identity is continually contested, with practical implications that become apparent in such recent conflicts as the Cherokee Freedmen controversy.[45] The scholarship presented here makes clear that these conflicts involve not only identity or racial politics but also have real legal, political, and economic implications, especially because of the importance of land to Indigenous sovereignty.

The important connection between Indigenous peoples and particular geographical locations is perhaps, more than any other factor, the reason for the uneasy fit of Indigenous studies with ethnic studies. As Chadwick Allen discusses in his *Blood Narrative: Indigenous Identity in American Indian and Maori Literary and Activist Texts*, a simple definition of Indigeneity as "original inhabitants" is inadequate for addressing particular historical and geographical circumstances that have led Indigenous peoples to differing positions with regard to one another and to colonial presences.[46] Alice Te Punga Somerville's discussion of Maori disidentification with American Indians reveals this inadequacy, pointing out the distinct histories that question the appropriateness of Indigeneity as a universal or global concept. Allen opts for the more specific term "Fourth World" to reference Indigenous minority peoples who "have been forced to compete for *indigenous* status with European settlers and their descendents eager to construct new identities that separate them from European antecedents."[47] Fourth World peoples, Allen continues, continually and collectively struggle for land, resources, languages, and cultures. Drawing on N. Scott Momaday's concept of "blood memory," Allen outlines a blood/land/memory complex, which "articulates acts of indigenous minority recuperation that attempt to seize control of the symbolic and metaphorical meanings of indigenous 'blood,' 'land,' and 'memory' and that seek to liberate indigenous minority identities from definitions of authenticity imposed by dominant settler cultures, including those definitions imposed by well-meaning academics."[48] The term "Fourth World," then, is political rather than simply descriptive.

Connecting Indigenous criticism with its necessary political ramifications has been central to the work of Indigenous nationalists, who over the past decade or so have called for theorists and critics of Native American literature to develop nation-centered approaches that further draw together historical, theoretical, and activist endeavors around the aim of political autonomy. Author and scholar Elizabeth Cook-Lynn laid much of the groundwork for this movement. In her fiction, poetry, and scholarly writings, especially her essays "The American Indian Fiction Writers: Cosmopolitanism, Nationalism, the Third World, and First Nation Sovereignty" and "American Indian Intellectualism and the New Indian Story," Cook-Lynn promotes Native writing that is ethical and responsible to Native communities, particularly in the issue of land redress.[49] Craig Womack takes up this call in his book *Red on Red: Native American Literary Separatism*, in which he argues for more attention in literature and criticism to tribally specific concerns, links literary sovereignty to the political realities of Native nations, and emphasizes Native-authored literary and critical texts grounded in Indigenous geographies.[50]

Womack builds on this material with his *American Indian Literary Nationalism*, coedited with Robert Warrior, who advocates for a historically and politically developed Native American intellectual sovereignty in his *Tribal Secrets* and *The People and the Word*, and Jace Weaver, who emphasizes "communitism" within a religious studies approach to Native literature in *That the People Might Live*. Womack, Warrior, and Weaver's volume continues the writers' efforts to assert the importance of political, historical, and social realities to Native American literature and criticism.[51] The collaboratively authored *Reasoning Together: The Native Critics Collective*, introduced with Womack's extended critique of theoretical texts in Native studies thus far, puts into practice this nationalist, communitarian model through essays that engage in dialogue with one another about an ethical Native literary criticism.[52] The theoretical model that these scholars offer has done much to draw attention to authors and poets who have been neglected in academia and who predate the much-heralded Native American Renaissance of the 1960s and 1970s.

This nationalistic approach also has its critics. In her book *Mapping the Americas*, Shari M. Huhndorf explains that Indigenous literary texts since the 1980s shift away from a nationalist orientation and toward a transnational perspective.[53] This more contemporary literature similarly addresses landownership and political control but framed in relationship to global flows of capital and empire, including alliances among tribes to resist these colonial forces. While pointing out postcolonial scholars' lack of attention to Indigenous studies, Huhndorf also offers the following critique of nationalism: "Although nationalism is an essential anticolonial strategy in indigenous settings, nationalist scholarship neglects the historical forces (such as imperialism) that increasingly draw indigenous communities into global contexts. The concern of nationalism with cultural and political restoration deflects questions about the economic, environmental, and social changes that ongoing colonization has brought to Native America."[54] Additionally, she suggests that nationalist literature has done little to counteract the patriarchal legacies of colonialism. She asserts, "Nationalist critics have devoted little attention to writing by Native women, especially those works that attend to issues of gender . . . The ways in which colonization has positioned indigenous women demand a feminist rethinking of Native politics and culture, a task to which nationalism is incomplete."[55] Huhndorf's work has influenced almost all of the essays included in this volume; yet, perhaps mediating between nationalist approaches and Huhndorf's critique, authors such as Andrea Smith and Molly Geidel have offered revised and/or expansive articulations of Indigenous nationalism, crafting a decolonial strategy that readily addresses the need to overcome gender strictures and more fully recognizes the roles class and labor have played in imperialism.

The transnational approach Huhndorf offers connects more with postcolonial studies than a nationalist paradigm does, particularly in its attention to cross-nationalist movements and its Marxist critique of capitalist imperialism. It is not surprising, however, that transnational Indigenous theory is uneasily allied with postcolonial theory, a mismatch of sorts that Chadwick Allen and Jace Weaver have soundly addressed. Most obviously, in the United States, there is no "post" to the colonized status of Native peoples as members of so-called domestic dependent nations, though tribes daily assert and seek to extend their sovereign rights. It is also important to note, as Renya K. Ramirez does in her book *Native Hubs: Culture, Community, and Belonging in Silicon Valley and Beyond*, that nationalist paradigms that privilege U.S. federal recognition are problematic as well, especially for many urban Indians, and this problem calls for more attention to Indigenous peoples who have not been granted this recognition.[56] Further, postcolonial scholars, especially those who place

Edward Said's classic model in a postmodern context, often focus perhaps too broadly on the subaltern's status as a minority, emphasizing hybridity as a cosmopolitan state of being beyond tradition and deemphasizing the postcolonial subject's capacity for resistance, at least in a tribal context that is more familiar to Indigenous peoples. In the aforementioned *Blood Narrative*, Allen parallels Huhndorf's work by offering a critique of this postcolonial neglect of Indigenous activism while also pushing theoretical work beyond U.S. tribal borders to illumine its global importance. Following Allen's lead, Jeanne Sokolowski shows how *Hiroshima Bugi*, by the ever-unsettling Gerald Vizenor, intervenes in debates about Native nationalism, creatively adapting those positions to locations outside of the United States and connecting them to a cosmopolitan Indigeneity.

These locations of Indigenous political and cultural sway outside of the continental United States are an important feature of our special issue, and we believe that they offer opportunities to develop a praxis for sometimes abstract notions of transnationalism or nationalism within a global context. Essays authored by Stephen Hong Sohn and Wen Jin display links—especially overlapping but distinct experiences of imperialism—between Indigenous peoples of the United States and peoples of other nations, while Ryan Burt's essay foregrounds mobility as a means of Indigenous liberation. This interplay between distant migration and historical and specific localities is a fruitful line of inquiry that, according to the authors of this special issue, is critical to understanding contemporary Indigenous experiences, in which attitudes toward place are part of anticolonial culture that tend toward claiming rootedness in homelands. To this end, each of the essays just mentioned points toward particular but shifting geographies, employing but critiquing typical definitions of concepts such as "citizenship," "cosmopolitanism," and "belonging." This foregrounding of migration and contact among peoples aside from a Euro/Native "first contact" narrative continues and extends valuable insights offered by scholars of Black-Indian studies, including William Loren Katz, Jack D. Forbes, Tiya Miles, Sharon Patricia Holland, and Daniel Littlefield.

In our taking up of the organizing concept of "contact" and conjunctural analysis, however, we do not suggest that Indigenous exactions of sovereignty in an international or cosmopolitan framework are inherently unstable or destined to become in Craig Womack's words, a "hybrid mess."[57] The essays collected here are ardent in their resistance to an all-encompassing or simplistically celebratory multiculturalism. Dean Saranillio's discussion of the artwork of Kēwaikaliko, for example, highlights the artist's exposure of the "Aloha for All" campaign as a tool of cultural genocide against Hawaiians. We identify in cultural studies aspects of Marxist theory that emphasize labor relations and the circulation of capital, important parts of imperial projects—and resistance to them—that, as Huhndorf has suggested, nationalist critiques have not yet fully addressed. Thus, in Jean J. Kim's analysis of imperial transformations of food in service to an invented illness, Danika Medak-Saltzman's reinscription of a photograph from the 1904 St. Louis Exposition, and Glen Mimura's discussion of Frank Matsura's postcards from Okanogan County, we may identify commodities that themselves encapsulate the fraught dynamics of colonialism.

The Spaces of the Pacific

This collection begins with essays that address the contact zone of the Pacific Islands, forging connections between studies of American imperialism abroad and Indigenous studies. The histories and politics of these island nations and territories in the Pacific Ocean are often radically different from and in tension with continental U.S. versions of racializing and colonizing Indigenous peoples. The conjunctural analysis offered by the essays emphasizes the importance of specificity for each moment of consideration. Hawai'i as a site of contact and Native Hawaiians as Indigenous people struggling for greater self-determination are just one example of important differences and complicated histories of interaction between Indigenous peoples and the U.S. government. Though sharing a similar status of colonial dispossession as American Indians, Native Hawaiians deal with different administrative bodies of federal and state governments.[58] An ongoing, contentious debate in the state, in fact, is about the Akaka Bill, which proposes that the U.S. government recognize Native Hawaiians as Indigenous people with the same relationship to the federal government that American Indians have.[59]

It is also worth noting in passing that Pacific Islanders, in the understanding of the continental United States, are often conjoined with Asian Americans in the identity formation "Asian Pacific Islander." Such a category, while collecting together peoples from places geographically contiguous, often elides important tensions and contrasts between Asian and Pacific Islander histories. Following the lead of scholar-activist Haunani-Kay Trask, others have begun to explore the concept of "Asian settler colonialism," probing how Asian Hawaiian constructions of belonging as "Locals" displaces Indigenous presence.[60] Even so, Asian Americans and Pacific Islanders on the mainland have at times seized this category to form broader coalitions for antiracist, anti-immigration projects. Writing of Asian American and Pacific Islander studies, Vicente Diaz states, "I think it is vital, in order to maintain the integrity of our respective struggles and projects, that our resolve to keep the differences clear and equal not reify in any way any of the categories in question."[61] Maintaining a balance between distinctiveness and shared struggle is important, even as we must refuse essentializing any of the categories. Some of the essays in this section approach Indigeneity in the Pacific by way of interactions with Asian Americans, while others emphasize the uniqueness of Indigenous struggles outside the frame of this Asian Pacific Islander category.

In this volume, Judy Rohrer's "Attacking Trust: Hawai'i as a Crossroads and Kamehameha Schools in the Crosshairs" calls us to acknowledge the specificity of colonial histories. Through discussion of disputes concerning programs serving Kanaka Maoli students in Kamehameha Schools, Rohrer uncovers the incompatibility of race-based notions of Indigeneity with the unique circumstances of Native Hawaiians. As Rohrer shows, by invoking color-blind ideology, some *haole* (white people) have miscast Native Hawaiian educational policies as illegal racial preferences, a strategy that not only erases Indigeneity but makes invisible the Japanese presence in this space. Addressing the same colonial dynamics from a different disciplinary perspective, Dean Saranillio, in his essay "Kēwaikaliko's *Benocide:* Reversing the Imperial Gaze of *Rice v. Cayetano* and Its Legal Progeny," draws attention to the artwork of Kēwaikaliko, which challenges the normalization of colonial violence against Indigenous Hawaiians. As Saranillio explains, Kēwaikaliko frames this adversity as a "legal lynching," opening up the rhetoric of civil rights while at the same time critiquing the misuse of that rhetoric to racialize and subsume Hawaiians under a multicultural umbrella.

Illustrating the complex dynamics of diaspora, Hokulani K. Aikau and Jo-Anna Poblete-Cross analyze two examples of a disrupted colonizer-colonized polarity. In her essay "Indigeneity in the Diaspora: The Case of Native Hawaiians from Iosepa, Utah," Aikau offers a personal account of the way in which a rigorous awareness of multipronged power relations challenges scholars such as herself to rethink their methodologies, incorporating greater understanding of "other actors on the scene." Reflecting on the implications of Native Hawaiians' claims to Goshute land at Iosepa, Utah, she cautions that Indigenous land claims may be multilayered and that colonial forces may come from unexpected sources, necessitating continual discussions about respectful behavior. Poblete-Cross calls for alliance across Asian immigrant and Indigenous Samoan populations in "Bridging Indigenous and Immigrant Struggles: A Case Study of American Sāmoa." Placing emphasis on much-needed discussion of labor within Indigenous studies, Poblete-Cross asserts that while the goals of different groups may be in tension, these groups may nonetheless find common ground in resisting imperial legacies.

Jean J. Kim and Stephen Hong Sohn both discuss the confluence of Indigenous peoples and Filipinos but from differing medical and literary perspectives. Kim's essay, "Experimental Encounters: Filipino and Hawaiian Bodies in the U.S. Imperial Invention of Odontoclasia, 1928–1946," displays the racialization of territorial medicine as practiced across intersecting borders. Remarking on a timely subject—Indigenous struggles for health care—Kim reveals the power of food as a tool for colonial invention of illness. Further expressing this link between Filipinos and Indigenous peoples, Sohn, in his "Los Indios Bravos: The Filipino/American Lyric and the Cosmopoetics of Comparative Indigeneity," recovers international commonality in the mistaken Spanish categorization of the many groups as "Indios" but revises the usual definitions of cosmopolitanism in describing this phenomenon, asserting that linkage does not collapse difference. Sohn finds in Luisa A. Igloria's poems creative invocation of Filipinos as global subjects, which, rather than reifying ethnic or nation-based affiliations, instead emphasizes overlapping experiences of imperialism across a range of historical experiences. Igloria's poetry thereby honors Indigenous experiences, Sohn argues, and somewhat ironically, proposes that the misnaming of "Los Indios Bravos" may inspire revolution.

"Unexpected" Indigenous Modernity

Following these essays on Pacific/Indigenous alternative contact, the book turns to unsettling renderings of Indigenous modernity in an international context. Influenced by the work of Philip Deloria, these essays highlight unexpected moments of Indigenous alliance, liberation, and anti-proscriptive action. Andrea Smith, in "Decolonization in Unexpected Places: Native Evangelicalism and the Rearticulation of Mission," describes the "secret history" of evangelical Indigenous and Third World peoples allied in global anticolonial aims. Smith thus traces redefinitions of evangelism and sovereignty in the development of ethical practices of nationhood. In this discussion, Smith answers Womack's call to address the ways Indigenous Christian viewpoints may inform ethical work and the strategies that they offer for decolonization.[62]

Next, Danika Medak-Saltzman and Ryan Burt reinterpret standard responses to the presence of Indigenous subjects in western imaginaries in their discussions of the 1904 St. Louis Exposition and Buffalo Bill's Wild West show. In "Transnational Indigenous Exchange: Rethinking Global Interactions of

Indigenous Peoples at the 1904 St. Louis Exposition," Medak-Saltzman relays new possibilities for foregrounding Indigenous perspectives in archival materials associated with Ainu and Tzoneca peoples. Continuing and extending a conversation begun by Rayna Green, Medak-Saltzman argues that previous methodologies applied to these materials mistakenly imply that Indigenous peoples are unknowable, thereby obscuring the unintended transnational encounters the fair produced.[63] Instead, Medak-Saltzman offers an alternative, global understanding of such world fairs. Burt similarly complicates "Indian expectations" in his study of the life and work of Luther Standing Bear in "'Sioux Yells' in the Dawes Era: Lakota 'Indian Play,' the Wild West, and the Literatures of Luther Standing Bear." An important implication of Burt's article is that the framework of "citizenship" is liberating rather than assimilative for Standing Bear. Centering understandings of individuality unique to Lakota people, Burt argues that mobility contributed to, rather than detracted from, Standing Bear's sense of Lakota identity.

In the next set of essays, James H. Cox, Alice Te Punga Somerville, and Glen Mimura question influential mythologies in their studies of how Indigeneity is co-opted within various contexts. Cox's "Mexican *Indigenismo*, Choctaw Self-Determination, and Todd Downing's Detective Novels" mines Downing's writings to uncover the author's refiguring of Mexican notions of *indigenismo*—a concept that incorporates Indigeneity into a unified national Mexican identity—to expose Indigenous peoples obscured by that concept. Cox emphasizes the local roots of these novels despite their international context and shows that this broader content connects with activism within the Choctaw Nation. Discussing a different discourse rooted in U.S. film westerns, Somerville follows this analysis of appropriated Indigeneity in "Maori Cowboys, Maori Indians," in which she analyzes Maori disidentification with American Indians. Like other authors in the volume, Somerville stresses the need for a specificity in Indigenous identifications that recognizes the intersections and divergences of local, regional, and national particularities. Her argument for allowing Natives to be themselves rather than "act like Natives" challenges scholars to make critical space for the work of Indigenes who may have been dismissed as assimilationists, and to resist colonial mappings of Indigenous identity. Glen Mimura, in "A Dying West? Reimagining the Frontier in Frank Matsura's Photography, 1903–1913," likewise challenges typical perceptions of Indigenous and immigrant behavior. Contrasting Matsura's body of work with that of Edward Curtis, Mimura shows that the Japanese photographer portrays Native Okanogan peoples not as resigned to extinction but rather as full participants in modernity on their own terms.

Nation and Nation-State

This volume ends with three essays in which Indigeneity is discussed as part of commentary on multiple nation-states, especially outside of the United States. Jeanne Sokolowski's "Between Dangerous Extremes: Victimization, Ultranationalism, and Identity Performance in Gerald Vizenor's *Hiroshima Bugi: Atomu 57*" demonstrates the Anishinaabe writer's attention to the difficulties of identity construction and his intervention in debates about Native nationalism. Sokolowski contends that Vizenor's unconventional novel, set in Japan, opens up the possibility for creatively adapted cultural traditions and positions apart from the traditional homeplace, developing as a rejoinder of sorts to iconic novels such as N. Scott Momaday's *House Made of Dawn* and Leslie Marmon Silko's *Ceremony*. In her essay "Toward a U.S.-China Comparative Critique: Indigenous Rights and National Expansion in Alex Kuo's *Panda Diaries*," Wen Jin interprets Kuo's text as exemplifying the potential for comparative insights when seeking perspective on encounters between Indigeneity and the nation-states that govern them, in this case concerning the United States and China. Foregrounding place as encapsulating tensions between colonial and anticolonial attitudes, Jin argues for diaspora as a mode of critique for understanding citizenship and belonging. Finally, Molly Geidel, in "'Sowing Death in Our Women's Wombs': Modernization and Indigenous Nationalism in the 1960s Peace Corps and Jorge Sanjinés' *Yawar Mallku*," analyzes the gender narratives involved in the dramatization of conflicts between anticommunist modernization doctrines espoused by the Peace Corps and Indigenous nationalists as represented in the Bolivian film *Yawar Mallku* (*Blood of the Condor*). Geidel concludes that activism must be freed of colonial gender strictures while working against development ideology.

Continuing the Exploration

Having explored "alternative contact" from various disciplinary and theoretical angles, we seek further discussions not only of the ways Indigenous studies continues to develop as a field but also of the transformative potential that greater attention to Indigeneity may hold for related areas of ethnic and American studies. The conceptual space we delimit in this project is admittedly sprawling and amorphous at the edges, but our hope is that the questions the authors raise in this volume will help spur additional research and conversations about our methodologies and assumptions. Further, we seek through this collection to join the theoretical with the practical and ethical. In other words, we have sought to underline the timeliness and relevance of our project for urgent matters at hand, as rhetorics of "borders," "illegals," and "aliens" saturate our current political climate. Having begun this project inspired by "new directions," perhaps it is fitting to close here with a call for others to create and share insights about still other conjunctures and to continue to remind us of the stakes of the work that we do. Our thanks go to editor Curtis Marez and the entire *American Quarterly* editorial board for allowing us the opportunity to foster this dialogue here.

Notes

The guest editors of this volume wish to thank Curtis Marez and Stephen Hong Sohn for reading and commenting on drafts of this introduction.

1. The New Directions in American Indian Research conference was established to foster research by graduate students and other junior scholars. It, importantly, offers a space for Native researchers and others studying American Indians to share their work in a supportive environment. For more information about the conference, please visit the Web site: http://gradschool.unc.edu/diversity/newdirections/.
2. Participants in the panels included Hokulani K. Aikau, Chadwick Allen, Ahimsa Timoteo Bodhrán, Ryan Burt, Jodi Byrd, Robert F. Castro, Karen Mary Davalos, Tol Foster, Elizabeth Guerrier, Jennifer Ann Ho, Margo Machida, Mark J. Miller, Renya Ramirez, Dean Saranillio, Jeanne Sokolowski, and Amy Stillman. Their contributions have greatly shaped our sense of this project, and we thank them for their participation.
3. We are also attentive to the fact that some Native studies scholars see their work as outside the scope of American studies. Alternately, many American studies scholars dismiss the centrality of Indigenous peoples and histories to the formation of the American nation. The essays in this volume cast a wide net in terms of addressing this second point by exploring multiple sites and histories of American nationalism and imperialism that are rooted in the relationship of the U.S. nation-state to American Indians and Pacific Islanders.
4. In this way, our project resonates with the work of scholars like Vijay Prashad, *Everybody Was Kung Fu Fighting: Afro-Asian Connections and the Myth of Cultural Purity* (Boston: Beacon Press, 2002), who trace connections between different non-European peoples outside the organizing schemas of Western modernity and globalization.
5. Philip J. Deloria, *Indians in Unexpected Places* (Lawrence: University Press of Kansas, 2004).
6. Dipesh Chakrabarty, *Provincializing Europe: Postcolonial Thought and Historical Difference* (Princeton, N.J.: Princeton University Press, 2000), 16.
7. Andrea Smith, "American Studies without America: Native Feminisms and the Nation-State," *American Quarterly* 60.2 (June 2008): 312.
8. Ibid., 311.
9. Kevin Bruyneel, *The Third Space of Sovereignty: The Postcolonial Politics of U.S.-Indigenous Relations* (Minneapolis: University of Minnesota Press, 2007), 20.
10. The curious and ambiguous phrase "domestic dependent nations" comes from the infamous *Cherokee Nation v. State of Georgia* Supreme Court decision in 1831. Chief Justice John Marshall coined the phrase to describe the way that Indigenous tribes existed simultaneously inside and outside the American nation-state, both recognized as sovereign governments and reduced to the status of a "ward" of the United States. For discussions of this case, see Bruyneel, *Third Space*, 3, and Priscilla Wald, "Terms of Assimilation: Legislating Subjectivity in the Emerging Nation," *Cultures of United States Imperialism*, ed. Amy Kaplan and Donald E. Pease (Durham, N.C.: Duke University Press, 1993), 59–84.
11. Gloria Anzaldúa, *Borderlands: The New Mestiza / La Frontera*, 2d ed. (San Francisco: Aunt Lute Books, 1999).

12. Mary Louise Pratt, "Arts of the Contact Zone," *Profession* 91 (1991): 33–40, quote on 33.
13. In *The Spectre of Comparison: Nationalism, Southeast Asia, and the World* (London: Verso, 1998), Benedict Anderson borrows Filipino nationalist hero José Rizal's phrase, "the spectre of comparison," explaining that this haunting is the inevitable comparison of Filipino cities to European ones, always to the detriment of the Filipinos. Like Chakrabarty's "provincializing Europe," this phrase helps identify the ways in which Indigenous peoples often must contend with Euro-American modernity in articulations of their own nations.
14. Stuart Hall, "What Is This 'Black' in Black Popular Culture?" in *Stuart Hall: Critical Dialogues in Cultural Studies*, ed. David Morley and Kuan-Hsing Chen (New York: Routledge, 1996), 465.
15. Elaine H. Kim, Margo Machida, and Sharon Mizota, eds., *Fresh Talk / Daring Gazes: Conversations on Asian American Art* (Berkeley: University of California Press, 2003).
16. Ibid., xiii.
17. We use scare quotes around the terms "illegal immigrants" and "illegals" to signal the fact that they are problematic terms, designating peoples as unlawful by virtue of their geographical displacement. The terms are nevertheless inescapable in many public discussions, and we use them when noting how others discuss the issue of immigration. Our preference is for the term "undocumented migrants" to clarify that these are people who simply lack U.S.-sanctioned documents like visas and green cards that would officially allow them to be in the country. Shifting the focus from immigration to migration also deemphasizes the centrality of the nation-state as the entity that holds ultimate authority over how people move within and between regions.
18. Randal C. Archibald, "Arizona's Effort to Bolster Local Immigration Authority Divides Law Enforcement," *New York Times*, April 21, 2010, online edition, http://www.nytimes.com/2010/04/22/us/22immig.html (accessed June 1, 2010).
19. Presidents Barack Obama and Felipe Calderón, "Remarks by President Obama and President Calderón of Mexico at Joint Press Availability," *White House* official Web site, Speeches and Remarks, May 19, 2010, http://www.whitehouse.gov/the-press-office/remarks-president-obama-and-president-calder-n-mexico-joint-press-availability (accessed June 2, 2010).
20. Gary Martin, "Obama to send 1,200 troops to border," *Houston Chronicle* Web site, Washington Bureau, http://www.chron.com/disp/story.mpl/metropolitan/7021486.html (accessed June 2, 2010).
21. Ibid.
22. For a list of cities and organizations that have approved boycotts of Arizona, please see "Who Is Boycotting (and Not Boycotting) Arizona?" *Arizona Republic*, May 30, 2010, http://www.azcentral.com/arizonarepublic/business/articles/2010/05/30/20100530biz-immigration-boycotts-list0530.html (accessed June 1, 2010).
23. "Mayor's Release on Arizona Travel Boycott," City of St. Paul, MN—Official Website, http://www.ci.stpaul.mn.us/index.aspx?NID=3895 (accessed June 1, 2010).
24. "Motion by Supervisors Gloria Molina and Zev Yaroslavsky," Los Angeles County Web site, June 1, 2010, http://molina.lacounty.gov/PDFs/06%20%2001%2010%20Arizona%20SB1070.pdf (accessed June 2, 2010).
25. "Boycott Intolerance," National Council of La Raza Web site, http://www.nclr.org/section/boycott (accessed June 2, 2010); emphasis in original. The statement announcing the boycott on behalf of the coalition is also available on the site at http://www.nclr.org/section/boycott_intolerance_petition.
26. Randal C. Archibold and Megan Thee-Brenan, "Poll Shows Most in U.S. Want Overhaul of Immigration Laws," *New York Times*, May 3, 2010, online edition, http://www.nytimes.com/2010/05/04/us/04poll.html (accessed June 2, 2010).
27. Daniel B. Wood, "After Arizona, Why Are 10 States Considering Immigration Bills?" *Christian Science Monitor*, May 10, 2010, online edition, http://www.csmonitor.com/USA/Society/2010/0510/After-Arizona-why-are-10-states-considering-immigration-bills (accessed June 2, 2010).
28. Arizona State Legislature, Senate Bill 1070, lines 36–45, http://www.azleg.gov/alispdfs/council/SB1070-HB2162.PDF (accessed June 1, 2010).
29. "Tohono O'odham Nation Opposes New Immigration Law," Tohono O'odham Nation official Web site, May 20, 2010, http://www.tonation-nsn.gov/press_releases_details.aspx?id=29 (accessed June 2, 2010).
30. Ibid., page 1, lines 11–15. The text of the resolution is included as an attachment to the press release.
31. Ibid., page 2, lines 15–18.

32. For news coverage of a protest action, see Babette Herrmann, "Protesters Stage Sit-in," *Indian Country Today* (June 3, 2010), http://www.indiancountrytoday.com/home/content/95117474.html (accessed June 16, 2010).
33. O'odham Solidarity Across Borders Collective, "End Border Militarization Contingent," May 26, 2010, Web site blog post, http://oodhamsolidarity.blogspot.com/2010/05/end-border-militarization-contingent.html (accessed June 1, 2010).
34. O'odham Solidarity Across Borders Collective, "Tucson: Indigenous Peoples Protest Against SB 1070 and HB 2281 Demonstration," May 16, 2010, Web site blog post, http://oodhamsolidarity.blogspot.com/2010/05/tucsonindigenous-peoples-protest-againt.html (accessed June 1, 2010). NEPA refers to the National Environmental Policy, and NAGPRA is the Native American Graves Protection and Repatriation Act.
35. Margo Tamez, "Congressman Raul Grijalva Urges Boycott of Arizona as Gov. Brewer Contemplates 'the Right Thing' to Do," NAISA official Web site blog forums, April 22, 2010, http://naisa.org/node/183 (accessed June 2, 2010).
36. The Maya, Mixtec, Nahuatl, and Zapotec are just four of the Indigenous peoples of the region. For some discussion of the politics of Indigeneity in Mexico, see Carmen Martínez Novo, *Who Defines Indigenous? Identities, Development, Intellectuals, and the State in Northern Mexico* (New Brunswick, N.J.: Rutgers University Press, 2006), and Shannon Speed, *Rights in Rebellion: Indigenous Struggle and Human Rights in Chiapas* (Stanford, Calif.: Stanford University Press, 2008).
37. Robert Warrior, "NAISA Letter to Governor Jan Brewer," NAISA Web site blog, April 26, 2010, http://naisa.org/node/189 (accessed June 1, 2010).
38. Robert Warrior, "NAISA Responds to Arizona SB 1070," NAISA Web site blog, April 25, 2010, http://naisa.org/node/188 (accessed June 1, 2010).
39. Robert Warrior, "NAISA Council Statement on the Annual Meeting in Tucson," NAISA Web site blog, May 2, 2010, http://naisa.org/node/212 (accessed June 1, 2010).
40. "Southern California Native Feminist Reading Group Letter to NAISA," NAISA Web site blog, April 28, 2010, http://naisa.org/node/196 (accessed June 2, 2010).
41. "Friday Protest 11:00: Native and Indigenous Peoples against SB 1070/HB 2281," NAISA Web site blog, May 16, 2010, http://naisa.org/node/277 (accessed June 1, 2010).
42. Arizona State Legislature, House Bill 2281, http://www.azleg.gov/legtext/49leg/2r/bills/hb2281s.pdf (accessed June 1, 2010): page 1, lines 12–16.
43. Ibid., page 1, lines 39–40; page 2, lines 6–9.
44. Jeff J. Corntassel, "Who Is Indigenous? 'Peoplehood' and Ethnonationalist Approaches to Rearticulating Indigenous Identity," *Nationalism and Ethnic Politics* 9.1 (2003): 75–100.
45. We refer here to the Cherokee Nation's vote to remove from tribal rolls descendents of Freedmen, who were African Americans enslaved by the tribe. See Circe Sturm's *Blood Politics: Race, Culture, and Identity in the Cherokee Nation of Oklahoma* (Berkeley: University of California Press, 2002); and Alan Ray's "A Race or a Nation? Cherokee National Identity and the Status of Freedmen's Descendants," *Michigan Journal of Race and Law* 12 (2007): 387–463
46. Chadwick Allen, *Blood Narrative: Indigenous Identity in American Indian and Maori Literary and Activist Texts* (Durham, N.C.: Duke University Press, 2002), 7.
47. Ibid., 9.
48. Ibid., 16.
49. Elizabeth Cook-Lynn, "The American Indian Fiction Writer: Cosmopolitanism, Nationalism, the Third World, and First Nation Sovereignty," *Wicazo Sa Review* 9.2 (Autumn 1993): 26–36. Cook-Lynn, "American Indian Intellectualism and the New Indian Story," *American Indian Quarterly* 20.1 (1996): 57–76.
50. Craig Womack, *Red on Red: Native American Literary Separatism* (Minneapolis: University of Minnesota Press, 1999).
51. Jace Weaver, Craig S. Womack, and Robert Warrior, eds., *American Indian Literary Nationalism* (Albuquerque: University of New Mexico Press, 2006); Robert Allen Warrior, *Tribal Secrets: Recovering American Indian Intellectual Traditions* (Minneapolis: University of Minnesota Press, 1995); Robert Warrior, *The People and the Word: Reading Native Nonfiction* (Minneapolis: University of Minnesota Press, 2005); and Jace Weaver, *That the People Might Live: Native American Literatures and Native American Community* (New York: Oxford University Press, 1997).

52. Janice Acoose et al., eds., *Reasoning Together: The Native Critics Collective* (Norman: University of Oklahoma Press, 2008).
53. Shari M. Huhndorf, *Mapping the Americas: The Transnational Politics of Contemporary Native Culture* (Ithaca: Cornell University Press, 2009).
54. Ibid., 3–4.
55. Ibid., 4.
56. Renya K. Ramirez, *Native Hubs: Culture, Community, and Belonging in Silicon Valley and Beyond* (Durham, N.C.: Duke University Press, 2007).
57. Acoose et al., *Reasoning Together*, 37.
58. The scholarly and activist work of Native Hawaiians is particularly trenchant in its critique of American imperialism. See Haunani-Kay Trask, *From a Native Daughter: Colonialism and Sovereignty in Hawai'i*, rev. ed. (Honolulu: University of Hawai'i Press, 1999); Noenoe K. Silva, *Aloha Betrayed: Native Hawaiian Resistance to American Colonialism* (Durham, N.C.: Duke University Press, 2004); and J. Kēhaulani Kauanui, *Hawaiian Blood: Colonialism and the Politics of Sovereignty and Indigeneity* (Durham, N.C.: Duke University Press, 2008).
59. For an analysis of Native Hawaiian opposition to the Akaka Bill, see J. Kēhaulani Kauanui, "Precarious Positions: Native Hawaiians and U.S. Federal Recognition," *The Contemporary Pacific* 17.1 (2005): 1–27.
60. For a collection of essays on this topic, see Candace Fujikane and Jonathan Y. Okamura, eds., *Asian Settler Colonialism: From Local Governance to the Habits of Everyday Life in Hawai'i* (Honolulu: University of Hawai'i Press, 2008). For a critique of the binary of Asian settler-Native Hawaiian emphasized in "Asian settler colonialism," see Seri Luangphinith, "Homeward Bound: Settler Aesthetics in Hawai'i's Literature," *Texas Studies in Literature and Language* 48.1 (Spring 2006): 54–78.
61. Vicente M. Diaz, "'To "P" or Not to "P"?': Marking the Territory Between Pacific Islander and Asian American Studies," *Journal of Asian American Studies* 7.3 (October 2004): 184. Diaz's essay appears in a special issue of the journal, vol. 7, no. 3, edited by Davianna Pomaika'i McGregor, titled "Weaving Together Strands of Pacific Islander, Asian, and American Interactions."
62. Craig S. Womack, "A Single Decade: Book-Length Native Literary Criticism between 1986 and 1997," in *Reasoning Together*, 91.
63. See Rayna Green, "The Pocahontas Perplex: Images of American Indian Women in American Culture," *Native American Voices: A Reader*, ed. Susan Lobo and Steve Talbot (New York: Longman, 1998).

Attacking Trust: Hawai'i as a Crossroads and Kamehameha Schools in the Crosshairs

Judy Rohrer

Hawai'i is a global crossroads of indigeneity and racialized communities, homeland and diaspora, nation and globalization, imperialism and sovereignty. A history of colonialism and neocolonialism, manifest today in tourism and militarism, has brought the islands very much inside the folds of empire (Hawai'i is both the most touristed and the most militarized of the fifty states). Yet, just over a hundred years ago, Hawai'i was its own independent nation, governed by indigenous principles and values, and organized as a constitutional monarchy that was overthrown in a U.S.-backed coup. Since this was an illegal action (followed by illegal annexation and statehood), many Kanaka Maoli (native Hawaiians) continue to live and believe in Hawai'i's sovereignty. They do not identify in any way as American, making their political position vis-à-vis the state and federal government ambiguous to say the least. Like many indigenous people, Kanaka Maoli fall to the bottom of every socioeconomic indicator—they are the most disadvantaged people in their own land.[1] And since the early 1990s they have faced an incredible backlash that exploits their precarious position, including attacks on the programs and entitlements established to try to remedy the colonial legacy.

Despite (or perhaps because of) this complex and rich history, Hawai'i is often overlooked by American studies, indigenous studies/Native American studies, postcolonial studies, and transnational feminist theory—fields that are just beginning to realize their productive and challenging interrelations. Because it does not neatly fit any existing model, the study of Hawai'i resides in an academic limbo. The islands are 2,500 miles from North America (and equidistant from Asia) and have a history that raises serious questions about their incorporation into (or occupation by) the United States and their assumed primary association with the North American continent. Kanaka Maoli were never organized into tribes and in many ways have more in common with other native Pacific Islanders than with Native Americans.[2] Hawai'i was taken off the

United Nations list of non-self-governing territories at the point of the contested statehood vote in 1959, moving it out of the category of decolonizing nations. American studies has been roundly criticized for undertheorizing the United States as an imperial power and for situating interventionism and imperialism as new phenomena.[3] Transnational feminist theory has been relatively silent regarding Hawaiian sovereignty, perhaps partly because of assumptions about what a nation looks like.

In this essay, I build on my previous work examining how haole (white people/whiteness in Hawai'i) is currently reestablishing itself as normative legal subject through the invocation of color-blind ideology and legal strategies that cast Native Hawaiian programs and entitlements as illegal racial preferences. Here I focus on recent litigation and political mobilization aimed at forcing Kamehameha Schools, by far the largest institution serving the Hawaiian community, to eliminate the preference it gives Kanaka Maoli students. My intention is neither to argue legal issues per se, nor to advocate for Kamehameha Schools. There are plenty of people doing both of those things. Instead I look at how those attacking Kamehameha Schools have constructed their narratives both inside and outside the courtroom in ways that dehistoricize and distort Kanaka Maoli struggles, reducing them to petty racial conflicts and constraining them to the arena of U.S. law.

Taking a cue from my free-diving, spear-fishing brother, I will apply a three-pronged approach in hopes of surfacing more material for a discursive analysis of the anti-Hawaiian backlash.[4] The power of language has always been clear to Kanaka Maoli. There is an old saying in Hawaiian, "I ka 'ōlelo ke ola, i ka 'ōlelo nō ka make," that roughly translates as "life is in the word [or language], death is also in the word."[5] First, I explore the pernicious use of civil rights law refracted through color-blind ideology to attack Native Hawaiian entitlements, and the acceptance of the civil rights framework by defenders of these entitlements. This is the anti-affirmative action strategy imported from the continent. Second, I want to examine the construction of a reactionary discourse specific to Hawai'i that mobilizes Kanaka Maoli cultural values and practices *against* Kanaka Maoli entitlements by claiming Hawaiianess for non-Hawaiians and purporting anti-Hawaiianness on the part of Kanaka Maoli. This is native cultural appropriation, haole style. Finally, I look at how these moves insistently racialize Kanaka Maoli, erasing their indigeneity and locking them into battle with constitutional and federal law, while simultaneously claiming a higher moral "race-neutrality" or post-race position for non-Hawaiians. Ironically, this post-race position is increasingly constructed through rhetoric claiming a grossly distorted simulation of Hawaiian culture, or "Aloha for All," as one group calls itself.

Before symbolically diving in with my three-prong spear, let me set the political and legal context for readers unfamiliar with Hawai'i. Kanaka Maoli represent about 20 percent of the population of Hawai'i, although that number is declining as many are forced to move to the continent because of the rising cost of living, at the same time non-Hawaiians are moving to the islands.[6] Since 1778 when Captain Cook arrived, Kanaka Maoli have faced the violence of colonization: disease, dispossession, loss of language and culture, governmental overthrow, subjugation, discrimination, and criminalization.[7] Beginning in the 1970s, Kanaka Maoli organized a cultural and political revitalization. They and their allies began language immersion schools, recovered and taught hula and other cultural practices, protested against military bombings of Hawaiian lands, and stepped up organizing for different forms of sovereignty or independence. Not surprisingly, the haole and non-Hawaiian power brokers became nervous and fomented a strong backlash, which by the 1990s included the legal strategy of attacking programs and entitlements benefiting Kanaka Maoli by charging illegal racial preference.

In 2000 the U.S. Supreme Court handed down a devastating decision in *Harold F. Rice v. Benjamin J. Cayetano*, 528 U.S. 495 (2000), hereafter referred to as *Rice*. This opened the floodgate of attacks against entitlements. Kanaka Maoli are supposed to have a "special relationship"—codified in numerous laws establishing programs and entitlements—with the state of Hawai'i and the federal government based on the overthrow of their government and the seizure of lands belonging to the Kingdom of Hawai'i. Those lands are now held in "public trust" and a fifth of the revenues generated from them are supposed to go into programs benefiting Kanaka Maoli. (There is an ongoing battle with the state over securing the full 20 percent.) These programs are administered by a state of Hawai'i entity, the Office of Hawaiian Affairs (OHA), trustees of which were voted for by native Hawaiians, since they are the beneficiaries.

Harold Rice, a fifth-generation haole of missionary descent, filed his lawsuit in 1996. Rice charged that OHA's Hawaiians-only voting restriction for trustees constituted unlawful racial discrimination. In a 7–2 decision in February 2000, the U.S. Supreme Court agreed with Rice, holding that the state violated the Fifteenth Amendment's ban on voting restrictions based on race. I have argued elsewhere that the Court was able to come up with this ruling by reading Kanaka Maoli indigeneity as race, adhering to a color-blind ideology, and glossing the history of the U.S. colonization of Hawai'i.[8] Since this decision, a number of lawsuits have been filed seeking to eliminate programs and entitlements for Kanaka Maoli. Most have attacked state programs, but now Kamehameha Schools is also in the crosshairs.

Kamehameha Schools is a multicampus private institution with an endowment of $6.8 billion serving between five thousand and six thousand preschool to twelfth-grade students in Hawaiʻi (and many others via community programs), making it the largest institution of its kind in the United States (assuming one thinks of Hawaiʻi as part of the United States). It was founded in 1887 as part of the Bishop Estate, an enormous land trust established from the will of Princess Bernice Pauahi Bishop, the last direct descendent of King Kamehameha I. Princess Pauahi was very concerned about the suffering of her people from the devastating effects of colonialism. She believed education was an important key to a better future. She instructed that Kamehameha Schools be established to provide "a good education" to boys and girls, giving preference to "Hawaiians of pure or part aboriginal blood."[9] Since there are far more Kanaka Maoli children than the schools can accommodate (approximately seventy thousand statewide), admitting a non-Hawaiian student necessarily means taking a "native slot." The will also indicates that assistance should be given to those who are "orphans or indigent," and so the schools have always heavily subsidized tuition in addition to providing further aid for those who need it. This is not to say that the institution is without fault; far from it, but that critique is not the focus of this essay.[10]

Kamehameha Schools Lawsuits

The Kamehameha Schools admission policy has become a prime target of attack, hit by three lawsuits since 2003. All three suits have been organized by the same cabal of lawyers who mobilize color-blind ideology both inside and outside the courtroom by calling for "equal treatment" and "equal protection" of racial groups. In popular discourse, plaintiffs and their supporters also undermine Kanaka Maoli claims to indigeneity by purporting to be Hawaiian, "representative of Hawaiʻi," or even more culturally Hawaiian than Hawaiians—strategies much more tentatively employed in the *Rice* case. These discursive moves construct non-Hawaiians, particularly haoles, as victims seeking redress.[11]

In the first case, the mother of a seventh-grade haole boy, Brayden Mohica-Cummings, was able to get her son admitted by claiming he was native Hawaiian on his application. When the school found out Mohica-Cummings had no Hawaiian ancestry, it tried to rescind its enrollment decision, but his mother,

Kalena Santos, fought back. Attorney John Goemans, who had orchestrated the *Rice* lawsuit (and who passed away in June 2009), happily took the case, charging that the admissions policy discriminates against non-Hawaiians. In public, however, Santos claimed her son was native because she was hānai (a traditional Hawaiian practice similar to adoption) by a Hawaiian stepfather. Since she believed she was Hawaiian via hānai, she argued that her son was also Hawaiian. In the December 2003 settlement, Kamehameha Schools agreed to allow Mohica-Cummings to remain enrolled in exchange for his mother dropping the suit.

The question of Mohica-Cummings's Hawaiianness, given the hānai status of his mother, led to much discussion and debate. Significantly for the study of neocolonial power relations, it opened up space for some haoles to admonish Hawaiians for not following their own cultural practice. This statement by Robert Rees (a conservative haole journalist) is a prime example, "Kamehameha Schools—Hawaii's pre-eminent guardian of Hawaiian culture and customs—rejected the great Hawaiian tradition of hānai in the name of preserving racial preferences."[12] Kamehameha Schools fought back, vigorously maintaining that their preference for Hawaiian students was based on ancestry or genealogy and not race, yet this argument had been rejected by the Supreme Court in *Rice*. The institution worked a public relations angle highlighting the multiracial composition of their population. As if casting them as cultural destroyers was not enough, attackers compared Kamehameha School officials and trustees to George Wallace and other white supremacists who barred the doors to the admission of Black students on the continent.[13] In this way, a haole boy and his mother were able to invoke the legacy of the civil rights movement, framing Hawaiians as unjust bigots.

It is worth noting that this lawsuit, bent on establishing white victimhood, was supported and funded by many of the same powerful haoles behind the *Rice* lawsuit. John Goemans, who convinced Harold Rice to play the role of plaintiff in the first place, served again as lead attorney. To defeat Kamehameha Schools, Goemans pulled in financial backing from three powerful, rich haoles: these included James Growney, heir to the Campbell Estate; Thurston Twigg-Smith, former owner of the *Honolulu Advertiser* (and crusader against Hawaiian rights and sovereignty); and Scott Wallace, former owner of Wallace Theaters.[14] Campbell and Twigg-Smith's fortunes were built directly through the dispossession of the Kanaka Maoli and the industrial development of Hawai'i.

The second lawsuit against Kamehameha Schools for the admission of, this time, an unnamed haole boy (*John Doe v. Kamehameha Schools*) was also filed by Goemans in 2003 and was settled to the tune of $7 million in May 2007.

Via media reports, the public was led to believe that the plaintiff's desire for anonymity was motivated by fear. As conservative attorney Bruce Fein wrote, "the social ostracism unleashed against persons in Hawaii who challenge the political correctness of Native Hawaiian preferences obligated the plaintiff to sue under a pseudonym 'John Doe.'"[15] It is this type of rhetoric that helps build the notion of the victimized non-Hawaiian. There was widespread nonviolent protest attended by diverse crowds against these largely unpopular lawsuits. In fact, Kanaka Maoli activism has a strong history of nonviolent protest, including legal demonstrations and civil disobedience actions. One march, organized by Kamehameha Schools and Hawaiian civic organizations, included more than ten thousand people, many wearing red shirts with the saying "Kū I Ka Pono—Justice for Hawaiians." Employing the well-worn trope of native savage, Fein and others worked hard to characterize these marches as "mob-like" and threatening.[16]

The suit moved between state court and the Ninth Circuit Court of Appeals for four years before lawyers for John Doe appealed an unfavorable (to them) circuit court decision to the U.S. Supreme Court. In May 2007, before the Supreme Court could announce whether it would hear the case and in order to protect themselves from a possible precedent-setting negative outcome similar to *Rice*, Kamehameha Schools settled confidentially. School officials immediately issued a statement calling the settlement "pono" (correct or proper, but not relating the amount) because it preserved the favorable Ninth Circuit court ruling and therefore the preferential admissions policy.[17] John Goemans again served as Hawai'i attorney for the plaintiff, along with Eric Grant in California, who had also represented Mohica-Cummings. Goemans leaked the $7 million figure to the media in February 2008, provoking an outcry against Kamehameha Schools from many native Hawaiians concerned that the huge settlement would invite more lawsuits.[18]

Hawai'i attorney David Rosen promised just that the day after the settlement was announced. He used the media and e-mail to solicit plaintiffs (a move of questionable legality now under scrutiny by the Hawai'i State Bar Association)[19] for yet a third attack on the Kamehameha Schools admission policy. In launching this new attack, Rosen said he thinks the "highest court in the land" should rule on the question and was disappointed that the John Doe suit was settled. He said he was not motivated by money and would take only one dollar in fees if the Kamehameha Schools lawyers did the same. He wrote, "Like many others in Hawai'i, I believe that consideration of an individual's national origin or race is immaterial for any reason other than human interest . . . We cannot return to the past or undo it." In his e-mail solicitation

Rosen promised "the identity of all of the plaintiffs will be kept extremely confidential" and "there will be absolutely no cost to the Plaintiffs."[20] He also claimed to be motivated by the good of the children, not wanting his own "growing up as second-class citizens in their own home."[21] In a few short sentences, Rosen vanishes indigenous difference, sweeps centuries of colonial violence under the rug, and claims victimhood for his haole children.

Rosen filed his new suit, along with Eric Grant, on behalf of four anonymous students in August 2008. Remarkably, the attorneys proudly admitted the suit was "essentially identical" to the original John Doe suit, the only difference being this time there were four Does and they promised not to settle. As Eric Grant stated, "the purpose of today's action is to obtain a definitive ruling from the Supreme Court that the [Kamehameha Schools] trustees' racially exclusionary policy violates our nation's civil rights law." Rosen and Grant not only describe the plaintiffs as "representative of Hawai'i" (read: not just haoles this time) but go even further to claim "they are Hawaiian in every sense save the merely genetic."[22] This statement reduces indigeneity from genealogy to genes in order to undercut indigenous claims and highlights the anti-Hawaiian sentiment behind the case and the overall attack on Hawaiian programs. I come back to this reductive racialization later.

The attorneys drove home the now familiar claim that Hawaiians are turning Hawai'i into a place rife with racial strife and discrimination. In this discursive twist, Hawaiian programs and entitlements are said to go against the "aloha spirit" because they are "divisive" and unfair to non-Hawaiians. Grant told the press, "our clients believe, and we agree with them, that such a ruling will have a significant impact in reversing unfortunate trends toward discrimination and even segregation in Hawaii."[23] Kamehameha Schools trustees countered: "It is deeply disturbing to see a Civil Rights law enacted to protect an oppressed population used to undermine Pauahi's desire to restore the vitality and health of her people, who were dispossessed in their own homeland."[24] Some alumni said they were happy to see the suit because it could settle the question once and for all.[25] The trustees showed a strong front, referencing the favorable Ninth Circuit decision, but *Rice* cast a much bigger shadow and that clearly made them and the community nervous.

As with the first John Doe case, the lawyers had argued that the plaintiffs feared retaliation from the public at large, but in October 2008 a U.S. District Court magistrate ruled that the plaintiffs had failed to show evidence of threats of physical or economic harm that would justify them bringing the case anonymously.[26] The magistrate ruled that, at most, the students could fear "social ostracization," and the public interest in knowing who they were outweighed this. Putting a sharper edge on it, one alumnus told the press, "The public and the Hawaiian community deserve to know the people that are attempting to essentially steal money from the legacy." The case was dismissed in March 2009 because the plaintiffs refused to identify themselves. Their lawyers immediately appealed to the Ninth Circuit Court of Appeals to enable them to continue anonymously.[27]

Use of Civil Rights Law to Attack Native Hawaiians

In the first prong of my analysis, I look at the framing of these lawsuits through the use of color-blind ideology. While these three suits against Kamehameha Schools are part of a larger legal strategy attacking programs, preferences, and entitlements granted to Kanaka Maoli, they have an important difference. Other suits attack state and federal programs, invoking the constitutional guarantees in the Fourteenth and Fifteenth amendments against racial discrimination. By contrast, the attorneys in the Kamehameha cases have tapped reconstruction law to build arguments for precluding private entities from granting preference. Essentially, these suits seek to outlaw not only public entitlements but also private programs and institutions benefiting native Hawaiians. The overlapping teams of lawyers base their cases against Kamehameha Schools on 42 U.S.C. § 1981,which was enacted as part of the Civil Rights Act of 1866, when, ironically, the Kingdom of Hawai'i was still an independent nation. The 1866 Act was aimed at protecting the citizenship rights of recently emancipated Black people, especially as they entered into private contracts for employment and housing with whites.[28] To use this law, aimed at helping Blacks out of slavery, *to keep Kanaka Maoli from helping themselves out of colonialism*, is an expression of color-blind ideology at its worst.

Marcus Daniel, a University of Hawai'i history professor, addressed this in commentary running in the *Honolulu Advertiser*:

> Whatever the faults of Kamehameha Schools (elitism for starters), it wasn't created to deprive white people of educational opportunity; it was created to provide opportunity for Native Hawaiians who had been deprived of educational opportunities by whites! Only to the willfully ignorant could such differences mean nothing. But in the resentful racial imagination of many American whites, the world is turned upside-down and whites become the "victims" of racial injustice.[29]

Here Daniel asks us to question the logic that assumes preferences or programs for Kanaka Maoli necessarily means disadvantages for non-natives; that attempts to provide opportunities for natives somehow necessarily deprive non-natives. Further, the "upside-down" nature of color-blind ideology is based in a refusal to admit the contemporary legacies of historical discrimination and inequality that make recuperative measures necessary, in this case, admissions preferences for Hawaiians.

Those who attack Hawaiian programs employ anti-affirmative action or "reverse discrimination" strategies that have also been used to roll back gains made by communities of color on the continent. This is not surprising, as the Hawai'i actors are tightly connected to continental right-wing groups and funding sources.[30] These strategies rely on a logic that insists the law be "color blind," even if our history and social and political institutions are not, and that labels as "racist" any acknowledgment of race or attempt to compensate for institutionalized racism. Daniel and others argue vigorously against this twisted logic, insisting that remedies to racial inequalities are necessary precisely because we continue to live in a culture of white supremacy, where the racial advantages conferred on whites are so naturalized that we tend not to see them.[31] While this counterargument is incredibly important and needs to continue to be made, it does not fully fit the situation in Hawai'i. Daniel accepts the continental racial framing of the context by situating native Hawaiians as one more persecuted racial group. That is both true and not true. Kanaka Maoli are an indigenous people who have been racialized via colonial processes. But an essential aspect of that racialization is the vanishing of their indigeneity.

So it is not just that Kanaka Maoli have been "deprived of educational opportunities by whites," for the broader picture is one in which education has been a central weapon of colonial violence. Additionally, while haole hegemony was responsible for educational inequalities up to around the time of statehood, in subsequent decades the Department of Education came to be increasingly controlled by local (especially Japanese) teachers and administrators who are also responsible for the mistreatment and educational failure of native students via cultural denigration, insistence on "standard English," reliance on Western educational methods, and tracking. Simply framing this as a racial struggle between native Hawaiians and haoles misses the complex indigenous-racial histories and politics in the islands that are part of Hawai'i's neocolonial present.

Not surprisingly, legal analysis of the lawsuits against Kamehameha Schools, even when sympathetic, often makes the same mistake. A piece in the *Harvard Law Review*, for example, states that "the Kamehameha admissions policy reflects a broad remedial mission to right historical wrongs that have left the Native Hawaiian community lagging behind other Hawaiian citizens academically, professionally, and financially."[32] Even if Kamehameha Schools has historically understood its mission as "remedial," many advocates today would frame it in the more politicized context of decolonization, which does not assume a goal of catching native students up to their peers in the colonizers' educational system. The reference to "other Hawaiian citizens" betrays this author's lack of understanding of the neocolonial environment, wherein Hawaiianness is far from unproblematic and citizenship is equally vexed. The late University of Hawai'i law professor Chris Iijima writes about how this framing was established with the *Rice* case:

> In the midst of the legal battle over the categorization of Native Hawaiians, a cacophony of popular media on the continent identified the issue in *Rice* as a purely "racial" case using traditional civil rights terms. The success of this obfuscation was almost inevitable in an environment uneducated about the complexities of Hawaiian history and culture, and accustomed to dealing with racial issues in simplistic and biological terms.[33]

It has been ten years since the *Rice* decision and Kanaka Maoli are under even more pressure than ever to account for themselves. As Hawaiian identity is increasingly surveilled and threatened, scholars such as Lisa Kahaleole Hall are pushing back: "We are Hawaiian at heart, history, and bone, in ancestor and child."[34] Hall and others refuse all boxes, instead insisting on a multifaceted, historicized yet not ossified, genealogical understanding of what it is to be Hawaiian. It is critical that those of us who are academics understand the very different histories behind civil rights organizing by African Americans and other communities of color struggling for full constitutional rights, and efforts by indigenous people to reclaim their cultures and nations. The late Vine Deloria Jr. reminds us of the unique political "no man's land" of American Indians:

> American Indians . . . stand outside the protections of the Constitution as tribes and only have partial protection as individual citizens. While Indian lands have become part of the United States, Indian communities have neither been allowed to remain isolated as independent political entities nor have they been granted full status within the American political system. Consequently, American Indians have been forced to live within a political/legal no man's land from which there seems to be no possibility of extrication.[35]

Deloria's representation of the political (non)status of American Indians applies to Kanaka Maoli as well, one significant difference being that the history of colonization of Hawai'i is much more recent, elevating hopes of "extrication" among many. Extrication from this state of political limbo is often framed in terms of self-determination or sovereignty (significantly, it is *not* framed as equality or full citizenship—the primary goals of civil rights movements).

"Sovereignty is the assertion that *what we are*—culturally, emotionally, and physically—is *what we prefer to be*."[36] As two other native scholars put it, "'separate but equal,' anathema to African Americans, with good reason, would please us greatly."[37]

Native Hawaiian scholar J. Kēhaulani Kauanui has written extensively on the legal conundrum faced by native Hawaiians. On this issue she concludes, "despite the expansive and changing notion of civil rights, as a political project it is insufficient for indigenous and other colonized peoples and the ongoing and often pressing questions of sovereignty and nationhood."[38] Moving this argument into the specifics of the issue at hand, the Web site SupportKamehameha.org states, "There is a critical difference between an affirmative action or diversity program and the efforts of a private institution to help an indigenous group almost wiped out by Western influence."[39] Kanaka Maoli continually struggle to bring attention to the specificity of their colonial history.

Using Hawaiianness against Hawaiians

Cultural appropriation is nothing new to Native Americans. Native scholars and activists have developed an advanced critique of the multiple ways indigenous cultures have been mined by the dominant culture looking at everything from anthropologists misusing indigenous knowledge, to Hollywood's creation of "the Red man," to indigenous DNA being taken without consent, to the "owning" of native "artifacts" by collectors and museums, to New Age "white shamans and plastic medicine men," to University of Illinois former mascot Chief Illiniwek, to all the wannabe Indians who claim a Cherokee princess in their family tree, to agribusiness and the pharmaceutical industry's patenting of native plants. And that's just the beginning. These practices demonstrate how appropriation has been integral to colonization, even when articulated otherwise. The second prong of my analysis explores the ways cultural appropriation is used to claim Hawaiianness for non-Hawaiians, specifically those attacking Kamehameha Schools.

Postcolonial and indigenous studies scholars have been instrumental in exploring the ways colonization operates through cultural processes, not simply through military, political, or economic force. One of the most persistent forms of appropriation is that of "playing Indian" or "going native," which occurs in many forms, including some mentioned above.[40] Non-natives "play Indian" by claiming native ancestry, indigenous knowledge, and/or by practicing native traditions. The motivations and intensions of these appropriations are complex and contradictory, but seldom are the consequences beneficial in the long term to native communities. Writing particularly about the Native American experience, Shari Huhndorf states:

> Throughout the twentieth century, going native has served as an essential means of defining and regenerating racial whiteness and a racially inflected vision of Americanness. It also reflects on the national history by providing self-justifying fantasies that conceal the violence marking European America's origins. The politics of going native, then, are extremely complex. Exhibiting profound ambivalence about America's past as well as about modernity, forms of going native also support European-American hegemony.[41]

While it may seem contradictory, white hegemony is supported by "playing Indian" because the practice accelerates the process of vanishing real Indians and their cultural knowledge. In his cutting critique of Kevin Costner's *Dances with Wolves,* Louis Owens makes this crystal clear: "from the beginning of the colonial enterprise, the European invader has simultaneously demonstrated (and continues to demonstrate) a perverse and almost grotesquely paradoxical yearning to be Indian, to inhabit not merely the continent but the original inhabitant as well."[42]

Kanaka Maoli have certainly not been spared these appropriative moves and haole hegemony has benefited. The appropriation of Hawaiian culture commingles with Orientalist ideas about Asia—a very large place, with many cultures—that are then conflated with the Pacific, an equally vast and heterogeneous region. The continual referencing of Asian Pacific Islanders (API), as if one could easily capture such a category, enables this confusion.[43] One of the most obvious examples can be found in tourist shows, which often contain a potpourri of dances and dress thrown together with little cultural referencing and lots of artistic license performed by various "Polynesian" dancers. Shows often end with an audience-participation number in which tourists are encouraged to "play Hawaiian" by enacting a hula with the "help" of "authentic" hula girls.

While most non-Hawaiian residents know enough not to participate in such blatant spectacles, some search for belonging via other means of appropriation. Haole residents in particular have sought to escape their haoleness by claiming to be kamaʻāina (literally "children of the land" but popularly reinterpreted to mean longtime resident), Hawaiian, or "Hawaiian at heart." Others have sought to diminish Kanaka Maoli claims to place by insisting that everyone in Hawaiʻi is an immigrant and therefore everyone has equal claim to the islands. The rhetoric mobilized around the attacks on Kamehameha Schools that chastises Hawaiians for not following their own cultural practices incorporates elements of both of these claims.

The statement by Robert Rees that Kamehameha Schools was "rejecting the great Hawaiian tradition of hānai" in the Mohica-Cummings case is brilliantly insidious. The move makes the anti-Hawaiian attackers seem both knowledgeable about, and protective of, Hawaiian culture (read: even more Hawaiian than the Hawaiians), at the same moment they seek to bring down one of its oldest institutions. Lisa Kahaleole Hall has written about this phenomenon:

> Those who do not claim to be literally Hawaiian often make a symbolic claim. "Hawaiians at heart" assume that knowing and appreciating Hawaiian culture is enough to transform them into being Hawaiian. Indeed, some have gone so far as to claim that they are more Hawaiian than actual Hawaiians, because they have greater cultural or language knowledge.[44]

Hall goes on to discuss how the "internalized fear, shame, and anger" instilled via colonization often impede strong identity claims and cultural practice by today's Hawaiians.[45] Understanding this history makes these accusations by non-Hawaiians even more difficult to stomach.

The notion that non-Hawaiians are needed to protect Hawaiian culture from Hawaiians is expressed even more broadly in the repeated claims that efforts to maintain admissions preferences are somehow anti-aloha, part of what Rosen calls "unfortunate trends toward discrimination and even segregation in Hawai'i." The unmooring of Hawaiian culture, and the "aloha spirit" in particular, allowing all an equal claim on Hawaiianness is not new. The discourse of racial harmony in the islands has long exploited "aloha" to shore up the construction of the islands as a racial paradise.[46] The same logics are followed here as with the claim that everyone is an immigrant. A good example of this is the anti-Hawaiian group "Aloha for All," whose powerful haole founders and funders include Thurston Twigg-Smith, H. William Burgess, and Ken Conklin.[47] They promote the notion that aloha is a free-floating "gift" from Hawai'i (and notably not Hawaiians) to the world. What *is* new to popular discourse is the direct charge that Hawaiian culture, including the principle/value/spirit of aloha, needs protection from Hawaiians. The Aloha for All Web site states:

> It is not in keeping with the spirit of Aloha for the government to give one racial group land or money or special privileges or preferences from which all other racial groups in Hawaii are excluded. Yet some of our Hawaiian neighbors support exactly this sort of preference, and to a degree, they have had it written into the state's constitution and laws . . . We believe that individuals of Hawaiian ancestry are just like the rest of us. Hawaiians are not a "people" separate from the state's other citizens.[48]

Cutting through to the heart of the matter, J. Kēhaulani Kauanui writes, "Aloha for All regards Native Hawaiians as only a race and wants to render invisible such land claims based on original occupancy and the sovereignty of the kingdom—and without further recourse to reclamation."[49] This insistent racializing of Kanaka Maoli is successful not simply through denial, that is, they are "not a 'people,'" but by going further and rewriting aloha as equal protection, thereby eviscerating its origins and transplanting it neatly within the myth of American democracy. Again from the Web site:

> Hawai'i's gift to the world is the Aloha embodied daily in the beautiful people of many races living here in relative harmony. Similarly, one of America's greatest gifts to the world is the principle that all citizens, regardless of race or ancestry, are entitled to the equal protection of the laws. That principle is incorporated into Hawai'i's Bill of Rights, which provides that no person shall be denied the equal protection of the laws because of race or ancestry. That principle also fits perfectly with the Aloha spirit and, in effect, makes Aloha part of the constitutional law of the United States.

We see how this statement invokes the ubiquitous origin story of U.S. democracy being founded on equality, which does the important work of rendering invisible the genocide, colonial violence, and slavery that marked the beginning of this nation. Andrea Smith calls this "the liberal myth that the United States is founded on democratic principles rather than being built on the pillars of capitalism, colonialism, and white supremacy."[50] The Aloha for All proponents laud Hawai'i state law, which we know to be contested, since the overthrow, annexation, and statehood processes were all illegal. Finally, "the Aloha spirit" is neatly rolled into the mix. This is done by first vaguely referencing it as having something to do with "beautiful people," "many races," and "relative harmony," making it sound like a Benetton ad, then distilling it to mean "equal protection," which is further narrowed to apply just to "race or ancestry."

Vanishing Indigeneity and Elevating Postracial America

If aloha is as American as apple pie and non-Hawaiians can better practice Hawaiian culture than Hawaiians, claims by Hawaiians are easily framed as unfounded demands for "race-based" special treatment. The two-stage attack against Kamehameha Schools I just detailed, which claims the admissions policy is racially discriminatory and then further claims that Hawaiians are undermining Hawaiian culture, is successful in so far as both of these moves vanish Kanaka Maoli indigeneity. The first move says Kanaka Maoli are a racial group and all racial groups should be treated equally. If Kanaka Maoli are simply one of a number of immigrant groups in the islands, they can make no unique claims. In fact, as this line of argument goes, any claims they make demonstrate that they have not evolved to a higher moral "post-race" position. This is the third prong of my analysis.

As Kauanui and others relentlessly argue, indigenous claims tie not just to U.S. political entitlements as civil rights claims do, but to sovereignty, and to international law, and to land. Many state and federal documents recognize the unique history of Kanaka Maoli but the 1993 Congressional Apology Resolution is the strongest and most significant recognition of Kanaka Maoli indigeneity and dispossession. The resolution clearly states that "the indigenous Hawaiian people never directly relinquished their claims to their inherent sovereignty as a people or over their national lands to the United States, either through their monarchy or through a plebiscite or referendum" (U.S. Public Law 103-150, November 28, 1993). Not only does this statement underscore Kanaka Maoli indigeneity, but it explicitly says that claims to *national* lands were never relinquished, thereby raising the question of international law. "Given that Hawaiian Kingdom sovereignty was not lost via conquest, cession, or adjudication, those rights to self-rule are still in place under international law."[51]

Many native Hawaiian activists have been struggling for decades to move the contest from the state and federal courts to international arenas. The success of color-blind ideology in keeping the argument about racial preferences and thus constitutional and federal law makes international arguments impossible to articulate, or seemingly ridiculous, when they are advanced. Haunani-Kay Trask writes: "The context of the U.S. Constitution is too small a framework in which to argue for sovereignty. An international frame of reference, one that invokes universal human rights, must be the context for discussion."[52]

The second offensive move implies we should get beyond race and simply celebrate the melting pot culture of the islands with no group, indigenous or otherwise, having any unique claims. Hawaiian claims to "preferential treatment" are disrupting the melting pot and threatening island culture itself. Hawaiians are cast as holding on to victim status rather than moving to the higher moral ground of race neutrality. Paternalism has always been part of colonization and it is clearly seen in the arguments about Hawaiians threatening their own culture. How convenient that non-Hawaiians, in particular haoles, are able to intervene and save the day, the culture, and the islands.

David Rosen's statement that his plaintiffs "are Hawaiian in every sense save the merely genetic" effectively incorporates both moves, racializing Hawaiians and claiming Hawaiianness for non-Hawaiians.[53] The phrase "merely genetic" not only (dismissively) racializes Kanaka Maoli, but it reinforces the common mistaken conflation of race with biology. The claim that the plaintiffs are "Hawaiian in every sense" that really matters is a direct assault on indigeneity and a clear appropriation of Hawaiian culture. It would be interesting to hear Rosen specify exactly how the plaintiffs are Hawaiian, but we can surmise that the answer would involve vague gestures at "aloha," having been born in the islands, mixed-race heritage, and perhaps even participation in hula or paddling or playing the ʻukulele. Clearly there is nothing wrong with any of these things, except insofar as they are used to "play Hawaiian."

The postracial argument of being "beyond race" is increasingly popular in the age of Obama, especially in the islands, where it has always been strong and is now even stronger with a "native son" in office. With the election of a Black man to the presidency, proponents of a color-blind ideology have new fodder for their argument. Obama's election is held up as proof that the United States is now in a postracial period wherein Martin Luther King's "dream" (King had many dreams, including an end to the war in Vietnam and economic justice, but his vision is nearly universally reduced to this one speech on racial equality) has been fulfilled and racial discrimination and oppression are things of the past. Legions of social scientists and social justice activists have amassed too much data on the increasing inequalities in this country for us to be fooled. Social justice continues to be the goal or "the dream," but we cannot get there without recognizing where we really are and how we got here. Even if we had racial equality, we still would not have justice for Kanaka Maoli or the other native peoples colonized by the U.S. government. This is why color-blind ideology is so dangerous and, further, why not recognizing the different histories of indigenous and racial groups forecloses any significant progress.

Unlike my brother's spearing, my three-pronged analysis does not end with the satisfaction of a clean, clear shot that neatly resolves everything. I can only hope to have added information and analysis to the discussion. It is hard to know what the ultimate outcome of these lawsuits will be, but if the latest case is actually heard by the Supreme Court as Rosen desires, many fear the worst. A ruling against Kamehameha Schools would be devastating, not just because it could topple the most powerful institution supporting Kanaka Maoli culture, but also because it would invigorate attacks against native Hawaiian public programs and strengthen anti-Hawaiian public perception. It would violently resolve the productive tensions of Hawaiʻi's crossroads in favor of homogenized empire. Challenging these attacks includes exposing a discursive strategy that racializes Kanaka Maoli, claims Hawaiianness for non-Hawaiians, and situates the non-Hawaiian, particularly the haole, both as *victim* of racial discrimination and *champion* of racial equality.

Notes

Thank you to the editorial board of the *American Quarterly*, and especially to Paul Lai and Lindsey Smith for their editorial support and for producing this volume. Mahalo nui to Dorrie Mazzone, Phyllis Turnbull, and RaeDeen Keahiolalo Karasuda for feedback on early drafts and tireless support.

All Web links listed below were accessed in fall 2009.

1. Economic Development and Tourism State of Hawai'i Department of Business, "2006: The State of Hawai'i Data Book: A Statistical Abstract," State of Hawai'i, www.hawaii.gov/dbedt/, 113; Sen. Dan Inouye and Sen. Daniel Akaka, "Native Hawaiian Health Care Improvement Reauthorization Act of 2007" (2007).
2. Along with other Pacific Islanders, some Kanaka Maoli scholars are involved in building the field of Native Pacific Cultural Studies. See Vicente M. Diaz and J. Kēhaulani Kauanui, "Native Pacific Cultural Studies on the Edge," *The Contemporary Pacific* 12.2 (2001): 315–41; Teresia K. Teaiwa, "L(o)osing the Edge," *The Contemporary Pacific* 13.2 (2001): 343–57; Geoffrey M. White and Ty Kawika Tengan, "Disappearing Worlds: Anthropology and Cultural Studies in Hawai'i and the Pacific," *The Contemporary Pacific* 13.2 (2001): 381–416.
3. Amy Kaplan, "Violent Belongings and the Question of Empire Today: Presidential Address to the American Studies Association, October 17, 2003," *American Quarterly* 56.1 (2004); Andrea Smith and J. Kēhaulani Kauanui, "Native Feminisms Engage American Studies," *American Quarterly* 60.2 (2008): 241–49.
4. Following the traditional sustenance practices of Kanaka Maoli, many in Hawai'i free dive (dive without scuba tanks) with Hawaiian sling three-pronged spears. A successful diver must know how to read the ocean and must have unfailing patience, enormous lung-capacity, and most important, a respect and caring for the land (malama 'āina). My brother, Joby Rohrer, has mastered the art and is busy teaching his kids.
5. Noenoe K. Silva, *Aloha Betrayed: Native Hawaiian Resistance to American Colonialism* (Durham, N.C.: Duke University Press, 2004), 169.
6. J. Kēhaulani Kauanui, "Diasporic Deracination and 'Off-Island' Hawaiians," *The Contemporary Pacific* 19.1 (2007): 137–60; Gordon Y. K. Pang, "Native Hawaiian Census Numbers Down," *Honolulu Advertiser*, Aug. 12, 2005.
7. For more on the history of colonization in Hawai'i, see Silva, *Aloha Betrayed*; J. Kēhaulani Kauanui, *Hawaiian Blood: Colonialism and the Politics of Sovereignty and Indigeneity* (Durham, N.C.: Duke University Press, 2008); Jonathan Kay Kamakawiwo'ole Osorio, *Dismembering Lāhui: A History of the Hawaiian Nation to 1887* (Honolulu: University of Hawai'i Press, 2002); Haunani-Kay Trask, *From a Native Daughter: Colonialism and Sovereignty in Hawai'i*, rev. ed. (Honolulu: University of Hawai'i Press, 1999); Lilikalā Kame'eleihiwa, *Native Land and Foreign Desires* (Honolulu: Bishop Museum Press, 1992).
8. Judy Rohrer, "Got Race? The Production of Haole and the Distortion of Indigeneity in the Rice Decision," *The Contemporary Pacific* 18.1 (2006):1–31.
9. Bernice Pauahi Bishop, "Bernice Pauahi Bishop's Will and Codicils," Kamehameha Schools, http://www.ksbe.edu/pauahi/will.php.
10. For more on Kamehameha Schools and Bishop Estate, see Samuel P. King and Randall W. Roth, *Broken Trust: Greed, Mismanagement, and Political Manipulation at America's Largest Charitable Trust* (Honolulu: University of Hawai'i Press, 2006); Gavan Daws and Na Leo o Kamehameha, *Wayfinding through the Storm: Speaking Truth to Power at Kamehameha Schools 1993–1999* (Honolulu: Watermark Publishing, 2009).
11. I use "haoles" as a plural term because this is common in Hawaiian Creole English (HCE), even though it is not grammatically correct in 'Ōlelo Hawai'i (Hawaiian language), the originating language of the term.
12. Robert M. Rees, "Hawaiian History Can't Be Reduced to Race," *Honolulu Advertiser*, August 31, 2003.
13. Rod Antone and Associated Press staff, "Kamehameha Sued over Its Admissions," *Star Bulletin*, June 26, 2003.
14. Rick Daysog, "Tycoons to Share Tab in Kamehameha Suit," *Honolulu Advertiser*, Dec. 3, 2003.
15. Bruce Fein, "Race Separation Ratified," *Washington Times*, Dec. 26, 2006.
16. Ibid.
17. Kamehameha Schools Trustees and CEO, "Trustee Message: Kamehameha Schools and 'John Doe' Settle Admissions Lawsuit," Kamehameha Schools, http://www.ksbe.edu.

18. Jim Dooley, "Kamehameha Settled at $7M," *Honolulu Advertiser*, February 8, 2008.
19. Star Bulletin staff, "Solicitation Upsets Lawyer Group," *Honolulu Star Bulletin*, May 30, 2007.
20. KITV, "Attorney Solicits Plaintiffs for Kamehameha Schools Lawsuit," April 3, 2008 (news report), http://www.kitv.com.
21. David R. Rosen, "Let High Court Hear Admissions Issue," *Honolulu Advertiser*, May 27, 2007.
22. Jim Dooley and Gordon Y. K. Pang, "Kamehameha Schools Again Being Sued over Admissions Policy," *Honolulu Advertiser*, August 7, 2008.
23. Star-Bulletin staff and Associated Press, "Kamehameha Schools Face Another Challenge to Admissions," *Honolulu Star-Bulletin*, August 6, 2008.
24. Kamehameha Schools Board of Trustees, "KS Sues John Doe for Breach of Contract; Receives Demand Letter Threatening New Lawsuit from Eric Grant," Kamehameha Schools, www.ksbe.edu.
25. Dooley and Pang, "Kamehameha Schools Again Being Sued."
26. Susan Essoyan, "Secret Plaintiffs Appeal Kamehameha Lawsuit," *Star Bulletin*, Mar. 6, 2009.
27. Ibid. In November 2010, the Ninth Circuit Court of Appeals denied the request for the rehearing on the issue of anonymity.
28. Kara M. L. Young, "Kamehameha's Hawaiians-Only Admissions Policy under 42 U.S.C. § 1981: A Permissible Pursuit of Practical Freedom," *Hawai'i Law Review* 26 (2003): 314–15.
29. Marcus Daniel, "Don't Hijack King's Message," *Honolulu Advertiser*, August 31, 2003.
30. J. Kēhaulani Kauanui reports that outside funding for the *Rice* case came from "Campaign for a Color-Blind America, Robert Bork, Americans against Discrimination and Preferences, the United States Justice Foundation, the Center for Equal Opportunity, the New York Civil Rights Coalition, and the Pacific Legal Foundation—all of which submitted legal briefs on his behalf. These extremely conservative right-wing think tanks have been central in a nationwide attack on affirmative action and other civil rights gains in the United States." J. Kēhaulani Kauanui, "Precarious Positions: Native Hawaiians and U.S. Federal Recognition," *The Contemporary Pacific* 17.1 (2005): 8.
31. The foundation of this argument comes from critical race theory (CRT), which maintains that law and legal discourse are significant players in the processes of social construction, particularly racialization. It exposes color-blind ideology as a white historical amnesia that pretends we live in a postracist society and therefore contends that race does not matter. See Kimberlé Crenshaw et al., eds., *Critical Race Theory: The Key Writings That Formed the Movement* (New York: New York Press, 1995); Francisco Valdes, Jerome McCristal Culp, and Angela P. Harris, eds., *Crossroads, Directions, and a New Critical Race Theory* (Philadelphia: Temple University Press, 2002); Ian Haney-López, *White by Law: The Legal Construction of Race* (New York: New York University Press, 1996).
32. "Ninth Circuit Holds That Private School's Remedial Admissions Policy Violates § 1981," *Harvard Law Review* 119 (2005): 666.
33. Chris K. Iijima, "Race over Rice: Binary Analytical Boxes and a Twenty-First Century Endorsement of Nineteenth Century Imperialism in *Rice v. Cayetano*," *Rutgers Law Review* 53 (2000): 114–15.
34. Lisa Kahaleole Hall, "'Hawaiian at Heart' and Other Fictions," *The Contemporary Pacific* 17.2 (2005): 412.
35. Vine Deloria Jr., "The Application of the Constitution to American Indians," in *Exiled in the Land of the Free: Democracy, Indian Nations, and the U.S. Constitution*, ed. Oren Lyons et al. (Santa Fe: Clear Light Publishers, 1992), 282.
36. Haunani-Kay Trask, *From a Native Daughter: Colonialism and Sovereignty in Hawai'i* (Monroe, Minn.: Common Courage Press., 1993), 264.
37. Steve Russell and Terri Miles, "One-Sided Interest Convergence: Indian Sovereignty in Organizing and Litigation," *Wicazo Sa Review* 23.1 (2008): 7.
38. J. Kēhaulani Kauanui, "Colonialism in Equality: Hawaiian Sovereignty and the Question of U.S. Civil Rights," *South Atlantic Quarterly* 107.4 (2008): 636.
39. SupportKamehameha.org, "About *Doe v. Kamehameha*," http://SupportKamehameha.org.
40. Philip Joseph Deloria, *Playing Indian* (New Haven, Conn.: Yale University Press, 1998); Rayna Green, "The Tribe Called Wannabee: Playing Indian in America and Europe," in *Visions of an Enduring People: A Reader in Native American Studies*, ed. Walter C. Fleming and John G. Watts (Dubuque, Iowa: Kendall Hunt, 2000), 215–41.
41. Shari M. Huhndorf, *Going Native: Indians in the American Cultural Imagination* (Ithaca, N.Y.: Cornell University Press, 2001), 5.

42. Louis Owens, "Apocalypse at the Two-Socks Hop: Dancing with the Vanishing American," in *Mixed Blood Messages: Literature, Film, Family, Place*, ed. Louis Owens (Norman: University of Oklahoma Press, 1998), 125. The film *Avatar* simply takes this "yearning" to go native one step further. (Thanks to Noenoe Silva for planting this idea and encouraging me to see the film.)
43. Lisa Kahaleole Hall, "Strategies of Erasure: U.S. Colonialism and Native Hawaiian Feminism," *American Quarterly* 60.2 (2008): 273–80.
44. Hall, "'Hawaiian at Heart' and Other Fictions," 410.
45. Ibid., 411.
46. Judy Rohrer, "Disrupting the 'Melting Pot': Racial Discourse in Hawai'i and the Naturalization of Haole," *Ethnic and Racial Studies* 31.6 (2008): 1110–25; Lori Pierce, "'The Whites Have Created Modern Honolulu': Ethnicity, Racial Stratification, and the Discourse of Aloha," in *Racial Thinking in the United States: Uncompleted Independence*, ed. Paul Spickard and G. Reginald Daniel (Notre Dame, Ind.: University of Notre Dame Press, 2004), 124–54.
47. Kauanui, "Colonialism in Equality," 645.
48. H. William Burgess, "Aloha for All," http://www.aloha4all.org/home.aspx.
49. Kauanui, "Colonialism in Equality," 646.
50. Andrea Smith, "American Studies without America: Native Feminisms and the Nation-State," *American Quarterly* 60.2 (2008): 309–16.
51. Kauanui, "Precarious Positions," 15.
52. Trask, *From a Native Daughter*, 38–39.
53. Dooley and Pang, "Kamehameha Schools Again Being Sued."

Kēwaikaliko's *Benocide*: Reversing the Imperial Gaze of *Rice v. Cayetano* and Its Legal Progeny

Dean Itsuji Saranillio

This artwork was created in October 2000. It was completed in a week and has been getting both positive and negative feedback. Grandma hates it.

—Kēwaikaliko, caption to *Benocide*

A Hawaiian artist who goes by the pseudonym Kēwaikaliko critiques the legal challenges emerging out of the 2000 *Rice v. Cayetano* Supreme Court decision in his artwork titled *Benocide.*[1] Rooted in a history of colonial dispossession, Kēwaikaliko created a loaded illustration that illuminates, from a Native Hawaiian epistemological vantage point, forms of colonial violence that are often rendered natural and normal in Hawai'i.[2] Central to the artwork is a Hawaiian man being lynched by then governor Benjamin Cayetano, Hawai'i's first governor of Filipino descent (1994–2002). At the feet of former governor Cayetano lies the bearded and bloodied skull of Sanford B. Dole,[3] the first colonial governor of the Territory of Hawai'i and president of the interim governments between the 1893 U.S. military-backed overthrow of the Hawaiian Kingdom and 1898 illegal U.S. annexation.[4] The lynching of the Hawaiian man takes place on a tree with leaves made of money and upon which Death, smoking crystal methamphetamine or "ice," is figured as its trunk. A *haole* (white) settler, and well-known political pundit, who has been seeking to dismantle all Hawaiian rights and entitlements, stands wearing a swastika-covered aloha shirt, patriotically waving the state flag of Hawai'i—which is closely similar to the flag of the Hawaiian Kingdom. Next to him is what I perceive to be a Hawaiian figured as a *pua'a*, or pig in western-style clothing. A *pua'a* with trickster-like qualities, perhaps a colluding Native, appears to be fondling the rear of the *haole* settler. Depicted in black and gray, and composing the ground beneath this mob, are Hawaiian women who appear in all manner of suffering. The black and gray envelop the green mountain that overlooks the urban sprawl of Waikīkī. Centered along the horizon is a nuclear mushroom cloud rising into the sky, a direct reference to nuclear testing in the Pacific and more specifically to the U.S. military's devastating impact in Hawai'i.[5]

Benocide was exhibited at the Honolulu Academy of Arts in an exhibition titled "*Nā Maka Hou*: New Visions" from May 13 until June 17, 2001. Featuring one hundred works of art by fifty-eight contemporary Hawaiian artists, the exhibition was designed to "communicate a new vision of Hawaiians in today's society."[6] Manulani Aluli Meyer, scholar of Hawaiian epistemology and education, explains the pedagogical and theoretical implications of Hawaiian art in her essay "Hawaiian Art: A Doorway to Knowing," which accompanied the *Nā Maka Hou* exhibition:

> Hawaiian art has always inspired me to enter doorways to deeper relationships, wider truths and vivid realities . . . We read in art the possibilities of our people, we dialog with history, we repent with shame, we wonder, we marvel, we wake up! We are educated through the poetry shared by these modern prophets of ancient knowing. We are changed. We are changed forever.[7]

Where ways of seeing are guided intimately by ways of knowing, which itself is shaped by a pedagogy of history, culture, and one's position within the cultural politics of the everyday, Meyer speaks to the use of art as a pedagogical tool. Art can thus provide discursive space to dialogue with different histories and various conditions of possibility, thus challenging viewers and their versions of reality. Far from the romantic images of Hawai'i peddled globally by a billion-dollar tourism industry, Hawaiian artwork such as *Benocide* defamiliarizes exotic images and official state histories of Hawai'i, showing how they facilitate a violent history of U.S. occupation. Kēwaikaliko thus literally offers a vision of Hawai'i that often goes unseen, even among Hawai'i residents, and is a clarion call to re-envision and re-imagine Hawai'i's contemporary situation.[8]

On February 23, 2000, the U.S. Supreme Court in *Rice v. Cayetano* struck down the Native-only voting scheme of the nine Office of Hawaiian Affairs (OHA) trustees. The Office of Hawaiian Affairs is a state agency responsible for managing and administering trust monies generated from the "ceded public lands trust" to Hawaiians.[9] The Court found OHA to be in violation of the U.S. Constitution's 15th Amendment and ruled 7–2 that OHA was a State of Hawai'i race-based agency, deeming the Native-only voting qualifications to be racially discriminatory.[10] As a result of the Court's declaration in the *Rice* decision, all federal and state programs benefiting Hawaiians as an indigenous people became vulnerable, and a series of legal challenges ensued.[11] In October of 2000 the Republican candidate for U.S. Senate, John Carroll, and Hawai'i

Kēwaikaliko, *Benocide*, 2000. Pastel and fluorescent marker on paper. Courtesy of the artist.

resident Patrick Barrett filed two separate lawsuits claiming racial discrimination, arguing that Hawaiian "entitlements" created by the constitution of the state of Hawai'i violated the Equal Protection Clause of the U.S. Constitution. These two lawsuits were consolidated and when combined they threatened to eliminate the Office of Hawaiian Affairs; all federal programs for Hawaiian health, education, and housing; Hawaiian gathering rights; and the Department of Hawaiian Home Lands.[12] Both cases were eventually thrown out of court for lack of standing once it was found that neither plaintiff had ever applied for a single Native program. In March of 2002, however, a group of sixteen self-proclaimed "multiethnic Hawaii Citizens" sued the state in the *Arakaki et al. v. Lingle* case. This case was reduced to a ruling on the constitutionality of OHA in U.S. District Court and was appealed to the 9th Circuit Court of Appeals. The Federal Court of Appeals issued a ruling on August 31, 2005, reaffirming that the plaintiffs could not challenge the constitutionality of federal spending but ruled that they were in standing as taxpayers to sue OHA.[13] Completed in October of 2000, when the *Carroll* and *Barrett* suits were filed, Kēwaikaliko's *Benocide* inserts into the historical record a challenge to the earlier lawsuits, but its critique applies to the entire string of legal assaults targeting Hawaiians. The artwork, indeed, questions the very legitimacy of a U.S. legal institution by visually showing how the rights exercised by the plaintiffs, and violence inflicted on Hawaiians through the *Rice* decision, are rights gained and structured through relations of colonial domination.

By situating the lynching in *Benocide* high on a scenic point in an affluent area of O'ahu known as Tantalus, the three in attendance obtain a sweeping and panoptic vision of both Honolulu and the lynched Hawaiian. Here a totalizing imperial gaze or "commanding view," one that implies a viewer with an elevated vantage point and the colonial authority to subject, discipline, and simultaneously objectify the colonized subject has direct bearing on both a reading of this artwork and its connections to the imperial gaze of the *Rice* decision.[14] As David Spurr notes in *The Rhetoric of Empire*, the ideology of the gaze is an "active instrument in construction, order, and arrangement" and its authority, similar to Foucault's Panopticon, relies on an "analytic arrangement of space from a position of visual advantage."[15] The gaze defines the subject by fixing its identity in relation to the observers, while also objectifying it within a "relation of power inherent in the larger system of order."[16] The logic underpinning the lawsuit and the Supreme Court's decision to identify the OHA voting scheme as "race-based" perceives race but renders Hawaiian sovereignty rights and a history of occupation invisible, consequently flattening the important historical and political differences between Hawaiians and non-Hawaiians. As J. Kēhaulani Kauanui explains: "Blood quanta classifications have consistently been used to enact, substantiate, and then disguise the further appropriation of native lands while they obscure and erase a discourse of specifically Hawaiian sovereignty and identity as a relation of genealogy to place."[17] Here, the dominant U.S. frameworks of race and citizenship trump Hawaiian articulations of indigeneity and genealogy, and the Native subject's claims to sovereignty, with land and resources at stake, are expelled for the supposed cause of equal rights. Spurr notes that "the superior and invulnerable position of the observer coincides with the role of affirming the political order that makes that position possible."[18]

Kēwaikaliko conveys visually his knowledge and view of contemporary Hawai'i by drawing attention to the hidden aspects of imperial power that underpin the legal assaults. Seeing how the imperial gaze attempts to remain unmarked, the artist is able to make such a gaze visible by turning the "observer into the observed," marking and calling attention to a color-blind visual optic and the violence it enacts.[19] In other words, through selective narrative framing, Kēwaikaliko uses the medium of visual art to draw connections between various historical references, thus theorizing the intersections and distinctions between race and indigeneity, while challenging the sanctity of U.S. jurisprudence by implicating it in maintaining a violent colonial order dependent on the subjugation of Hawaiians. By highlighting visuality, this essay traces how *Benocide* appropriates a gaze blind to Hawaiian indigenous birthrights and turns it upon settlers and collaborative Hawaiians through the artist's use of historically legible images and the spatial configurations of a lynching.

The site of the lynching, generally known as Tantalus, is a place marked by a settler genealogy of colonial erasure and authority. Exemplifying an imperial gaze, the Hawaiian name for Tantalus, *Pu'u 'Ōhi'a*, was effaced when the students from Punahou School, an elite private school created in 1841 to educate white missionary children separate from Hawaiians, renamed this place after a figure in Greek mythology.[20] The marking of *Pu'u 'Ōhi'a*, which literally means "the mound of the *'ōhi'a* tree," is identified through the use of the twisted *'ōhi'a* in the artwork. Using place and landscape as an archive of history, Kēwaikaliko's choice to locate the lynching at this popular lookout points to the historical link between the colonial authority that underpins the imperial gaze in the *Rice* decision and the overthrow of the Hawaiian Kingdom. Many of the men who were influential and actively involved in processes of economic and political disenfranchisement, including the overthrow, graduated from Punahou School. Sanford B. Dole, for example, who was both born at the school and graduated from there in 1864, is drawn at the feet of Cayetano. The plaintiff Harold Rice is himself a graduate, whose ancestor William Harrison Rice was one of the first missionaries who helped found the school. Another Rice patriarch, William Hyde Rice, helped draft the Bayonet Constitution in 1887 disenfranchising from vote all Asians and a majority of Hawaiians through income, property, and literacy requirements, thus strengthening white settler control of the government.[21] Indeed, while the current Rice claims discrimination as a U.S. citizen without the "requisite ancestry" to vote in Native-only elections, Kēwaikaliko provides specificity to such abstractions by highlighting the familial and institutional genealogy of Harold Rice and his family's political involvement in events that helped establish a colonial order and its accompanying epistemes.[22] In this way, Kēwaikaliko juxtaposes two competing genealogies with very different claims to history about Hawai'i, and the colonial authority obscured through notions of abstract equality that are necessary to the imperial gaze of the *Rice* decision are given significance.

While in the drawing Cayetano is physically hanging the Native, he does not look at the lynching, but rather looks to the *haole* settler for recognition of his act.[23] This is a subtle but apt illustration of the performative role that Cayetano as a Filipino American played in order to maintain his political power and inclusion. Eiko Kosasa and Ida Yoshinaga, founders of the group Local Japanese Women for Justice (LJWJ), exposed the chain of command in the state when soon after the U.S. Supreme Court ruled in favor of the plaintiff in the *Rice* case, Hawai'i's senator Daniel Inouye issued a statement to the Office of Hawaiian Affairs and Governor Benjamin Cayetano requesting the removal of all trustees who were voted into office.[24] Inouye instructed in his letter, "I believe that the Governor has authority under a separate State of Hawai'i statute to appoint interim trustees so that the important work of the Office of Hawaiian Affairs need not be interrupted."[25] Cayetano, under Senator Inouye's instructions, called for the nine trustees to step down voluntarily or risk OHA's termination, and then appointed his own trustees to office. As Kosasa and Yoshinaga point out, "the intended result of Inouye's statement was to facilitate the control of OHA by the state and away from the electoral process."[26] In *Benocide*, the *pua'a* and Cayetano choose not to look at the lynching but instead to the *haole* settler as they work within the constraints of the system and struggle for subordinate supremacy. In other words, to reword David Spurr's statement, the imposing but vulnerable position of a minority within a political position of colonial power coincides with the role of affirming the colonial order that makes their position possible.

Kēwaikaliko's use of a lynch mob to visually represent settler colonialism in Hawai'i helps us to see how the current multicultural order, celebrated by state ideology as devoid of racism, was achieved through an inaugural moment of racist and colonial violence. Providing historical depth to the scene, Kēwaikaliko places at Governor Cayetano's feet the bloodied skull of Sanford B. Dole, the first colonial governor appointed to administer the Territory of Hawai'i (1900–1903). As mentioned above, Dole was president of both the Provisional Government (1893–1894) and the Republic of Hawai'i (1895–1898), two settler governments motivated ideologically by white supremacy and formed after the U.S.-backed overthrow of the Hawaiian Kingdom in January of 1893. Cayetano is positioned over Dole's remains and appears to have Dole's blood on his hands. Dole's position beneath the feet of Cayetano can be understood as a historical reference to the transfer of political power from the largely white-led Republican Party to the predominantly (East) Asian American–dominated Democratic Party. Resulting from a general and popular desire for social change in Hawai'i, coupled with the important support from labor unions and the cultural valorization of the primarily Japanese American 442nd Regiment and 100th Battalion in World War II, the liberal Democratic Party in 1954 captured from the Republicans a majority of seats in the legislature in what would be termed the "Democratic Revolution." The so-called Democratic Revolution is often narrated as the moment when liberal multiculturalism displaced a white racial dictatorship in Hawai'i. Ronald Takaki notes that Asian American struggles against the *haole* oligarchy reflected a new consciousness, "a transformation from sojourners to settlers, from Japanese to Japanese Americans."[27] Takaki goes on to say that Asian Americans "by their numerical preponderance . . . had greater opportunities [than did Asian Americans on the U.S. continent] to weave themselves and their cultures into the very fabric of Hawaii and to seek to transform their adopted land into a society of rich diversity where they and their children would no longer be 'strangers from a different shore.'"[28] Roger Bell, on the other hand, observes in his study of the Hawai'i statehood movement that Hawaiians after statehood had become "strangers, in their own land, submerged beneath the powerful white minority and a newly assertive Asian majority."[29] This seeming contradiction might be helpful for framing and disaggregating the different forms of oppression that these groups were contending with and moving against. Here Hawaiian and Asian American oppressions are "overlapping without equivalence," where these groups are each historically oppressed but their specific forms of oppression cannot be equated.[30] Thus it is important to understand how these forms of oppression are structured differently within the complex relations of power constituting the settler state.

The contest between representative figures Dole and Cayetano historically frame the art piece. In what Haunani-Kay Trask describes as an "intra-settler struggle for hegemony,"[31] the victor holds the noose. Cayetano stands where Dole once stood, exercising political power, which is made possible only by maintaining Hawaiian political subjugation. As Trask explains:

> While Asians, particularly the Japanese, come to dominate post-Statehood, Democratic Party politics, new racial tensions arise. The attainment of full American citizenship actually heightens prejudice against Natives. Because the ideology of the United States as a mosaic of races is reproduced in Hawai'i through the celebration of the fact that no single "immigrant group" constitutes a numerical majority, the post-statehood euphoria stigmatizes Hawaiians as a failed indigenous people whose conditions, including out-migration, actually worsen after statehood. Hawaiians are characterized as strangely unsuited, whether because of culture or genetics, to the game of assimilation.[32]

While Cayetano was not a popular governor among the many Asian American communities in Hawai'i, he and the Democratic Party are often touted as symbols of Asian success at assimilation and especially an Asian American civil rights struggle against white racist exclusion.[33] The collective desires for equality and empowerment within a U.S. political system by marginalized groups—represented here by Dole's remains at Cayetano's feet—constitute crucial components of a complex hegemonic colonial structure that often is never interrogated relative to ambitions for liberal inclusion. Such desires for liberal inclusion often takes the U.S. possession of contested indigenous lands and resources as a given, functioning to obscure and normalize U.S. occupation within a liberal and domestic U.S. civil rights discourse. While conservatives are criticized for enacting anti-indigenous lawsuits, the very naming of the art piece *Benocide* speaks to the collaborative role liberal Democrat "Ben" Cayetano has played in attempts to eliminate Hawaiian indigeneity. In response to the *Rice* decision, for instance, Cayetano stated publicly: "I've lived in Hawai'i long enough to feel I'm Hawaiian."[34] Situating "Filipino American" subjectivities within a genealogy of white supremacy and genocidal conquest, Dylan Rodríguez argues that a particular " 'Filipino American' commonsense" posits a "social ambition of nationalist multiculturalist raciality, while also inducing a Filipino American sociality that cannot (and must not) engage the always violent and terrorizing analytics of raciality."[35] That ambition for facilitating liberal inclusion through multiculturalism leads to an unwillingness or inability to engage with a history of U.S. genocidal occupation of the Philippines, and extends to a difficulty or unwillingness to contend with similar structures of violence in other sites including Hawai'i. Rodríguez contends that Filipinos are uniquely, though not exclusively, positioned to contend with racial death and disaster in a way that finds historical connections to other peoples faced with genocidal white supremacist racial ordering.[36] In this context, however, Cayetano becomes the symbol of a liberal multicultural state in Hawai'i maintaining his position by protecting a colonial order as the first Filipino American governor in the United States, thus facilitating "new modalities of American hegemony, across scales and historical moments."[37]

As critical projects that examine the entangled formations of settler colonialism and occupation in Hawai'i grow, scholarship examining Asian Americans in Hawai'i also have the potential to be transformed by engaging with the history of Native Hawaiians.[38] While Asian American history usually begins with Western colonialism/imperialism's displacement of peoples from Asia, or at the point of entry to the Americas or the Pacific, Asian American histories are seldom placed in relation to an indigenous history of dispossession by the United States. Though the effects of land dispossession and genocide against Native Americans and Hawaiians are acknowledged, indigenous histories are often written in past tense, as memorialized moments that are rarely used to interpret relations of force in the present. Asians in Hawai'i had much to agitate against as they were used as exploitable labor in a variety of industries and simultaneously marked as perpetual "foreign threats." This exclusion actually helped to discipline desires for further inclusion into the U.S. nation, often defined in opposition to representations of Native Hawaiians as primitive. Thus, the legal designation at different times of different Asian groups as "aliens ineligible to citizenship" helped to justify exclusionary laws pertaining to immigration and naturalization.[39] At the same time, the 1893 overthrow of the Hawaiian Kingdom and illegal annexation to the United States was possible because of the cultural work that designated Hawaiians, like other colonized peoples, "unfit for self-government."[40] Here American Orientalism positioned Asian Americans among other things as "ineligible to citizenship," and combating this designation by seeking inclusion into the settler nation helped to reaffirm Hawaiians' designation as permanently "unfit for self-government."[41] Andrea Smith explains in her concept of the "three pillars of white supremacy" that different communities are not affected by white supremacy in the same way. Understanding a groups' particular racial positioning and the logics of these oppressions—capitalist exploitation (slavery), war (Orientalism), and genocide—poses questions as to how otherwise noble efforts to combat one's own form of oppression can lead unwittingly to participating in the oppressive logic of another. In this instance, the continued existence of a settler state relies on racial projects whose goal is equality in the United States with white settlers. This should not be mistaken for an argument that civil rights are irrelevant, but rather that the scope and effects of such struggles can be expanded to take into account the movements of indigenous peoples. As Patricia Williams argues, "what is needed, therefore, is not the abandonment of rights language for all purposes, but an attempt to become multilingual in the semantics of each other's rights-valuation."[42]

By holding the noose and looking to the *haole* settler, former governor Cayetano also represents the collusion of the state of Hawai'i with the legal assaults. The state of Hawai'i has always been in a peculiar position of having to defend Native "entitlements" from suit while being negligent in administering these same "entitlements." In *Benocide*, Cayetano lynches the Hawaiian on a tree with leaves made of money. The 1959 Admissions Act, which admitted Hawai'i as a state, transferred an estimated 1.8 million acres of original Hawaiian crown and government lands from the federal government to the state of Hawai'i. In what was to be called the Ceded Public Lands Trust, "the betterment of the conditions of Native Hawaiians" was listed as one of its five responsibilities, and 20 percent of the revenue gained by these so-called ceded lands was to be transferred from the state of Hawai'i to another state agency, the Office of Hawaiian Affairs (OHA), which was established in 1978. In 1991 the Hawai'i Advisory Committee to the United States Commission on Civil Rights stated that both the territory and state of Hawai'i had been negligent for seventy-three years in fulfilling their fiduciary duties as trustees of the Ceded Public Lands Trust. In 1990 the Hawai'i State Legislature passed Act 304 to provide a mechanism for determining the amount of ceded land revenues owed to OHA. This law specified that OHA was entitled to 20 percent of revenue from the ceded lands. Three years later, the state paid OHA $19 million and agreed to make annual revenue payments. OHA filed a lawsuit in 1994 to resolve all remaining back-payment issues. On September 12, 2001, the Hawai'i Supreme Court ruled that Act 304 conflicted with the 1998 "Forgiveness Act" passed by Congress, which prohibited further payment of airport revenues for claims related to ceded lands, and was therefore invalid. The high court, however, reaffirmed OHA's right to benefit from the ceded lands trust. Based on the ruling, Governor Cayetano ordered state departments to stop payments to OHA. He instead offered to settle the issue of repayment in 1999 with a global settlement of $251 million and 360,000 acres of ceded lands, but OHA declined.[43]

In *Benocide,* across from Cayetano stands the caricature of a well-known *haole* settler wearing a swastika-covered aloha shirt, waving the state of Hawai'i flag, and clutching a bundle of documents under his arm. He represents a group, Aloha for All, that has been using the precedent set by the *Rice* decision to dismantle all Hawaiian "entitlements." Aloha for All is partially supported by the Campaign for a Colorblind America, a national group that challenges affirmative action programs across the United States.[44]

> We believe that individuals of Hawaiian ancestry are just like the rest of us. Hawaiians are not a "people" separate from the State's other citizens. They are not a "tribe," not a "sovereign nation." They are one among many ethnic groups in the state, entitled to the same respect we give all those groups and their varied cultures—but not more.[45]

Of the three—Cayetano, the *pua'a,* and the *haole* settler—the *haole* settler is the only one who looks at the lynched Hawaiian directly. His "color-blind" epistemology, however, makes the materiality of Hawaiian history and indigeneity hidden in plain sight. By reading the representations of the institutions that structure his worldview, symbols of a U.S. nation-state—the state flag and U.S. legal documents—show how the values they represent render occupation and indigenous issues ideologically invisible. In placing the swastikas, a symbol of a genocidal and fascist nation-state, on the *haole* settler's aloha shirt, *Benocide* forces one to see how a neoconservative "Aloha for All" ideology contributes to the cultural genocide of Hawaiians.

The *haole* settler holds in his left hand the state of Hawai'i flag, which is visually similar to the flag of the internationally recognized Hawaiian Kingdom. The flag has since been recoded as the state of Hawai'i flag that remains under the imposed legal and ideological framework of the United States and its Constitution. The possession of the Hawaiian nation's flag in the settler's hand symbolizes colonial control over the state, and the flag's hidden double meaning—both the successful occupation and the simultaneous obfuscation of this act—is exposed. Under the settler's right arm is a bundle of documents representative of his groups' control of the U.S. legal system. This group has been using the precedent set by the *Rice* decision in order to legally terminate, or lynch, an indigenous political category held by Hawaiians. In Justice Anthony Kennedy's opening remarks to his opinion on the *Rice* case, he applies the 15th Amendment of the U.S. Constitution to Hawaiians and finds their relationship to the state of Hawai'i to be race based:

> A citizen of Hawaii comes before us claiming that an explicit, race-based voting qualification has barred him from voting in a statewide election. The Fifteenth Amendment to the

> Constitution of the United States, binding on the National Government, the States, and their political subdivisions, controls the case.[46]

By focusing the gaze upon Rice's race and citizenship, the court is able to, as Judy Rohrer writes, "render indigenous claims inarticulable by racializing native peoples, while simultaneously normalizing white subjectivity by insisting on a color-blind ideology."[47] Indigenous rights are thus subsumed under a category of race, providing other potential plaintiffs with the groundwork to seek the further erasure of indigenous rights from Hawai'i through appeals to the 15th Amendment of the U.S. Constitution. Haunani-Kay Trask argues that the U.S. Constitution itself actually facilitates indigenous dispossession:

> As indigenous peoples, we are all outside the Constitution, the settler document that declares ownership over indigenous lands and peoples. Since the Constitution is an imposed colonial structure, nothing therein prevents the taking of Native lands or the incorporation of unwilling Native peoples into the United States.[48]

This history of political dispossession and forced inclusion into the United States is key to understanding the problematic logic of the *Rice* decision and its legal progeny. In his dissenting opinion to the Court, Justice Stevens points out, "It is a painful irony indeed to conclude that native Hawaiians are not entitled to special benefits designed to restore a measure of native self-governance because they currently lack any vestigial native government—a possibility of which history and the actions of this Nation have deprived them."[49]

Tying these images together is the settler and his group's "Aloha for All" campaign as represented by swastikas on an aloha shirt. By juxtaposing these symbols with anti-Black lynchings, the artist makes comparisons that challenge neoconservative appropriations of African American civil rights discourse and do two things. First, they show how violence and injustice can be legitimized through the legal system of a nation-state. In Martin Luther King Jr.'s "Letter from Birmingham Jail" he writes that "we should never forget that everything Adolf Hitler did in Germany was 'legal' and everything the Hungarian freedom fighters did in Hungary was 'illegal.'"[50] King's referencing of Nazi Germany's legal genocide revealed the laws upholding segregation as also legal but unjust. King thus encouraged pastors critical of his nonviolent activism to look past the state as inherently just and question how the legal system can codify violence. Kēwaikaliko makes a similar move here. By evoking Nazi Germany, he shows how the 'Aloha for All' project of applying the 15th amendment to Hawaiian entitlements as legitimizing a violent termination of Hawaiian rights and their standing as indigenous peoples.

Secondly, Kēwaikaliko's referencing of "genocide," in the title *Benocide*, for instance, compares the systematic genocide committed by Nazi Germany to the cultural genocide committed through the termination of an indigenous category. By comparing these acts, the artist reveals the systemic and material forms of violence committed against Hawaiians. Hawaiian playwright Alani Apio uses the term "cultural genocide" to describe the legal challenges in his 2001 *Honolulu Advertiser* newspaper commentary, "A Thousand Little Cuts to Genocide."

> The things many of you say and do amount to 1,000 little cuts against us. And these cuts represent a subversive, long-standing cultural genocide against the Hawaiian people. Cultural genocide against the Hawaiian people.
>
> Nobody executes us. No one lynches us. No government enslaves our children or rapes our women. No citizenry chains us up and drags us from the backs of pickup trucks. No homicidal maniac gassing us. Just 1,000 little cuts to our self-esteem, self-identity, cultural pride—to our souls.[51]

The genocide referenced is a systemic form of anti-Hawaiian violence often rendered natural and normal.[52] It is the lynching of a Hawaiian nation and indigenous way of life, which makes Hawaiians distinct from settlers. According to Apio, "people with Hawaiian blood may still be here, but my culture—distinct and unique from everyone else—will have bled to death." Recent scholars theorizing settler colonialism and genocide have conceptualized physical and cultural genocide as not mutually exclusive processes but as "two-sides of the same coin."[53] According to Patrick Wolfe, historical campaigns for assimilation and extermination of Native peoples were mutually constitutive, each informed by the same "logic of elimination." For instance, Wolfe shows that General Paul Sheridan's white supremacist call to Native American genocide, "The only good Indian, is a dead Indian," was endorsed by the founder of the Carlisle Boarding School for Indian youth, Captain Richard Pratt, who argued in a revised maxim: "Kill the Indian in him and save the man."[54]

Where the plaintiffs in the legal challenges portray themselves as victims of state racism, the metaphor of a lynching takes us to the very emergence of the 15th Amendment in 1870 to challenge a narrative of settler victimhood. In the late nineteenth century, African American intellectuals and activists such as Ida B. Wells, Pauline Hopkins, and others demonstrated that the hysteria surrounding alleged sexual offenses by African American men against white women were imaginary, and that lynching was a form of racial terror used to uphold a white racial order and arrest African American social mobility.[55] As W. Fitzhugh Brundage remarks in his work on African American lynching in the South:

> Rather than punish criminals, lynchers actually sought to crush black economic aspirations, squelch black activism, and perpetuate white hegemony . . . Once the myths were discredited, they [Black activists] believed, lynching would be understood for what it was—a crude and brutal tool of white supremacy.[56]

By describing the legal assaults as a lynching of Hawaiians, the myths of "racial discrimination" and settler victimhood are reversed, visually representing the lawsuits as a means to terrorize and discipline a Hawaiian community that has been mobilizing effectively to rectify the continued U.S. violation of Hawaiian national sovereignty. Historian of Hawai'i Jonathan Kamakawiwo'ole Osorio called the legal challenges a reactionary backlash to a Hawaiian movement that had created "widespread discussion and acknowledgment" of the 1893 overthrow of the Hawaiian Kingdom.[57] It was not until 1996, three years after the largest demonstration in Hawai'i's history protesting the illegitimate overthrow of the Hawaiian nation, that the *Rice* case was filed. The 2000 *Carroll* and *Barrett* cases were both thrown out of court after it was revealed that neither had applied to any Native programs. According to Chris Iijima, that fact confirms that "the *Barrett* and *Carroll* lawsuits were not motivated by any particularized concern for Hawai'i, or its people, or even to redress any real harm to any of its citizens. These lawsuits were simply the application of a generalized right-wing ideology about the nature of race relations to the circumstances of Hawai'i."[58] Threatened by a Hawaiian movement for self-government, the legal assaults were a means of reaffirming a colonial order by attacking Hawaiian "entitlements" and resources. And while the plaintiffs in the lawsuits imagine themselves as continuing the work of civil rights leaders such as Martin Luther King Jr., the historically created system of asymmetrical economic, political, and cultural power in Hawai'i is maintained, not challenged, by their actions.

The metaphor of a lynching shows how Black and Native communities are commonly terrorized, through legal and extralegal means, for challenging a hierarchical racial and colonial order. But there are also representations that point to the distinct genealogy and specific responsibilities Hawaiians have to Hawai'i. Haunani-Kay Trask explains the familial relationship that Hawaiians hold with Hawai'i:

> As the indigenous people of Hawai'i, Hawaiians are Native to the Hawaiian Islands. We do not descend from the Americas or from Asia but from the great Pacific Ocean where our ancestors navigated to, and from every archipelago. Genealogically, we say we are descendents of Papahānaumoku (Earth Mother) and Wākea (Sky Father) who created our beautiful islands.

> From this land came the *taro*, and from the *taro*, our Hawaiian people. The lesson of our origins is that we are genealogically related to Hawai'i, our islands, as family.[59]

Kēwaikaliko's other artwork, titled *Papa A Me Wākea* features the progenitors *Papa* (Earth Mother) and *Wākea* (Sky Father) and shows how both the sky and the land are gendered in *Benocide*. In *Benocide*, they are both represented as suffering. *Wākea* is striated and colored yellow and magenta with a nuclear mushroom cloud rising in it, and below, *Papa*, the green patches of land, is enveloped in black and gray with Native women shown suffering and fighting, some within the crimson red blood. The Native man is raised into the sky by the noose and is separated from the land via the noose of the state, creating displacement and interruption. In his left hand he is holding dirt, struggling to be released from the noose and returned to the land, thus reuniting political sovereignty with land and resources. The clenched fist also cautions us against viewing the lynching as complete. In this historical moment he is not yet dead but is still struggling against being lynched.[60] In the tree there is an *'iole*, or rat, that seeks to free the lynched Hawaiian by chewing at the noose.

Another figure that highlights these distinctions is the *pua'a*; however, its thoughts and actions remain ambiguous. The *pua'a* can be seen as either fondling the settler's rear or, as Vicente M. Diaz has suggested, picking his pocket. He is a *pua'a* with *kino lau*, a shape-shifter who could be read as a greedy, colluding pig to be loathed or a pig with the potential to ruthlessly defeat his enemies, like the pig-god Kamapua'a. Lilikalā Kame'eleihiwa writes about Kamapua'a and the characteristics of a pig nature:

> Defiant of all authority, bold and untamed, he recalls the pig nature that lies dormant in most people. He is the primeval reveler, lusting after life, he is the creature eagerly sucking at a mother's breast. Treacherous and tender, he thirsts greedily after the good things in life—adventure, love, and sensual pleasure. Kamapua'a is a hero to Hawaiians because he recognizes no societal restraint, and we love him for it.[61]

In the drawing, the *pua'a* is in a position to free the lynched Hawaiian, but perhaps because he is not actively protecting political and cultural indigeneity, the *pua'a* is figured as colluding with the lynch mob. Like Cayetano and the *haole* settler, the *pua'a* is drawn with short, round, and stubby features. The lynched Hawaiian man, however, is drawn to scale. In the face of Hawaiian suffering and occupation, the commonly propagated and highly romanticized representations of Hawai'i (more than 7 million tourists yearly) have as much relevance as a cartoon, but one with very real material effects on Hawai'i's ecology and people.[62]

Kēwaikaliko's work forces the viewer to see the often uncomfortable and harsh realities of U.S. control of Hawai'i while asking one to bear witness to the contemporary situation of Hawaiians. This, I would assert, is the principal purpose of positioning the viewer of the art piece as a spectator to the lynching. In much the same way that lynchings throughout the United States were viewed publicly and necessitated general public support or at least silent complicity, we view the lynching as it happens, implicating us in the symbolic lynching of Hawaiians. Positioning the viewer in this way, the artwork poses a difficult question: What are you going to do about this? As Manulani Aluli Meyer asserts:

> We speak to you in shapes, colors, and metaphors. We view angles distinctly; we prioritize contours differently; we have different politics based on our experience of rape, pillage, and transformation. We are speaking in the language of imagery and you are learning more about the passion and priorities of a people. The time demands it of all of us. And I believe we are ready to listen.[63]

While it is far easier to see the blindness of the past than it is to see the blindness of the present, *Benocide* offers a vision of Hawai'i that reveals the current consequences of a racial episteme blind to indigeneity. *Benocide* visually narrates what often goes unseen, particularly in a place propagated by advertisements for tourism and U.S. cinematic and television portrayals that render colonial violence unimaginable. Hawaiian artwork such as Kēwaikaliko's *Benocide* demystifies the illusions of American benevolence, revealing the current violent material effects of the continued U.S. occupation of Hawai'i.

Notes

1. My deep appreciation to Kēwaikaliko for allowing me to use his artwork. No biography available due to request for anonymity by artist.
2. For an examination of Hawaiian epistemology and ontology see Manulani Aluli Meyer, *Ho'oulu: Our Time of Becoming* (Honolulu: 'Ai Pōhaku Press, 2003).
3. Kēwaikaliko, interview with artist , October 30, 2003.
4. The annexation of Hawai'i was accomplished through the Newlands Resolution, which did not possess the required two-thirds vote from the U.S. Senate. Furthermore, as the research of Noenoe Silva shows, by 1897 there was a critical mass of Hawaiian nationals who were opposed to annexation. The Native Hawaiian population was estimated at near 40,000 and signatures on petitions opposing annexation totaled 38,000. See Noenoe K. Silva, *Aloha Betrayed: Native Hawaiian Resistance to American Colonialism* (Durham, N.C.: Duke University Press, 2004), 123–63.
5. See Phyllis Turnbull and Kathleen Ferguson, *Oh, Say Can You See?: The Semiotics of the Military in Hawai'i* (Minneapolis: University of Minnesota Press, 1999); Setsu Shigematsu and Keith L. Camacho, *Militarized Currents: Toward a Decolonized Future in Asia and the Pacific* (Minneapolis: University

of Minnesota Press, 2010); Teresia K. Teaiwa, "Bikinis and Other S/pacific N/oceans," reprinted in *Militarized Currents: Toward a Decolonized Future in Asia and the Pacific*; Stewart Firth, *Nuclear Playground* (Honolulu: University of Hawai'i Press, 1987).

6. Momi Cazimero, "Art Is a Window," in *Nā Maka Hou: New Visions—Contemporary Native Hawaiian Art*, edited by Momi Cazimero, David de la Torre, and Manulani Aluli Meyer (Honolulu: Honolulu Academy of Arts, 2001), 11.
7. Manulani Aluli Meyer, "Hawaiian Art: A Doorway to Knowing," in *Nā Maka Hou*, ed. Cazimero, de la Torre, and Aluli Meyer.
8. The caption that accompanies this piece warns against a reading that would represent *Benocide* as speaking on behalf of all Hawaiians. Given that his grandmother "hates it" and the artwork has been getting "both positive and negative feedback," I do not wish to argue that all Hawaiians view the court cases in the way that my reading of *Benocide* does. In addition, my purpose in reading this text is not to claim expertise in Hawaiian cultural knowledge. Instead, my interest lies in its rich observations of the intricate power relations operating in Hawai'i as it visually narrates the complex interrelations among whites, Asian Americans, and Native Hawaiians in contemporary Hawai'i. As a settler of Filipino and Japanese ancestry, I wish to pay careful attention to my own subjectivities and limitations. It is in this spirit that I read Kēwaikaliko's *Benocide*, keeping in mind the important differences between Natives and settlers, while knowing that there are other readings of this piece that I may not be able to see. See Karen Kosasa, "Thefts of Space and Culture: Kimo Cashman's *Kapu* Series," *History of Photography*, ed. Lynn Ann Davis (Autumn 2001): 279–87.
9. See M. K. Mackenzie, *Native Hawaiian Rights Handbook* (Honolulu: Native Hawaiian Legal Corporation, 1991).
10. Gavin Clarkson, "Not Because They Are Brown, but Because of *Ea*: Why the Good Guys Lost in *Rice v. Cayetano*, and Why They Didn't Have to Lose," *Michigan Journal of Race and Law* 7 (Spring 2002): 317–56.
11. J. Kēhaulani Kauanui, "Precarious Positions: Native Hawaiians and U.S. Federal Recognition," *The Contemporary Pacific* 17.1 (2005): 9.
12. The *Barrett* and *Carroll* cases were consolidated on December 15, 2000. *Carroll*, at 1234n1.
13. Ken Kobayashi, "Lawsuit Filed to Open OHA Seats to All Races," *Honolulu Advertiser*, July 26, 2000.
14. Mary Louise Pratt, *Imperial Eyes: Travel Writing and Transculturation* (New York: Routledge, 1992).
15. David Spurr, *The Rhetoric of Empire: Colonial Discourse in Journalism, Travel Writing, and Imperial Administration* (Durham, N.C.: Duke University Press, 1993), 15–16.
16. Ibid., 17.
17. J. Kēhaulani Kauanui, "The Politics of Blood and Sovereignty in *Rice v. Cayetano*," *PoLaR* 25.1 (May 2002): 110.
18. Spurr, *Rhetoric of Empire*, 16.
19. Homi Bhabha, "Of Mimicry and Man: The Ambivalence of Colonial Discourse," *The Location of Culture* (New York: Routledge, 1994), 127.
20. Punahou School, *Punahou Jubilee Celebration, June 25–26, 1891* (Honolulu: Hawaiian Gazette Company, 1891), 99. President Barack Obama also attended this school.
21. Edward Joesting, *Kauai: The Separate Kingdom* (Honolulu: University of Hawai'i Press, 1984), 175–76; Christine Donnelly, "*Rice:* It's about Protecting the Constitution, Not 'Racist'," *Honolulu Star-Bulletin*, February 23, 2000.
22. Justice Anthony Kennedy, "Opinion," *Rice v. Cayetano* (98-818) 528 U.S. 495.
23. Mieke Bal, "Seeing Signs: The Use of Semiotics for the Understanding of Visual Art," in *The Subjects of Art History: Historical Objects in Contemporary Perspectives*, ed. March A. Cheetham, Michael Ann Holly, and Keith Moxey (Cambridge: Cambridge University Press, 1998), 81.
24. U.S. Senator Daniel Inouye, press release, Statement of Senator Inouye on the Supreme Court's Ruling in *Rice v. Cayetano*, February 23, 2000.
25. As cited in Ida Yoshinaga and Eiko Kosasa, "Local Japanese Women for Justice Speak Out Against Daniel Inouye and the JACL," *Honolulu Advertiser*, February 6, 2000, and reprinted in *Asian Settler Colonialism: From Local Governance to the Habits of Everyday Life in Hawai'i*, ed. Candace Fujikane and Jonathan Y. Okamura, 295–96 (Honolulu: University of Hawai'i Press, 2008).
26. Ibid.

27. Ronald Takaki, *Strangers from a Different Shore* (New York: Back Bay Books, 1998), 171.
28. Ibid., 176.
29. Roger Bell, *Last among Equals: Hawaiian Statehood and American Politics* (Honolulu: University of Hawai'i Press, 1984), 293.
30. For an analysis of how Homi Bhabha's phrase "overlapping without equivalence" can be given a "settler" inflection, see Anna Johnston and Alan Lawson, "Settler Colonies," in *A Companion to Postcolonial Studies*, ed. Henry Schwarz and Sangeeta Ray (Malden, Mass.: Blackwell, 2000), 374.
31. Haunani-Kay Trask, "Writing in Captivity: Poetry in Time of De-Colonization," in *Navigating Islands and Continents: Conversations and Contestations in and around the Pacific*, ed. Cynthia Franklin, Ruth Hsu, and Suzanne Kosanke (Honolulu: University of Hawai'i Press, 2000), 17.
32. Haunani-Kay Trask, "Settlers of Color and 'Immigrant' Hegemony," in *Asian Settler Colonialism*, ed. Fujikane and Okamura, 47.
33. Benjamin J. Cayetano, *Ben: A Memoir, from Street Kid to Governor* (Honolulu: Watermark Publishing, 2009). An article in the *Fil-Am Courier* also describes Cayetano as "the son of immigrants from Kalihi to Washington Place . . . the American Dream come true." Zachary Labez, "Mabuhay . . . and Salamat, Ben" *Fil Am Courier*, December 16–30, 2002.
34. As quoted in Candace Fujikane, "Foregrounding Native Nationalisms: A Critique of Antinationalist Sentiment in Asian American Studies," in *Asian American Studies After Critical Mass*, ed. Kent Ono (Boston: Blackwell, 2004), 81. Cayetano's remark aired on KITV and other Hawai'i television stations on September 19, 2000.
35. Dylan Rodríguez, *Suspended Apocalypse: White Supremacy, Genocide, and the Filipino Condition*, (Minneapolis: University of Minnesota Press, 2010), 96.
36. Ibid., 194.
37. Ibid., 35.
38. As the research and legal actions of scholar Keanu Sai have shown, the Hawaiian Kingdom may have been overthrown, but subjects of the nation had in fact never officially relinquished their national sovereignty. The political consequence of this reality is that it places past and present Hawai'i under the formal category of "occupation," rather than a "colonized" territory, a status with equally different legal implications. I contend that "occupation" and the concept of "settler colonialism" (not to be equated with "colonized" territory) are not two irreconcilable polarizing frameworks, but are actually both pertinent to an understanding of the uniqueness of Hawai'i's situation and the multiple tactics that the United States has utilized to dominate Hawai'i. Thus, Keanu Sai's framework, which examines international law, sovereignty, and occupation at the legal level, provides a clear understanding of the illegitimacy of the occupying United States, while a discussion of settler colonialism, at the level of power relations, can help to describe the form of power that was used to normalize such occupation. Moreover, these forms of power were also used to establish a violent rationale through which Hawaiians are relegated to being permanently "unfit for self-government," while settlers (Asian and haole), although contentious with one another, are afforded the masculine and intellectual capacity to turn "primitive" Hawaiian lands into "modern" and "democratic" societies. In other words, Hawai'i's patterns of settlement and legal and sovereign legacies, and the colonial discourses of dominance that enabled them, share characteristics of both settler colonialism and nation under occupation. See Keanu Sai, "A Slippery Path towards Hawaiian Indigeneity: An Analysis and Comparison between Hawaiian State Sovereignty and Hawaiian Indigeneity and Its Use and Practice in Hawai'i Today," *Journal of Law and Social Challenges* 10 (Fall 2008): 101–66; Keanu Sai, "The American Occupation of the Hawaiian Kingdom: Beginning the Transition from Occupied to Restored State" (PhD diss., University of Hawai'i at Mānoa, December 2008). For scholarship engaging different approaches and tactics to questions of law, occupation, and sovereignty see Jonathan Kamakawiwo'ole Osorio, "Kū'ē and Kū'oko'a (Resistance and Independence): History, Law, and Other Faiths," *Hawaiian Journal of Law and Politics* 1 (Summer 2004): 92–113; J. Kēhaulani Kauanui, "The Multiplicity of Hawaiian Sovereignty Claims and the Struggle for Meaningful Autonomy," *Comparative American Studies* 3.3 (2005): 283–99. For scholarship examining Hawaiian nationhood outside of state-based models, specifically around anarcha-indigenist principles, please see Noelani Goodyear-Ka'ōpua, "Kū'oko'a: Hawaiian Independence and Affinity," *Affinities: A Journal of Radical Theory, Culture and Action*, forthcoming in 2010.
39. Ian Haney Lopez, *White By Law: The Legal Construction of Race*, tenth anniversary ed. (New York: New York University Press, 2006), 56–76.

40. Ralph Kuykendall, *The Hawaiian Kingdom: The Kalakaua Dynasty, 1874–1893* (Honolulu: University of Hawai'i Press, 1967), 634.
41. For instance, on April 9th 1893, a little over two months after the U.S. backed overthrow, Japanese plantation laborers submitted a petition that did not to oppose the overthrow of Hawai'i but rather, demanded their electoral participation in the new settler government, stating that they were the "physical and intellectual equals of any of the other foreigners." Likewise in 1894, the Chinese in Hawai'i sent a petition, signed by hundreds of people, also seeking their right to participate in the new settler government. Virgilio Menor Felipe writes that the term "Kanaka," which usually means Hawaiian, was used as a slur by Filipinos to also mean "'boy' or servant." Furthermore, in a study conducted in the 1950s, Joseph C. Finney argued that the "primitive stereotype" defined common views of Hawaiians as "lazy." As one woman listed as Japanese said: "You see the Hawaiians are . . . popularly known to be lazy, and they don't have a tradition for literacy and they're not the conscientious type, industrious type." See Kathleen Dickenson Mellen (1895–1969), MS 19, Bishop Museum Archives; "A Petition signed by several hundred Chinese will be presented to the Councils today, asking that the Chinese in Hawaii be given the voting franchise," *Pacific Commercial Advertiser*, May 17, 1894; Virgilio Menor Felipe, *Hawai'i: A Pilipino Dream* (Honolulu: Mutual Publishing, 2002), 198; Joseph C. Finney, "Attitudes of Others Toward Hawaiians," 79, Hawaiian and Pacific Collections University of Hawai'i, Mānoa; Ty P. Kāwika Tengan, *Native Men Remade: Gender and Nation in Contemporary Hawai'i* (Durham, N.C.: Duke University Press, 2008), 45.
42. Patricia J. Williams, "Alchemical Notes: Reconstructing Ideals from Deconstructed Rights," in *Critical Race Theory: The Cutting Edge* (Philadelphia: Temple University Press, 2000), 84.
43. Debra Barayuga, "OHA Sues to Resume Land Revenues: The Agency Says That the State Failed in Its Fiduciary Duties as Trustee of the Lands," *Honolulu Star Bulletin*, July 22, 2003.
44. Donnelly, "*Rice*."
45. See the Aloha for All Groups' Web site at http://www.aloha4all.org/.
46. Justice Anthony Kennedy, "Opinion," *Rice v. Cayetano* (98-818) 528 U.S. 495.
47. Judy Rohrer, "'Got Race?': The Production of Haole and the Distortion of Indigeneity in the *Rice* Decision," *The Contemporary Pacific* 18.1 (Spring 2006): 1.
48. Haunani-Kay Trask, *From a Native Daughter: Colonialism and Sovereignty in Hawai'i*, rev. ed. (1993; Honolulu: University of Hawai'i Press, 1999), 26.
49. Justice Stevens, "Opinion," *Rice v. Cayetano*, 9.
50. Martin Luther King Jr., "A Letter from Birmingham Jail," in *The Conscious Reader*, ed. Caroline Shrodes, Harry Finestone, and Michael Shugrue (New York: Macmillan, 1974), 542.
51. Alani Apio, "A Thousand Little Cuts to Genocide," *Honolulu Advertiser*, February 25, 2001.
52. For an examination of anti-Black genocide and the "normalized absence of concern" that accompanies it, see João H. Costa Vargas, *Never Meant to Survive: Genocide and Utopias in Black Diaspora Communities* (New York: Rowman & Littlefield, 2008), 9–14.
53. Caroline Elkins and Susan Pederson, "Settler Colonialism a Concept and Its Uses," *Settler Colonialism in the Twentieth Century* (New York: Routledge, 2005), 3.
54. Patrick Wolfe, "Settler Colonialism and the Elimination of the Native," *Journal of Genocide Research* 8 (December 2006): 397; Patrick Wolfe, *Settler Colonialism and the Transformation of Anthropology: The Politics and Poetics of an Ethnographic Event* (New York: Cassell, 1999), 175–76.
55. Hazel V. Carby, "'On the Threshold of Woman's Era': Lynching, Empire, and Sexuality in Black Feminist Theory," in *Feminist Postcolonial Theory: A Reader*, ed. Reina Lewis and Sara Mills (New York: Routledge, 2003).
56. W. Fitzhugh Brundage, introduction to *Under Sentence of Death: Lynching in the South*, ed. W. Fitzhugh Brundgage (Chapel Hill: University of North Carolina Press, 1997), 5.
57. Osorio, "Kū'ē and Kū'oko'a," 95.
58. Chris Iijima, "New Rice Recipes: The Legitimization of Continued Overthrow," *Asian-Pacific Law and Policy Journal* 3.2 (Summer 2002): 390.
59. Trask, "Settlers of Color," 45.
60. Here I am using Mieke Bal's notion of "semiotics as caution." Mieke Bal, "Seeing Signs: The Use of Semiotics for the Understanding of Visual Art," in *The Subjects of Art History: Historical Objects in Contemporary Perspectives*, ed. March A. Cheetham, Michael Ann Holly, and Keith Moxey (Cambridge: Cambridge University Press, 1998), 81.

61. I thank J. Kēhaulani Kauanui for pointing out this connection and reference to me. Lilikalā Kame'eleihiwa, *A Legendary Tradition of Kamapua'a: The Hawaiian Pig-God* (Honolulu: Bishop Museum Press, 1996), x.
62. See www.hvcb.org.
63. Manulani Aluli Meyer, "Hawaiian Art: A Doorway to Knowing," in *Nā Maka Hou*, ed. Cazimero, de la Torre, and Meyer, 12.

Indigeneity in the Diaspora: The Case of Native Hawaiians at Iosepa, Utah

Hokulani K. Aikau

> It is Tuesday night and I have just arrived at the Iosepa Association Executive Board meeting. When I arrive, the board members are already in a heated discussion about a conflict they are having with the landowner, Chris Robinson of the Ensign Group. The conflict is over the board's desire to expand the footprint of the Iosepa Historical Site and the landowner's determination to block all further expansion. At one point in the discussion, one of the board members pulls out a topographical map of Iosepa and the surrounding area while another clears off the table. They lay the map out on the table as we all gather around. Uncle Richard, a former Iosepa Association president traces the boundaries of the Bureau of Land Management (BLM) parcels, then the boundaries of the Ensign Group properties, and then the area marked as part of the state historical site. They begin to strategize about how they could expand if either the BLM or the Ensign Group could be persuaded to "return" some of the land. Throughout the discussion the members repeat an impassioned declaration that this is "our" land and that both the Ensign Group and the BLM should return the land to "us."

This essay is a meditation on the central contradiction of the opening scene: the board members are indigenous peoples from Oceania strategizing to reclaim land in Utah, which they feel is "theirs."[1] Recently I started to reflect on the implication of what it means to claim the land as "ours," when it is not "ours" any more than it belongs to the Bureau of Land Management (BLM) or Chris Robinson of the Ensign Group, who currently owns and operates a ranch on private and public land. In this essay, I examine the stories that the Polynesian Latter-day Saints who gather annually at the Iosepa Festival held at Iosepa, Utah, tell about this place as a way to understand why and how they make a claim to the land.[2] I will trace how the stories told about Iosepa perform a kind of memory work that is simultaneously indigenous, religious, and settler-colonial, to name only three vectors of power examined here. My objective is to think through the political implications of indigenous peoples who settle in the diaspora and who self-identify as part of an indigenous struggle to reclaim our land "at home." What should our responsibilities be to the peoples whose land we dwell upon? What roles can or should indigenous peoples in the diaspora play in Native struggles to reclaim territory and regenerate cultural and spiritual practices? I do not have a prescriptive answer but offer some suggestions for what my community could do to live in a more responsible way on the land of the Skull Valley Goshute peoples.

Admittedly, I did not make the connection between the actual land we called "ours" and the Skull Valley Band of the Goshute tribe, whose homeland it is, until I started putting a proposal together to host an archaeological field school at Iosepa. The archaeological field school was a collaborative project I started with a colleague who specializes in Native American and Pacific archaeology at the University of Hawai'i at Mānoa. He and I had several conversations about Iosepa, a Native Hawaiian settlement established in the late nineteenth century in Goshute territory. He was instantly intrigued and suggested we develop a field school that incorporated oral histories and an archaeological dig. Our research question asked how nineteenth-century Native Hawaiians immigrants adapted to the Utah environment, geography, and ecology. We planned to focus on a canal, built in 1908, which redirected water from fresh water springs and streams in the mountains down into the town. We wanted to know the degree to which the canal system for Iosepa resembled an 'auwai, an irrigation system that redirects and controls the flow of stream or river water to lo'i kalo (taro water gardens). Unfortunately, the project did not get beyond the proposal stage. However, the process of thinking through methodological and ethical issues of doing Native Hawaiian research in the diaspora raised additional questions about our responsibilities to the indigenous peoples upon whose land we live. It was not until I started to contemplate the possibility of digging in the dirt that I asked, how deep do we have to dig before the stories buried there—and the material objects unearthed—stop being about Iosepa, Polynesians, and Mormonism and begin to be about the Goshutes?

Indigenous Settler Colonial Dialogics

The literature on indigenous immigrants living in the diaspora tends to focus on their continued relationship to the homeland. These studies also focus on generational issues that emerge when subsequent generations, born in the "host" country, attempt to makes sense of their connection to an imagined homeland.[3] My investigation of a Polynesian Mormon community in Utah asks how we maintain our indigeneity not only in relationship to home but also to the native peoples upon whose lands we dwell. When we shift our analytical gaze from the homeland to alternative contact narratives, we must also recalibrate the way we see and understand the articulation of settler-colonialism with indigeneity. The example of two waves of Mormon Polynesian migration to Utah, which occurred a century apart, offers an evocative case for interrogating these linkages. First, I describe the early history of Mormon settlement in the Great Basin as an example of unconventional colonialism. The Mormon settlement pattern and Indian-Mormon relations provide a context for understanding how the nationalist project of building Zion morphed into a colonial project of dispossession and exploitation. Second, this historical context sets the stage for the arrival of the first Native Hawaiians to immigrate to Utah. In this instance the religious discourse of return to an ancient homeland is articulated with a belief that Native Americans and Native Hawaiians are lineal descendents of Israel. Finally, this story is about how contemporary Polynesian Saints remember the past as they strive to build an ideal life in Utah's harsh desert climate. What is remembered and why? How is a collective memory of this history expressed, discussed, and performed annually at the Iosepa Festival?

The literature on settler-colonialism offers one possible analytical frame by which to make sense of the opening vignette. Within a settler-colonial framework this scene can only be read as a contradiction, as it is founded upon the dialectic between native/settler and colonized/colonizer. This binary frame, although quite useful for understanding the history of dispossession and colonization by the Church of Jesus Christ of Latter-day Saints (the LDS church) and the United States government, forecloses the potential for considering the role of other actors on the scene. Adorno's critique of dialectics as a problem of frame, not content, offers an alternative interpretation of the opening scene. Contradiction, he argues, arises when an aspect of identity, a characteristic, a category fails to fit within the dialectical frame. That is to say, within a dialectical framework, that which does not fit, the contradiction, will continually "appear divergent, dissonant, negative for just as long as the structure of our consciousness obliges it to strive for unity."[4] According to a settler-colonial framework, the board members could be seen as settlers whose claim to land perpetuates colonial processes of dispossession. However, the settler-colonial frame cannot accommodate the diasporic indigene: the natives who have been exiled from their homeland and who carry their own history of dispossession, exploitation, and expropriation with them as they settle in the diaspora.

If we apply a dialogical analysis to the opening scene, what becomes visible are indigenous peoples who draw upon a set of shared experiences and stories engaging in strategies to reclaim a particular kind of relationship to the land. I understand indigeneity to be a political category that recognizes both the connection of autochthonous peoples to their "sacred history, ceremonial cycles, language and ancestral homelands" as Jeff Corntassel redefines it, and the international alliances and interconnections among peoples who identify as indigenous.[5] Indigeneity, then, is a broad category that reflects shared experiences of struggle against dispossession, exploitation, and expropriation as well as a point of view grounded in the particular cosmology and history of peoples that emerge out of their primordial relationship to a place.

David Gegeo defines indigeneity in similar terms. As Kwara'ae and Lau from Malaita Island, in the Solomon Island archipelago, the foundation of Kwara'ae identity is grounded in an understanding of place that is the existential foundation for identity. "Space," by contrast, he says, "has to do with the *location* where a Kwara'ae person may be at any given time as necessitated by contemporary conditions. . . . Space is the location a Kwara'ae person occupies while in motion or in circulation."[6] Place, one's relationship to an existential foundation that includes an original homeland and genealogy, to name only two of the eight characteristics of place describe by Gegeo, then, is carried with a Kwara'ae regardless of where that person travels. Thus, Kwara'ae people do not stop being indigenous when they migrate; rather, they carry their place—indigenous identity—with them to new spaces. Gegeo's point is not to overly romanticize indigeneity, but to challenge the pernicious notion that indigenous people who do not live in our homeland become less native the longer we are away from "home." J. Kēhaulani Kauanui's discussion of off-island Hawaiians resonates with Gegeo's. Using kalo, the primary food source of Native Hawaiians and the cosmological older sibling of Kanaka 'Ōiwi Hawai'i, as a metaphor, she makes the case that off-island Hawaiians remain rooted in place even when planted in foreign soil. Within this figuring, indigeneity is grounded to an original source through genealogy even when migration routes take us away from that original place.[7] When the opening scene is interpreted from this vantage point, what we see is indigenous people trying to protect the bones of their ancestors who are buried in Goshute territory, while also providing a cultural foundation for the next generation of diasporic indigenes. As I will demonstrate, the board members and others who attend the annual Iosepa Festival draw upon broad understandings of indigeneity as well as religious narratives that reiterate settler-colonial discourses to understand their relationship to the land.

Goshute Dispossession: The High Price of Building Zion in Utah

The Goshute Nation is part of the larger Shoshone-speaking language group prominent in the intermountain west. It is also composed of two groups, the Deep Creek tribe (now part of the Confederated Tribes of the Goshute

Reservation), located on the Utah-Nevada border approximately sixty miles south of Wendover, Nevada, and the Skull Valley Band, whose original territory stretched from the Great Salt Lake in the north, south to the southern border of Utah Lake, east to the Oquirrh Mountains, and west to the Steptoe Mountains in what is now eastern Nevada. Historians describe the Skull Valley Band as indicative of the style of life needed to survive the arid desert of the Great Basin.[8] During aboriginal time, the Skull Valley Band was organized into small familial groups who subsisted on gathering and reseeding berries, grasses, and root vegetables; hunting small animals; and eating insects. On occasion, families would organize hunting parties for large game, and during the winter months several family units would gather near piñon pine forests, where they would share resources and supplies. As with other indigenous peoples, their intimate and cosmological relationship to the land and their understanding of where and when to find food and water allowed the Skull Valley Band to thrive from time immemorial in one of the most arid deserts on the North American continent.[9]

The dispossession of the Skull Valley Band of Goshute is a story that began a half century before the first Polynesian pioneers arrived in Utah. According to Ned Blackhawk's history of the violence that produced the American West, the Goshute nation had been struggling against New Mexican colonialism since the 1830s, specifically the slave trade: equestrian tribes, such as the Ute, would use their relative strength to kidnap and sell tribal members in return for guns and other commodities of the frontier economy. Although the slave trade persisted until the 1860s, the Goshute nation would experience the impact of western expansion in indirect, although no less devastating, ways.[10]

In 1847, when the first wave of Latter-day Saint settlers arrived in the Salt Lake valley, the Goshute lifestyle, like that of other Shoshone tribes, was already experiencing pressure from settlers moving through the territory on their way to the California gold rush. Although these settlers had no intentions of establishing permanent settlements, they disrupted the fragile balance in this ecosystem. They cut down piñon pine trees and burned them for fuel and let their cattle feed off grasses and roam freely, contaminating water sources with their feces. Despite these added ecological pressures, the Goshute were able to maintain some semblance of their subsistence economy until 1863, when the power struggle over land was firmly established in the hands of United States federal Indian agents. The 1863 treaty between the United States and the Shoshone nation granted overland travel through their territory. Although the Shoshone did not cede land to the United States, they did agree to participate in an initiative to relocate tribal members to farms, where they would learn western styles of agriculture. The Indian farm initiative was the precursor to reservations for the Goshute. Between 1864 and 1912, on several occasions the U.S. government attempted to remove the Goshute from their territory to as far away as Oklahoma, but again, their knowledge of the desert allowed them to resist until a reservation was established in their original territory. The boundaries of the reservation were formally recognized by the U.S. Congress in 1917, coincidentally the same year the Iosepa colony was disbanded and the property sold.[11]

The Church of Jesus Christ of Latter-day Saints played a critical role in the dispossession of the Goshute and other tribes from their homelands. What makes their involvement unique, however, has to do with the distinctive history of this quintessentially American religious faith. Through the religious principle of gathering Saints to Zion and the religious mythology that Native Americans were a lost tribe of Israel, LDS leaders and their followers rationalized their interactions with Indians even as they dispossessed and exploited them.

The church was founded by Joseph Smith Jr. in 1830 and built upon the principle that he restored Christ's true teachings and the authority of the priesthood to the earth. Missionary work was paramount to the future of the faith, as all people needed the "saving ordinances of salvation as performed by men who had the authority of the priesthood, as restored through Joseph Smith."[12] Once converted, these Saints were then asked to join their co-religionists in a religious community called a Gathering Place. Max E. Stanton describes this early era of the church as "the Gathering of Zion."[13] The gathering principle linked two dominant discourses of the time: a religious millennial discourse that the end of days was upon them, which made the act of gathering an urgent preparation for this eventuality, and an American nationalist discourse of manifest destiny. According to Mormon immigration historian William Mulder, the gathering principle to Zion, not polygamy, was the first and fundamental covenant made between the faithful and the Lord. For the newly converted, the holy waters of baptism and the laying on of hands at confirmation held the promise of gathering in Zion. It produced, Mulder writes, "a strange and irresistible longing which ravished them and filled them with a nostalgia for Zion, their common home."[14] In 1830, Zion was still only an imagined community, but as Mulder notes, Smith believed it would be built in the West on the edge of civilization in Indian country. It was in the open, emptied lands of the frontier where the promise of an ideal life in the service of the Lord could be actualized.

Kirkland, Ohio, and Nauvoo, Illinois, were two early attempts at building Zion. But the hostility and violence exacted on the Saints by their "gentile" neighbors inspired the Mormons to migrate further west, beyond the reach of the United States, where they could build the Kingdom of God without persecution. "Building the Kingdom," Mulder explains, "meant providing an environment that would regenerate the adult and rear the young so that they would never know themselves otherwise than as Saints."[15] Brigham Young, second president and prophet of the church, led the Saints across the plains and into the Rocky Mountains. Upon seeing Salt Lake valley on the horizon he declared, "This is the Place." For the Mormons, the Great Basin was ideal for their purposes of building Zion: in 1847, it was beyond the legal reach of the United States, and after the Mexico-American war its distance from centers of power made federal interventions sporadic.

The LDS settlement of what is now the state of Utah could be described as an example of "unconventional colonialism." Ilan Pappé uses this concept to describe late-nineteenth-century Zionism historically and thematically.[16] What makes Zionism an "unconventional" form of colonialism and parallel to Mormonism is that both movements were initially nationalist. Like Zionism, Mormon rhetoric describes the gathering process as a return to an ancient homeland, a Zion, where the faithful could build the Kingdom of God on earth. Salt Lake valley became an imagined homeland that Saints, who had no single mother country, would travel across oceans and lands to reach. Their arrival would demonstrate their faithfulness to the gospel of Christ and secure land—the ultimate covenant made with the Lord. Although the intent of the gathering principle was not colonial, as it was rationalized by religious doctrine and a desire for the freedom to practice their beliefs without fear of reprisal, as more Latter-day Saints set out for Zion, the pressure to make more and more land available for white Mormon settlement necessitated the removal of native peoples from their territories. In contrast to the rapture-filled descriptions of Zion documented in Mulder's history of Mormon migration to Utah are the stories of violence and dispossession enacted by these same Mormon settlers and federal Indian agents against local tribes. Through dispossession and exploitation, Mormonism, like Zionism, became in practice a colonialist project.

LDS settlers migrated to the Great Basin in the 1840s at a historical moment described by Blackhawk as the pre-reservation era. Violence in the form of conflict between equestrian and non-equestrian tribes, as well as the increased pressures over land and resources spurred by western American expansion, characterizes the political and social climate of the era.[17] Although historians agree that Mormon-Indian relations were considered less violent than federal Indian policy, and, indeed, Brigham Young is quoted as saying it is "better to feed the Indians . . . than it is to fight them," it is equally important not to romanticize Young's statement.[18] As Blackhawk describes, Young's reluctance to use federal agents to manage Indian affairs was motivated by a desire to keep the U.S. government out of LDS church political affairs. During this period, Young was committed to establishing the sovereign nation of Deseret, governed by a theocracy of which he would be head. The presence of U.S. Indian agents provided surveillance of the church and undermined Young's authority as president of Deseret. But the marginalization of federal Indian agents had two consequences: first, it meant that federal policies of removal or extermination did not affect intermountain tribes until the 1860s, and second, when conflicts between settlers and Indians erupted, Mormon settlers did not look to federal agents to manage their problems but organized their own retribution. Direct violence by Mormon settlers was most commonly enacted against Ute tribes, who responded to the economic collapse of their ecosystem due to western migration and Mormon settlement by raiding and terrorizing settlers. Blackhawk argues that these attacks were not intended to massacre settlers but were a strategy to destabilize the communities and to "procure stock, cattle, and horses," the currency of a settler-colonial economic system.

Young's religious belief that Indians were a lost tribe of Israel can also be attributed to his stand against full-scale genocide. The religious mythology of Native Americans as descendents of a lost tribe of Israel is authorized by the *Book of Mormon.* For Latter-day Saints the *Book of Mormon* is considered a second testament of Christ's church on earth and chronicles the rise and fall of an ancient civilization that existed on the American continent between 600 BC and AD 400. It documents the lives of a group of Israelites who fled the Holy Land and made the American continent their home. The majority of the volume follows the lives of the descendents of Lehi, the patriarch of these Israelites and father of three sons, Nephi, Laman, and Lemuel; Nephi would become the leader of a great civilization and his people would be called Nephites. What makes this text theologically important is that Christ established the full teachings of his church with Lehi, and those teachings were perpetuated by his loyal son Nephi. Laman and Lemuel were not content following the leadership of their younger brother and organized a rebellion against him and his religious principles. Their initial efforts failed. Laman, Lemuel, and their followers were banished to the wilderness and "cut off from the presence of the Lord."[19] The apostates were given a second punishment, a curse directly from the Lord:

> Wherefore, as they were white, and exceedingly fair and delightsome, that they might not be enticing unto my people the Lord God did cause a skin of blackness to come upon them.

> And thus saith the Lord God: I will cause that they shall be loathsome unto thy people, save they shall repent of their inequities.[20]

The curse of a skin of blackness was extended to all of the descendants of Laman and Lemuel. Since Laman became the leader of these banished and cursed people, they would be known as Lamanites. Embedded in this scripture is both the explanation of the curse and the solution for overcoming it—through repentance and baptism the curse could be lifted and one could become "white, and exceedingly fair and delightsome" once again. The curse of blackness was both literal—a punishment exacted on Lamanites—and metaphoric, as blackness became a symbol of an individual's wicked actions. Throughout the *Book of Mormon*, stories abound that chronicle many battles between the Nephites and Lamanites, but ultimately, the Lamanites defeat the Nephites. Native Americans are believed to be descendants of Lamanites, who, at one time, had the fullness of the gospel of Christ but rejected it.[21] According to R. Warren Metcalf, this cosmological narrative informed Mormon-Indian relations and produced a paradox for church leaders.[22] On the one hand, Lamanites were the lineal descendants of the house of Israel and Mormons had an obligation to return the gospel to their fallen cousins. On the other hand, Indians were a clear and present obstacle to the Gathering of Zion.

Polynesian Pioneers and the Establishment of Iosepa

The first Native Hawaiian Saints arrived in Utah in the late 1880s during the reservation era, when Utah's Indians had been formally dispossessed of their lands and removed to reservations that were only a small fraction of their original territories. In many ways these Polynesian pioneers, as they are remembered by contemporary Polynesian Saints at Iosepa, were similar to their U.S. and European co-religionists. They too were captured by the spirit of gathering and left their native country to lend their labor to building the Kingdom of God. During my interview with William K. Wallace III, he explained that the gathering principle was not just figurative. For his grandma and grandpa, who met and married while living in Iosepa, it was literal. "My grandpa," he tells me, "was one of the carpenters and masons who helped when they were building and constructing the temple."[23] But for these Polynesian Saints, the spirit of gathering was also resonant with their experience as members of the church in Hawaiʻi.

The story of how and why the first Polynesian pioneers migrated to Utah begins in the 1840s when Mormon missionaries attempted to establish a mission in the Society Islands. Although initially successful, the LDS church would not have a substantial presence in Oceania until 1850, when the Sandwich Island Mission was established in Hawai'i. Although the missionaries' primary objective was to spread the gospel among the American population, their efforts were squashed by anti-Mormon propaganda. Instead, they began sharing the gospel with Native Hawaiians, who showed much more interest in their message. Three historical events—a religious vision, the purchase of Lā'ie for the purpose of gathering, and the dissatisfaction Native Hawaiians felt toward Protestant prohibitions against various cultural practices—explain why the LDS church was able to take root in Hawai'i. For the Polynesians I interviewed, the vision that established a theological link between Native Hawaiians, Native Americans, and the *Book of Mormon* was central to how they understood both their membership in the church and their identity as Polynesian Mormons. George Q. Cannon, one of the first ten missionaries to Hawai'i, had a vision wherein he was told that Native Hawaiians, and by extension Polynesians, were descended from the House of Israel. In essence, this vision expanded the religious and racial mythology of Native Americans as a lost tribe to include Native Hawaiians and by extension all Polynesians.

The first Hawaiian Saint to travel to Utah was Jonatana Nāpela, also the first Native Hawaiian convert in Hawai'i, who accompanied George Q. Cannon upon his return home from his mission.[24] Individual Hawaiians would follow over the next two decades, but their visits were sporadic and temporary. Beginning in the 1880s, the number of Hawaiian immigrants to Utah would increase gradually, and unlike their predecessors, who were temporary visitors, these immigrants intended to remain in Zion and contribute their labor and faith to the construction of the Salt Lake City temple. The relaxing of emigration laws by the Hawaiian Kingdom, land dispossession, and exploitation by the sugar plantation economy can explain, in part, why Hawaiian Mormon migration increased during this period; however, there is more to the story. Indeed, Robert A. Stauffer's comparison between the Iosepa colony population lists and land title holdings in Kahana valley on the island of O'ahu indicate that at least one-third of those emigrants were landowners. Instead, what appears to motivate Hawaiian migration is the spirit of gathering.

According to Dennis H. Atkin, "by mid-1889 approximately seventy-five Hawaiian Church members had migrated to Salt Lake City."[25] These early Hawaiian immigrants initially settled in communities north of Salt Lake City, but because of problems with integrating into the larger white community and racial discrimination, the presidency established a separate settlement for Hawaiian Latter-day Saints about seventy-five miles southwest of Salt Lake

City in Skull Valley. The town would be called Iosepa, after Joseph F. Smith, the second councilor in the First Presidency of the church at the time. In 1901, he became the president and prophet of the church until his death in 1919. The Hawaiian Saints honored Smith by naming the town after him, but the name was also a way to remember the ties that bound him to the people of Hawai'i. Smith had had a long history of ministering to the Hawaiian people, first as a missionary who served in the Sandwich Island Mission, where he was an outspoken advocate for continued growth of the mission in Hawai'i. Later in his life, he spent a significant amount of time in Lā'ie while in exile from Utah for his continued practice of polygamy.

The establishment of the Iosepa settlement resembled many of the characteristics of other Mormon settlements in Utah and Hawai'i. In May 1889, three former American missionaries to Hawai'i, along with three Hawaiians, went in search of a place where the Hawaiian Saints could live in peace and prosperity. They selected the ranch in Skull Valley because it was far enough away from Salt Lake City to protect the Hawaiians from discrimination but close enough for the Saints to travel to the temple, although it was a three-day trip by horse and wagon. In addition, the settlement had the potential to become self-sufficient, as the settlers would earn a living as laborers for the church-owned Iosepa Agriculture and Stock Company. The company provided year-round labor for the Hawaiian Saints. During the winter they tended to cattle, sheep, and pigs and during the summer they farmed hay, wheat, barley, and other grains that were sold to local ranchers as feed. In a kind of sharecropper style, Hawaiians would live in homes owned by the church, buy their groceries at church-owned stores, and get paid in church-printed script. This system was not unfamiliar to the Hawaiian Saints.[26] In 1865, the LDS church bought the ahupua'a (a pie-shaped land division that stretches from the mountains to the sea) of Lā'ie, approximately six thousand acres, which became the mission headquarters. In 1868, the mission started cultivating sugar cane, and by the turn of the twentieth century, Lā'ie functioned as a sugar plantation and colony of the LDS church.[27] In Hawai'i, the sugar was grown and milled locally, then sent to Salt Lake City where it was marketed and sold. Funds were then returned to the mission president who was responsible for maintaining a balanced budget for the mission. At Iosepa, profits from ranching and farming were also managed by the mission president who also served as company manager. However, one difference between Hawai'i and Utah was that in Utah, Hawaiians were able to use their labor potential in the city and on nearby ranches as leverage for higher wages. Atkins lists at least three occasions when workers organized strikes for higher wages and succeeded. Although it took a decade for the settlement to become economically viable, as they welcomed a new century, the Hawaiians had reason to celebrate as Iosepa was a thriving town.

The organizational structure of the settlement also resembled the hierarchical structure of settlements in Hawai'i. As Atkin writes, "The colony remained under the direct responsibility of the First Presidency with a president appointed by them to reside over the colonists. . . . The leader of Iosepa held a unique dual position as president of the Church organization of the colony and manager of the company."[28] The layout of the town and its establishment also echoed the founding of other Mormon settlements. The town was surveyed and plots of land for houses, a schoolhouse, a store, and a chapel were laid out and constructed on a square grid. At the center of Iosepa was a town square called Imilani Square. The streets branching off from this centralized area were given Hawaiian place names, such as Lā'ie Avenue and Honolulu Avenue, thus mnemonically connecting Hawai'i and Utah.[29] The community was primarily composed of Hawaiians; however, Atkin's research also identifies the permanent white residents as the president of the colony, his assistant, and the schoolteacher, as well as two other white men who had married Samoan women and whose families also resided in Iosepa. Since Hawaiians were in the majority, their customs tended to shape the atmosphere and everyday experiences of the community. For example, because the climate made it impossible to grow kalo, the root from which poi—a principle component of a Hawaiian diet—is made, they made poi from fermented wheat flour, calling it poi palaoa (palaoa being the Hawaiian word for flour).

In 1917, the church disbanded the settlement and made arrangements for the Hawaiian Saints to return to Hawai'i. Atkin suggests that Hawaiian Saints did not want to leave Iosepa and resisted as long as they could. He also identified a clear discrepancy between the official reasons for closing the settlement and the reality. Four arguments were made to rationalize the decision to close Iosepa. The first was that leprosy posed a threat to the larger community and the settlement needed to be closed for the safety of public health. The second was that the ranch was no longer profitable and needed to be sold. The third concern was that the Hawaiians had been weakened by disease and would be better off at home, where they could be cared for properly. And fourth, some argued that the Hawaiians continued to struggle with adapting to the climate and working conditions and this made the return to the islands appealing.

Atkin argues that none of these reasons was plausible. His research indicates that since the turn of the twentieth century the ranch had been quite productive and profitable, the community no longer suffered from leprosy or other serious illness, and that after a few winters, the Hawaiians had adapted quite well to the climate and their new home. The more likely reason for closing the ranch, he argues, was that a temple was being built in Hawai'i and the Hawaiian Saints would be able to conduct temple work in the islands, where relevant genealogical records were more easily accessible. A second factor was President Joseph F. Smith's declining health. Smith worried that after his passing there would be no one to look out for the Hawaiians' interests. One could infer from President Smith's concern that the discrimination that faced Hawaiian Latter-day Saints in the 1880s had not subsided over time, but in fact, they were vulnerable to the whims of white church leaders.

William K. Wallace described the removal of the Hawaiian Saints from Iosepa as "our trail of tears."[30] I was a bit surprised that he used this reference. It is an apt description of how the Hawaiian Saints were forcibly removed from Iosepa; however, he did not ask me to remember this historical event as dispossession and expropriation enacted on his grandparents by a colonial organization. Rather, I am to remember that these Polynesian Saints are important because they never lost faith in the gospel. Despite the discrimination they experienced, the hardships of living in the desert, and the forced migration back to Lā'ie, these Saints did not lose their faith. In fact, Wallace stressed, their experiences only strengthened them, and it is this strength that we should remember.

The Annual Iosepa Festival and Kuleana

The collective struggle and the perseverance of the first Polynesian pioneers are central themes at the annual Iosepa Festival, an event that brings together Polynesian cultural activities and performances to honor and remember the Polynesians who settled there in the 1880s. The Iosepa Festival takes place over the Memorial Day weekend. The main events of the festival happen on Saturday, but families who plan to camp the entire weekend begin arriving as early as Thursday. Saturday begins with a Hawaiian sun-raising chant and a Mormon prayer followed by a flag-raising ceremony conducted by Polynesian members of the U.S. military, who solemnly raise the national flags of the Polynesian Islands. These three events—Hawaiian oli, Mormon prayer, and recognition of Polynesian nationalism—mark the opening of the Iosepa Festival. Craft booths, hula, and Hawaiian language lessons, musical and dance performances by hālau hula (hula schools), from Utah, California, and on occasion, Hawai'i; and informational presentations by Hawaiian organizations begin at 10:00 am and continue throughout the day. The festival officially ends with a potluck lū'au (feast), including pork, beef, and sweet potatoes cooked in an imu (the Hawaiian term for an underground/earthen oven) provided by the Iosepa Association. For those families who camp or plan to stay through the evening, more entertainment awaits them. As the day ends and the sun sets, fire-knife performers entertain the crowd as the DJ prepares for the dance, a highlight of the weekend for the youth and their parents. On Sunday morning, the large pavilion is transformed from dance club to chapel in preparation for LDS church services in which the congregation is invited to publicly share their testimony of the truthfulness of the gospel and reflections about Iosepa.

When I asked my dad why he and my mom took our family to Iosepa every year, he replied, "Kuleana." He and mom wanted to get together with friends and do something for Hawaiians. I ask, what do you mean by doing things for Hawaiians? He responds, "We wanted to take care of them." By "them," he means the Hawaiians who are buried in the cemetery and whose spirits still reside in the desert. So each year we would pile into the station wagon, loaded down with food, gardening tools, mosquito repellent, and kids, to spend Memorial Day cleaning the cemetery. With pride dad remembers, "When we were done the place looked real nice."[31] Kuleana, a key theme in his rationale for the annual trip to Iosepa, embodies a cultural value of responsibility that is perpetuated at the festival. Kuleana can be translated as responsibility, but it also means authority and right. Within a Hawaiian worldview, everyone has kuleana and one's kuleana is based on one's relative position in any given context.[32] At Iosepa there are families whose kuleana to this space is genealogical—they have iwi kupuna (the bones of ancestors) buried there. Then there is the kuleana that is communal, such as my family's responsibility. We are not lineal descendants of the iwi kupuna buried in the cemetery, but we have been taught that as Hawaiians living near these iwi we have a kuleana to mālama (care for) them as though they were our own. To be sure, there is a thin line that divides our cultural practices from being pono (proper) and being maha'oi (intrusive and rude). As I explore below, there were times when our actions have crossed the line.

Within a Hawaiian worldview, iwi kupuna are sacred.[33] The place where they are buried, the kulāiwi (burial site) is also sacred. When my dad said we went to Iosepa so we could do something for Hawaiians, I understood that clearing the debris from around the graves, righting fallen headstones, and fixing the fence were ways to honor the kupuna. Today, a central aspect of the Iosepa Festival is beautifying the cemetery. The families of iwi kupuna care for their ancestors while other families volunteer to be responsible for cleaning a specific grave and making lei for the headstone. Over the years many improvements have been made to the cemetery: trees have been planted around the perimeter, irises have been planted at each grave site, boundaries made of concrete have been poured to demark each grave, the fence has been improved so cows can no longer trample on the graves, and each year fresh lei are made for each headstone. A crude water-catchment system has been set up to water the trees and flowers in the cemetery.

At Iosepa, the kuleana people have to mālama the iwi kupuna reflects an indigenous Hawaiian understanding of the relationship between kānaka (people), iwi, and ʻāina (land). As Ayau and Tengan describe it, the burial of iwi is a reflection of a broader Hawaiian cosmology and genealogy of the interdependent relationship between the iwi, the kulāiwi, and the living. "The burial of iwi" they explain, "results in the physical growth of plants and the spiritual growth of mana [spiritual power]. The living descendants feed off the foods of the land and are nourished spiritually by the knowledge that the iwi kupuna are well cared for, and in their rightful place."[34] The Iosepa Festival is a community that has been built around the kulaiwi that nourishes and sustains the people who gather there.

But Ayau and Tengan are describing cultural practices and understandings that take place in Hawaiʻi, not Utah. Caring for the iwi kupuna at Iosepa is an act that relies on a dialogical and fluid understanding of indigeneity in the diaspora, an understanding that is about "the place from which we see the world, interact with it, and interpret social reality," as Gegeo argues, and less about political status, blood, and geography. "The term *indigenous*," Gegeo explains, "has been used in a variety of ways in third-world and minority people's struggles against invasion, colonialism, and political oppression."[35] Whereas Kauanui's example is figurative—the metaphoric planting of kalo roots in foreign soil—at Iosepa it is literal; the iwi of kānaka have been buried in Goshute tribal soil. And herein is the tension. On the one hand, caring for the iwi kupuna at Iosepa is an act that performs an indigenous identity—it reflects a Native Hawaiian sensibility of the cycle of life and the interdependence of people, land, and spiritual power. Additionally, within this context, kuleana is also reckoned based on indigenous notions of family, in which "kinship," according to Linnekin, "is readily attributed to those who behave like relatives."[36] Since tending to the iwi kupuna and the kulāiwi are behaviors attributed to family members, legal definitions of lineal descent and natal birth are displaced by dialogical, indigenous notions of family based on responsibility and relationship. In this instance, to mālama the iwi kupuna is an example of diasporic indigeneity grounded in Native Hawaiian burial practices and familial affiliations.[37]

Despite the importance of caring for the iwi kupuna, my community has not extended our current understandings and narratives to include our kuleana to the ancestors of the Goshute who may be buried in the same soil. According to Greg Johnson, one underlying assumption about historic Native Hawaiian burial practices is that one's "rights to land were symbolized by the right to bury upon it."[38] Thus, within an indigenous framework, the place of one's birth and death, presumably the same place, establishes one's right to live on and from the land. Land in this context is ʻāina, that which feeds, the source of physical and spiritual nourishment.[39] But making an indigenous claim to land in Utah, even when done within an indigenous framework of kuleana and mālama the iwi kupuna, is predicated upon forgetting a prior indigenous relationship to the same land, namely that of the Skull Valley Goshute tribe. To be sure, since the cemetery is recognized by the state, rights to bury the dead at Iosepa are sanctioned by law not culture. However, as the opening scene suggests, contemporary Polynesian claims to the cemetery and surrounding land are made on cultural and religious grounds—cultural in the context of caring for the iwi kupuna and religious in the context of their membership in the LDS church. The line that divides pono actions from hewa (wrong) ones is thin. By drawing attention to when, where, and how we claim land, my actions may be interpreted as disrespectful of my elders. However, it is my kuleana as a scholar and analyst to point out to my elders and others that when we claim the land as "ours," we have crossed the line between pono and hewa. I believe it is pono to mālama the iwi kupuna, and I fully support the continuation of this cultural practice, because when we gather together to perform this act of memory we nourish ourselves spiritually, emotionally, and physically. However, when we take the next step and use these cultural practices to make larger claims for land, then we are being mahaʻoi and need to reevaluate our kuleana. Kuleana is a cultural principle we can use to guide us as we continue to negotiate the relationships and power dynamics in the diaspora.

A Few Lessons from the Imu

A second important event at the festival is the lūʻau on Saturday evening. Preparations begin early in the morning as a small group of men meet at the imu site. The imu is men's work at Iosepa, a carryover, perhaps, from Hawaiian cultural practices at the turn of the nineteenth century, when food preparation and eating was divided along strict gender lines, or perhaps it is a remnant of a gendered division of labor evident at the Polynesian Cultural Center in Lāʻie, Hawaiʻi, where many of the Polynesians who attend Iosepa once worked and learned the art of imu cooking.[40] Although there are regional and familial variations to imu cooking, at Iosepa a shallow hole is dug, hard woods are arranged volcano-style with a vent in the middle that will be used to light the fire and, on top of the wood, lava rocks are stacked. In Hawai'i, dried coconut husks would be used as tinder to ignite the fire, and beside the imu pit banana stumps would be crushed and stacked, banana leaves and ti (*Cordyline terminalis*) leaves would be sorted and stacked, and burlap sacks would be soaking in water. But at Iosepa, there are no banana trees or ti plants, and lava rocks are not readily available. Instead of banana stumps and leaves, which keep the food from being charred on the blazing hot lava rocks and make the steam that will cook the food, the association gets several boxes of cabbage and lettuce leaves from local grocery stores. Finally, at dawn on Saturday morning, a small group will gather watercress, which grows wild in a nearby freshwater spring.

The freshwater spring is about a mile north of Iosepa and about a half mile from the highway. The place is not visible from the road, and as you drive into the small valley, the landscape transforms from sparse sagebrush, spindly grass, and salty sand to a lush oasis of dense piñon pine, shrub oak trees, and wild flowers. The dark green of the watercress is a stark contrast in this desert landscape and the fresh spring water bubbling out of the ground looks refreshingly cool. Even in the early morning one feels the temperature rising. Typically when writers describe Iosepa in their magazine, newspaper, or academic journal articles, they juxtapose the harsh arid desert of Skull Valley, and its forbidding name, to the tropical paradise of Hawai'i. However, what is eclipsed by this contrast is the beauty in the Utah desert and the deserts in Hawai'i. The place where we gather watercress is a paradise in the desert. When I visited this site with my parents, they told me that this was the place where one of the two Hawaiian families who did not return to Hawai'i lived after they were forced out of Iosepa. The family was able to survive in large part because of the freshwater spring that supplied us with watercress for our imu. Folks at Iosepa learned the exact location of the spring when the grandchildren of these Polynesian pioneers started researching their family's history. The imu is not merely an example of perpetual cultural adaptation in the diaspora, but the process of gathering watercress is also experienced as a way to pay homage to the Hawaiians who used their cultural knowledge to do more than survive.

Decolonizing Our Stories or Unsettling Indigenous Settler Colonialism

As Geoffrey White explains about the politics of memory, "if representations of history (or, more generally, the past) mediate social relations and identities, then they become tools for shaping those identities and, in a more fundamental way, determining which identities obtain public recognition and validation through acts of memory."[41] At the Iosepa Festival, we are encouraged to remember those aspects of the history of Iosepa that reiterate a positive relationship between our Polynesian identity and religious membership. Thus, the process of remembering the Hawaiian pioneers becomes a project of articulating, yoking belief in LDS gospel with unquestioning obedience to the leadership and their decisions. Thomas King writes, "The truth about stories is that that's all we are."[42] We are the collective composition of the stories that are told. In indigenous contexts, stories provide the foundation upon which a people establish and legitimate their connection to their ancestors, the land, the spiritual world, and the universe. The stories told at Iosepa about the first Polynesian pioneers allow those of us who attend the festival to reorient ourselves to ancestors, land, and spirituality but in the sometimes hostile Utah climate.

For the people I interviewed, attending the annual Iosepa Festival is experienced as a contemporary gathering place where adults regenerate themselves and young people are raised to know themselves as Polynesian Latter-day Saints. Iosepa is a place where they were emotionally nourished and fortified so that at the end of the long weekend they could return to communities where many felt isolated, misunderstood, and lonely. Another way to interpret the act of honoring the perseverance of the first Hawaiian immigrants is self-referential. Utah was an inhospitable place for Hawaiians at the turn of the twentieth century, and as the century was coming to a close, the climate was still quite hostile to many Polynesian Saints.

Families who were the first Polynesians to move into predominantly white neighborhoods reported feeling alienated and misunderstood by the white members of their religious communities. His voice barely a whisper and his body hunched down in the sofa, Uncle Joe expressed how the first few years living in St. George, Utah, were some of the hardest years of his life. Uncle Joe was born and raised on Maui. At age eleven he left home to attend Kamehameha Schools on O'ahu, a private school started in 1887 as a boarding school for Native Hawaiian children. After graduation he attended Church College of Hawai'i and went on a Mormon mission to the Arizona/Utah Indian Mission. At the conclusion of his mission, he returned to Lā'ie but did not return to school. Instead, he worked at the Polynesian Cultural Center while simultaneously performing in a band in Waikīkī. When his dreams of making it big in the Waikīkī music scene were not actualized, he and his wife moved to St. George, Utah.

His body language and the story he told of this move reflect how incredibly painful a time it was for him. He felt that he had to become a different person when he moved to Utah because the white people in his community did not understand him. He recalls having a few friends who were attending Brigham Young University in Provo, but it was a four-hour drive from St. George so visits were rare. He remained lonely and misunderstood until he started going to Iosepa in the late 1970s. At one point in the interview, he spoke of these annual pilgrimages to the old settlement as having saved his life. It is the place he still goes to "recharge his battery." At Iosepa he can be himself. "I can talk as fast as I want and throw out as much pidgin and someone will know exactly what I'm saying."[43] Although this story explicitly highlights his feelings of exclusion in his white community and feelings of connection at Iosepa, the story was told during the interview about a time when he was losing faith. In this instance, the adversity he experienced did not strengthen his testimony, as the narrative of obedience and perseverance intends, but reflects how difficult it was for Hawaiians to migrate to the Utah desert.

When I heard Uncle Joe talk about needing to recharge his batteries and retreat to Iosepa from his everyday life, I heard a story of struggle against institutionalized forms of racism, and yet there was no mention of racism. Instead, the stories told are about the first Polynesian pioneers and their ability to overcome adversity, which serves as an allegory for contemporary Polynesians trying to survive the hostility of living in the Utah desert. But these stories are not only about survival. They also have a quality that resembles what Gerald Vizenor calls survivance. "Native survivance," he writes, "is an active sense of presence over absence, deracination, and oblivion; survivance is the continuance of stories, not a mere reaction, however pertinent."[44] The stories that are told about the first Polynesians to settle in Utah are an attempt to overcome "the unbearable sentiments of tragedy" and racism, loneliness, and being misunderstood and ostracized while also referencing, although not acknowledging, a larger structure of inequality and dominance within Mormonism.

The stories told at the Iosepa Festival are intended to regenerate and to reiterate a Polynesian Mormon identity that is faithfully obedient and persevering. In substantiating this identity, we delete, erase, and silence those aspects of the stories that would ask us to question the authority and decisions of church leaders. For example, what we do not hear are the stories about how the Polynesian Saints refused to leave their home or the part of the story in which the LDS church leaders force them to leave by damning the canal that brought fresh water to the town. We also do not hear about the two families who decided to actively go against the church leadership and stay in Utah. One family stayed in Utah for a few more years but eventually returned to Hawai'i, while the other never went back "home." This family severed its ties to the church and retreated into the surrounding mountains, where they lived independently for several years. When they were finally forced out of the mountains, the family members did whatever they had to do to survive, including assimilating into the dominant society. It was only after the grandchildren and great-grandchildren from this family started attending the Iosepa Festival that they began the process of recovering their history and learning the connections they had to Hawai'i, the LDS church, and their own identity as Hawaiians. It is from the stories recovered by this family that we learned where to find watercress in the desert.

What is at stake in this remembering and forgetting? Although I continue to consider myself part of the Polynesian community in Utah, today I am writing from my ancestral territory of Hawai'i. In Hawai'i, scholars have begun the critical work of expanding the binary of settler-colonialism beyond the colonizer/colonized, and settler/native, white/nonwhite dualities to include nonwhite immigrants who become settlers in this colonized space. As Candace Fujikane writes, Asians are settlers in Hawai'i. They may not have been active agents of U.S. occupation of Hawai'i, but the "narratives of Japanese settlement and its affirmation of U.S. democracy actually serves the ends of the United States as a settler state and its occupation of Native lands."[45] At Iosepa, certain stories, those that reference faithfulness, obedience, and perseverance, are told and retold, becoming "renarrativized" so as to produce a particular kind of Polynesian Mormon identity as well as a historic affiliation to the land.[46] For example, hearing the story about where to find watercress feels like a reverberation of mo'olelo (stories) used as mnemonic maps that tell us where, when, and how to use the natural resources in a given ecosystem. The story allows us to feel grounded in the space in which we find ourselves by tapping into our preexisting relationships to place. However, this is only part of the story. What my community stops short of asking is, from *whom* did that family learn to find fresh water and edible greens in the desert?

As I return to my community and continue to participate in the Iosepa Festival, I struggle to engage in a process of unsettling our settler-colonial tendencies. We must continually ask, what is our place? What is our kuleana? What histories and stories of places do our children need to know to live more responsibly on the land of the Goshute? Unsettling settler-colonialism is uncomfortable, and I know these will be very difficult conversations to have with my elders, family, and friends. However, unsettling ourselves has the potential to reconnect us to the Goshute tribe. The first Polynesian Saints to Utah must have learned where to find fresh water and wild watercress from the Goshute. What kind of relationship did the Polynesian settlers and the Skull Valley Goshute have? Did they feel connected to each other because they shared similar cosmological connections to land? Did they socialize? Did they trade? Did they marry and have children? What were the ties that bound these two indigenous peoples together in the desert? In the late 1970s, one woman set out to substantiate the relationship she believed must have existed between the Hawaiians and the Goshute tribe. She drove past the turnoff to Iosepa and kept driving until she reached the reservation. At the reservation, she asked around to find out if anyone still held stories about the Hawaiian settlers. She was directed to an old man living in a trailer who, she learned, was part Hawaiian. She spent the day with him, listening to stories about how he attended holiday celebrations at Iosepa and how the Hawaiian band would perform on the reservation. I think it is the kuleana of my community to fill in the empty spaces of our stories so that we do not perpetuate narratives of Polynesian Mormon settlement that reaffirm U.S. and LDS dispossession of native lands.

Finally, unsettling settler-colonialism is also about returning land to native peoples. As the opening vignette illustrates, the Iosepa Association Executive Board members have an active agenda to expand the footprint of the state historical site. They draw upon indigenous and religious narratives to authorize their claim for land. I utilize the Hawaiian cultural value of kuleana to point to those moments when land claims are pono and when they become hewa. As a scholar committed to reclaiming indigenous territorial boundaries and knowing that many in my community share similar commitments, I believe it is imperative that we reflect critically on how we claim the land. We could go one step further and rather than reclaim land for our benefit, we could work with the Skull Valley Goshute tribe to help them reclaim their land. Doing so could mean we do not get to expand the footprint of the Iosepa historical site, but it might be a first step in reestablishing a relationship with the people whose land has nourished us spiritually, emotionally, and physically. It is my belief that this would be pono.

Notes

Mahalo nui loa—thanks very much—to my family and community who care for me and for whom I hope I honor with these words. I also want to thank Charles R. Lawrence, III, and the Junior Faculty Seminar for their feedback on an early draft of this article, and Noenoe Silva and Noelani Goodyear-Kāʻopua for their support and editing skills.

1. The opening quote is from my field notes, May 15, 2001.
2. I use the term Polynesian, recognizing full well that the division of Oceania into three regions (Micronesia, Melanesia, and Polynesia) was and continues to serve a colonial, anthropological, and racial project. I use it, however, because this is the term the people I interviewed used to describe themselves and their relationship to the LDS Church.
3. J. Kēhaulani Kauanui, "Diasporic Deracination and 'Off-Island' Hawaiians," *Contemporary Pacific* 19.1 (2007): 138–61; Yen Espiritu, *Home Bound: Filipino American Lives across Cultures, Communities, and Countries* (Berkeley: University of California Press, 2003); Jean Barman, *Leaving Paradise: Indigenous Hawaiians in the Pacific Northwest, 1787–1898* (Honolulu: University of Hawaiʻi Press, 2006); Tevita Kaʻili, "Tauhi va: Nurturing Tongan Sociospatial Ties in Maui and Beyond," *Contemporary Pacific* 17.1 (January 24, 2005): 83–114.
4. Theodor W. Adorno, *Negative Dialectics*, trans. E. B. Ashton (New York: Continuum, 1995), 5.
5. Jeff Corntassel, "Who Is Indigenous? 'Peoplehood' and Ethnonationalist Approaches to Rearticulating Indigenous Identity," *Nationalism & Ethnic Politics* (2003): 91.
6. Gegeo, 494–95. David Welchman Gegeo, "Cultural Rupture and Indigeneity: The Challenge of (Re) visioning 'Place' in the Pacific," *The Contemporary Pacific: A Journal of Island Affairs* 13.2 (2002): 492.
7. J. Kēhaulani Kauanui, "Off-Island Hawaiians 'Making' Ourselves at 'Home': A (Gendered) Contradiction in Terms," *Women's Studies International Forum* 21.6 (1998): 681–93.
8. Laura Laurenson Byrne, "Federal Indian Policy in Utah, 1848–1865," http://content.lib.utah.edu/u?/uaida,4930 (accessed March 4, 2010).
9. "Goshute," http://indian.utah.gov/utah_tribes_today/goshute.html (accessed March 2, 2010).
10. Ned Blackhawk, *Violence over the Land: Indians and Empires in the Early American West* (Cambridge, Mass.: Harvard University Press, 2006).
11. Ibid.
12. R. Lanier Britsch, *Moramona: The Mormons in Hawaii* (Lāʻie, Hawaii: Institute for Polynesian Studies, Brigham Young University, 1992), 5.
13. Max Stanton, "A Gathering of Saints: The Role of the Church of Jesus Christ of Latter-day Saints in Pacific Islander Migration," in *A World Perspective on Pacific Islander Migration: Australia, New Zealand, and the USA* (Kensington, Australia: Center for South Pacific Studies, University of New South Wales, and the Bureau of Immigration Research, 1993), 23.
14. William Mulder, *Homeward to Zion: The Mormon Migration from Scandinavia* (Minneapolis: University of Minnesota Press, 2000), 18.
15. Ibid., 19.
16. Ilan Pappé, "Zionism as Colonialism: A Comparative View of Diluted Colonialism in Asia and Africa," *South Atlantic Quarterly* 107.4 (2008): 612.
17. Blackhawk, *Violence over the Land.*
18. Ibid., 239.
19. *Book of Mormon*, 2 Nephi 5:20.
20. Ibid., 2 Nephi 5:21–22.
21. I contend that although the racialization process underlying this narrative of Nephites and Lamanites appears to be mutable, in practice, whiteness continues to have supremacy in the organizational structure of the church.
22. R. Metcalf, *Termination's Legacy: The Discarded Indians of Utah* (Lincoln: University of Nebraska Press, 2002).
23. William K. Wallace III, interview with the author, August 7, 2001, Lāʻie, Hawaiʻi.
24. Britsch, *Moramona.*
25. Dennis H. Atkin, *A History of Iosepa: The Utah Polynesian Colony* (unpublished manuscript, 1958), 73.
26. Ibid.

27. Britsch, *Moramona.*
28. Ibid., 85.
29. For a discussion of the significance of naming and place names within a Hawaiian epistemology, see Mary Kawena Pukui, E. W. Haertig, and Catherine A. Lee, *Nānā I Ke Kumu*, vol. 1 (Honolulu: Hui Hānai, 1972).
30. Wallace interview.
31. Ned Aikau, personal communication with author, September 29, 2007.
32. See also Sam L. No'eau Warner, "Kuleana: The Right, Responsibility, and Authority to Speak and Make Decisions for Themselves in Language and Cultural Revitalization," *Anthropology & Education* 30.1 (1999): 63–93; Julie Kaomea, "Contemplating Kuleana: Reflections of the Rights and Responsibilities of Non-indigenous Participants," *AlterNatives* 5.2 (2009): 78–99.
33. Pukui, Haertig, and Lee, *Nānā I Ke Kumu.*
34. Edward Halealoha Ayau and Ty Kāwika Tengan, "Ka Huaka' o Nā 'Ōiwi: The Journey Home," in *The Dead and Their Possessions: Repatriation in Principle, Policy, and Practice,* Cressida Fforde, Jane Hubert, and Paul Turnbull, eds., (London: Routledge, 2002).
35. Gegeo, "Cultural Rupture and Indigeneity," 492.
36. Jocelyn Linnekin, *Sacred Queens and Women of Consequence: Rank, Gender, and Colonialism in the Hawaiian Islands* (Ann Arbor: University of Michigan Press, 1990), 148.
37. See also Graham Harvey and Charles D. Thompson Jr., introduction to *Indigenous Diasporas and Dislocations,* edited by Graham Harvey and Charles D. Thompson Jr. (Burlington, Vt.: Ashgate, 2005),1–12.
38. Greg Johnson, "Genealogy and the Limits of Articulation: Identity Claims and Law in Contemporary Hawai'i" (unpublished paper, 2009 [permission granted by author via e-mail]).
39. Lilikalā Kame'eleihiwa, *Native Land and Foreign Desires: How Shall We Live in Harmony?* (Honolulu: Bishop Museum Press, 1992).
40. See Ty Kāwika Tengan's work for a full description of how the kapu religious and political system informed gendered social relations in Hawai'i during the late eighteenth and early nineteenth centuries. Ty Kāwika Tengan, *Native Men Remade: Gender and Nation in Contemporary Hawai'i* (Durham, N.C.: Duke University Press, 2008).
41. Geoffrey White, "Epilogue: Memory Moments," *Ethos* 34.2 (2006): 331.
42. Thomas King, *The Truth about Stories: A Native Narrative* (Minneapolis: University of Minnesota Press, 2003), 2.
43. Joe Apo, interview with the author, March 12, 2001, Las Vegas, Nevada.
44. Gerald Vizenor, "Aesthetics of Survivance: Literary Theory and Practice," in *Survivance: Narratives of Native Presence,* ed. Gerald Vizenor (Lincoln: University of Nebraska Press, 2008), 1–24.
45. Candace Fujikane, "Introduction: Asian Settler Colonialism in the U.S. Colony of Hawaii," in *Asian Settler Colonialism: From Local Governance to the Habits of Everyday Life in Hawai'i,* ed. Candace Fujikane and Jonathan Y. Okamura (Honolulu: University of Hawai'i Press, 2008), 1–42.
46. Grant Farred, "The Unsettler," *South Atlantic Quarterly* 107.4, Setter Colonialism (2008): 791–808.

Bridging Indigenous and Immigrant Struggles: A Case Study of American Sāmoa

JoAnna Poblete-Cross

In American Sāmoa today, lines are being drawn between immigrants from Western Sāmoa, Tonga and the Philippines, and the indigenous population. A close study of the 2007 Future Political Status report, as well as the responses to the closure of the Chicken of the Sea tuna cannery, demonstrate how anti-immigrant sentiment has grown, along with fears over the stability and survival of the local economy. Such tensions between American Sāmoans and these Pacific and Asian immigrant workers have masked potential synergies in the struggles of both groups. This article provides preliminary suggestions toward a dialogue on how the goals of colonized indigenous groups might be combined with those of exploited working-class immigrants living in the same region.

Indigenous studies has focused on making the sovereignty and cultural perspectives of native groups central to academic analyses.[1] According to Vicente Diaz and J. Kēhaulani Kauanui, Pacific Native studies "involves at least two interconnected fronts: the identification and dismantling of colonial structures and discourses variously conceptualized and theorized, and cultural reclamation and stewardship."[2] Such an emphasis is necessary to understand the historical colonial context and complex issues facing indigenous groups. Scholars of indigenous studies also prioritize the needs and goals of their communities of study. Duane Champagne claimed that "the primary focus of indigenous studies should concentrate on defining, analyzing, theorizing, making policy, and supporting indigenous nations."[3] Issues surrounding immigrant rights further complicate such research. Academics such as J. Kēhaulani Kauanui have discussed the incongruities between immigrant and indigenous rights.[4] Topics like citizenship are seen as tangential, inconsistent with, and completely separate from indigenous rights. Nevertheless, there may be fruitful ways in which the struggles of immigrant workers could also support the anticolonial projects of indigenous groups. The plight of immigrant groups should not subordinate the fight for indigenous rights. However, both groups could benefit from acknowledging their shared colonial connections to the United States.

This essay demonstrates how indigenous groups and Pacific and Asian immigrants in American Sāmoa are part of the same imperial legacy. After becoming an unincorporated territory of the United States in 1900, American Sāmoa and its people were ignored by the U.S. government for sixty years. When the government finally started to invest in the region in the 1960s, U.S. officials encouraged and supported the development of a single-industry economy, tuna canning, through government subsidies. U.S. corporations recruited immigrants from Western Sāmoa, Tonga, and the Philippines to fill their numerous manual labor positions.[5] Today, all groups in the region worry about the economic impact of the closure of the Chicken of the Sea cannery. U.S. colonialism in American Sāmoa created the current economic crisis in the region and the existing immigrant population. Both immigrants and American Sāmoans were subjugated to the political and economic interests of U.S. empire.

This work provides a critical space to acknowledge, connect, and coordinate the concerns of indigenous and other marginalized groups. Each group could benefit from collaborations to understand, address, and contest colonial and imperial structures that have constrained their lives on a daily basis. Both groups have a historical basis for joining together and fighting against continued U.S. imperialism in the region. This essay does not seek to equate Pacific and Asian immigrants with American Sāmoans. However, I do hope to redirect the anger surrounding the closing of the cannery away from these immigrant groups and toward the neoliberal policies that brought these non-American Sāmoans to the region in the first place.

In the later part of the nineteenth century, the United States, Germany, France, and Great Britain began claiming land in the South Pacific. By the 1870s, German businessmen had established themselves in the western part of the Sāmoa Islands, about 200 miles northeast of New Zealand and 2,600 miles south of Hawai'i. The British had a consul general in the region, and the United States gained exclusive access to the deep water port of Pago Pago. From 1884 until 1898, these Western nations became involved in a tense balancing act of power and control over these islands. In 1889, a devastating hurricane destroyed both U.S. and German fleets in the area. After this event, the Western nations agreed to give the western islands of Sāmoa to Germany, the eastern islands to the United States, Tahiti and Tonga to France, and New Zealand to Great Britain. These agreements, known as the Berlin Act, went into effect on June 14, 1889, solidifying Western colonial rule in the region.

On April 17, 1900, the *matai* (chiefs) of Tutuila formally ceded the islands of Tutuila and Aunu'u to the United States. In the Deed of Cession, the signers stated that the "declaration is accepted by us with glad hearts . . . we do also cede and transfer to the Government of the United States of America the Island of Tutuila and all things there to rule and to protect it. We will obey all laws and statutes made by that Government or by those appointed by the Government to legislate and to govern. Our whole desire is to obey the laws that honor and dwelling in peace may come to pass in this country."[6] This submission to U.S. rule was based on U.S. Commander B. F. Tilley's promise that "the authority of Sāmoan chiefs, 'when properly exercised, will be upheld.'"[7] Unlike other Western powers in the region, the United States seemed more willing to incorporate Sāmoan forms of governance in their territorial rule. Eastern Sāmoan leaders consequently turned over ultimate authority of the region to the United States government in exchange for the protection of their land tenure system and cultural practices.

Within two weeks of the cession, Commander Tilley, who also became the first governor of American Sāmoa, developed the basic ordinances that preserved Sāmoan authority at the village level and established overarching U.S. Naval authority in the region. Promulgated on April 30 and May 1, respectively, Regulations 4 and 5 are considered "the two most important regulations that Tilley issued during his tenure as Governor/Commandant of the Naval Station."[8] Notice No. 4, known as the Native Lands Ordinance, strictly limited land ownership in the region to either Sāmoans or the government. This restriction prevented the purchase of indigenous land by private foreigners, thus avoiding the exploitation of these lands by independent Western businessmen. The U.S. federal government, however, could acquire land freely. Notice No. 5 applied U.S. laws to the territory, as long as they did not conflict with Sāmoan customs. This rule also stated that "the governor, for the time being, of American Sāmoa is the head of the government. He is the maker of all laws, and he shall make and control all appointments" (Notice No. 5, RG 284, T1182, Roll 1). The federally appointed governor held complete control over the region. But indigenous forms of governance, such as village, county, and district councils, remained untouched by the U.S. Naval administration. American Sāmoans consequently maintained the same political, economic, social, and cultural institutions that they practiced prior to the arrival of the U.S. military. These customs included descent-based land tenure and adjudication of issues by community elders, known as the *matai* system. However, the wording of these initial ordinances also left room for interpretation and change. The preservation of Sāmoan political power was ultimately provisional, subject to change based on the observations and decisions of U.S. government officials.

American Sāmoans, like many other indigenous peoples, have had complicated forms of affiliation with the United States. Since the beginning of relations with the U.S., American Sāmoans have emphasized the protection and preservation of their culture, land, and ways of life.

Any study of native peoples should be cognizant, mindful and respectful of the group's specific needs and goals. According to Diaz and Kauanui "the inseparability of land and blood," or the strong "kinship ties between people and land" are fundamental principles for Pacific Natives.[9] Such connections are apparent among American Sāmoans, where "one of the most important responsibilities of any *matai* is serving as trustee of family land."[10] The guarding of land rights has always been the central tenet of American Sāmoan relations with outsiders. Any threats to land rights are seen as obstacles to the continued preservation and function of Sāmoan life.

In American Sāmoa, land belongs to the entire *'āiga*, or extended family, instead of the *matai* or any one person. The *matai* gain their positions from election by the entire *'āiga*. All political, social, and economic decisions are filtered through the leaders of each *'āiga*. In addition to land issues, the *matai* are also "responsible for maintaining family unity and harmony, promoting participation in religious or church-related activities, and insuring the family's children are educated."[11] The judgments of the *matai* are considered final and absolute. Tongan and Filipino immigrants, however, are not included in, and hence not beholden to, the Sāmoan belief system and local forms of governance.

Some American Sāmoans have worried about the impact that immigrants who are not governed by Sāmoan culture and principles, or *f'aa sāmoa*, might have on their society. According to the 2007 Future Political Status (FPS) report, "while some are married to Samoans and live as Samoans, most aliens live outside the Samoan system."[12] The differential ethnic backgrounds of Filipino and Tongan immigrants do not require them to follow Sāmoan laws or verdicts. This variation in cultures is seen as a major hazard to conventional Sāmoan lifestyles. The report continues, stating that "the number of people in American Samoa living outside of the matai system, and the size of the economy under their control continues to grow. That is a clear threat to the system."[13] Non-Sāmoans are viewed as external, thus undesirable, groups that could jeopardize the traditional way of functioning in the islands. The report also claimed that immigrants have placed severe pressure on land, increased the cost of government services, overloaded social services, dominated business opportunities and skilled jobs, as well as committed some of the most serious crimes. Such anti-immigrant sentiments stem from changes in social life presumably created by the migration, settlement, and integration of Tongans and Filipinos into the region.

These fears, however, have roots in the form and structure of the U.S. colonial presence in the region. The infiltration of Western ideas and practices, such as private property, consumerism, and individualism, contradict the basic tenets of American Sāmoan life. When the U.S. military drastically increased its activity and personnel in the islands during World War II, American Sāmoans were rapidly introduced to Western goods and lifestyles. They started to listen to Western music, wear Western-style clothing and eat Western food. Such intense exposure to U.S. products and ideas stopped abruptly with the end of the war. However, this brief period made a lasting impact on American Sāmoans. Since that time, many have left American Sāmoa to take advantage of better opportunities in education, employment, and metropolitan lifestyles in other parts of the United States.[14] According to the 2000 U.S. Census, 133,000 Sāmoans lived outside of American Sāmoa at the time of the census.[15] With a total population of 50,545 Sāmoans in American Sāmoa, more than 72 percent currently live elsewhere.

Despite significant outmigration and the shift of younger generations toward Western lifestyles, the 2007 FPS Commission did not recommend any change in the region's relationship with the United States. While the FPS Commission found that *American* Sāmoans wanted to "remain part of the American family of states and territories," they also wanted to make sure that "a chosen status will not adversely affect customs and culture, and the perpetuation of the Samoan language."[16] Such a statement demonstrates the continued subordinate and dependent position of American Sāmoa to the United States. Executive Order No. 10264 placed the secretary of the Department of Interior in charge of American Sāmoa in June 29, 1951. Even though a 1983 law now requires U.S. congressional approval for all amendments to the American Sāmoan Constitution, the Department of Interior still has legal control to invalidate other forms of legislation created by the American Sāmoan government. To further guard Sāmoan land and culture, the FPS Commission recommended that the special protective provisions for lands and titles in the region's constitution be affirmed by an act of the U.S. Congress without any change to their present political status. Such legislation would ease concerns over the ultimate authority that the Department of Interior maintains over American Sāmoa.

American Sāmoan desires to remain part of the United States while sustaining native forms of governance and culture, suggests a contradictory positionality. They rarely speak out against the United States and often actively support continued U.S. colonial relations, as long as their cultural practices are maintained. Since the U.S. government had very little interest in American Sāmoa until World War II, and only limited involvement after that, American Sāmoans have not felt the direct and obvious impact of U.S. colonialism in their daily lives. They did not lose local control of their islands or have to subordinate their practices to U.S. rule. Compared to the aggressive colonization of other Pacific Islands and the near-obliteration of American Indian lifestyles in the continental United States, U.S. rule in American Sāmoa seemed quite accommodating. Consequently, the degree of animosity toward the United States has varied among American Sāmoans.

In fact, American Sāmoans tend not to associate U.S. colonialism with the area's economic underdevelopment. Instead of critiquing U.S. colonial government authority and policies toward the region, local animosity often focuses on Pacific and Asian immigrants, whose lives are just as much subsumed to the interests of the U.S. empire as American Sāmoans' are. Immigrants from Tonga and the Philippines entered the region only after being recruited to work in the U.S.-subsidized tuna canneries. These groups migrated mainly because of the job opportunities.

In both the public hearings for the 2007 FPS Commission and reactions to the Chicken of the Sea (COS) / Samoa Packing cannery closure in 2009, immigrants have become scapegoats for the larger U.S. imperial and neoliberal practices that have dramatically changed the lives of American Sāmoans, as well as shaped the circumstances facing immigrant workers in the region. During the FPS Commission's public study tour throughout American Sāmoa and nine cities in the United States with significant American Sāmoan populations, the main goal was to evaluate options for the future political status of American Sāmoa. Beyond this issue, the commissioners found that "the threat of being overwhelmed—loss of identity and loss of future opportunities—has become very unsettling to most American Samoans."[17] In these hearings, numerous American Sāmoans throughout the U.S. empire made passionate calls for immediate immigration reform.

Members of the American Sāmoan government (ASG) also supported the idea that immigration was a crisis threatening the well-being of American Sāmoans. On May 7, 2009, American Sāmoa's governor, Togiola Tulafono, established a Territorial Population Commission. Executive Order No. 005-2009 stated that population pressure "is one of the most significant threats to our natural resources, our island and thus our current and future quality and way of life . . . foreign migrants strain our basic social services and significantly modify the composition of our population, based on the fact that nearly half of the current population of American Samoa was not born here."[18] This order was promulgated just six days after COS announced the closure of its cannery facility in American Sāmoa, which employed 87 percent, or 1,892, non-American Sāmoan workers.

According to ASG representative Taotasi Archie Soliai, "the sudden announcement by COS Samoa Packing that it will be shutting down its operation as of September is cause for alarm and concern in several areas, one of which is immigration."[19] He continued, "I am particularly concerned that if prompt action is not taken . . . our already serious overstayer problem will only multiply, placing additional strain on our limited resources."[20] One result of the cannery closure involved a greater focus on the negative impact of immigrants on American Sāmoa's public services.

This fear over the harmful presence of foreigners was also reflected in the comments posted by readers of the online version of the local daily newspaper, the *Samoa News*. One anonymous poster stated that "non-citizens can then go back to their countries and we regain American Samoa for American Samoans. What's so hard about that? Less strain on our schools, roads, crime rates, and of course, the environment."[21] The fear over limited resources was directly connected to predictions of economic downturn as a result of the COS closure. Governor Togiola claimed that this "single industry meltdown has caused havoc with the business community and many businesses are facing possible downsizing or closure . . . it is predicted that as many as 7,500 people will lose their jobs during this year."[22] Another *Samoa News* article commented that the cannery closure "impact on the community will include drastic hikes in food costs, because shipping costs will go up—due to the fact that the container vessels will be without shipments" from the cannery.[23] These very real concerns about the economic impact of the cannery closure easily combined with anti-immigrant attitudes. One anonymous reader proclaimed that "this is a great opportunity to return American Samoa to American Samoans. Let them all go back to where they came from so we can get back to our ideal population."[24] These kinds of anti-immigrant comments prioritized the needs of American Sāmoans and failed to acknowledge the simultaneous suffering of exploited foreign workers who would face unemployment and financial hardships in the coming months.

The FPS report further stated that "there is a growing concern among native American Samoans that too many foreign nationals come to American Samoa and give birth to children who then become U. S. Nationals—equating them to children of native American Samoans. These new nationals, born of two alien parents, are entitled to participate in the political and social life of the Territory. They can run for office and may even be governor."[25] This statement presented such access for immigrants as a major threat. In American Sāmoa, issues of sovereignty and citizenship for native groups versus immigrants often conflict. American Sāmoans want to maintain a level of autonomy from the United States, and would like the choice to become U.S. citizens, but they also do not believe American Sāmoan status or rights should be provided to non-American Sāmoans living in the islands. While American Sāmoans can see the benefit of U.S. citizenship for themselves, and believe they have the right to such status, they rarely believe non-American Sāmoans should get the same kind of flexibility and accommodation in the islands. Tied to the land by blood and kinship, indigenous groups often struggle to establish their ultimate right to benefits in their region from colonial settlers. While such goals are important and necessary, these efforts can also overlook the struggles and oppressions of other marginalized groups in the same area. In American Sāmoa, a focus on indigenous rights can eclipse the grave problems facing migrant cannery workers from Western Sāmoa, Tonga, and the Philippines.

A History of the Canneries

As stated, immigrants from Western Sāmoa, Tonga, and the Philippines came to American Sāmoa primarily to support the fish processing industry. In addition to federal grants that total about $63 million each year, most of the income in the islands has been from the tuna canneries.[26] This business was established in the region in October 1948, when Harold C. Gatty, a well-known aviator and businessman of the time, made plans to set up a $1,500,000 tuna cannery in American Sāmoa. The initial plan called "for an annual output of 125,000 cases of tuna at the beginning, with an eventual yearly capacity of 350,000 cases . . . The tuna cannery will be the first industry of its kind in Samoa."[27] By 1955, products from the Van Camp Sea Food cannery accounted for 80 percent of the region's total exports: $1,016,438.40 of $1,270,548.[28] In 2008, StarKist and Chicken of the Sea had a combined total of five thousand employees and generated a thousand tons of canned tuna per day, worth $400 million a year. These canneries were the two largest fish-processing plants in the world.

When plans for the first cannery began in 1948, "Samoans were consulted and approved the enterprise. Initially it will provide work for 150 Samoans. Not more than 10 non-Samoans may be employed in the plant."[29] Even at this early stage of development, there was tension over the nationality of the cannery workers. American Sāmoans did not want foreigners to profit from this industry more than themselves. But as this labor-intensive industry grew, American Sāmoans began to look down upon cannery work. Consequently, the tuna companies started bringing in immigrants to process the fish.

When canneries are in production, they must function twenty-four hours a day. The multistep process involves difficult manual labor at every stage. First, frozen fish are unloaded onto broad platforms under the blazing sun. Workers must hunch over to sort the fish by size with a hatchet-type pick. Another group of laborers transport the fish into the freezing cold-storage warehouses. Next are the arduous and dangerous stages of defrosting and deboning the fish. Then there is the swift canning, sterilizing, and packaging of the final products. There are two 12-hour shifts for cannery workers. Conditions are smelly, wet, hot (unless one works in cold storage), deafening (from the noise of machinery), exhausting (from standing for an entire shift), and dangerous (from the heat of steaming processes, the quick and sharp knives for processing, and the powerful and potentially crushing packaging machines). Until 2007, cannery workers in American Sāmoa were paid less than four dollars an hour for this grueling work.

The U.S. federal government used its historical accommodation of Sāmoan cultural practices as the pretext for not encouraging other industries in the region. The U.S. Navy "made no general request for bids for the establishment of industries in areas under its control because of its responsibility to insure that the economy and customs of the Samoans are not disturbed."[30] For more than fifty years, the navy maintained minimal operations in Pago Pago harbor. Besides using the area as a coaling station and supply stop for military ships crossing the Pacific, the U.S. federal government did not invest any additional money or time in the region.[31] Not until July 1961, when Clarence Hall wrote a scathing article about poverty-level conditions in American Sāmoa for *Readers Digest,* did the United States focus on improving economic and social conditions in the region.[32] But these projects only lasted until 1967 and focused on upgrading public infrastructure and social services. None of these programs aimed to diversify the economic base or industries in the region. Such circumstances resulted in American Sāmoa's continued financial dependence on tuna canneries.

American Sāmoans also developed a dependent attitude toward the fish-processing plants over the years. As part of American Sāmoa's neoliberal subjugation to the canning industry, tuna companies in the region created and perpetuated fears that the local economy would collapse without the presence of these businesses. In March 1956, Vaiinupo J. Ala'ilima testified at a U.S. House Education and Welfare subcommittee in Washington, D.C., to plead against any policy of keeping wages down to attract industries to American Sāmoa. He believed the application of the national minimum wage standard of one dollar an hour would "protect our people from being exploited for cheap labor and likewise slow down the industrialization of our little country."[33] In the same newspaper article, the Van Camp Sea Food Company stated that it might need to leave the islands if required to pay one dollar an hour. As the only industry in American Sāmoa at that time, Van Camp employed three hundred island women for their tuna packing plant. The cannery's casual comment about a potential shutdown if Ala'ilima's campaign succeeded in raising wages instilled fear among the general public and government officials alike. This subtle threat ended up convincing the federal government not to raise wages.

Fifty-four years later, in March 2008, the director of commerce and tourism, Falesiu Eliu Paopao, argued that if the canneries left, so would the majority of jobs. He explained that such changes would "be an impact, a great impact, to American Samoa because about 80 percent of the jobs, our economy is depending on those two canneries."[34] Throughout the existence of commercial fish processing in American Sāmoa, the fear of losing this industry has lurked in the back of people's minds. Rumors or references to the closure of canneries could trigger panic and fear about the economy's ability to function and survive. This fear also fostered anti–minimum wage talk throughout the last sixty years of cannery presence in the islands. Despite the environmental pollution caused by the canning process and the substandard pay of the industry, American Sāmoan residents viewed these tuna companies as essential to the stability of the region's economy and the continuation of their own lifestyles. As a result, American Sāmoa has made many accommodations to tuna companies to retain their business.

Instead of focusing on the negative impacts of the canneries in the region, some American Sāmoans have engaged in exploitative actions and negative rhetoric toward immigrant cannery workers. In the oral histories I conducted in 2008, some American Sāmoans downplayed the animosity native groups had toward immigrant cannery workers. But there were also different reactions to Pacific Islander immigrants than to those from Asia. Most American Sāmoans I interviewed saw their cultural similarities with cannery workers from Western Sāmoa. One interviewee said, "We're all one culture, we're cousins."[35] Since immigrants from Western Sāmoa share common cultural values and practices with American Sāmoans, their presence was seen as more tolerable than that of Tongans or Filipinos. Sometimes negative feelings toward Sāmoan immigrants were abated by familial, clan, or village connections. In fact, American Sāmoans often sponsored relatives from Western Sāmoa to work in the canneries. Despite such familial ties and common cultural backgrounds, Sāmoans from Western Sāmoa are still seen as outsiders, or subordinate to American Sāmoans.

Every immigrant to American Sāmoa must be sponsored by either an employer or an individual American Sāmoan, defined as someone of 50 percent or more Sāmoan blood and born in the region. The individual sponsor must pay a deposit large enough to transport the immigrant back home if necessary. The sponsor is also responsible and liable for immigrants who overstay their visas or break any laws. Sponsors are not supposed to accept any form of payment or compensation from their wards. Even with this rule, some sponsors have exploited their wards. In exchange for their legal support, some American Sāmoans expect their charges to provide services around the house, such as cleaning or cooking. Beyond the expectation of household work, some sponsors have pressured wards into giving them part of their cannery salary as compensation for acting as their guarantor. If workers refuse to pay their benefactors or provide domestic services, sponsors sometimes threaten to withdraw their petition of support, which would result in deportation. In this context, some immigrant cannery workers not only provide critical labor for the main industry in the region; they also supply domestic services and financial support to their sponsors.

In spite of their central roles in the regional economy and the domestic households of a number of American Sāmoan sponsors, Pacific and Asian immigrants are often viewed negatively in the region. The FPS Commission attributed the start of foreign entry into the region to the establishment and growth of the tuna canneries in the 1950s and 1960s. According to the commission's report, "policy planners and lawmakers knew and accepted this heavy presence of Western Samoans and Tongans because it was critical to the success of both the canneries and the construction industry. There were groans about the growing number of aliens, but we had to have them in order to realize the opportunities in economic development. Today's dilemma is different."[36] While migration was always frowned upon, earlier labor recruitment from other Pacific Islands was viewed as a natural consequence of the labor-intensive canning process. In more recent times, however, attitudes toward immigrants have been less accepting.

Current fears about immigration in American Sāmoa have focused on people from Asia and the Philippines. The FPS report stated that "Congress needs to be informed about the effects of the present growing situation on limited land and absence of natural resources, and the need to protect the customs and traditions of the Samoa people against the strong assault of foreigners and their cultures."[37] American Sāmoans worry that "if the present trend continues, the children of the native American Samoans may soon become a minority in their own home."[38] Like the fear over diminishing resources in the islands, American Sāmoans also worry about an invasion of foreigners who will take over their land and culture. Such apprehension drives anti-immigrant sentiment, alarmist rhetoric and calls for corrective action.

While foreign laborers have migrated from Western Sāmoa, Tonga, and the Philippines, there are also visible Chinese and Korean immigrant populations in American Sāmoa that work in the grocery and restaurant industries.[39] Anti-immigrant rhetoric in newspaper reports, at government hearings, and in comments on newspaper articles rarely specify which groups they are discussing. The lack of distinction demonstrates the wide swath of people vulnerable to anti-immigrant sentiments in American Sāmoa.

As a result of the anti-immigrant perspectives that emerged from its hearings, the FPS Commission recommended that the ASG enact laws to "further restrict alien entry and residence in the territory."[40] The commission also recommended that U.S. national status be given only to children of American Sāmoan parents. Even though immigrants to American Sāmoa have contributed much to the daily functioning of the canneries and the general economy, such involvement is not acknowledged. As servants of neoliberalism, their labor has kept tuna plants running while their salaries have supported local business, such as restaurants, stores, and banks. Despite these important roles, foreigner cannery workers receive low pay, encounter dangerous working conditions, experience exploitation from some sponsors, and endure anti-immigrant rhetoric.

The fears of a swarming and unemployed immigrant population heightened on May 3, 2009, when COS / Samoa Packing announced the closure of its cannery on September 31, 2009. The shutdown cut about two thousand jobs in the region. In the three months after the announcement of the cannery closure, 627 Web posts were logged for the eighty-four *Samoa News* articles that discussed the demise of the fish-processing industry in the region. A variety of issues have developed from stories covering the shutdown of COS and subsequent implications. Many people expressed how they always knew the canneries would leave. One anonymous reader stated that

> for years there have been rumors that the canneries may or may not move out . . . it's like the entire economy of American Samoa are in the hands of the canneries and its owners. So in reality, the canneries have and always had the power to make or break the economy here in American Samoa. . . . The Governor was asked if there was an alternative government plan in place in the event the canneries do leave, including a way to help the laid off workers, the

governor's reply was, "We do not have an alternative plan. There is no way we can employ [all] these folks. We have no other cannery."[41]

This post reflects the long-held fear over cannery closures and public consciousness of American Sāmoa's dependence on this industry. While most were not surprised about the shutdown, many were shocked that the ASG had no plan to deal with the closure. Another reader named "The Maverick" stated that "we knew this was coming, but no safety net nor any alternative plans in place . . . What now? . . . Nothing was in place for these folks, what a catastrophe and a national nightmare, that for these 2000+ workers and possibly total 5000 will be no longer employed. They have failed, the Governor, ASG government Leaders, the Fono and the Congressman."[42] Many other readers expressed similar kinds of disappointment with American Sāmoan officials. These people believed poor planning and lack of leadership by either the governor or the representative to the U.S. Congress resulted in the current situation.

The federally mandated minimum wage increase of 2008 became another hotly debated issue connected to the cannery closure. American Sāmoa's minimum wage was slated to increase fifty cents each year until reaching a level "generally applicable in the United States."[43] On May 25, 2009, salaries for cannery work were increased to $4.76. Both the ASG governor and the American Sāmoa Chamber of Commerce president believed the imposition of continental U.S. wage standards on this small Pacific Island region would have a negative impact on the fish-processing industry.[44] Other *Samoa News* readers believed that minimum wage increases had nothing to do with the cannery closure. Instead, they blamed COS for taking advantage of better tax incentives in Georgia, as well as automation of the canning process.[45] Regardless of the ultimate factors that resulted in the closure of the COS plant in Pago Pago, the loss of this cannery will have major long-term impacts on the region's economy.

Soon after the announcement of the COS closure, rumors spread that the second cannery in the islands, StarKist, might also shut its doors. While Governor Togiola requested a meeting with this company's leaders upon hearing about the COS closure, there was no immediate official statement about the future plans of this business in the islands. Then on July 23, 2009, StarKist announced it would be laying off about 350 workers as part of their plan to make the Pago Pago cannery viable in the long term. These layoffs, combined with the closure of the COS cannery, motivated the governor and members of the private sector to develop a petition asking President Barack Obama to reverse minimum wage increases in the region, except for the initial fifty-cent increase in 2008, and to reinstate a Special Industry Committee to determine minimum wage rates in the territory. While much debate occurred about this petition, with vocal supporters and opponents, it garnered more than 12,000 signatures from American Sāmoan residents. This petition, in addition to letters written by Governor Togiola and American Sāmoan congressional representative Eni F. H. Faleomavaega requesting assistance from members of the U.S. Congress and Department of Interior, resulted in the visit of a congressional delegation to American Sāmoa on August 4 and 5, 2009. The six-member delegation examined the tuna fishing and processing industries and considered what needed to be done to keep StarKist in the territory. The petition and letters also resulted in an on-site visit from the Government Accounting Office (GAO) to conduct a study on the impact of minimum wage hikes in American Sāmoa. This three-member team conducted a series of hearings with the public, businesspeople, and the government between August 17 and August 31, 2009. After the earthquake and tsunami on September 29, 2009, GAO senior officials conducted a follow-up visit between January 25 and January 28, 2010, to see how conditions in the islands had changed since the natural disaster. This final report, which was published in April 2010, was more representative of the economic situation in the islands than the previous GAO report of 2007.[46]

In the meantime, Congressman Faleomavaega introduced a bill to the U.S. Congress on September 16, 2009, "to provide American Sāmoa with employment stabilization and economic development assistance."[47] Hearings for this legislation continued through the winter of 2010. On December 16, 2009, President Barack Obama signed a federal law postponing the next fifty-cent minimum wage increase from May to September 30, 2010. The remaining cannery, StarKist, also requested and received a three-month tax exemption from the ASG Tax Exemption Board between the months of January and March 2010. According to the senior manager of StarKist Corporate Affairs, the "minimum wage increase is one of several factors that are combining to make American Samoa no longer globally competitive for the tuna industry."[48] Depending on the outcome of the ASPIRE bill StarKist may or may not stay in American Sāmoa.

Coming Together

While the long-term prospects for the StarKist cannery remains unclear, the tuna-processing industry has presented an interesting contradiction in American Sāmoa. On the one hand, fish canneries have been the only successful major industry in the area. The American Sāmoa economy is largely dependent on the taxes, salaries, and other investments provided by these companies. On the other hand, most American Sāmoans see cannery work as beneath them, and so the majority of workers in the canneries are immigrants to the region from Western Sāmoa, Tonga, and the Philippines. These cannery workers are often spoken of and treated negatively. There are few alliances over the common devastation that the demise of the fish-processing industry will wreak on both immigrant cannery workers and American Sāmoans. All groups will face higher utility and food prices, unemployment, decreased revenue for social services, and a generally depressed economy. For everyone, these problems resulted from an imperially imposed, neoliberal ideology that encouraged the development of a single industry in American Sāmoa and deprived the economy of any resilience.

When the news of the cannery closure spread, many American Sāmoans reacted with anti-immigrant rhetoric. One *Samoa News* reader named "concerned AmSamoa citizen" said "just to make it plain and simple for the ASG. Send all those illegal immigrants back to their country of origin."[49] Other readers supported assistance only to American Sāmoans who were laid off. One anonymous reader stated

> where is the great tragedy if the canneries close? . . . The first and foremost responsibility of the ASG and US Government is to AMERICAN Samoans, then our cousins and neighbors. It is not the sole responsibility of American Samoans or our Government to spend the time or taxpayer dollars (to our own detriment) to find new employment for workers who came here from another country to work for a local business that is now closing. Those businesses have responsibility along with sponsors and all the individuals who left their homes and came here of their own volition.[50]

Others urged the deportation of unemployed immigrants. In another anonymous post, one reader spoke about the 31,500 registered aliens from Western Sāmoa, wondering

> how many came here originally to work for the canneries, don't any longer but found somebody to sponsor them, and remained? Of those 31,500 how many work "under the table" and don't pay taxes? How many have been or are on WIC and food stamps? How many have had children born here out of wedlock and have their kids in and out of LBJ [Tropical Medical Center] or crammed into our schools? How many have cars on our roads? . . . I could go on about the physical burden on our local infrastructure but I'd be stating the obvious."[51]

Regardless of their similar cultural backgrounds, these commentators spoke negatively about helping Western Sāmoan cannery workers above the needs of American Sāmoans.

But shared imperial repression could also unite American Sāmoans and immigrant laborers. Scholars such as Todd R. Ramlow provide some guidance on ways to start bridging indigenous and immigrant struggles in the same time and place. In his analysis of Gloria Anzaldua's classic work *Borderlands / La Frontera* and David Wojnarowicz's *Close to the Knives*, Ramlow argues that groups should "reject the limitations of dualism and connect to others across fields of difference, rather than being immobilized by the fantasy of normate physical and national unity . . . rethink dominant ideals of singular, unitary, autonomous identity; in doing so they offer a revisioning of subjectivity that might produce a resistant politics of multiplicity."[52] Ramlow encourages different minoritized groups to move beyond identity-based distinctions and seek out connections among each other in the context of larger organizational forms of domination and control. Instead of speaking negatively about foreign cannery workers, perhaps the energy of anti-immigrant natives could be more productively channeled into figuring out how to, for example, diversify American Sāmoa's economy while undoing the region's dependence on the tuna industry fostered by imperialist neoliberalism.

Another way American Sāmoans and immigrant workers could come together would be to acknowledge and address the similar oppressions they both face from either U.S. or corporate domination. American Sāmoans are subject to the will of the U.S. federal government in a similar way that immigrant cannery workers are subject to the will of the fish-processing industry. The legal status of both groups is dependent on the continued cooperation of U.S. officials and big business, respectively. The withdrawal of support for either the cultural preservation of American Sāmoans, or the employment of foreign laborers, would place each group's way of life into a tailspin. American Sāmoans would be extremely upset if their traditions were ruled illegal by the U.S. administration and consequently banned. In the same way, immigrant workers were devastated to learn that they were losing their jobs and means of living. Each group engages in significant struggles with macro-structural institutions, and the lives of both are rendered precarious as a result of these institutions' powers. Each group could benefit from acknowledging the challenges facing the other and thinking of ways to join together to rally for more equitable relationships with the United States and big business in the islands.

Some *Samoa News* readers have already expressed compassion and sympathy for cannery workers. The response of one reader, "SATANI 4M SCO DA SCO," to anti-immigrant sentiment was: "So what if more foreigners are in AS? We need to start pointing out the similarities b/n the foreigners and the indigenous ppl instead of separating them. These foreigners need to be able to vote and have their voices heard as well because all you have in AS is a bunch of corrupt ppl running the whole show while the rest of the people just settle with meager, unfulfilling lifestyles. They struggle in a situation they almost have no way to escape. Now can you tell me if that is fair."[53] An emphasis on similar forms of oppression has the potential to unite indigenous and immigrant groups to fight for more beneficial economic and social practices for all people in the region.

A focus on human rights could also help unite the multiple exploited groups in American Sāmoa. Rosa Linda Fregoso's definition of human rights is useful for the American Sāmoan context. She states that "the more progressive formulation is linked to a global justice project that considers human (civil) rights to be indivisible and inseparable from economic rights to food, health care, and shelter. It is a perspective that calls for the transformation of social structures, and that defines the 'global problem' facing human beings as both 'suffering and systematic disenfranchisement from collaborative self governance.'"[54] Hannah Arendt provided another useful definition of human rights when she said, that "the right to have rights, or the right of every human being to belong to humanity, should be guaranteed by humanity itself."[55] Overall, human rights can be defined as "'substantive and indivisible': the right to work and the right to a life free from violence and torture."[56] Whether indigenous or immigrant, people of all races, classes, ages, genders and sexual orientations should have access to the same basic rights for living. This focus is not so much political as it is humanist. As one *Samoa News* reader named "Sole" stated, "we are all of the Human race. Let's pull each other up, it's our God given humanity."[57] Sole provides a glimpse into how a humanist approach could unite American Sāmoans and immigrant workers in the region.

Fregoso also suggests strategic ways to merge local and global human rights concerns. She explains how in the Mexican border town Ciudad Juárez, Las Muertas de Juárez campaign incorporated human rights discourse into symbolic actions, "integrating emotive with cognitive understandings," as well as "choreographed cultural politics of visibility."[58] The campaign combined Catholic religious imagery and ideas with Mexican fears of shame and activated "a discourse of global human rights in a locality by giving voice to rights violations."[59] In a similar way, the deep religiosity of Sāmoans could be used to think more broadly about human rights for all people in American Sāmoa. According to the CIA *World Factbook*, 100 percent of the American Sāmoan population claims affiliation with some form of Christianity.[60] Pointing out the contradictions between anti-immigrant sentiment and biblical passages proclaiming God's concern for immigrants, temporary laborers, and the exploited could encourage some native people to seek more cooperation with foreigners in the islands.[61] Another powerful concept in American Sāmoa is that of *f'aa sāmoa*, or the Sāmoan way of life. This practice includes the prioritization of "the *'āiga* (kin group) . . . and principles of *tautua* (service), *fa'alavelave* (obligations), *alofa* (love, compassion), and *fa'aaloalo* (respect) in kinship relations."[62] *F'aa sāmoa* is a central tenet of Sāmoan culture and the lack of *f'aa sāmoa* could be a great source of shame. Combining Christian beliefs with the love, respect, and compassion of *f'aa sāmoa* could be a potential symbol for unifying immigrants and indigenous groups in American Sāmoa.

Some posts to the *Samoa News* already illustrate this potential. J. Kalepo Fanua stated, "I would like to respond to the writer who brought up the issues of immigration. Let's not ourselves practice racism. Let's not be exclusionary and be God-toting in the same breath. It's not becoming of the Samoan hospitality that we try and market to the world. It's also not Samoan, at least from where I'm sitting."[63] Another reader claimed that

> without our SAMOAN CULTURE we are practically nothing before the eyes of the good Lord. Of course, God, not the United States of America, created Samoan as one of the group of peoples in the universe. Needless to say, and, as you well know, Tutuila, Manu'a, Upolu and Savaii or Saua to Falealupo, have the same culture, language, skin color, thinking pattern or human characteristics, all of which are God's creation in His own image. Are you complaining about this? . . . It does not mean that you have to point one finger to Upolu, Savai'i, Koreans, Vietnamese and other human race. We ought to make the best out of the world we live in before our last breath . . . and we must always thanks the Lord for even allowing us to be here.[64]

From these examples, we can see how Sāmoan cultural traditions and religiosity could merge with larger human rights concerns to unite the struggles of American Sāmoans with immigrant workers in the region.

On the flip side, there were some highly charged negative responses to these humanistic suggestions. One anonymous reader reacted to Sole's comment by saying

> Sole . . . it's not a matter of ancient ancestry (you only need to go back to 17 Apr 1900/14 Jul 1904), compassion and charity, it's a matter of citizenship and laws and why they exist. "Send them home mode" is not about lack of compassion it's about survival and quality of life. Wake up and smell the coffee Sole, American Samoa has been more than charitable it's been taken advantage of and it's about to implode.[65]

Once again, this comment demonstrates the strong belief that resources are limited in the region and that the needs of American Sāmoans should take priority over all others.

Even those who acknowledged the important role of immigrants in the region still expressed anti-immigrant beliefs. Pio Tulouna agreed that foreigners "contributed to the island's economy. However, if alternate work opportunities are not available, and their permit does not allow them to remain, then they have to go."[66] American Sāmoans have valid concerns about scarce resources and violations of immigration laws. However, anti-foreigner sentiment does not resolve the greater institutional issues that caused such problems in the first place. It will be a difficult and lengthy struggle to persuade indigenous groups to consider a multigroup unification against larger economic and social structures. Yet such a struggle is essential if either group is to truly reckon with the forces of domination and control in the region.

By highlighting the negative impact of U.S. colonialism on the economic situation in the region, American Sāmoans do not have to give up their connections to the United States. Instead, they could tap into the dual patriotism discussed by Michael Elliott, wherein American Indians can be both anti-American and patriotic because of their historical colonial history with the United States. He explained how "American Indians are "outraged at the U.S. history of colonization while still supporting contemporary efforts to protect the United States."[67] In the same way, American Sāmoans can justly call out the United States for subjecting their region to underdevelopment while still maintaining ties with the region. Criticizing U.S. imperialism could also be seen as exercising their rights to freedom of speech and dissent, fundamental tenets of U.S. democracy.

While American Sāmoans have been subjected by the United States, they can also subject others. As an oppressed group with ties to the land, they possess powerful ideological tools for acknowledging the need to act justly toward non-Samoans in their region. The current economic environment will provide a long and tough road for both American Sāmoans and foreign cannery workers. But there is great potential for a strong and unified movement of all residents in American Sāmoa if they can work together against macro-structural issues to remove the imperial and colonial constraints that impact their daily lives.

Notes

1. See Duane Champagne, "Theory and Method in American Indian Studies," *American Indian Quarterly* 31.3 (Summer 2007): 353–72; Vicente Diaz and J. Kēhaulani Kauanui, eds., "Native Pacific Cultural Studies on the Edge," Special Issue, *Contemporary Pacific* 13.2 (Fall 2001): 315–42; Epeli Hau'ofa, "Our Sea of Islands," in *A New Oceania: Rediscovering Our Sea of Islands*, ed. E. Waddell, V. Naidu,

and E. Hau'ofa, 2–16 (Suva: Beake House, 1993); Noenoe Silva, *Aloha Betrayed* (Durham, N.C.: Duke University Press, 2004); Sylvia Escárcega Zamarrón, "*Trabajar haciendo*: Activist Research and Interculturalism," *Intercultural Education* 20.1 (February 2009):39–50.

2. Notice No. 5., Record Group 284 (RG 284), Records of the Government of American Samoa, Records of the Governor's Office, 1872–1961, National Archives and Records Administration, Pacific Branch, San Bruno, T1182, Roll 1.
3. Champagne, "Theory and Method in American Indian Studies," 366.
4. J. Kēhaulani Kauanui, "Colonialism in Equality: Hawaiian Sovereignty and the Question of U.S. Civil Rights," *South Atlantic Quarterly* 107.4 (Fall 2008): 635–50.
5. Per the 2000 Census, 36.1% out of a population of 57,291 people were foreign born. *2000 Census of Population and Housing, Social, Economic, and Housing Characteristics PHC-4-AS, American Samoa* (Washington, D.C.: Census Bureau, 2003), 50. There were 1,598 Tongans and 792 Filipinos in 2000. There were 50,545 Sāmoans that year, but no distinction was made between American Sāmoans and Western Sāmoans.
6. Deed of Cession, RG 284, T1182, Roll 1.
7. Commander Tilley to Mauga Moimoi, December 6, 1899, RG 284, T1182, Roll 1.
8. J. Robert Shaffer, *American Sāmoa: 100 Years Under the United States Flag* (Honolulu: Island Heritage, 2000), 117.
9. Diaz and Kauanui, "Native Pacific Cultural Studies on the Edge," 318–319.
10. Shaffer, *American Sāmoa*, 42.
11. Ibid.
12. *Final Report* (Utulei: Future Political Status Study Commission of American Samoa, 2007), 45. This report provides an overview of American Sāmoan perspectives about various political, economic, and social issues in the region. The commission conducted exhaustive public hearings in American Sāmoa, San Diego, Oceanside, Los Angeles, San Francisco, Tacoma, Seattle, Laie, Honolulu, and at the Kuhio-Kalihi Association of Senior Citizens.
13. *Final Report*, 48. Many of the report findings were based on the opinions provided by hearing participants. Little statistical evidence was provided to support these claims.
14. For more perspectives on Sāmoan migration, see Sa'iliemanu Lilomaiava-Doktor, "Beyond Migration: Samoan Population Movement (*Malaga*) and the Geography of Social Space (*Vā*)," *Contemporary Pacific* 21.1 (Spring 2009): 1–32; Unasa L. F. Va'a, "Searching for the Good Life: Samoan International Migration," http://unpan1.un.org/intradoc/groups/public/documents/EROPA/UNPAN019859.pdf (accessed August 28, 2009); Ilana Gershon, "Compelling Culture: The Rhetoric of Assimilation among Samoan Migrants in the United States," *Ethnic and Racial Studies* 30.5 (September 2007): 787–816; Barbara Burns McGrath, "Seattle Fa'a Samoa," *Contemporary Pacific* 14.2 (Fall 2002): 307–40.
15. United States Census Bureau, Census 2000, Summary File 1 (SF 1) 100-Percent Data, Table PCT 10: Native Hawaiian and other Pacific Islander alone or in combination with one or more races and with one or more Native Hawaiian and other Pacific Islander categories for selected groups.
16. *Final Report*, 42.
17. *Final Report*, 45.
18. Tina Mata'afa, "Executive Order Establishes Territorial Population Commission," *Samoa News*, May 19, 2009.
19. Fili Sagapolutele, "Taotasi Requests Info from AG on Immigration Status of Cannery Workers," *Samoa News*, May 28, 2009.
20. Ibid.
21. Anonymous response to Fili Sagapolutele, "COS Samoa Packing Announces Sept. 30 Shut Down with More Than 2,000 Jobs Affected," *Samoa News*, May 2, 2009 (posted May 2, 2009, at 6:39 p.m.).
22. Fili Sagapolutele, "Petition to President Obama on Min Wage Circulates," *Samoa News*, July 2, 2009.
23. Fili Sagapolutele, "Min Wage Petition Drive Only Doing Well in Eastern District," *Samoa News*, July 13, 2009.
24. Anonymous response to Fili Sagapolutele, "Taotasi Requests Info from AG" (posted May 29, 2009, at 5:00 p.m.).
25. *Final Report*, 62–63.
26. Currently, American Sāmoa government jobs account for close to 50 percent of the employment in the islands.

27. "$1,500,000 Cannery Is Slated for U.S. Samoa," *Honolulu Star Bulletin*, October 5, 1948.
28. Shurei Hirozawa, "Samoan Economy Improves Since Gov. Lowe Took Over," *Honolulu Star Bulletin*, December 16, 1955.
29. "$1,500,000 Cannery."
30. Ibid.
31. Multiple military governors asked for funding to establish social services, such as schools and hospitals, but funding was often denied.
32. Clarence Hall, "Samoa: America's Shame in the South Pacific," *Readers Digest*, July 1961, 111–16.
33. "Don't Industrialize Samoa, Native Son Pleads at Hearing," *Honolulu Star-Bulletin*, March 10, 1956.
34. "American Samoa's Congressman to Introduce Bill on U.S. Citizenship for Locals," *Solomon Star News*, March 19 2008.
35. Anonymous interview, May 10, 2008. In May 2008, I interviewed 20 individuals in American Sāmoa, including American Sāmoans of different ages, Western Sāmoan and Filipino cannery employees, government workers, and local community leaders.
36. Ibid.
37. *Final Report*, 63.
38. Ibid.
39. According to the 2000 Census, there were 329 Chinese and 200 Koreans in American Sāmoa. *2000 Census of Population and Housing*, 1.
40. *Final Report*, 45.
41. Anonymous response to Fili Sagapolutele, "Cannery Job Losses Will Have Domino Effect," *Samoa News*, May 4, 2009 (posted May 4, 2009, at 2:42 p.m.).
42. The Maverick response to Fili Sagapolutele, "Cannery Job Losses" (posted May 4, 2009, at 6:21 p.m.).
43. See "Wage Rates in American Samoa," Wage and Hour Division, Employment Standards Administration, U.S. Department of Labor: http://www.dol.gov/ESA/minwage/americanSamoa/ASminwage.htm (accessed August 30, 2009).
44. See Fili Sagapolutele, "Chamber Head Pleads with Congress to Delay Next Min Wage Hike," *Samoa News*, May 26, 2009. Fili Sagapolutele, "Cannery Job Losses."
45. See Maverick response to Fili Sagapolutele, "Monday Hike Will Put Min Wage at $4 Plus," *Samoa News*, May 23, 2009 (posted May 26, 2009, at 5:28 p.m.). COS received a strong economic incentive package to open up canning facilities in Georgia. While they will be paying their workers a higher hourly rate those in the continental United States, they will employ only about 200 workers as compared to the 2,147 workers in American Sāmoa. The cost to transport the supplies needed to can tuna, such as tin, cardboard, labels, and plastic wrap, as well as the cost to ship the finished product to U.S. markets, will be lower. Also, the fish will be cleaned in Vietnam by 1,000 employees who work for about 25 cents an hour.
46. The 2007 report was based on telephone interviews with government officials and local business leaders. Without visiting the islands, the GAO officials recommended the establishment of minimum wage increases to meet continental U.S. standards.
47. This bill is known as the American Samoa Protection of Industry, Resources, and Employment Act, or the ASPIRE Act. http://www.opencongress.org/bill/111-h3583/show (accessed January 27, 2010).
48. Fili Sagapolutele, "StarKist Samoa Shuts Down for Usual End of Year Downtime," *Samoa News*, December 23, 2009.
49. Concerned AmSamoa citizen response to Fili Sagapolutele, "Taotasi Requests Info from AG" (posted June 2, 2009, at 6:11 p.m.).
50. Anonymous response to Fili Sagapolutele, "COS Samoa Packing" (posted May 4, 2009, at 6:59 p.m.).
51. Anonymous response to Fili Sagapolutele, "COS Samoa Packing" (posted May 4, 2009, at 12:12 p.m.).
52. Todd R. Ramlow, "Bodies in the Borderlands: Gloria Anzaldua's and David Wojnarowicz's Mobility Machines," *MELUS* 31.3 (Fall 2006): 180–81.
53. SATANI 4M SCO DA SCO response to "The Average American Samoan Is Not Who You Think," *Samoa News*, May 13, 2009 (posted May 18, 2009, at 9:52 a.m.).

54. Rosa Linda Fregoso, "'We Want Them Alive!': The Politics and Culture of Human Rights," *Social Identities* 12.2 (March 2006), 130.
55. Hannah Arendt, *The Origins of Totalitarianism* (San Diego: Harcourt, 1968), 294.
56. Fregoso, "We Want Them Alive!" 131.
57. Sole response to Fili Sagapolutele, "COS Samoa Packing" (posted May 3, 2009, at 12:37 p.m.).
58. Fregoso, "We Want Them Alive!" 120.
59. Ibid., 121.
60. CIA, *The World Factbook*, https://www.cia.gov/library/publications/the-world-factbook/geos/aq.html (accessed August 29, 2009).
61. For example, Leviticus 19:33–34 states, "When an alien lives with you in your land, do not mistreat him. The alien living with you must be treated as one of your native-born. Love him as yourself, for you were aliens in Egypt." *Holy Bible*, NIV thinline reference Bible (Grand Rapids: Zondervan, 2002), 108.
62. Lilomaiava-Doktor, "Beyond Migration," 7.
63. J. Kalepo Fanua response to Fili Sagapolutele, "COS Samoa Packing" (posted May 3, 2009, at 10:37 p.m.).
64. Anonymous response to Fili Sagapolutele, "Taotasi Requests Info from AG" (posted June 3, 2009, at 5:24 a.m.).
65. Anonymous response to Fili Sagapolutele, "COS Samoa Packing" (posted May 4, 2009, at 12:12 a.m.).
66. Pio Tulouna response to Fili Sagapolutele, "Taotasi Requests Info from AG" (posted May 29, 2009, at 7:34 a.m.).
67. Michael A. Elliot, "Indian Patriots on Last Stand Hill," *American Quarterly* 58.4 (December 2006): 1010–11.

Experimental Encounters: Filipino and Hawaiian Bodies in the U.S. Imperial Invention of Odontoclasia, 1928–1946

Jean J. Kim

Inside a pamphlet richly illustrating the activities of the Ewa Health Center, a pilot industrial health project located on a sprawling eleven-thousand-acre Hawaiian sugar plantation on the island of O'ahu, appears a collection of tables and photographs spread across a page under the bold label "ODONTOCLASIA." A graph in the upper left corner of the page reports the incidence of this disease and enumerates dental cavities in groups of plantation infants from the ages of six months to six years. Another graph charts the number of cavities in the teeth of 1,610 kindergarten children by race. Together, these tables indicate that the rate of tooth decay increases throughout children's development from infancy to school age, and also that a group categorized as "Orientals" suffered the highest incidence of dental disease. The remaining seven inserts on the page display gross specimens, or diagnostically revealing postmortem dissections, clinical photographs of children's mouths, an x-ray, several cross sections of eroded tooth enamel, and six photos of jagged, protruding teeth from the dissected jaws of puppies who were placed on an experimental diet.[1]

These photos juxtapose a number of contrasting conditions—animal and human, diseased and healthy, dead and alive. Captions beneath the human and animal specimens highlight the distinctions and hint at the research protocols framing the study and visual representation of odontoclasia, a disease that one researcher described as a "type of dental decay which is ravaging the teeth of the babies and young children of Hawaii."[2] Two photographs among the seven clusters of morbid clinical images feature children whose disease had been successfully arrested. In a didactic manner, using all capital letters, the pamphlet's author claims that odontoclasia could be cured by the substitution of "COW'S MILK, TARO, SWEET POTATO, AND MEAT-VEGETABLE PUREE" for an unidentified, dangerous food item that had been implicated in this disease. The dissected jaws and rotten teeth of two Hawaiian babies, one who died at eight months and another who died at eighteen months, illustrate the deadly power of this dangerous food. Captions also direct readers' attention to the soft and chalky diseased enamel covering the teeth embedded in these young jaws. The lower incisor of a seven-week-old Filipino baby who could not be saved by a vitamin supplement after she had been breast-fed suggests the potentially fatal connection between maternal and infant nutrition. The incisor of an unborn baby whose mother died of nephritis indicates a relationship between the mother's kidney disease and fetal bone and tooth degeneration.

Out of the sixteen photos depicting human subjects, only three feature living children. Only four images disclose the racial background of their subjects, and only two racial designations—Hawaiian and Filipino—appear with any of these images. Other data on the Ewa experiments and the composition of the plantation workforce support the inference that the majority of children enrolled in plantation health studies were ethnically Japanese. This focus on the two smaller groups of participants in these studies—Hawaiians and Filipinos—suggests their status as special subjects of medical interest within the racial representation of odontoclasia. It also signals the way that Hawaiians and Filipinos, as indigenous subjects of U.S. imperialism, figure into territorial medicine.

Starting in 1928, animal modeling, microscopic and x-ray imaging, and the local presence of multiple immigrant, ethnic, indigenous, and colonial migrant groups animated the visual and empirical linkage between the teeth of puppies and the teeth of babies as part of the basis for modernizing medicine in the U.S. territory of Hawai'i.[3] The colonial medical archive further transformed immigrant and indigenous bodies into objects of comparison, establishing sites of alternative contact that are endemic to the U.S. Pacific empire and its imperial epistemologies. In 1930, comparative surveys of indigenous diets informed doctors' recommendation of *poi*, a starchy Hawaiian staple, as a dietary antidote to odontoclasia. At face value, doctors' and nutritionists' recommendation of *poi* consumption appears to be a novel endorsement of indigenous foodways at a time predating contemporary efforts by native American and indigenous scholars around the world to study and reinstate traditional food cultures to support indigenous health. A critical examination, however, reveals odontoclasia and doctors' recommendation of *poi* consumption to be consistent with existing imperial power relations in Hawai'i, which was a U.S. colony from 1898 to 1959.

The diagnosis of odontoclasia, represented by intimate images of infants' and children's teeth rotted down to black stumps, was made possible by the science of nutrition in national and imperial contexts. The biomedical emphasis on the cultural rather than structural etiology of odontoclasia, along with teleological assertions that Hawaiian health was implicitly threatened by "modernity," were ultimately dangerous to Hawaiian and Filipino health. They tended to marginalize indigenous health problems as matters of insufficient assimilation, and obscured the ways both the culture and the economy of U.S. imperialism were implicated in high rates of morbidity and mortality. Critical analysis of the colonial invention of odontoclasia makes visible the power of imperial politics, new scientific fields, and comparisons between indigenous and racialized migrant bodies in the constitution of colonial medical pathology. They also suggest alternative genealogical sites of contact between indigenous struggles for health care in Hawai'i, the Pacific, North America, Africa, and Asia.

Nutrition, Nation, and the Imperial Governmentality of Food

Advances in biology, chemistry, and physiology after 1800 made possible the analysis of exact components of food and their relationship to human growth and development. These sciences produced new normative physiological principles that homogenized bodies across disparate contexts while simultaneously producing new ways of conceptualizing cultural difference and supporting imperial inequalities. Starting in 1850, interdisciplinary researchers in France, Germany, and the Netherlands, and later in England, Japan, and the United States, used surveys and the laboratory to evaluate food composition, its metabolic consequences, and its relationship to normative health outcomes. Politically, nutrition became important as the modern welfare state accorded prominence to the scientific, social, nutritional, and policy dimensions of food. In the United States, nutrition also figured in industry, as employers and city and federal governments sought to determine the lowest possible wages that could sustain a scientifically healthy standard of living. Researchers studied diets in Chinese railroad camps, on Georgia plantations, in urban slums, on Indian reservations, and in boarding schools between 1885 and 1910.[4] Nutritionists, doctors, and policymakers also codified national standards of food safety, consumption, and nutritional content as guidelines to popular eating during the twentieth century. Internationally, organizations such as the League of Nations, the World Health Organization, and the United Nations' Food and Agriculture Organization have further directed foreign policy attention to the political and health implications of food.[5]

Nick Cullather argues that during the first half of the twentieth century, the calorie, as a measure of the amount of heat and human energy that could be produced by quantities of food, "allowed Americans to see food as an instrument of power, and to envisage a 'world food problem' amenable to political and scientific intervention." Along with quantitative measures of standards of living, wealth, education, and population, the calorie made possible the comparative evaluation of the status of states and empires, and the reduction of group and social life into universal measures. Architects of foreign policy believed that numbers provided "explanatory rigor," which native informants, who were previously important to international relations, could not approximate. The calorie, according to Cullather, also shaped U.S. military ration policies and relief efforts in Europe after World War I, and calorie counts guided international humanitarian relief after World War II.[6]

As a universalizing abstraction, Cullather argues, the calorie facilitated a movement away from emphasis on the cultural and qualitative character of food as its governmental function gained prominence.[7] What he neglects to explain, however, is that at the same time the calorie made possible rough calculations of relative hunger and satiety around the world, the discovery of vitamins and new epidemiological patterns of dietary deficiency disease reasserted cultural differences in patterns of food consumption domestically and across colonial dependencies and suggested the centrality of culture to understanding nationally distinct foodways. Even nutritional scientists who implicitly asserted the political neutrality of normative standards for evaluating food could not obviate the ways they fundamentally depended upon and mobilized cultural ideas and assumptions that changed over time.[8] Further, the science of nutrition produced increasingly narrow and standardized national and international dietary recommendations that had cultural consequences.

Global migration and the spread of imperial economies throughout the world by 1900 intensified cultural conflicts that were embedded within the science and politics of eating. Colonial settlement and labor migration brought populations and diverse foodways side by side in colonies and in metropolitan centers. On the U.S. continent, professional opinions of the quality of ethnic immigrants' diets shifted from criticism, as an offshoot of prevalent patterns of xenophobia, to acceptance by the 1920s, emulation and admiration during the interwar years and World War II, and passive marginalization within national postwar dietary guidelines.[9] Judy Perkin and Stephanie F. McCann note that by 1956, the United States Department of Agriculture began recommending four food groups as "the major cornerstone of government advice with regard to the consumption of a nutritionally adequate diet." They argue that the agricultural industry has played a major role in homogenizing official nutritional advice in the United States since then.[10]

Studies of colonial nutrition were contemporaneous with the first industrial dietary surveys in the United States, and they transformed popular thinking about the governmentality, or behavioral and rational rules, of food. Throughout Asia, beriberi, a disease that can affect the nervous system, cognition, memory, speech, ambulation, and major organs, reached epidemic proportions by the middle of the nineteenth century. Because of its affect on colonial armies and indigenous laboring populations, it gained the attention of specialists in tropical medicine, who began scientifically seeking its modes of transmission, cause, means of treatment, and modes of prevention. Through studies in the Japanese navy, Philippine and Indonesian prisons, Malay labor camps and army barracks, and plantations, scientists and doctors found this disease to be caused by a dietary deficiency in thiamine, or vitamin B1.[11]

This research was critical in illustrating the political significance of the biochemistry of food and metabolism to health after decades during which colonial sanitarians attended to foods primarily as potentially infectious articles carrying organisms that might cause disease. The study of beriberi was also important to the field of nutrition; one outcome was scientists' recognition of a category of food substances known as "vitamins." This discovery moved smoothly from specific Asian colonial contexts and bodies to metropolitan *habitus*, where it affected popular understandings of the relationships between food, human growth, and health. According to Victor Heiser, a former officer with the U.S. Public Health and Marine Hospital Service and director of the Rockefeller Foundation's International Health Board, the scientific principles of nutrition animated hopes that other diseases that, like beriberi, had "caused extraordinary havoc among the rice-eating peoples of the Far East," were subject to prevention and elimination.[12]

By the 1920s, colonial medical officials continued to study indigenous diets and the endemic health problems they were associated with in addition to epidemics, which were the centerpieces of late nineteenth-century colonial medicine. Robert McCarrison of the Indian Medical Service concluded from his nutritional research in jails, military barracks, and famine relief camps that poor diets, chronic morbidity, and susceptibility to infection were related, and that further research was necessary.[13] Recent studies of metropolitan and colonial diets together influenced the League of Nations' sponsorship of research in the 1920s and 1930s that resulted in the first international table of dietary standards.[14] Warwick Anderson points out that in the late 1920s, U.S. researchers drew together military hygiene and colonial public health in the

Philippines as they studied what natives ate in an attempt to figure out how to better adapt white soldiers to the tropics.[15] They also began to consider the possibility that physical differences between races were caused by nutritional differences that could be corrected through dietary interventions.[16]

Michael Worboys argues that the imperial discovery of colonial undernutrition and malnutrition in the 1920s quickly reproduced colonial logics by explaining indigenous hunger and malnutrition as caused by cultural deficits rather than by structural consequences endemic to the politics and economics of imperialism itself.[17] In 1926, John Boyd Orr of the British Rowett Institute of Nutrition and Health and John Gilks of the Medical Department in Kenya conducted a widely influential survey comparing the diets and physiques of the Masai tribe, which subsisted primarily on meat, and the Kikuyus, who lived on a vegetarian diet. Orr and Gilks initially extended principles governing the relationship between diet and disease from Europe to the colonies to suggest that the problem of malnutrition was precipitated by adverse structural changes that included monoculture, an export economy, disruption to indigenous food production, and colonial failures.[18]

Within a few years, however, European policymakers reinterpreted colonial undernutrition as a widespread problem that was caused by indigenous ignorance and general backwardness rather than structural imperial transformations.[19] Worboys argues that Orr and Gilks were able to come to their conclusion in part because of their "geographical and professional" isolation from European centers of laboratory science.[20] Practically, structural explanations for colonial malnutrition were widely unpopular among colonial administrators because they simply begged for interventions that were too expensive and unwieldy to implement, especially during the Depression.[21] The cultural explanation of colonial malnutrition and undernutrition, on the other hand, implicitly supported the expansion of metropolitan medical authority and power over indigenous populations.[22] In this way, cultural explanations of colonial dietary disease have supported imperial practices and institutions.

The U.S. Colonial and Cultural Invention of Odontoclasia

The medical research on odontoclasia in Hawai'i maintained continuities with earlier colonial studies on the nutritional consequences of the dietary consumption of mechanically polished white rice and the regional systems of food distribution that had been implicated in the epidemiology of beriberi. Contemporary colonial studies on diet and tooth decay included research based in British Kenya and Tristan da Cunha, and the U.S. Panama Canal Zone.[23]

Studies of odontoclasia also drew together two predominant patterns of food research, one focusing on epidemiological patterns of nutrition, and the other on smaller subgroups viewed as facing particular dietary health risks. In 1928, odontoclasia became increasingly observable through research on varying immigrant health and ethnic foodways, and it was based on the comparative study of three forms of U.S. imperial indigeneity that converged in Hawai'i through intercolonial migration, contact, and cultural exchange.

In 1928, Nils Larsen, an American trained pathologist of Swedish descent, initiated several research projects at Ewa Plantation Company, a prosperous enterprise located on the island of O'ahu and the home to more than four thousand people.[24] The medical work that framed the invention of odontoclasia was organized through the Queen's Hospital, the territory of Hawai'i's largest medical center. Larsen gained an appointment as director of the Queen's Hospital in 1922 through his wife's family connections.[25] In this position, Larsen immediately began working to transform Queen's into a modern medical institution with an active research department. Between 1923 and 1928, this research department studied cancer, the composition and value of green coconut meat as a baby food, the sun's ultraviolet rays, tooth decay, hay fever, Kahn and Wasserman tests for syphilis, acidophilus, and fish poisoning.[26] Of the many projects Larsen worked on in the department, the most comprehensive was on tooth decay and nutrition among children living on Hawai'i's sugar plantations. In 1930, Larsen also became the sugar industry's medical advisor after promising to apply modern health-care techniques to raise plantation standards of living and to enhance workers' productivity in a cost-efficient manner.[27] After two years of research on tooth decay starting in 1928, what was known as the Ewa Health Project expanded to encompass greater attention to infant hygiene and the broader impact of nutrition on community welfare. A model community health institute known as the Ewa Health Center became the interface for administering health interventions, supervision, and experimental feedings from the Ewa Health Project starting in 1930.[28]

Larsen was prominent in introducing the disease of odontoclasia to local, national, and international medical communities, while Martha R. Jones, who earned a PhD in physiological chemistry from Yale in 1920, directed the Ewa Plantation Health Project and its odontoclasia studies from 1929 to 1936. She came to Hawai'i with a lifelong interest in nutrition and health based on her own childhood dietary indulgences, tooth decay, and susceptibility to infections.[29] In 1926, Jones and dental researcher F. V. Simonton published a paper on changes in the teeth of dogs that were experimentally placed on a diet that included sulfuric acid.[30] The following year, Simonton published a paper continuing his research on gum disease while Jones took a leading role in the plantation studies of the relationship between diet and tooth decay as a research associate at Queen's Hospital. In contrast to contemporary studies of the physical action of food and acid-producing bacteria on tooth surfaces as a cause of decay, Jones and Larsen's dietary hypothesis, which they pursued with Honolulu dentist George Pritchard, conceptualized "active tooth decay [as] an indicator of metabolic fault," caused by certain foods after they were broken down in the body through digestion.[31]

Jones and Larsen believed odontoclasia was a particularly important disease to understand because it was a sensitive index of the general nutritional status of children living on plantations. Jones claimed that it was "associated with high infant mortality, diseased tonsils, stunted growth, susceptibility to disease, and abnormal development of the jaws, nasal, and other facial bones which often lead to a succession of ills which persist throughout life."[32] In 1939, Larsen, Pritchard, and director of the Ewa Health Clinic Charles Wilbar argued that "dietary intake," but more particularly the "oriental diet" high in white rice, was the main factor in setting groups with good and poor teeth apart.[33] They claimed that two groups that were relatively free from dental decay included "Hawaiian children on the primitive diet" and "white children who come from higher economic groups in Honolulu."[34] Researchers reported that children on experimental diets experienced half the rate of tooth decay, and that the causes of tooth decay were complex, but cure was possible by "a return to the type of diet employed by the ancient Hawaiians." They further claimed that this diet could broadly solve many of the economic, health, and social problems of the community.[35] This intertwining of an indigenous dietary panacea and an immigrant dietary menace provided a unified instance for researchers to declare authority over both native Hawaiian and Asian migrant bodies.

In the early years of transforming odontoclasia into a human disorder, Martha Jones and George Pritchard evaluated dietary survey data and comparisons of three populations in Hawai'i who were indigenous to three U.S. colonies—the Philippines, Hawai'i, and Samoa—to identify alternative foods that could remedy the problems caused by heavy consumption of white rice. They first illustrated the extensiveness of odontoclasia among children living in Hawai'i, classifying their observations by race, age, and urban or rural residence. They found that urban Japanese children and a smaller sample of rural Japanese children known to eat large quantities of white rice exhibited the highest rates of tooth decay, with over 97 percent showing dental disease. Rural Samoans, on the other hand, had the best teeth, with 80 percent free of decay. Urban Caucasians and urban Hawaiians ranked second and third, respectively, with 55.6 percent and 50 percent free of decay. Rural Filipino tooth decay was about 10 percent higher than that of urban Hawaiians. Rural Hawaiian children exhibited higher rates of dental decay than both Filipinos and urban Hawaiians, with only 38 percent having teeth free of decay.

When the tests were controlled by country of birth, Jones and Pritchard found a startling phenomenon. Foreign-born rural Samoan and Filipino children had far healthier teeth than all groups of children born in Hawai'i. The Samoa-born children's teeth were 95.4 percent free from decay, and Philippine-born children's teeth were 88.2 percent free from decay.[36] As part of nearly three decades of anti-tuberculosis work and a decade of Americanization, public health professionals promoted uniquely American dietary customs, especially the consumption of milk beyond infancy and early childhood, within poor and immigrant communities. The nearly perfect teeth of children born in two relatively less modern U.S. colonies, and their high rates of dental decay once they began to live under the putatively more healthful context of Hawai'i challenged nascent imperial medical expectations. However, rather than recognize this pattern of indigenous dental disease as a sign of potential failures within U.S.-dominated health institutions or as a result of structural inequalities leading to poverty and limited food options within Hawai'i's colonial monoculture economy, Jones, Larsen, and Pritchard chose to frame dental disease within an existing medical paradigm for recognizing and correcting faulty immigrant hygiene and cultural practices.

As a way to solve odontoclasia, Jones, Larsen, and Pritchard proposed replacing white rice, the primary carbohydrate in the diets of rural Asians and Hawaiians with *poi* or steamed taro, the starchy staple also found in Samoan diets that could be responsible for their nearly perfect teeth. Jones and Pritchard explained that rural Hawaiians suffered high rates of dental decay despite their familiarity with *poi* because they had begun eating white rice in its place. This comparison of indigenous and immigrant diets molded the nutritional experiments at Ewa Plantation around efforts to determine the harmful effects of a white rice diet, and to discover feasible, cost-effective, and more nutritious dietary substitutes for white rice. Researchers at the Ewa Health Center also continued to promote cow's milk as an archetypically American dietary tool for protecting children's health, as well as sweet potatoes, which they observed in the relatively healthful diets of Okinawan plantation laborers.

Experimental research on diet and tooth decay at Ewa Plantation would not have been as elegant in design if it were not for the patterns of colonial labor migration and racial diversity intersecting through Hawai'i's sugar industry. These experiments capitalized on the racial makeup of plantations, ethnic dietary variations, climatic factors, and easy access to a relatively stable population. The isolation of rural plantations also allowed researchers to administer controlled dietary supplements to identify nutrients relevant to the development of odontoclasia and to successfully rule out the competing theories about tooth decay in the dental literature. They found that vitamin D, B, and C supplements failed to prevent tooth decay.[37] Vitamin A seemed to have some beneficial but unclear effect, so doctors recommended it to pregnant women to promote healthy fetal bone development.[38] Heredity was ruled out as a factor in tooth decay because dental health was mutable across generations. Hawaiians, with a group history of excellent tooth and bone development according to European and American colonial accounts, were susceptible to rampant tooth decay once they adopted the "Oriental diet," and Filipino children in Hawai'i had high rates of tooth decay while co-ethnics in the Philippines did not.[39] Climate, or the "tropical factor," could not explain tooth decay, because residents of Hawai'i exhibited a range of excellent to poor teeth. Roughage could not explain tooth decay, since Hawaiian *poi* and cooked white rice had a similar texture, but were associated with low and high rates of tooth decay, respectively. Sugar consumption also could not explain tooth decay, because some of the children in Hawaiian plantation studies consumed large quantities of sugar, but had good teeth, while others with low sugar consumption exhibited severe decay.[40] Researchers referred to diets with higher amounts of taro, fruits, and vegetables as "good," and those with higher amounts of rice or bread as "bad." *Haole*, or local northern European and American, diets never systematically became the basis for scientific study, because foods such as white crackers, macaroni, and oats cost too much for most laborers to obtain, and because *haoles*, regardless of what they ate, had better nutrition and better dental health than Japanese, Filipino, and Hawaiian children.

After one year, the Ewa Health Center's programs found wide acceptance among the majority of Japanese and Japanese American parents, who quickly enrolled their infants and children in feeding programs that they subsidized with fees. In addition to feeding programs, the health center also ran a dental clinic in the local school to gain access to children's dental status, and its workers identified underweight children through the third grade for enrollment in classes that encouraged them to gain weight by eating special foods and observing regular rest periods.[41] Additional Ewa health initiatives provided education on the relationship between nutrition and health through school curricula and adult classes.[42]

The feeding programs were also associated with extensive physical measurement, observation of mothers and infants, and instruction. Researchers even conditioned plantation babies as ideal experimental subjects and willing participants in scientific experiments by substituting newborn infants' mother's milk once each day with a beta lactose formula in plantation hospitals. This bottle-feeding carried no therapeutic rationale, and its only objective was to train infant palates at the youngest age possible to accept the health center's formula, and to later prefer foods the center prepared, recommended, and distributed.[43] The center's training of mothers to act as ideal laboratory subjects was also evident in rewards available to parents who followed professional recommendations and were able to substantiate this by their children's achievement in their first year of life of the average length and weight of white or *haole* children living in Honolulu.[44]

Along with other advice, Ewa Health Center staff directed mothers to feed their children *poi*, explaining that it was highly assimilable, even by sick babies, and that it contained substances that were necessary for children's proper growth. Mothers were also shown graphs, X-rays, differently sized rats fed on experimental diets, and how urine samples could reveal whether mothers had fed their children unhealthy, dangerously acidic rice rather than healthy, alkaline *poi*. The center's focus on the dangers of white rice consumption, in addition to highlighting Japanese immigrants' dietary deficiency, also supported the sugar industry's competitiveness in a tight food market. As a primary cause of tooth decay, white rice shifted attention away from the role of sugar in causing cavities, and the health center also helped promote wider use of sugar cane and sugar cane by-products as nutrition supplements through an infant formula mixed with cane syrup, and the addition of an eight-inch-long piece of sugar cane to schoolchildren's lunches to supplement the minerals in their diet.[45] The center's recommendation of alternative foods as a remedy for odontoclasia also demanded relatively little financial outlay from plantations because it pushed most of the costs of health reform back onto workers and their families.

In 1936, Martha Jones abruptly left the Ewa Health Project over conflicts with Larsen. Larsen, meanwhile, continued to publish studies on odontoclasia and to expand nutritional work on plantations by serving as the chair of a plantation-wide Central Nutrition Committee in 1939. This body facilitated changes plantations could adopt to help consumers purchase and also grow foods consistent with the principles of balanced scientific eating. Until his death in 1964, Larsen was closely associated professionally with plantations. Additional nutritional interventions the Ewa Health Center eventually supported included recommendation of fruits and vegetables for all children at school meals, truck gardening, cooking classes for school girls, and vitamin-enriched soy sauce for single men and adults less likely to change their dietary habits.[46]

Comparative Indigeneities and Cultural Appropriations: The Poi Thesis and the Marginalization of Hawaiian and Filipino Health

The etiology and therapeutic interventions researchers identified to cure odontoclasia ultimately had dangerous consequences. They animated colonial myths and outlined a set of culpabilities in the development of disease that elided the impact of imperial U.S. land and economic politics on Hawaiian and Filipino health. Nils Larsen, who gave odontoclasia its widest publicity, was a key figure in bridging the realm of medicine and the culture of U.S. imperialism. Despite his belief that his perceptions of cultural difference were neutral—neither critical nor affirming—Larsen's anthropological and historical commentary on Hawaiian civilization decontextualized Hawai'i's past and established a normative medical teleology that placed Hawaiians in a special category that was not temporally coeval with other groups. By classifying them as "ancient" and healthy only within a context that no longer existed, he placed them on an inevitably downward spiral toward extinction that began with Western contact in 1778. This and other features of the nosology of odontoclasia and the thesis that *poi* could restore Hawaiian health and cure this disease served to further marginalize Hawaiians and Filipinos.

Throughout his career, Larsen was interested in travel, world cultures, art, and medicine. He immigrated to the United States from Sweden in 1890 with his family at the age of three and later studied agriculture and medicine, working as an intern in New York City and serving as a medical officer in the army before coming to Hawai'i, where he remained for the rest of his life. Hawai'i had been a U.S. territory for more than two decades when Larsen arrived in 1922, and he considered this to be an opportune time for great cultural and social transformations, of which his modernization of the Queen's Hospital to meet American Medical Association standards by 1924 was a part.[47] As a physician, he was interested broadly in territorial public health, which included tuberculosis and infant mortality prevention, milk safety, improved health care on plantations, birth control, hospital deliveries, and sex education. As a pathologist, he was fascinated by medical anomalies and eager to find novel diseases within Hawai'i's uniquely diverse population. He also conceived of medicine in broad terms and supported alternative cures such as electroshock therapy and the therapeutic use of estrogen to lessen the symptoms of menopause in women before this application was officially approved.[48] He also enjoyed photography, playwriting, and etching. Like other doctors coming to Hawai'i, Larsen considered himself poised on a relatively uncharted U.S.

epidemiological frontier that seemed to invite innovative study and novel experimentation.

Based in part on his agricultural training prior to entering medical school, Larsen was also immediately curious about Hawaiian medicinal herbs, from which his interests expanded to encompass Hawaiian medical history, archaeology, bones, corpses, and artifacts as clues to the character of Hawaiian civilization. His avid quest for greater knowledge of Hawai'i and his relationship to Hawaiians were marked by contradictory desires and tendencies. Unlike a previous century of physicians who deeply criticized Hawaiian hygiene, Larsen portrayed Hawaiian medical knowledge as extensive and empirically sound.[49] He even pointed out that it was superior to its Western counterpart during most of the nineteenth century. In 1933, he accompanied John Warriner, a patient and fellow Hawaiian artifact investigator on a trip to explore a cave at Kaunakakai, Molokai'i. As a souvenir of their discovery of an ancient burial site, Larsen collected a string of beads from around the neck of an elderly Hawaiian woman whose corpse had been laid to rest there. When Hawaiian crew members of the ship ferrying him home suggested that rough weather and water were caused by his taking of the amulet, he obliged their recommendations by tossing the artifact into the ocean.[50] In another instance, he abided Hawaiian critics and enlisted prominent Hawaiian community leaders to conduct a ceremony to restore damaged *mana* that was disturbed by his use of a word offensive to Hawaiians in a play that cataloged Hawai'i's ethnic medical pluralism. In 1951, he continued to promote his own authority as a translator, curator, and cultural broker by explaining ancient Hawaiian medical history to cosmopolitan doctors visiting Hawai'i to attend a Pan-Pacific Surgical Convention. He also later committed himself to the preservation of Hawaiian medical *heiaus*, or traditional healing sites.[51]

Ultimately, his interest in "ancient" knowledge was part of his attempt to more fully understand evolutionary categories of human development and the precursors to his own modern life and professional thought. Just as he was interested in extrasensory perception, or ESP, because he considered it a form of arcane communication that could highlight the evolution of contemporary speech, he was also interested in Hawaiian medical history because he believed that it could be periodized into stages and organized into a typology, and ultimately, that it would model for contemporary observers the stages through which all medicine moved to reach the status of Western scientific modernity.[52] Larsen also used Hawaiian and immigrant bodies and histories of illness to underscore Western medicine's advances and value. His research motives and lack of understanding of the impact of imperial political and economic factors in Hawaiian susceptibility to illness contributed to his gross simplification of the causes of Hawaiian population decline.

Today archaeologists, biologists, and physicians agree that the Hawaiian population was affected by relatively few and largely benign pathogens prior to European and Asian contact. As a consequence, the Hawaiian population had little genetic resistance to and protection from the pathogens for which foreigners carried immunity, which contributed to much higher rates of mortality among Hawaiians from diseases that travelers, merchants, and laborers introduced. Political, economic, and demographic transformations in Hawai'i also contributed to the epidemiological aftermath of foreign contact.[53] These factors can be divided between direct causes of death and causes of declining birth rates.[54] Among the new infections to reach Hawai'i, those affecting the reproductive system, such as syphilis and gonorrhea, and infections affecting infants, had some of the greatest impact.

Other factors included internal migration from healthful communities and households to port towns, where new dangers included inadequate housing, poverty, insufficient sanitation, crowding, contaminated food and water, and risks of contracting sexually transmitted infections. Other contributing sociological factors to Hawaiian mortality included the loss of the traditional family units that had previously emphasized the importance of child care, and the abolition of traditional *kapus*, or behavioral proscriptions, that had ensured higher levels of hygiene and sanitation.[55] Diversion from traditional food cultivation practices by urban labor also caused food shortages and contributed to malnutrition and susceptibility to severe cases of infectious disease. Psychological stressors further compounded physiological strains and ailments.[56] With continuous continental in-migration throughout the nineteenth century, Hawaiian out-migration, and stronger ties to foreign markets and economies, Hawaiians continued to face high rates of mortality from infectious disease and endemic health risks into the twentieth century. Hawai'i's precontact population estimates range from 100,000 at the low end to between 800,000 and 1 million at the highest.[57] By 1896, the Hawai'i census revealed 31,019 Hawaiians and 8,485 part-Hawaiians.[58]

As twentieth-century observers frequently described the declining health of Hawaiians, for two decades after annexation, U.S. colonial public health activities were focused more on general sanitary measures, proper registration of vital statistics, and epidemic surveillance. By the 1920s, however, the Board of Health was becoming more aware of infant mortality. From 1922 to 1924, Larsen was involved in a public campaign supported by the Queen's Hospital,

Tripler Army Medical Center, officials from the Board of Health, and Lorrin Thurston, editor of the *Honolulu Advertiser*, to raise standards for milk safety in Honolulu as a means of protecting infant health.[59] In 1925, the Board of Health established a Bureau of Infant and Maternal Hygiene using funds allocated under the Shepard-Towner Act to direct public health efforts to reduce infant and maternal mortality rates. By the late 1920s, Larsen worked with the Palama Settlement, Hawai'i's largest settlement house, where women from Hawai'i's elite white families brought their training from Chicago's Hull House and London's Toynbee Hall to bear on territorial social welfare.[60]

In 1929, shortly after the inauguration of the Ewa Health Project, rural areas showed much higher rates of infant mortality than did urban Honolulu and Hilo. Odontoclasia, a new disorder emerging at this time, correlated with high rates of infant mortality and threw into relief the poor epidemiological status of Hawaiians and Filipinos. Larsen comparatively accounted for similarities and departures in these two groups' health patterns through a paradigm of natural indigenous extinction and potential rehabilitation through imperial assimilation in a 1946 article with the jarring title "The Hawaiian Says Goodbye."[61] In this essay, Larsen extended an abstract law of indigenous Hawaiian disappearance to argue that Hawaiians and other indigenous groups, as "relatively simple" in cultural terms, had been subordinated by an "overbearing" culture because the former could not adequately adapt to modern global circumstances. As a consequence, he explained, Hawaiians lost "inner pride," which contributed to their failures to govern themselves and to thrive in a modern world.[62] Within this framework, Larsen implied that medically devised interventions to rehabiltate Hawaiian health might, but would not necessarily, arrest their disappearance. He illustrates this using comparisons between Hawaiian and Filipino health patterns from the 1920s to the 1940s.

Larsen begins by asserting that Filipinos and Hawaiians maintained relatively comparable health statuses during the 1920s based on both groups' high rates of tuberculosis infection and their exceptionally high rates of infant mortality. In 1923, infant mortality for Filipinos was the highest in the territory, at a rate of 366 deaths per thousand births. Hawaiian infant mortality was the second highest, at 305 deaths per thousand. For the territory as a whole, the infant mortality rate was 139.1 per thousand.[63] In subsequent decades, according to Larsen, Filipino health improved greatly while Hawaiian health remained poor. Larsen's explanation of this disparity was that Filipinos obtained better nutrition due to their concentration on plantations, where they also enjoyed access to health care for industrial workers. Conversely, Hawaiians failed to make similar gains because of their avoidance of American medical institutions.

This assertion attributes to industrial medicine the power to save entire populations from extinction, and implies that a consequence of failure to adopt U.S. industrial and medical hygiene, on the other hand, was death. By appropriating Hawaiian medical history and connecting Hawaiian extinction to poor decision making about food and adoption of the wrong commensalities, or lines of food sharing with other working-class and poor Asians rather than with "ancient" Hawaiians, Larsen further suggests that their epidemiological outcomes are partly volitional and grounded in improper cultural proclivities.

What he elides in this cross-cultural teleology of indigenous disappearance and potential rehabilitation are the many demographic and social factors that separated Hawaiians and Filipinos to render comparisons between them untenable. These two groups differed along lines of sex, citizenship, and marital status, and Filipinos as a group were skewed toward young and healthy people in their prime working and reproductive years. Further, the colonial migration and mobility patterns of Filipinos selectively improved Filipino health statistics through multiple levels of screening and exclusion. Between February 1932 and May 1933, the sugar industry intensified its return of all classes of Filipinos, including the sick, indigent, disabled, and families considered likely to become a public charge because of their size. These repatriates totaled 5,196 persons.[64] In 1930, two years before these repatriations, the rate of Hawaiian and Filipino infant mortality had comparably improved to a rate of 206 infant deaths per thousand births for Hawaiians and 190 deaths per thousand births among Filipinos. In 1945, the Filipino infant mortality rate declined to 29.5, while the Hawaiian rate only fell to 100 deaths per thousand births.[65] Larsen cites this as evidence of plantation medicine's efficiency, but he ignores the impact of other factors on these figures, such as extensive repatriations, the aging of this population, and Filipino exclusion after 1934, when Filipinos were transformed juridically from "nationals" to "aliens" with the end of formal U.S. imperialism in the Philippines and the extension of immigration exclusion laws to Filipinos.

A closer look at the epidemiology of tuberculosis in Hawai'i further indicates that medical exclusion rather than imperial medical efficacy lowered rates of morbidity and mortality among Filipinos. On the U.S. continent, tuberculosis was most likely to affect people under the age of twenty, but in Hawai'i, the largest number of cases were found among people of prime working age, between twenty and forty years of age. The occupation with the highest prevalence of tuberculosis was that of laborer, a category in which Filipinos predominated.[66] Further, as numbers of Filipinos testing positive for tuberculosis declined, they still died at disproportionately high rates from this disease.[67] Given the economic, political, and social context of tuberculosis, a disease that is precipitated by poverty, crowding, and malnutrition, epidemiologists and historians have referred to it as a "social disease." These social factors in the transmission and deadliness of this disease also signal the dangers of plantation employment and reveal the inaccuracies in Larsen's claim that plantation medicine prevented Filipinos from following a general indigenous trajectory toward extinction.[68]

Larsen's recommendation of *poi* as a health remedy was also quite conservative and more conventional than it may appear to contemporary observers familiar with criticisms of culturally inappropriate and ineffective standardized nutritional guidelines.[69] According to some sociologists and anthropologists, growing acceptance of another group's unique foodways is an indication of favorable feelings toward that group, just as their rejection of foreign foods is an indication of xenophobia.[70] In Hawai'i, there existed a history of missionary acceptance of chiefly Hawaiian food rituals, and shared meals were one of the ways American missionaries and merchants socialized with Hawaiian elites. In Elsie Wilcox's childhood home, Japanese and Chinese servants were trained to prepare Hawaiian feasts for her elite family, while they rarely served their own ethnic cuisines to their employers. For special occasions, or in the presence of guests, Wilcox's family would serve *poi*, raw seasoned and chopped *lomi* salmon, *kalua* pork roasted in a traditional Hawaiian underground oven known as an *imu*, and *laulau* made by steaming pork or fish in taro leaves.[71] Roger Abrahams cautions against the overly sanguine assumption that culturally pluralistic palates are an indication of growing egalitarianism by pointing out that "to the contrary, eating other people's foods has often been a sign of their having been subjugated."[72]

Ewa researchers' promotion of *poi* consumption was also consistent with imperial structural inequalities. Recently, researchers from a number of interdisciplinary vantage points have begun to reassert the scientific value and ecological, economic, and cultural advantages of indigenous foods over globalized commodity foods.[73] They define "traditional foods" in a dynamic way to include foods indigenous groups have traditional knowledge about and which they have access to locally through cultivation or harvesting. Traditional foods can also include items that are used by nonindigenous people. Conversely, "market foods" are those that are circulated and that enter into the diets of indigenous people through global industrial retail channels.[74] According to this definition, *poi* could move from being a traditional to a market food if Hawaiians lost sovereignty over the production of this dietary staple. Contemporary indigenous food researchers and activists understand traditional foods and indigenous health in far more complex ways than the Ewa researchers did. They recognize malnutrition as a structural condition, and understand that poverty, discrimination, and marginalization can interfere with access to traditional foods.[75] In Hawai'i, *poi* risked becoming a market food as planters considered cultivating taro on lands they had removed from sugar cane growth to comply with production restrictions stipulated by the Agricultural Adjustment Administration in 1934. Ready supplies of *poi* also became increasingly important in a military context as Japanese aggression in China signaled potential regional warfare that could disrupt rice exports to Hawai'i. On plantations, *poi* consumption helped to accommodate workers to the existing low wage structure, and dietary reforms suggested that poor health was an individual matter caused by one's faulty behavior. U.S. sovereignty, security, and commercial use of Hawaiian land, rather than Hawaiian tradition, ultimately buttressed doctors' promotion of *poi.*

As a departure from patterns established in the colony of Hawai'i, on the U.S. continent, health officials who were contemporaries of Larsen and Jones conceptualized nutritional deficit disorders and their solution in broader structural terms. Federal public health officials framed the problem of pellagra, a nutritional deficit disease endemic to the U.S. South, as an illness precipitated by environmental crises that disrupted agriculture following "financial depression in the South for many years" due to low cotton prices.[76] The primary preventive measure to thwart an epidemic of pellagra according to U.S. Public Health Service agents who surveyed a flooded area in Mississippi in 1927 was "[a] farming program of diversified crops" in addition to livestock industries, and "community or plantation dairies and truck patches" in areas that were inundated by water.[77] They proposed a number of long-term strategies to prevent the recurrence of pellagra among poor white and African American tenant farmers because unlike infectious disease, they explained, nutritional deficit disorders were harder to fix because they were the result of poverty.[78] Although solutions to these diseases overlapped in many ways, professionals understood that treatment of pellagra encompassed the wider ecological and economic recovery of the South.[79]

The worst pitfall of the *poi* thesis and the imperial accounts of Hawaiian and Filipino history and health that animated it is that they ultimately marginalized Hawaiian and Filipino welfare by naturalizing myths of Hawaiian extinction and Filipino salvation through imperial hygiene. Teleological trajectories of Hawaiian disappearance and colonial blood quantum rules that defined Hawaiian identity through genetics to reduce their numbers in the census were not conducive to informed and substantive approaches to Hawaiian health needs.[80] They also encouraged static misrepresentations of dynamic Hawaiian adaptation, resistance, and political struggles throughout more than a century of foreign settler colonialisms and imperial expropriation and contests over land usage. Inaccurate accounts of Filipino health were also reproduced through claims that plantation medicine saved Filipinos from indigenous trajectories of extinction by properly educating them in modern hygiene. Patterns of Filipino mobility, morbidity, and the epidemiology of tuberculosis in this group suggest instead that exclusion rather than successful medical treatment and U.S. imperial tutelage on plantations was responsible for improvements in their health. In 1933 and 1934, Edna Wentworth studied the home economy and living standards of 101 Filipino families at Ewa Plantation, and found that 25 of the 36 undernourished families were in "a twilight zone of nutritional instability" because of poverty rather than irresponsibility in budgeting.[81] Plantation life clearly posed specific public health risks to Filipinos that escaped critical attention; and for all groups living in the territory, malnutrition carried important structural underpinnings that the research on odontoclasia ignored.

Conclusion

Structurally and discursively, New Deal agricultural policies such as the Jones-Costigan Act, anthropological narratives of indigenous health and population decline, poverty, and increased child health surveillance intersected in the act of looking into the diseased mouths of children and infants in Hawai'i and seeing in their place the sulfuric acid–ravaged teeth of dogs from veterinary dental studies. The late nineteenth-century science of nutrition established terrains of cultural difference and human normativity simultaneously, and it enabled medical nosologies that made productive comparative use of racial and indigenous difference to inform the invention of a unique childhood dietary disease, known as odontoclasia, that medically recapitulated and legitimized cultural and political narratives of U.S. imperial power. The comparative dental and health trajectories of Filipino, Hawaiian, and Samoan children residing in Hawai'i gave plantation health researchers an opportunity to advance a typology of indigenous decline, and to promote *poi* as a panacea to prevalent health problems putatively caused by cultural preferences for white rice as a dietary staple. Projecting the inevitable extinction of indigenous Hawaiian people, colonial medicine proceeded to appropriate indigenous food in the service of an imperial plantation economy based in the exploitation of racialized labor.

Throughout all Pacific island nations during the twentieth century, traditional systems of food production were replaced by commercial cash-crop agriculture, underdevelopment of local food sectors, dependence on imports, and the additional change of urbanization. Local tastes and food preferences also changed as ethnic groups encountered each other, and as U.S. federal welfare assistance and food aid during the 1960s allowed imported foods, including cheap processed carbohydrates and low-grade meats, to be paid for with food stamps.[82] Under globalization, food more than ever continues to be an important instrument of power. Patterns of imperial dependency and indigenous illness are important because they impact so many parts of the world, and they constitute a point of shared global indigenous political alliance. Comparisons across contexts illustrate the critical importance of structural and sovereign measures in supporting indigenous health.

Nutritional researchers in Hawai'i, on the other hand, were almost always reductionistic in the ways they represented eating habits. They often simplified good and bad diets and overlooked the internal diversity of what groups actually ate. Their narrowly technocratic solution of education in *poi* consumption to prevent and treat diseases stemming from malnutrition was driven in part by the industrial context of this medical research. As noted above, the etiology of odontoclasia as a disease caused by consumption of high amounts of white rice drew critical attention away from sugar as a factor in causing tooth decay, and the medical promotion of *poi* similarly furthered colonial commercial agriculture and imperial appropriations of Hawaiian land. After 1934, entrepreneurs attempted to market taro grown on land taken out of sugar production by U.S. federal restrictions in the form of breads, *poi*, or a beverage called Tarorco. The promotion of *poi*, in other words, helped reproduce and expand forms of imperial domination. Through the many ways this disease reinforced existing power relations, the story of odontoclasia ultimately demonstrates how food and disease nosologies can be instruments of hegemony.

Just as biomedical experts are clearly never fully disinterested in explaining disease and bodily difference, their purchase on authority in this area has likewise never been fully complete. For nearly two decades, researchers from Hawai'i introduced odontoclasia to audiences in Vienna, Tokyo, Manila, Bangkok, and Chicago.[83] Reports of this diagnosis also reached U.S. doctors more generally through articles published in the *Journal of the American Medical Association*, *Dental Cosmos*, *New York State Dental Journal*, and the *American Journal of Diseases of Children*.[84] In 1939, Larsen delivered a paper based on local nutrition work at the annual meeting of the Far Eastern Association of Tropical Medicine in Hanoi. In 1946, however, 104 children arriving from the war-torn Philippines helped to seal the inauspicious fate of the diagnosis of odontoclasia. These children defied the principles of the etiology of this disease that positively correlated healthy teeth with optimal nourishment. Having clearly sustained prolonged dietary deficiency and malnourishment, only 11 percent of these children showed evidence of tooth decay.[85] Over the next several years, this and other contradictions such as local Filipino and Hawaiian children's improved health and continued high incidence of dental decay, forced Larsen to revise, reformulate, and ultimately abandon his odontoclasia thesis. The last publication that claimed odontoclasia existed appeared in an article by G. N. Davies in 1956, and Louis J. Baume and Jean Meyer referenced it again in 1966.[86] Since then, it has remained in the World Health Organization's International Classification of Diseases as a dental disorder, but it has lost its clinical and discursive power in Hawai'i. Today, generations of immigrants have grown up with *poi* and recognize it as a healthful food item. *Poi* consumption alone, however, has never been capable of guaranteeing good health, and Hawaiians continue to be exceptionally underserved by existing health-care institutions in Hawai'i.

Notes

1. "Ewa Health Project," Castle Foundation Papers (Hospitals—Honolulu, correspondence), Mission Houses Museum Library, Honolulu, Hawai'i, n.d.
2. Nils P. Larsen, "Is the Acid Base Balance an Important Dietary Factor?" *Transactions of the Hawaii Medical Association* (1934): 70.
3. F. V. Simonton and Martha R. Jones, "Odontoclasia," *Journal of the American Dental Association* 72 (1927): 439–50.
4. Nick Cullather, "The Foreign Policy of the Calorie," *American Historical Review* 112.2 (April 2007): 343.
5. Stephen Mennell, Anne Murcott, Anneke H. van Otterloo, *The Sociology of Food: Eating, Diet, and Culture* (Thousand Oaks, Calif.: SAGE, 1992), 35, 36.
6. Cullather, "Foreign Policy," 337–39.
7. Ibid., 338–39.
8. Mennell, Murcott, and von Otterloo, *Sociology of Food*, 115.
9. Susan Kalcik, "Ethnic Foodways in America: Symbol and the Performance of Identity," in *Ethnic Foodways in the United States: The Performance of Group Identity*, ed. Linda Keller Brown and Kay Mussell (Knoxville: University of Tennessee Press, 1984), 42–43; Judy Perkin and Stephanie F. McCann, "Food and Ethnic Americans: Is the Government Trying to Turn the Melting Pot into a One-Dish Dinner?" in *Ethnic and Regional Foodways*, ed. Brown and Mussell, 241.
10. Perkin and McCann, "Food and Ethnic Americans," 238.
11. Judith P. Swazey and Karen Reeds, *Today's Medicine, Tomorrow's Science: Essays on Paths to Discovery in the Biomedical Sciences* (Washington, D.C.: U. S. Department of Health, Education, and Welfare, Public Health Service National Institutes of Health, 1978), 29; K. Takaki, "Three Lectures on the Preservation of the Health Amongst the Personnel of the Japanese Navy and Army," *Lancet* 1 (1906): 1369–74; R. R. Williams, *Toward the Concept of Beriberi* (Cambridge, Mass.: Harvard University Press, 1961), 19–25; and see Kenneth J. Carpenter, *Beriberi, White Rice, and Vitamin B: A Disease, a Cause, and a Cure* (Berkeley: University of California Press, 2000).

12. Victor Heiser, "The Influence of Nutrition on the Diseases of Middle and Old Age," *Scientific Monthly* 49.4 (October 1939): 310.
13. Michael Worboys, "The Discovery of Colonial Malnutrition Between the Wars," in *Imperial Medicine and Indigenous Societies*, ed. David Arnold (New York: St. Martin's Press, 1988), 212–13, 215.
14. Mennell, Murcott, and von Otterloo, *Sociology of Food*, 78.
15. Warwick Anderson, *Colonial Pathologies: American Tropical Medicine, Race, and Hygiene in the Philippines* (Durham, N.C.: Duke University Press, 2006), 43, 49.
16. Cullather, "Foreign Policy," 355.
17. Worboys, "Colonial Malnutrition," 208.
18. J. L. Gilks and J. B. Orr, "The Nutritional Condition of the East African Native," *Lancet*, March 12, 1927, 560–63; J. B. Orr and J. L. Gilks, *Studies of Nutrition: The Physique and Health of Two African Tribes*, Special Report Series no. 155 (London: Medical Research Council, 1931); and Worboys, "Colonial Malnutrition," 211–12.
19. John Sharpless, "Population Science, Private Foundations, and Development Aid: The Transformation of Demographic Knowledge in the United States, 1945–1965," *International Development and the Social Sciences: Essays on the History and Politics of Knowledge*, ed. Frederick Cooper and Randall Packard (Berkeley: University of California Press, 1997), 184–86; Worboys, "Colonial Malnutrition," 213, 214.
20. Worboys, "Colonial Malnutrition," 215.
21. David Arnold, "Introduction: Disease, Medicine and Empire," *Imperial Medicine and Indigenous Societies*, ed. David Arnold (New York: St. Martin's Press, 1988), 21.
22. Worboys, "Colonial Malnutrition," 214.
23. Edward Mellanby, "A Lecture on the Relation of Diet to Health and Disease," *British Medical Journal* 1.3614 (April 12, 1930): 677–81; Worboys, "Colonial Malnutrition," 215; "Tristan da Cunha," *Dental Cosmos* 69.1 (January 1927): 115; Robert W. Chapix and C. A. Mills, "Dental Caries in the Panama Canal Zone," *Journal of Dental Research* 21 (1942): 55–59.
24. Register of the Ewa Plantation Company, HSPA Archives. Census figures for July 1932 appear in "Health Project," Hawaiian Mission Homes Library.
25. "Nils Paul Larsen," *Physicians' Files*, Mamiya Medical Heritage Center (Honolulu: Hawaii Medical Library, 1995–2000).
26. "Research at Queen's," *Queen's Vision* 3.3 (March 1977): 1.
27. Rodman Miller, "Plantation Doctor," *Hawaii Medical Journal* 54.11 (November 1995): 791.
28. Martha Jones, "H.S.P.A. Research Health Project Report of Dietary Observations Carried on at Ewa Plantation 1932–1933," bulletin no. 1 (Honolulu: Honolulu Star-Bulletin), 7, 10.
29. "Martha R. Jones, PhD, Bibliography," Price-Pottenger Nutrition Foundation, 2003–2009, http://www.ppnf.org/catalog/product_info.php?products_id=66 (accessed August 31, 2009).
30. Martha R. Jones and F. V. Simonton, "Changes in the Alveolar Process about the Teeth in Dogs on Experimental Diets," *Proceedings of Social Experiments in Biology and Medicine* 33 (1926): 734–39; F. V. Simonton, "The Etiology of Parodontoclasia," *Journal of the American Dental Association* 14 (1927): 1767–1828.
31. Larsen, "Acid Base Balance," 72; Alfred C. Reed, "Vitamins and Food Deficiency Diseases," *Scientific Monthly* 13.1 (July 1921): 78.
32. Jones, "H.S.P.A. Research Health Project," 14.
33. Martha Jones, Nils Larsen, George Pritchard, "Odontoclasia: A Clinically Unrecognized Form of Tooth Decay in the Pre-School Child of Honolulu," *Dental Cosmos* 72.5 (1930): 439; Nils Larsen, "Tooth Decay in Relation to Diet and General Health," *JAMA* (July 3, 1948): 835; Martha Jones, Nils Larsen, and George Pritchard, "Dental Disease in Hawaii: Can Unerupted Teeth Decay?" *JAMA* 99.22 (November 26, 1932): 1852.
34. Nils P. Larsen, George P. Pritchard, and C. L. Wilbar, "Ten Year Study on Tooth Decay," *Transactions of the Hawaii Territorial Medical Association* (1939): 125, 126.
35. Ibid., 129; Jones, "H.S.P.A. Research Health Project," 20.
36. Martha R. Jones and George Pritchard, "Original Communications; Dental Disease in Hawaii," *Dental Cosmos* 72.7 (July 1930): 698.
37. Jones, Larsen, and Pritchard, "Dental Disease in Hawaii," 1852.
38. Larsen, "Tooth Decay in Relation to Diet," 836. See P. E. Boyle, *Journal of Dental Research* 13 (1933): 39; S. B. Wolbach and P. R. Howe, *American Journal of Pathology* 9 (1933): 275; Martha Jones, Nils

Larsen, George Pritchard, "Dental Disease in Hawaii: Relationship Between Bone and Tooth Development in Infants," *American Journal of Diseases of Children* 45 (April 1933): 789–98.

39. Larsen, "Tooth Decay in Relation to Diet," 832.
40. Ibid., 836.
41. Jones, "H.S.P.A. Research Health Project," 16.
42. By the middle of 1933, 92 percent of eligible babies and 58 percent of kindergarten children enrolled in a voluntary school lunch program. Eighty-five percent of participants brought their children to the center daily. Jones, "H.S.P.A. Research Health Project," 7, 10, 14–16.
43. "Infant Diet at Ewa Health Center," *Plantation Health Bulletin* 1.1 (July 1936): 1.
44. Jones, "H.S.P.A. Research Health Project," 15.
45. Charles Wilbar, "Health Report," *Proceedings of the Fifty-eighth Annual Meeting of the Hawaiian Sugar Planters' Association* (Honolulu, 1938), 91, 92, 95.
46. "Nutrition on the Plantations," *Plantation Health Bulletin* 3.1 (1938): 6.
47. "Nils Paul Larsen," *Physicians' Files.*
48. Janine A. Powers, "From Medicine to Art: Nils Paul Larsen (1890–1964)" (PhD diss., University of Hawai'i, 2003), 142.
49. Ibid., 63–64. Nils Larsen, "Kahunas' Means for Curing on Exhibition," *Honolulu Advertiser*, November 18, 1951.
50. Larsen, "Kahunas' Means," 116.
51. Nils Larsen, "Rededication of the Healing Heiau Keaiwa," *Annual Report of the Hawaiian Historical Society Honolulu* (1951): 7–16; Powers, "From Medicine to Art," 68, 133.
52. Nils Larsen, "Phallic 'Temple' of Molokai," *Paradise of the Pacific*, May 1945, 6; Powers, "From Medicine to Art," 157.
53. O. A. Bushnell, *Gifts of Civilization: Germs and Genocide in Hawai'i* (Honolulu: University of Hawai'i Press, 1993), 275–76.
54. Ibid., 275.
55. Ibid., 293–95.
56. Ibid., 289–90.
57. Ibid., 6–7.
58. Francis John Halford, *Nine Doctors and God* (Honolulu: University of Hawai'i Press, 1954), 284.
59. "A Brief History of the Campaign for Better Milk in Honolulu," Nils P. Larsen Papers (unprocessed), C. S. Judd Collection, Mamiya Medical Heritage Center, Hawai'i Medical Library, folder "Correspondence, Memos, Notes."
60. Margaret Catton, *Social Service in Hawaii* (Palo Alto, Calif.: Pacific Book Publishers, 1959), 42.
61. Nils Larsen, "The Hawaiian Says Goodbye," *Plantation Health Bulletin* 11.2 (October 1946): 20.
62. Ibid., 20.
63. Ibid.
64. "The HSPA and the Labor Problem in Hawaii," presented before the Senate on April 13, 1933, by J. K. Butler, May 29, 1933, H.S.P.A. Archives, KSC box 23, folder 28, 10.
65. These statistics, but not the context, are reported by Larsen in "The Hawaiian Says Goodbye," 20.
66. J. S. B. Pratt, "Report of the President," *Board of Health Annual Report* (Honolulu, 1914), 32–33. Bruno Lasker recognized that critics cited unfavorable working conditions on plantations in the high rates of morbidity among Filipinos in *Filipino Immigration to the Continental United States and to Hawaii* (Chicago: University of Chicago Press, 1931), 187–88.
67. Both Filipinos and Hawaiians were disproportionately affected by tuberculosis. In 1910 Hawaiians were the most affected by TB, but in 1933, TB caused the greatest proportion of deaths among Filipinos. L. L. Sexton, "Report of the Anti-Tuberculosis Bureau," *Board of Health Annual Report* (Honolulu, 1910), 159.
68. Jean J. Kim, "Empire at the Crossroads of Modernity: Plantations, Medicine, and the Biopolitics of Life in Hawai'i, 1898–1946" (PhD diss., Cornell University, 2005), 274–363.
69. Perkin and McCann, "Food and Ethnic Americans," 238–39.
70. Kalcik, "Ethnic Foodways," 41.
71. Judith Dean Gething Hughes, *Women and Children First: The Life and Times of Elsie Wilcox of Kaua'i* (Honolulu: University of Hawai'i Press, 1996), 23.
72. Roger Abrahams, "Equal Opportunity Eating: A Structural Excursus on Things of the Mouth," *Ethnic Foodways in the United States: The Performance of Group Identity*, ed. Linda Keller Brown and Kay Mussell (Knoxville: University of Tennessee Press, 1984), 34.

73. Harriet V. Kuhnlein, Bill Erasmus, and Dina Spigelski, eds., *Indigenous Peoples' Food Systems: The Many Dimensions of Culture, Diversity, and Environment for Nutrition and Health* (Rome: Food and Agriculture Organization of the United Nations Centre for Indigenous Peoples' Nutrition and Environment, 2009).
74. Ibid., 3–4.
75. Ibid., 4.
76. "Pellagra Epidemic Threatens," *Science News-Letter* 12.334, September 3, 1927, 148.
77. Ibid., 147.
78. Ibid.
79. Ibid.
80. J. Kēhaulani Kauanui, *Hawaiian Blood: Colonialism and the Politics of Sovereignty and Indigeneity* (Durham, N.C.: Duke University Press, 2008), 36–52.
81. Edna Louise Clark Wentworth, *Filipino Plantation Workers in Hawaii: A Study of Incomes, Expenditures, and Living Standards of Filipino Families on an Hawaiian Sugar Plantation* (San Francisco: American Council, Institute of Pacific Relations, 1941), 105, 204–5.
82. Penelope Schoefel, "Social Change," in *Tides of History: The Pacific Islands in the Twentieth Century*, ed. K. R. Howe, Robert C. Kiste, and Brij V. Lal, 362–64 (Honolulu: University of Hawai'i Press, 1994).
83. Larsen, "Odontoclasia," 375.
84. Jones, Larsen, and Pritchard, "Odontoclasia," 439–50; Martha Jones, Nils P. Larsen, and George Pritchard, "Dental Findings in Pre-School Polynesian, Japanese, and Filipino Children in Rural Districts on the Island of Oahu," *Dental Cosmos* 72.6 (June 1930): 574–77; Martha Jones and George Pritchard, "Factors in Dental Decay in Preschool Children of Certain Races Resident in Honolulu and Rural Hawaii," *Dental Cosmos* 72.7 (July 1930): 685–99; Nils P. Larsen, Martha Jones, George P. Pritchard, "Dental Decay as an Indicator of a Dietary Fault," *American Journal of Diseases of Children* 48.6 (1934): 1228–33; Jones, Larsen, and Pritchard, "Dental Disease in Hawaii," 1852; and Nils Larsen, "Odontoc1asia," *New York State Dental Journal* 14.7 (August-September 1848): 375–82.
85. Larsen, "Tooth Decay in Relation to Diet," 836.
86. Louis J. Baume and Jean Meyer, "Dental Dysplasia Related to Malnutrition, with Special Reference to Melanodontia and Odontoclasia," *Journal of Dental Research* 45 (1966): 726–41; *ICD-DA: Application of the International Classification of Diseases to Dentistry and Stomatology*, 3rd ed. (Geneva: World Health Organization, 1995), 64.

Los Indios Bravos: The Filipino/ American Lyric and the Cosmopoetics of Comparative Indigeneity

Stephen Hong Sohn

When the Spanish first arrived in the Philippines, they made the mistake of calling the various peoples they had discovered *indios*, thinking that they had disembarked in some part of the East Indies. This fascinating conflation had the effect of connecting Filipinos more broadly to other populations mistakenly called Indians. In a recent lyric turn, Filipino American poets have been probing the ways in which Filipino diasporic subjects might be contextualized within this larger frame that links them with various indigenous groups, based upon a problematic but shared semantic moniker. This article addresses a cosmopoetics of comparative indigeneity, illuminating its valences primarily through a reading of Luisa A. Igloria's collection *Juan Luna's Revolver*.[1] While Igloria boasts numerous publication credits and distinctions, having won the National Book Award for Poetry within the Philippines multiple times, only her two most recent poetry collections, *Trill & Mordent* and the aforementioned *Juan Luna's Revolver*, have been published in the United States. Despite her status, then, as one of the most prolific and distinguished contemporary diasporic Filipino American writers, her work has not yet been the center of much critical attention. I focus on Igloria's tactical construction of the lyric "I" within *Juan Luna's Revolver*, a poetic personage that shifts in subject position from one poem to the next, moving readers to various geographical locations and temporal periods. This article elucidates the centrality of Igloria's poetic project as imperative not only to Asian Americanist cultural and poetic critiques, but also for American studies at large, especially as her work advances a unique comparative race axis that juxtaposes the racial formations of Filipinos and American Indians. The poetry collection clarifies how spectacle, exhibition, and performance became cultural domains upon which the colonial enterprise could subjugate, classify, and compare indigenous bodies.

What are the greater stakes in these cosmopoetics of comparative indigeneity? On the one hand, thinking through *Juan Luna's Revolver* helps contextualize the larger move Filipino American poets have made to query the grounds of Filipino subjectivity, especially as it relates to indigenous populations. Indeed, Igloria is one of a group of poets, including Barbara Jane Reyes, Eric Gamalinda, and Bino Realuyo, who have considered Filipino Americans alongside American Indians.[2] While space here is too limited to fully critique the larger Filipino American lyric body, the interventions of Igloria and other poets are of great import to the shifts in American studies and contemporary poetry more broadly. In a special issue of the *Publications of the Modern Language Association of America* (*PMLA*) devoted to comparative racialization, Shu-mei Shih cautions that studies of comparative race might elide particular intersectional axes: "The calls to go beyond the black-white binary in American race studies are more likely to result in new insights on Asian Americans and Latinas/os (Alcoff) than on other people of color, especially American Indians. In other words, some terms may appear more readily triangulatable than others, while some may just disappear or fade into the background, as happens with the binary model."[3] Whereas Asian American studies has only recently begun to explore comparative race in earnest, it has tended to function so far through what Colleen Lye has called the "Afro-Asian analogy,"[4] where Bill V. Mullen's work on Afro-Orientalism, Helen Jun's articulation of Black Orientalism, and Daniel Y. Kim and Daryl J. Maeda's studies of Afro-Asian masculinities have loomed large.[5] The work of these poets elucidates how other comparative frames might be employed to analyze Filipinos and American Indians as populations exemplary of interrelated, but not necessarily transparently parallel, racial formations in certain historical and cultural circumstances. I focus on Igloria's collection as a paradigmatic example of the ways in which lyric poetry serves to resist the potential elision of American Indians within comparative race frameworks, and to further elucidate how racial binaries fail to account for the inherently complex nature of colonial enterprises. In these ways, Igloria's collection illuminates the racial intersections of Filipinos and American Indians, while her cosmopoetics of comparative indigeneity remind us that racial lenses must be considered in diasporic scope as American and Spanish racial ideologies cross national boundaries, bodies, and waters, and emerge in different temporal and geographical contexts.

The complexity of the Asian American poetic terrain also reminds us of the connections between poetic forms and material histories. Primarily following the theories on ethics conceptualized by philosopher Emmanuel Levinas, literary critic Xiaojing Zhou has argued, "The lyric 'I' in Asian American poetry, more often than not, is a socially and culturally defined other, represented as the outsider, the foreigner, deviant from the norm, and positioned as marginal or subordinate. At the same time, Asian American poets reclaim otherness as irreducible alterity, as a form of resistance and intervention, which entails new perspectives on self and other, and generates new possibilities for using language, image, and poetic form."[6] For Igloria, the lyric "I" is exactly the productive space of interrogation, but Zhou's conception of irreducible alterity finds an interesting resonance within the cosmopoetics of comparative indigeneity. Indeed, Igloria's poetry raises questions such as who has the privilege to speak, and what experiences must be highlighted? By risking a poetics of appropriation, *Juan Luna's Revolver* illustrates that the lyric must be able to accommodate a crowd of subjectivities, to move across time and space, and to embody a continually shifting and mobile vantage point from which to depict the intricacies of history, race, ethnicity, nationality, and colonialisms.

While the term *indigenous* is not without its own intricacies and nuances, I employ it to name the earliest known inhabitants of a particular geographical region, in contrast to later settlers, immigrants, and colonizing bodies. In many cases, *indigenous* also implies that such populations have maintained a certain sense of cohesion and distance from the mainstream or hegemonic culture. Here, I will investigate indigenous populations in comparative scope, especially as Igloria's collection places Filipinos and Filipino indigenous populations in dialogue with American Indians. According to James Clifford, "Indigenous movements are positioned, and potentially but not necessarily connected, by overlapping experiences in relation to Euro-American, Russian, Japanese, and other imperialisms. They all contest the power of assimilationist nation-states, making strong claims for autonomy, or for various forms of sovereignty. In recent decades, positive discourses of indigenous commonality have emerged, drawing together this range of historical predicaments."[7] In likewise fashion, this article investigates how Filipino American poets such as Igloria mobilize representations of "indigenous commonality" from a transnational perspective that compares and contrasts a broad "range of historical predicaments."

Igloria uses lyric poetry to animate history such that it can be interrogated from a variety of subject positions and geographic temporalities all within one collection, without recourse to narrative unity. By offering this multipronged perspective, Igloria honors the complexity of the indigenous experience that she purports to excavate. She continually decenters the lyric "I" through historical meditations that contextualize Filipino and American Indian oppressions within a transnational scope. I begin by establishing how Igloria's collection lyrically links the Filipino revolutionary group known as *Los Indios Bravos* with American Indians who toured with Buffalo Bill's Wild West Show in the late nineteenth century. I then situate *Juan Luna's Revolver* in relation to another comparative framework in which indigenous Filipinos came to be associated with American Indians and other *native* groups during the 1904 Louisiana Purchase Exposition. The final section analyzes a sonnet series that concludes Igloria's collection. Here, the 1904 fair is lyrically reimagined through the presence of various indigenous figures, such as Igorot tribesmen and the legendary Apache warrior Geronimo. *Juan Luna's Revolver* shows us how lyric poetry mobilizes transnational historical reconstructions that yield new possibilities for comparative analysis in the juxtaposition of Filipinos and American Indians. The entire article clarifies the centrality of visual regimes in the comparative racialization of indigenous populations, especially as such groups were collectively exhibited, expected to perform, and finally, to reaffirm the moral stance of empire building.

Los Indios Bravos

Juan Luna's Revolver spotlights Filipinos as global subjects and how their movements across oceans and continents trouble any discrete considerations of ethnic or nation-based affiliations. The collection's title refers to the Filipino painter Juan Luna, part of a cadre of Manila-based painters, artists, and writers who traveled to Europe to showcase their work in the late nineteenth century. Luna was most famous for his large painting titled *The Spoliarium*, which depicted injured gladiators being taken off the field of battle for what was surely to be their deaths. The spoliarium was the structure wherein Romans stripped and burned the bodies of gladiators after they had been killed. Given the fact that many gladiators were recruited only after having been prisoners of war, the Roman Empire's policy to employ such figures through the violence and spectacle of large-arena fighting certainly finds parallels to the various ways in which the colonial subject becomes routed into visual frameworks, across a wide variety of historical epochs. By naming the collection after Juan Luna, Igloria participates in a poetic excavation in which the lyric "I" exists as a vantage point from which to view the past. Through this lyric speaker, the reader is continually encouraged to consider power relations that surface in the process of representation and memorialization, wherein museums and exhibitions operate as locales in which difference, oppression, and objectification become amplified.

In the poem "Luces," the lyric speaker positions the collection in relation to the Spanish imperial enterprise. Here Igloria explores the centrality of the *ilustrados*—the Spanish-influenced Filipino elite who often traveled abroad for schooling—to the project of the Filipino revolution. This group included the aforementioned Juan Luna as well as José Rizal, famously noted for his resistance to the U.S. occupation of the Philippines. When Rizal "traveled to Europe he made it a point to visit libraries, museums, and art gallaries [*sic*]. He sought to enlighten himself on the history of the country he visited and to observe and understand the ways of life of the common people, their customs, their traditions."[8] While the *ilustrados* could have been critiqued for an assimilationist approach that glorified the image of the colonial masters, the excerpt from Vicente L. Rafael's book *The Promise of the Foreign* that opens "Luces" articulates how "mimicry" can simply be a tactic.[9] In this context, the *ilustrados* possessed an understanding of their own political leanings, one that outwardly seemed to suggest support for the "civilizing project" promoted by Spanish colonizers but that nevertheless masked another motivation: to place the "foreign . . . outside of oneself."[10] Consequently, dress, manners, and even food become merely equivocal concessions to Spanish colonial power, not evidence that they shifted their attention away from national and cultural independence.

Like many of the other poems included in *Juan Luna's Revolver*, "Luces" has a focused historical context: the celebration of the short-lived First Philippine Republic emblematized by the successful assembly of the Malolos Congress. The poem opens with the speaker simply observing her surroundings from a position above a courtyard, with no hint that the lyrics will eventually confront the struggles endured for Filipino independence. In this respect, the speaker finds history, politics, and the question of the *native* in a simple courtyard, adorned in this case with a stone sculpture of a duck. The lyric speaker takes a moment to tell the reader that she is thinking of "*pâté / de foie gras* not from hunger, but because / I have been teaching about the Malolos Convention / of 1899."[11] An individual who makes the connection between stone ducks and pâté de foie gras might not only be read as someone looking for a bite to eat, but also as a person knowledgeable about European cuisine. This cultural capital seems to distinguish the speaker, marking her as a cosmopolitan consumer with a taste for the richest foods. Instead, the reference to the pâté de foie gras generates another line of significations that carries her back to a reconceptualization of the Malolos Convention, where the question of nativism is reconstituted. The speaker employs the word *native* in this poem in a double sense, especially in light of earlier poems included in *Juan Luna's Revolver* (e.g., "In the Clothing Archive" and "Letras y Figuras") in which the *native* is meant to invoke the backwardness of the Filipino. Here, what is foreign is not Filipino but French cuisine, even as it could indicate class cosmopolitanism. Indeed, the value placed on such food is further clarified by the speaker's consideration of Rizal's "favorite breakfast," *sardinas secas*, a dish he did not disavow after schooling in Paris, nor repudiate even with the availability of Spanish gourmet fare in the Philippines.[12] Everywhere in this poem, Igloria's lyrics serve up the attraction of the colonial powers, whether it is through musical forms (the waltz), new food amenities (ice, and with it butter), and highly prized objects (crystal), all as evidence of the Philippine Republic's presumed embrace of its colonial heritage.[13] However, the lyric speaker goes on to explain that the importation of valued foods or commodities from colonial powers does not sway Rizal, or the other revolutionaries, who come from a variety of different backgrounds and who, in the last line of the poem, are called "*los indios bravos.*"[14]

It was while Rizal and others were in Paris that the term *indios bravos* took on its own revolutionary potential, "transforming the traditional Spanish gibe into a badge of honor."[15] According to Vicente L. Rafael, "while attending the Paris Exposition of 1899, Rizal and his fellow Filipinos saw a Wild West show featuring American Indians performing various skills on horseback. Impressed not only by their daring but also by the enthusiastic applause they received from the crowd, the Filipinos decided to form a mutual-aid association and call it *Los Indios Bravos.*"[16] Rafael elaborates that "Rizal himself had suggested the name thinking to subvert the racist designation *indio* used by the Spaniards to refer to native Filipinos. Referring to themselves as 'brave Indians' coincided with their interest in fencing, gymnastics, martial arts, and weight lifting—again, ways of marking their bodies apart from their colonial counterparts."[17] E. San Juan Jr. calls the resignification of the term *indios* "a bold paradigm shift, a transvaluation of meanings and values, linked to a wider political-cultural movement of profound radical change among subject-peoples."[18] While there is a masculinist impulse undergirding Rizal's revolutionary group, one observes how a resistance project is keyed into Igloria's poem "Luces."[19] The poem advances the way in which convention attendees could still imagine "the idea of a nation," focusing on the future of an independent Philippines, one predicated on the emergence of revolutionary organizations like *Los Indios Bravos.*[20] At the same time, the resignification of the term *indios* implies the overlapping and concurrent histories of colonial brutality, for as Sharon Delmendo explains, "in his recuperation of the *Indio*, a term derogatorily used to designate native Filipinos during the Spanish colonial period, Rizal transplanted to the Philippines the United States' ideological construction of American Indians. Rizal's conceptualization of a symbolic fraternity between the American Indian and the Philippine *Indio* ironically prefigured the United States' export of the military tactics and racial attitudes developed through the U.S. Indian Wars to the Philippines in 1898."[21] Whereas Delmendo notes the ways in which the American Indian and the Philippine *Indio* could be constructed as savage, Rizal's interpretation clarifies how "symbolic fraternity" could lead to alternative reconstructions of derogatory racial terminologies.

While "Luces" alludes only to the historical moment in which Rizal and his contemporaries found inspiration in American Indian culture and resistance, Igloria's collection moves forcefully into the cosmopoetics of comparative indigeneity with the poem "Black Elk in Paris." It begins with the speaker considering the proliferation of celebrity culture and the appropriation of cultural artifacts such as jewelry. Like "Luces," the poem contains a lyric speaker who actuates a rupture in both time and space. In this case, the lyric speaker's entry into different historical contexts and geographies emerges through reading the *Chicago Tribune*, which contains a photograph of wax statues in the likenesses of Angelina Jolie, Brad Pitt, and daughter Shiloh. Jolie's neck is adorned with "a single strand of cowrie shells/corded on leather"[22] at which point the speaker observes:

> Such trinkets
> might have been the wampum Buffalo Bill Cody
>
> made his Indians thread—Sitting Bull,
> Chief Joseph, Geronimo, Black Elk,
>
> even Rains-in-the-Face (reputed to be
> the man who killed Custer), Ghost Dancers
>
> made to choose between prison
> or joining the Wild West Show.
>
> In that carnival standing in for the dusty frontier,
> Rizal and his friends admired
>
> staged battles and skirmishes, war paint
> and feathered regalia. *Why should we resent*
>
> being called Indios by the Spaniards?
> *Look at those Indios from North America . . .*
>
> Let us be like them. We shall be Indios Bravos!
> It's said that Black Elk, an Oglala Sioux,
>
> had traveled to London to meet Queen Victoria.
> He missed the boat taking the Wild West Show

> back to America, but found work with other
> traveling exhibitions.[23]

This sequence, which reimagines Rizal's experience watching Buffalo Bill Cody's Wild West, establishes an association between Filipinos, who sought independence in part under Rizal, and American Indians, who attempted to resist federal encroachment on Native lands. At the same time, however, the poem accents the complicated nature of representation and spectacle. As the speaker suggests, Sitting Bull and Black Elk experienced significant difficulties carving out a life after the brutal suppression of indigenous resistance movements, and their inclusion in such shows was encouraged by federal officials who sought to sequester these charismatic leaders from their respective reservations.[24] Of Sitting Bull's participation, L. G. Moses explains: "He endured the taunts and boos of the crowd who associated him with Custer's death at the Little Bighorn. From all reports, he bore the insults impassively—or with greater dignity than those who screamed their insults."[25] Like Sitting Bull, Black Elk similarly found the touring show a challenging milieu, but for his own reasons. As Sarah J. Blackstone reveals, "travel, though paid for by Cody, was hard on the Indians. They were put in railroad cars that were stuffy and noisy and in the steerage of boats to cross the Atlantic. Black Elk was very frightened and distressed by his voyage to England with Buffalo Bill in 1887."[26] To add to the complications, Black Elk became stranded in England when the show closed and he remained in Europe until he was reunited with the tour when it returned to Paris for the 1899 exposition.[27] The tour experience for Black Elk was far from the entertaining spectacle that audiences saw.[28]

But how did Rizal view the Wild West show? On the one hand, as scholars such as Blackstone have argued, Wild West shows encouraged audiences to accept as inevitable the marginalization and mistreatment of Indian peoples. At the same time, Rosemary K. Bank's critique of the Wild West tour show provides a divergent viewpoint: "From the Grand Review introducing 'Buffalo Bill's Wild West and Congress of Rough Riders of the World,' through its seventeen acts, to the farewell salute by the entire company, the show underscored the presence, rather than absence, of Indians and the frontier. Present as evidence were people and things to materially attest to the reality of Indians and frontiers."[29] Although the staged performances highlight a narrative in which American Indians find themselves subjugated under white power, Bank's argument dramatizes how Rizal could have identified with the struggles embodied by Sitting Bull, Black Elk, and others, where the fight to retain one's homeland could be associated with Filipino revolutionary aspirations. The Paris exposition's locale outside of the Philippines and the United States presents an intriguing middle space, brokering the complex global intersection of asymmetrical power relations. Because Rizal and his fellow *ilustrados* observe the Wild West show as spectators and as customers, they stand in contrast to the American Indian performers, many of whom were recruited for the show even as they were considered prisoners of war. As colonial subjects, Rizal and his fellow Filipino contemporaries, such as Juan Luna, were relatively privileged in their ability to export to the Philippines the example of anticolonial resistance offered by the American Indians.

The poem's ultimate question, "Who knew that a year later, / a hundred and forty-six *Indios* would die defending Wounded Knee, or that far away in the east, / other *Indios* were plotting a revolution, signing their names in their own real blood,"[30] returns to the links that might form between those subjugated under colonialism and empire building. Sitting Bull's support of the Ghost Dance movement would result in his death in 1890, just prior to the massacre at Wounded Knee.[31] Six years later, José Rizal would be executed for allegedly engaging in treasonous acts against the Spanish government. Both Rizal and Sitting Bull function as racialized synecdoches; their deaths symbolize the incredible setbacks experienced by indigenous groups resisting colonialism and domination. The lyric speaker considers both individuals and the populations they come to represent under the same term, *indios,* thereby linking their revolutionary activities under a unified umbrella that speaks to the cosmopoetics of comparative indigeneity. Whether in the (American) West, or in the (Filipino) East, or in a thirdspace (Paris), these *indios* rise up and attempt to challenge those who have dominated them. Even as "Black Elk in Paris" concatenates Filipinos and American Indians, the speaker's attention to Rizal's spectatorship and American Indian incarceration serves to complicate any simple parallel between two racialized populations. In this way, a cosmopoetics of comparative indigeneity honors comparative race linkages while still highlighting situational asymmetries.

The Igorots Go to the 1904 World's Fair

In the poetry collection's first section, *Juan Luna's Revolver* advances Filipinos as *indios* in ways that link them to American Indian populations. The first section also posits a lyric speaker, often the conduit through which these associations can be mobilized, who can yet be temporally and spatially distant from the particular historical and geographical contexts excavated in each poem. The collection serves to displace the exceptionality of the lyric "I," whose own predicaments and challenges are configured alongside larger structural frameworks that associate history, racialization, colonialism, and indigeneity. The following three sections in *Juan Luna's Revolver* gradually alter the emphasis of comparative indigeneity by exploring the variegated nature of the Filipino *indio*, especially centering on the Igorots.[32] Igloria increasingly employs lyric monologues that engage the "voice" of different speakers. The lyric reconstruction, hallmarking the lives of such exhibitionary subjects, comes with a certain appropriative danger that Igloria nevertheless risks in order to expose how Filipino indigeneity complicates reified notions of the primitive or the barbaric. Hence, I ultimately focus on textual readings from the final section, "Postcards from the White City," in which Igloria challenges the conflation of all Filipinos as *indios,* thereby nuancing the various positionalities of Filipino subjects under colonial domination.

One of the most provocative poems included in this final section, "Descent," crystallizes the cosmopoetics of comparative indigeneity. "Descent" begins with a brief factual excerpt that tracks the movement of Filipinos as global commodities bearing the imprint of exotic locales: "In 1904 more than 1100 indigenous Filipinos were transported to St. Louis, Missouri, to serve as live exhibits at the World's Fair and Exposition."[33] The preface reminds us that Filipino indigeneity must be continually reconsidered with respect to geography and temporality. In a study of the 1904 World's Fair and Exposition, historian William Everdell recounts, "Members of several of [Filipino] indigenous peoples, including Moro, Bagobo, Visayan, and Igorot, were deconcentrated on a 47-acre military-run reservation right on the fairgrounds."[34] The word *indigenous* here is perhaps used more loosely than today, but certainly, the thought was that these Filipinos were all *natives,* just of varying degrees. The partitioning of the Filipino "live" exhibits therefore was meant to emphasize the levels of refinement attained, with the Visayans being represented as the most cultured, in contrast to the Igorot and Negrito groups. The classification systems employed to distinguish the Filipino populations at the fair dovetailed with the rise in the disciplines of anthropology and ethnography and the traction that social Darwinism had attained by this time. However, Filipino groups were ultimately circumscribed by an insurmountable racial divide; the line between the savage and the civilized was clearly defined. In the context of this human exhibit, it was the U.S. that could stand tall as the nation that tamed the savage; here, the exhibit's project to tame the native Filipino was instructive as evidence of the power, influence, and moral character of U.S. colonialism.

Despite the fact that some Filipinos might have held their own views of what constituted a true savage, a perspective certainly influenced by the high degree of colonial contact that specific portions of the Philippines experienced, the way in which different Filipinos were exhibited rendered them all as barbaric others.[35] In a study of Carlos Bulosan's stories set in the Philippines, Joel Slotkin articulates how one group of Filipinos might have seen another: "Many Filipinos, whether because of traditional rivalries or assimilation into Spanish or American culture, also divided the people of the archipelago into civilized and savage. In northern Luzon, the region in which Bulosan grew up, the Igorots of the highlands were one of the major groups that both Americans and Filipino lowlanders considered uncivilized. In fact, the Igorots became emblematic of savagery and the rejection of mores that governed the behavior of other groups in the region."[36] *Juan Luna's Revolver* deconstructs the image of the supposedly savage Igorot in two ways. First, the collection highlights the influence of colonial ideology on Filipinos as it becomes routed into the Igorots' status as less evolved. Second, the collection shows that the Igorot exists at an incoherent nexus where difference is both excoriated and commodified. At this paradoxical juncture, the savagery projected on the indigenous body is abjected. In "Hill Station," the lyric speaker begins the poem from a geotemporal context that shifts the collection back to the beginning of the U.S. colonial occupation of the Philippines. While the Igorot is supposedly the primordial figure who cannot assimilate, the lyric speaker recalls that the "American officials" who had moved there "would not give up their top hats, their cravats / their coat-tails, waistcoats and wool trousers / those yards of skirts and heavy petticoats."[37] The inflexibility toward dress is not simply a means of retaining class and status, as it clashes against the "choking heat" of the tropical Filipino climates.[38] Such dress seems obsolete, indeed, perhaps even backward. Nevertheless, the poem, set in Baguio City, ends with a shift to the contemporary moment, where the lyric speaker, here more closely resembling a double for the poet, observes:

> Boys
>
> in my fourth grade class had names like Monroe Gawigawen
> and Jefferson Palpallatoc. They were of Igorot stock, again
> what you might call *native*. Other children taunted them,
>
> those who thought themselves more citified, more cleansed of
> savage origins.[39]

Whereas the poem's earlier sections include lyrics devoted to the way in which the American colonials attempted to alter the culture of the groups they encountered in the Baguio City area, the conclusion sees a regime of value that recalls Slotkin's critique that the Igorot came to be representative of the "savage." The process that Igloria draws out in the poem relies upon the lyric speaker crossing vastly different temporal moments to illustrate how gradations in racial difference offered up by the Americans become mapped onto Filipino culture itself. By rejecting their Igorot classmates, the other children suggest that, as colonial subjects, they have been interpellated by racial ideologies that move transnationally and maintain their presence across time.

The dilemma posed by the Igorot's status as the ultimate savage reaches its apotheosis in "Descent," which employs the lyric perspective of an Igorot woman who has lost contact with her lover, presumably one of the thousand or so indigenous Filipinos transported to St. Louis in 1904. The poem therefore tracks her journey down a mountainside as she looks for her husband and reflects on her inability to make contact with him. The poem then shifts to her eventual settlement with two Westerners, likely Americans, who have taken it upon themselves to civilize her. Her initial rejection by the coastal Filipinos is made apparent as she notices how "[f]aces gawked / as I walked past. To them I was a stranger, / dark and not to be trusted; my woven skirt a red-striped / carnival tent that might open to what they / could not imagine."[40] Her monstrosity is illuminated through her "woven skirt," which she compares to a "red-striped carnival tent," bespeaking the dangerous spectacle she embodies. At the same time, one must connect the "carnival tent" image to the historical note that precedes and appears encrypted in the lyrics themselves, as her husband is on display in such a circus-like atmosphere in the United States. The "circus" extends transnationally, shifting to the Philippines, where race and difference have come to colonize the landscape. The reference to her "dark" skin represents another racializing marker that associates particular colors with barbarity and backwardness. Her status as savage at first seems undermined in the presence of the Westerners, as she is baptized by them and given garments that "covered [her] breasts and arms." However, the lyric speaker notes that these articles of clothing "I took off only when, eventually I posed for him— / my dark breasts artfully concealed under an arrangement of necklaces, agate, and carnelian."[41] The Igorot's ability to be civilized is therefore not the project finally undertaken; her nakedness instead becomes the subject of documentation and visual appreciation. Indeed, the spectacle of her savagery appears at two poles, one scorned by the lowlander Filipino groups and another objectified by the Westerners, who each in their own way find a means to subjugate the Igorot woman's body within a racializing regime.

In the detailed note that concludes the poem, Igloria provides more context for "Descent," describing the creation of the Philippine Reservation at the 1904 world's fair: "The Filipino bodies at the fair made up half—and the largest—contingent of *native* bodies. Live exhibits of Filipinos, Ainu, American Indians, and pygmies, were meant to illustrate the development of nations from savagery to civilization, and America's role as new imperial power."[42] Even as "Descent" focuses most specifically on the experience of one Igorot woman, the civilizing project enacted by the husband and wife pair speaks more broadly to the American view of indigenous groups at the time. According to Gerald A. Finin,

> throughout much of the Spanish period, Spaniards referred to lowland 'natives' of the Philippines as *indios.* Americans, as they arrived during the early part of the century, appear to have frequently translated the concept of Indios into one akin to 'Indians,' which led them to assume that they were basically dealing in the Philippines with the same 'kind' of people found on North America's western frontier.[43]

In this way, the placement of the Filipino groups at the world's fair alongside other indigenous groups represents one of the primary associative axes highlighted by this last section in *Juan Luna's Revolver.* Indeed, the indigenous Filipinos were then symbolically connected to American Indians as a population that required domination and pacification, groups that collectively demonstrated the supposed appropriateness of colonial ventures.

The Cosmopoetic Sonnet Series

In the poems, conceived as a sonnet series that mirror the collection's fourth section title, "Postcards from the White City," the simultaneity of time and space provides a useful comparison point between Filipino diasporic subjects respectively living in the early twentieth and twenty-first centuries. This sonnet sequence begins with a quotation from the song "Meet Me in St. Louis," which focuses attention on the 1904 world's fair held in St. Louis, Missouri. Like "Black Elk in Paris" and "Descent," this poem elucidates the ways in which native Filipinos might be placed in the larger category of indigenous peoples throughout the globe. This dynamic viewpoint does not represent a simple equation among two racialized populations. Instead, these connections are nuanced as Igloria includes sonnets from the perspective of indigenous subjects who would have been present at the fair as part of the live exhibits. While a number of sonnets from "Postcards from the White City" are set during the fair, I concentrate on those that most explicitly advance a cosmopoetics of comparative indigeneity. I reproduce the first here:

World's Fair, St. Louis, Missouri; 1904

Here, where we were almost nothing,
on the banks of the Arrowhead River
they mapped the unruly forest, laid down
promenades and columns. Lights flickered
from dusk to dawn, their arctic glow eating
at the cone of darkness. The darkness was to become
extinct. Was to perish. The previous year, the first
flight in Kitty Hawk, North Carolina.
The first time a girl tiptoed round-mouthed
and pulled the cord that tripped
a light switch on—In Lancaster, Kentucky
she watched as her hands washed themselves
in light, blue like gentian violet, their shadows
swimming like a pair of fish.[44]

Many of the sonnets are notable for the intertwining use of collective lyric speakers, the "we," as well as the unitary lyric speaker, the "I." Although the "we" seems to refer to the indigenous Filipino tribes transported to the fair, the argument could likewise be made that the "we" more largely represents the various indigenous groups exhibited. Here, the "Arrowhead River" refers to the body of water that was used to separate the Filipinos from other groups. At the same time, Igloria employs specific diction here to call to mind various indigenous groups that were represented at the 1904 fair. The very word *arrowhead* suggests a range of historical periods in the Americas, including those long before European colonization, reminding readers of the connection being made among the different live exhibitions. In addition, the reference to "arctic light" resonates with the fact that Inuit tribes, an indigenous group located in the Arctic region, were often represented at these international exhibitions, including the 1904 world's fair.

The shift away from an early twentieth-century lyric persona abruptly alters the poetic context of "Postcards from the White City." In the middle section of the series, the sonnets move to the contemporary period, where a lyric speaker finds herself gazing upon different museum exhibitions and artifacts. The first of the "contemporary" sonnets is set at the Smithsonian Institution in the summer of 2002 and considers the complexities of fossilization and artifactualization. Beginning with the question, "What are the soft parts of the body?" the lyric speaker understands the importance of contextualizing the artifacts that stand in for peoples and cultures that have long past died.[45] Indeed, an urgent recovery must be made. In the process of fossilization, the "soft parts of the body" are the least likely to remain preserved, but they are also what the lyric speaker argues must be "foraged," out of terrains that might not necessarily yield such elements so easily.[46] The artifact, "deed of sale," calls attention to the ways in which indigenous groups ranging from the Ainu to the Igorots to American Indians could be bought and sold as commodities for these international exhibitions.[47] The "threshing floor," a surface that is used in processing grain, hints at agricultural labor, as do references to "winnowing" and the "repeated motion of the hand."[48] Ultimately, however, the indigenous experience itself is absent. Consequently, the sonnet enacts a series of grotesque comparisons to emblematize how native lives must be excavated and embodied, resisting a myopic gaze focused solely on cataloguing fossilized fingernails or "hair-plaits."[49] The perspective of the sonnet thus stands in contrast to exhibition contexts that frame indigenous subjects like "tagged and numbered fish," where humanity is stripped away and evolutionary development is questioned.[50] Here, the contemporary lyric speaker avoids a reductive gaze, attempting instead to "find the white medallions of the dissected body," to reconfigure and reconstruct the context and cultures of past communities and peoples. This sonnet is vital in establishing the importance of comparative indigeneity, as the agricultural references and anthropological vocabulary all serve to render a wholesale categorization of the *native* as a site through which American empire finds traction. The lyric speaker therefore reminds us that alternative modes of recovery and knowledge production must be engaged.

Moving beyond the reductive gaze that positions the indigenous body as an artifact to be observed, the sonnet series moves back to the 1904 world's fair and into lyric persona poems from that time period. The final sonnet is characterized by its confrontational tone in that it challenges a young and presumably white fairgoer's ennui over the exhibitions. Whereas many of the earlier 1904-based sonnets seem to be tied particularly to the presence of indigenous Filipinos, here the poem references a larger indigenous collective. The lyric speaker challenges the young fairgoer by suggesting that she take the place of Geronimo, perform her "*native*-ness" for the crowds, and likewise experience the problematic contractual obligations associated with participating as a live exhibit. The shift in the speaker's position is interesting, because it would seem to be another fairgoer, someone attuned to unmasking the contexts lurking behind the apparently banal, circus-like atmosphere that has already bored the girl. One wonders about the possibility again of the contemporary lyric speaker intruding here, moving from the twenty-first century museum visits in the previous two sonnets back to the time and place of the 1904 fair. This sonnet thus becomes an imaginative reconstruction of the past. In a study of colonialism and indigeneity, Richard Drinnon recalls Geronimo's pivotal place at the fair: "The 'little brown people' were the pagan Igorots Ida McKinley had so earnestly wanted to save and Worcester and the other commissioners had just shipped from the islands for the edification of their compatriots on the mainland. Unhappily, no one seems to have thought to take a snapshot of the Igorots' historic meeting with Geronimo—perhaps the latter's guard got in the way."[51] According to Nancy J. Parezo and Don D. Fowler, by this period, Geronimo had already been attuned to entertaining spectators, but his experience with the Igorots was singular; as Parezo and Fowler explain, "he was fascinated by the Igorots," and they add that "their nakedness bothered [Geronimo], as it did many Indians, and he thought that they should not have been allowed to come."[52] The accuracy of Parezo and Fowler's account, though, can be challenged by Frederick Turner in his new introduction to *Geronimo: His Own Story, as Told to S. M. Barrett*, in which Turner asserts that the tone of the entire recounting cannot always be ascertained: "As to the accuracy of the whole [autobiography], let us say to begin with that Geronimo, for reasons of his own, did not choose to tell Barrett everything. He was, after all, still a prisoner of war, and he was a bitter man who regretted to the end of his life that he had surrendered to Miles rather than fighting it out in the mountains. Considering his treatment in subsequent years, one cannot much blame him."[53] Following Turner's lead, one can surmise the very distinct possibility that Geronimo's disdain for the Igorots could be read from a different vantage point.

As a result, I turn briefly to the ways that Geronimo's autobiographical reflections prefigure a politics of comparative indigeneity. In reference to Geronimo's comment that "I am glad I went to the Fair. I saw many interesting things and learned much of the white people. They are a very kind and peaceful people. During all the time I was at the Fair no one tried to harm me in any way,"[54] Frederick Jackson Turner notes, "The reader should recall here that Geronimo was not without guile. His statements about white culture often have the appearance of cutting several ways."[55] Something similar could be said about Geronimo's account of the Igorots, whom he refers to as "little brown people at the Fair that the United States troops captured recently on some islands far from here."[56] While the phrase, "little brown people," might seem to racialize the Igorots in a derogatory way, this phrase is juxtaposed with the reference to U.S. military, which "captured" these indigenous populations and transported them to the fair under duress. This experience certainly mirrors Geronimo's own as well as that of many of his American Indian counterparts as prisoners of war, forced into their performative positions in Wild West shows. His autobiography thus enacts a politics of comparative indigeneity and must therefore be carefully interpreted with respect to its complicated subtexts.

Geronimo seems to express a particular dislike for the Igorots. He recounts that they

> did not wear much clothing, and I think that they should not have come to the Fair. But they themselves did not seem to know any better. They had some little brass plates, and they tried to play music with these, but I did not think it was music—it was only a rattle. However, they danced to this noise and seemed to think they were giving a fine show.[57]

Here, Geronimo's reflections could imply, on the one hand, that the Igorots do not exhibit any self-consciousness in relation to their naked bodies, demonstrating a kind of uncivilized manner. Details concerning their musical skills suggest a crude cultural background, one that Geronimo seems to find disappointing. Geronimo's relative dissatisfaction with the music produced and dance performed by the Igorots suggests an implicit critique of the Igorots' role at the fair, where they are exhibited not for the cultural enrichment of fairgoers, but rather for the spectacle of their savagery and their simplicity. This moment is one that reflects Geronimo's larger perspective concerning the way indigeneity can signify to the masses that travel throughout the fair grounds. As himself an indigenous prisoner of war often on display, Geronimo's view of the Igorots undermines the supposed righteousness of the American colonial project to master, imprison, and exhibit indigenous populations.

Geronimo ends his reflections concerning the Igorots by contextualizing their presence at the fair: "I do not know how true the report was, but I heard that the President sent them to the Fair so that they could learn some manners, and when they went home teach their people how to dress and how to behave."[58] This statement is curious because Geronimo does not place a value judgment on the rumored report, so it seems impossible to discern whether he agrees or disagrees with the president's supposed rationale. In the context of his possible desire to cultivate goodwill with the White House, we might imagine that Geronimo sides with the president, but reading these statements through the lens of coded satire makes apparent another important interpretation. Recall, for example, Geronimo's references to whites at the fair: "I am glad I went to the Fair. I saw many interesting things and learned much of the white people. They are a very kind and peaceful people. During all the time I was at the Fair no one tried to harm me in any way."[59] On the one hand, it as if Geronimo himself performs the part of the *native* subject that has become civilized through the process of attending the fair. On the other hand, given Geronimo's lengthy battle with American forces over tribal lands, his description of "white people" as peaceful is particularly ironic, suggesting that, based on past experience, it is a notable surprise that no one tried to hurt him, and that it is in fact whites who may need to learn how to be peaceful and "civilized" by observing indigenous peoples. The question of "manners" is therefore reflected back at those who have forcibly captured indigenous populations and made them perform in shows, whether in the form of the Igorot's music making or the American Indian "roping contests."[60] Geronimo's statements concerning the Igorot exhibits therefore seem to constitute a kind of reverse ethnography, one critiquing American fairgoers as barbaric and violent through their consumptive habits.

Geronimo's politics of comparative indigeneity can be put into conversation with Igloria's sonnet as it details how American Indian prisoners of war existed as spectacularly figured evidence of American supremacy. As the lyric speaker imagines the bored fairgoer, "I'd like to have drawn her deeper in, drop / her on a buckskin hide with instructions: / Instead of Geronimo, how about you / fill this exhibit hall with miniature bows / and blunted arrows? They'll sell for copper / coins before sundown."[61] Here, the nonchalant attitude of the young female fairgoer is challenged as the lyric speaker asks her to take the place of Geronimo, as a figure required to perform indigeneity. Igloria's sonnet sequence focuses on indigenous alignments, where both the Igorots and Geronimo function as objects of display and consumption. Within the sonnet, Geronimo's inclusion serves to reframe the Filipinos exhibited at the fair from the perspective of comparative indigeneity, where savagery could be observed in multiple sites and contexts. While Geronimo had the chance to observe the Igorots, almost as a fairgoer himself, historical accounts remind us that his appearance at the fair was not completely voluntary, and according to Anne Maxwell, he symbolized "a spectacle of defeated warriorhood."[62] In this respect, Igloria's sonnet sequence serves not to silence Geronimo's specific experiences, but to reveal the collective racial ideology that posited the unheralded domination of American Empire over indigenous peoples, both American Indian and Filipino Igorot, through their status as living exhibits.

Ars Cosmopoetica

Locating the material contexts that bring the Filipino American lyric speaker into conversation with other histories, geographies, and subjectivities is central to the project of *Juan Luna's Revolver*, offering what literary critic Sunn Shelley Wong would call "particular situated knowledges (knowledges that know something from somewhere and that are sometimes congruent, sometimes conflictual, and always partial)."[63] Consequently, the collection demonstrates how the politics of performance and spectacle underlying Buffalo Bill's Wild

West shows and the 1904 Louisiana Purchase Exposition, as routed into lyric, actuate a multifocal trajectory for situating American Indians and Filipinos as racial subjects comparatively configured under the imperial gaze. If cosmopoetics offers the lyric poet the artistic creativity to move through time and space, across nations and oceans, it is in the service of the kind of mobility and fluidity not offered to the many indigenous subjects that appear as central figures in these poems. Critiquing such cultural productions also dramatizes the need for continuing studies that situate Filipinos and American Indians under the rubric of comparative indigeneity.

Notes

I would like to thank Jeanne Sokolowski, Jean Kim, Gina Valentino, Haerin Shin, Samantha Tieu, Long Le-Khac, the special issue editors, and the *American Quarterly* editorial board for reading drafts of this article. A special acknowledgment must be made to Luisa A. Igloria, who read this piece in its entirety and who granted permissions to republish poetic excerpts from *Juan Luna's Revolver.*

1. Luisa Igloria, *Juan Luna's Revolver* (Notre Dame, Ind.: University of Notre Dame Press, 2008).
2. Barbara Jane Reyes makes extensive connections to American Indian and Filipino indigenous groups in her collection *Poeta en San Francisco.* For more limited examples, see the poem "Plan B," from Eric Gamalinda's *Amigo Warfare,* and "The Discovery of Skin," in *The Gods We Worship Live Next Door.* Barbara Jane Reyes, *Poeta en San Francisco* (Kaneohe, Hi.: Tinfish, 2006); Eric Gamalinda, *Amigo Warfare* (Cincinnati: Cherry Grove Collections, 2007); Bino Realuyo, *The Gods We Worship Live Next Door* (Salt Lake City: University of Utah Press, 2006).
3. Shu-mei Shih, "Comparative Racialization: An Introduction," *PMLA* 123.5 (October 2008): 1351.
4. Colleen Lye, "The Afro-Asian Analogy," *PMLA* 123.5 (October 2008): 1732–36.
5. See Daniel Y. Kim, "Do I, Too, Sing America? Vernacular Representations and Chang-rae Lee's *Native Speaker,*" *Journal of Asian American Studies* 6.3 (2003): 231–60; Bill V. Mullen, "Du Bois, *Dark Princess,* and the Afro-Asian International," *Positions: East Asia Cultures Critique* 11.1 (2003): 217–39; Daryl J. Maeda, "Black Panthers, Red Guards, and Chinamen: Constructing Asian American Identity through Performing Blackness," *American Quarterly* 57.4 (2005): 1079–103; Helen H. Jun, "Black Orientalism: Nineteenth-Century Narratives of Race and U.S. Citizenship," *American Quarterly* 58.4 (2006): 1047–66.
6. Xiaojing Zhou, *The Ethics and Poetics of Alterity in Asian American Poetry* (Iowa City: University of Iowa Press, 2006), 19.
7. James Clifford, "Indigenous Articulations," *Contemporary Pacific* 13.2 (2001): 468–90, esp. 472.
8. Nicolas Zafra, *José Rizal: Historical Studies* (Quezon City: University of the Philippines Press, 1977), 167.
9. The concept of "mimicry" has been the subject of much postcolonial theorization, the most prominent of which might be from Homi Bhabha's *The Location of Culture* (New York: Routledge, 2004).
10. Igloria, *Revolver,* 22.
11. Ibid.
12. Ibid.
13. Ibid., 22–23.
14. Ibid., 22.
15. See Sharon Delmendo, *The Star-Entangled Banner: One Hundred Years of America in the Philippines* (New Brunswick, N.J.: Rutgers University Press, 2004); León Ma Guerrero, *The First Filipino: A Biography of José Rizal* (Manila: National Historical Institute, 2006), 120.

16. See Rafael, "Nationalism, Imagery, and the Filipino Intelligentsia in the Nineteenth Century," *Critical Inquiry* 16.3 (1990): 591–611, esp. 605–6; E. San Juan Jr., *Balikbayang Sinta: An E. San Juan Reader* (Quezon City: Ateneo De Manila University Press, 2008); Antonio de Morga, "Sucesos de las Islas Filipinas," in *The Philippine Islands, 1493–1803*, vol. 15, ed. Emma Helen Blair, James Alexander Robertson, and Edward Gaylord Bourne, 25–288 (Cleveland: Arthur H. Clark, 1904); Austin Coates, *Rizal: Philippine Nationalist and Martyr* (New York: Oxford University Press, 1968), 175; Gregorio F. Zaide, *José Rizal, Asia's First Apostle of Nationalism* (Manila: Red Star Book Store, 1970), 169, 172,173; Disdado G. Capino, Ma. Minerva A. Gonzalez, and Filipinas E. Pineda, *Rizal's Life, Works, and Writings: Their Impact on Our National Identity* (Quezon City, Philippines: JMC Press, 1977), 33, 112; Laura Wexler, *Tender Violence: Domestic Visions in an Age of U.S. Imperialism* (Chapel Hill, N.C.: University of North Carolina Press, 2000), 45; Paul A. Rodell, *Culture and Customs of the Philippines* (Westport, Conn.: Greenwood, 2001), 13.
17. Rafael, "Nationalism," 606.
18. San Juan Jr., *Balikbayang Sinta*, 59.
19. Rafael, "Nationalism, Imagery," 606.
20. Igloria, *Revolver*, 24.
21. Delmendo, *Star-Entangled Banner*, 17.
22. Igloria, *Revolver*, 31.
23. Ibid., 32.
24. See Bobby Bridger, *Buffalo Bill and Sitting Bull: Inventing the Wild West* (Austin: University of Texas Press, 2002), 12; Robert A. Carter, *Buffalo Bill Cody: The Man Behind the Legend* (New York: Wiley, 2000), 282; and Joseph Manzione, *"I am looking to the North for my life"—Sitting Bull, 1876–1881* (Salt Lake City: University of Utah Press, 1991).
25. L. G. Moses, *Wild West Shows and the Images of American Indians, 1883–1933* (Albuquerque: University of New Mexico Press, 1996), 27. Numerous accounts of Sitting Bull's participation in the Wild West shows have been written; I list a partial bibliography here: Elizabeth S. Bird, *Dressing in Feathers: The Construction of the Indian in American Popular Culture* (Boulder, Colo.: Westview, 1996), 41; R. L. Wilson and Greg Martin, *Buffalo Bill's Wild West: An American Legend* (New York: Random House, 1998), 60–61; Joy S. Kasson, *Buffalo Bill's Wild West: Celebrity, Memory, and Popular History* (New York: Hill and Wang, 2001), 171–73; Sam A. Maddra, *Hostiles? The Lakota Ghost Dance and Buffalo Bill's Wild West* (Norman, O.K.: University of Oklahoma Press, 2006); Sandra Sagala, *Buffalo Bill on Stage* (Albuquerque: University of New Mexico Press, 2008), 172. See also Ryan Burt's article in this issue, "'Sioux Yells' in the Dawes Era: Lakota 'Indian Play,' the Wild West, and the Literatures of Luther Standing Bear."
26. Sarah J. Blackstone, *Buckskins, Bullets, and Business: A History of Buffalo Bill's Wild West* (New York: Greenwood, 1986), 87; and Adam Lebowitz, "Myth in *Black Elk Speaks* and *Aterui*: The Empowering Matrix," *Comparative Literature Studies* 37.2 (2000): 87–100, esp. 89.
27. John Gneisenau Neihardt, *The Sixth Grandfather: Black Elk's Teachings Given to John G. Neihardt*, trans. Raymond J. DeMallie (Lincoln: University of Nebraska Press, 1984), 6. See also Joseph G. Rosa and Robin May, *Buffalo Bill and His Wild West* (Lawrence: University Press of Kansas, 1989), 144; Hilda Martinsen Neihardt, *Black Elk and Flaming Rainbow: Personal Memories of the Lakota Holy Man and John Neihardt* (Lincoln: University of Nebraska Press, 1999), 73; Kasson, *Buffalo Bill's Wild West*, 189; Alan Gallop, *Buffalo Bill's British Wild West* (Stroud, U.K.: Sutton, 2001), 101–2, 112–13, 155; Bridger, *Buffalo Bill and Sitting Bull*, 353; Louis S. Warren, *Buffalo Bill's America: William Cody and the Wild West Show* (New York: Alfred A. Knopf, 2005), 360; Maddra, *Lakota Ghost Dance*, 94, 156. Two of the most prominent fictional reconstructions of Black Elk's experiences in Europe include James Welch, *The Heartsong of Charging Elk* (New York: Doubleday, 2000); and Kate Horsley, *Black Elk in Paris* (Boston: Trumpeter, 2006). Black Elk's experience is most prominently depicted in the controversial text *Black Elk Speaks*, which recounts his meeting with Queen Victoria, an event Igloria references in her poem.
28. See also Daniel Francis, *The Imaginary Indian: The Image of the Indian in Canadian Culture* (Vancouver: Arsenal Pulp, 1992), 95; Ray Broadus Browne and Pat Browne, eds., *The Guide to United States Popular Culture* (Bowling Green, O.H.: Bowling Green State University Press, 2001), 911; Robert W. Rydell, *Buffalo Bill in Bologna: The Americanization of the World, 1869–1922* (Chicago: University of Chicago Press, 2005), 30; Dee Brown, *Bury My Heart at Wounded Knee: An Indian History of the*

American West (New York: Macmillan, 2007). Igloria's poem also references Geronimo and Chief Joseph. According to Stephen McVeigh, "At Theodore Roosevelt's 1905 inauguration celebration, the star attraction, other than the President himself, was Geronimo." Stephen McVeigh, *The American Western* (Edinburgh, U.K.: Edinburgh University Press, 2007), 27. In relation to Chief Joseph, see Kent Nerburn, *Chief Joseph and the Flight of the Nez Perce: The Untold Story of an American Tragedy* (New York: HarperCollins, 2005), 390.

29. Rosemarie Bank, "Representing History: Performing the Columbian Exposition," *Theatre Journal* 54.4 (2002): 589–606, esp. 603.
30. Igloria, *Revolver*, 32.
31. Part of the danger attributed to the Ghost Dance by the United States Federal Government was that it was a pan-tribal movement, one that could potentially unite various groups together under the rubric of a revolutionary resistance.
32. William Henry Scott, *On the Cordillera: A Look at the Peoples and Cultures of the Mountain Province* (Manila: MCS Enterprises, 1969), 155.
33. Igloria, *Revolver*, 93.
34. William R. Everdell, *The First Moderns: Profiles in the Origins of Twentieth-Century Thought* (Chicago: University of Chicago Press, 1997), 216.
35. At the time that the Igorots were transported to the 1904 World's Fair and Exposition, there was some controversy as noted here: James A. Le Roy, *Philippine Life in Town and Country* (New York: Oriole Editions, 1973), 17.
36. Joel Slotkin, "Igorots and Indians: Racial Hierarchies and Conceptions of the Savage in Carlos Bulosan's Stories of the Philippines," *American Literature* 72.4 (2000): 843–66, esp. 846.
37. Igloria, *Revolver*, 91.
38. Ibid.
39. Ibid.; emphasis in the original.
40. Ibid., 93.
41. Ibid., 96.
42. Ibid. There are varying scholarly accounts of this global indigeneity. For example, see: Miya Elise Mizuta, "'Fair Japan': On Art and War at the Saint Louis World's Fair, 1904," *Discourse* 27.1 (2006): 28–52, esp. 38.
43. Gerard A. Finin, *The Making of the Igorot: Ramut ti Panagkaykaysa dagiti taga Cordillera (Contours of Cordillera Consciousness)* (Quezon City, Philippines: Ateneo De Manila University Press, 2005), 25. See also Carol Ann Christ, "'The Sole Guardians of the Art Inheritance of Asia': Japan at the 1904 St. Louis World's Fair," *Positions: East Asia Cultures Critique* 8.3 (2000): 675–709, esp. 679–680.
44. Igloria, *Revolver*, 83.
45. Ibid., 85.
46. Ibid.
47. Ibid.
48. Ibid.
49. Ibid.
50. Ibid.
51. Richard Drinnon, *Facing West: The Metaphysics of Indian-Hating and Empire-Building* (Oklahoma City: University of Oklahoma Press, 1997), 341.
52. Nancy J. Parezo and Don D. Fowler, *Anthropology Goes to the Fair: The 1904 Louisiana Purchase Exposition* (Lincoln: University of Nebraska Press, 2007), 115. Geronimo's presence was not completely voluntary, as William Everdell explains in *The First Moderns*, 215. See also Angie Debo, *Geronimo: The Man, His Time, His Place* (Norman, O.K.: University of Oklahoma Press, 1989), 415; Alexander B. Adams, *Geronimo: A Biography* (New York: G. P. Putnam's Sons, 1971); and David Roberts, *World of Fairs: The Century-of-Progress Expositions* (Chicago: University of Chicago Press, 1993).
53. Frederick Turner's introduction to *Geronimo: His Own Story, as Told to S. M. Barrett* (New York: Plume, 1996), 38.
54. Ibid., 160, 162.
55. Ibid., 162.
56. Ibid., 160.
57. Ibid., 160.
58. Ibid., 160.

59. Ibid., 160, 162.
60. Ibid., 135.
61. Igloria, *Revolver*, 86.
62. Anne Maxwell, *Colonial Photography and Exhibitions: Representations of the Native and the Making of European Identities* (London: Leicester University Press, 2000), 123.
63. Shelly Sunn Wong and Cristanne Miller, "Unnaming the Same: Theresa Hak Kyung Cha's DICTEE," in *Feminist Measures: Soundings in Poetry and Theory*, ed. Lynn Keller, 43–68 (Ann Arbor: University of Michigan Press, 1995), esp. 63.

Decolonization in Unexpected Places: Native Evangelicalism and the Rearticulation of Mission

Andrea Smith

> Decolonization is the intelligent, calculated, and active resistance to the forces of colonialism that perpetuate the subjugation and/or exploitation of your minds, bodies, and lands, and it is engaged for the ultimate purpose of overturning the colonial structure and realizing Indigenous liberation . . . But make no mistake: Decolonization ultimately requires the overturning of the colonial structure. It is not about tweaking the existing colonial system to make it more Indigenous-friendly or a little less oppressive. The existing system is fundamentally and irreparably flawed.

> Colonization is violence and violation of the most extreme sort. Colonization is theft and rape and murder and cannibalism on the grandest scale. Colonization is genocide. We should understand that there are indeed people with a heart for decolonization in the churches, in business, even in the military as well as in schools, colleges and seminaries, even if . . . the systems themselves are . . . malignant, delivered over to the enemy as tools or weapons of colonization. Even so, it is not for us to somehow share power with the colonizers.

In Native studies, many scholars propose "decolonization" as a guiding principle for Native scholarship and activism. In this first quote (above) from *For Indigenous Eyes Only: A Decolonization Handbook*, Waziyatawin Angela Wilson and Michael Yellow Bird outline their understanding of decolonization.[1] They call on community members and scholars to go beyond a politics of inclusion to build a world in which Native peoples are not governed by a settler colonial state. They further call on Native peoples to deconstruct the manner in which their own political and social imaginaries are shaped by the processes of colonization. Many other scholars similarly argue that Native communities live in a colonial relationship with the United States government, and hence the fundamental challenge these communities face is to dismantle this relationship. The call for decolonization is extended to the academy as well—we must "indigenize the academy"[2] and "decolonize methodologies."[3]

This work generally presumes a non-Christian framework for decolonization, because the imposition of Christianity within Native communities is understood as part of the colonial process. But interestingly, some Native evangelicals are reading the same works cited above and are also applying decolonization as a guiding principle for biblical faith. At the 2007 Native American Institute of Indigenous Theological Studies (NAIITS) conference, Robert Francis, author of the second quote above, gave a keynote address centering on the need for decolonization. According to Francis, colonization can be defined as "what happens when one people invades the territory of another people, appropriating the territory as their own, asserting control over and actually or essentially destroying the original inhabitants through outright murder, hegemonic subjugation, enslavement, removal, or absorption into the society and culture of the colonizers."[4] Ironically, it is the shared history of missionization that Native peoples have endured with indigenous and third-world communities globally that has inspired a politics of global anticolonial solidarity as well as a politics of decolonization with regard to U.S. and Canadian settler states.

This article will focus on one "unexpected place" for indigenous decolonization—Native evangelical leaders and organizations that circulate through NAIITS. Philip Deloria notes in *Indians in Unexpected Places* that part of the legacy of colonialism is to mark the presence of indigenous peoples within contemporary society as inherently anomalous,[5] because, as Anne McClintock argues, Native peoples exist in a supposedly anachronistic space, anterior to post/modernity.[6] Consequently, according to Deloria, "expectations" exist in terms of "the colonial and imperial relations of power and domination existing between Indian people and the United States"[7] whereby Native peoples are simply not supposed to exist in any meaningful way within U.S. society, because the United States' colonial imaginary depends on their perpetual absence. In looking at Native evangelicals in particular, we are left with a double anomaly. First, Native peoples, marked as "primitive," are not supposed to be Christian without becoming less Native. Second, Native evangelicals, because they are deemed less Native by virtue of supporting colonization, cannot have an interest in decolonization. In taking up Deloria's analysis, I am focused less on his project of articulating Native peoples within the context of modernity (although we can certainly understand Christian mission as an aspect of modernity). Rather, "expectation" within the context of colonialism always places Native peoples within an anterior relationship to humanity itself such that they can exist only as ethnographic objects, assimilated by discourses presumed to be owned by those in the dominant culture rather than as actual producers, shapers, and theorizers of those discourses.

Of course, there are many works that focus on how Native peoples have articulated visions of self-determination through the language of Christianity. Liberation theology has also rearticulated Christianity to support social justice struggles (although indigenous Christians have frequently been marginalized within that discourse). However, Christian *evangelicalism* in particular, has generally articulated itself as hostile to the interests of liberation theology and largely served as an apologist for colonialism and capitalism rather than as its critic. Building on Deloria's work, this article is another "secret history of the unexpected"[8]—a project that indicates "the complex lineaments of personal and cultural identity that can never be captured by dichotomies built around crude notions of difference and assimilation, white and Indian, primitive and advanced."[9]

NAIITS was launched to provide masters and doctoral graduate degrees for Native leaders in the area of contextualized evangelical missions. This perspective critiques standard missiological approaches that have presumed that indigenous peoples must reject all indigenous cultural and spiritual practices in order to become Christian, because indigenous practices are presumed to be "pagan" or demonic. Some examples of this standard approach can be reflected in the work of mega-church pastor Dick Bernal, who argues in *American Spirituality Mapped* that Native cultural practices are "a clever scheme of Satan to seduce the naïve."[10] NAIITS intervenes in this colonialist discourse by positioning Christianity as generally harmonious with indigenous culture rather than as its radical opposition. In addition, NAIITS creates forums for dialogue and engagement with other emerging indigenous theological streams, including the varieties that are emerging in Native North America. NAIITS has developed partnerships with Asbury Theological Seminary in Wilmore, Kentucky, as well as several denominational and nondenominational organizations, colleges, and seminaries.[11] In her genealogy of NAIITS, Jeanine LeBlanc situates it within the larger call in Native studies to decolonize/indigenize the academy. Citing the work of Taiaiake Alfred, she argues for the importance of the academy fundamentally changing its structures and policies in light of the colonial realities faced by Native peoples. She further notes that NAIITS positions itself in dialogue with indigenous peoples within a larger global context of those who are similarly interested in academic decolonization.[12] Several organizations are affiliated with NAIITS, such as Wiconi International and Eagles' Wings Ministries. The conferences sponsored by NAIITS bring together Native peoples in the United States into conversation with Native peoples globally as well as Christians from the third world. This global framework in turn has inspired a varied discourse on decolonization and how it might impact Native evangelicals in particular and Native communities in general.

This article emerges from (1) ethnographic participation in NAIITS events, (2) interviews with key members and participants, and (3) a survey of materials produced by NAIITS members. To work against the ethnographic entrapment of Native peoples within the academy, where Native peoples are *expected* to be studied but are not expected to theorize on their own behalf, I employ the methodology of "intellectual ethnography" and focus on the analysis proffered by Native evangelicals. In my research, I seek to avoid the colonial "ethnographic imperative" that would strive to make Native communities more knowable to non-Natives. Rather, I seek to identify resistance strategies within Native communities that will be helpful in promoting Native sovereignty struggles in particular and social justice in general. In addition, rather than render Native people as objects of my study, I wish to position them as subjects of intellectual discourse. Rather than study Native people so that we can know more about them, I wish to illustrate what it is that Native theorists have to tell us about the world we live in and how to change it. The point of an intellectual ethnography then is not primarily to make broad claims about the communities that are its focus; rather, the intention is to investigate the possibilities and pitfalls of fostering resistance struggles in Native evangelical communities.[13] Consequently, I cite their analysis at length so that their ideas can be more fully understood. Quotations that are not cited in this article are from the interviews I conducted with NAIITS members.

Missionization, Globalization, and Decolonization

As I have discussed in previous work, Native peoples have become more visible within white-dominated evangelical circles through their participation in the "race reconciliation" movement within conservative evangelicalism.[14] This movement began in the early 1990s with the goal of fostering racial unity among evangelical Christians. The purpose of race reconciliation, as advocate Tony Evans puts it, is to "establish a church where everyone of any race or status who walks through the door is loved and respected as part of God's creation and family."[15] One of the rationales for fostering race reconciliation is to involve people of color in general and Native peoples in particular in Christian missionization programs.[16] For instance, Native evangelical Craig Smith suggests that Native peoples in the United States and Canada need to be incorporated into Christianity in order to facilitate the missionization of indigenous peoples in other parts of the world. Native peoples, he contends, more easily evade the "imperialist American" label and thus more successfully convert other indigenous peoples.[17] Ironically, however, the inclusion of Native peoples within missionization programs also has the consequence of bringing Native peoples into conversation with other colonized peoples and vice versa. At the NAIITS conferences, these conversations between Native peoples in North America and indigenous peoples globally, as well as peoples from the third world, have promoted cross-national dialogues on the impact of colonization and on strategies for decolonization.

An example can be found in the keynote address from the 2007 NAIITS conference, held in Sioux Falls, South Dakota, by Charles Amjad-Ali (Lutheran seminary professor and presbyter of the Church of Pakistan). Amjad-Ali likened colonialism in South Asia to the forms of colonialism experienced by Native Americans, and explained that the survival of Native Americans is an inspiration to all colonized peoples. "Truly in all humility and awe I say that in that sense you have been our salvation. Because of what happened to you, not only have we survived, but we have learned how to survive under the current global hegemony."[18] He then critiqued the United States' claim to be a multicultural nation: "America has made claims of multiculturalism and plurality of identities for a long time . . . In this metaphoric melting pot, the Native Americans, whose land was stolen, were never to be incorporated, nor were African Americans whose labor was stolen, ever to be a part of it."[19] He unapologetically criticized the complicity of Christendom in genocide and slavery, which has "allowed the whites to go on pretending that no wrong was committed in the theft of the land and even of labor since this was the way God had planned the matter . . . If people were killed, maimed, decimated, oppressed, dislocated, etc., this was part of the predestined reality and not because some wrongs were committed . . .We forget that the cross was an instrument of torture, murder, and political oppression." He then concluded that all Christians have a biblical mandate to oppose and organize against imperialism.[20]

At the 2004 NAIITS conference, Tite Tiénou (professor at Trinity Evangelical Divinity School and formerly dean of the Faculté de Théologie Evangélique de l'Alliance in Abidjan, Côte d'Ivoire, West Africa) contended that the consequence of Christian mission is that Christianity is becoming "de-westernized."[21] Consequently, "Christians in Africa, Asia, and Latin America, indeed indigenous Christians everywhere, are able to defend themselves when accused of being agents of westernization and puppets in the hands of foreigners whose intention is the destruction of local cultures and religions."[22] However, while the church is becoming less Western, Tiénou argues that the theological and intellectual production of the church is still centered in the West.

> I contend that Christian theology and scholarship will remain "provincial" as long as some major challenges continue unaddressed [such as] the perception of indigenous Christian scholars as purveyors of exotic raw intellectual material . . . Indigenous theologians are . . . relegated to the museums of theological curiosity just like their cultures. We are then left with this: the West claiming to produce universal theology and the rest writing to articulate fundamental theology that will make [them] equal partners in the theological circles that determine what is theologically normative.[23]

In this regard, we can see Tiénou's words as a call to "decolonize methodology" within evangelicalism. NAIITS has similarly been involved in such calls, questioning the tendency within many evangelical churches to condemn all Native spiritual and cultural practices as heretical and pagan. States one Anita Keith, a staff person with NAIITS:

> So the traditional people, that's just another way that Creator is teaching us how to relate to Him—here is my story and here is how you can love me. You can smudge, you can Sundance, and in that process I will commune with you. And some people can do the Sundance without integrity and God will not meet them. And others can do it with a very pure heart and God will meet them there. Some people study the Bible without integrity, and slam people with it, and try to have other people live it out, and God will not meet them. But if they read the word with integrity, God will meet them there. So it's a form, it's a function, it's just another vehicle. Thinking the panorama of worshiping is absolutely wonderful, and to say that you're way is wrong—that's not good . . .
>
> I have no problem with moving from traditional way of worshiping, sweat, Sundance, or any of those ceremonies. There is no demonic in it, it's all about Creator, and us connecting to Him.

Thus ironically, while evangelicals have been missionizing the world's indigenous peoples, these peoples are simultaneously redefining what it means to be an evangelical.

Decolonizing Methodology

Despite the controversies and disagreements that exist within NAIITS, as will be discussed in the next sections, it is clear that NAIITS articulates "decolonization" not simply as theological or political content, but as a methodology for doing theological work. First, NAIITS has been in critical conversation with the emergent movement within evangelicalism. This reformist movement within evangelicalism employs methods of theological conversation rather than boundary setting. That is, rather than articulate a set of boundaries that defines who is and who is not an evangelical, the emergent movement, undergirded by postmodern thought, understands that while there may or may not be an inerrant scripture, there is certainly no inerrant reader of it. Consequently, while this movement may see a theological center around which to organize, its goal is not to exclude those who do not fit within the evangelical boundary, but to engage in theological conversations with all who are willing to engage. Brian McClaren, one of the leaders of this movement, headlined the 2009 NAIITS conference. He called on evangelicals to move from a position of certainty to one of comfort with not knowing all the answers in advance. Terry LeBlanc, one of the primary organizers of NAIITS, similarly states that one cannot have a true dialogue if one presumes an outcome before the conversation is started.

In that spirit, NAIITS conferences are primarily organized around conversations rather than lectures. A goal of NAIITS is to have everyone able to engage in discussion regardless of educational training or professional standing. In addition, those who speak at conferences or who write in the NAIITS journal are not identified by professional title. Adrian Jacobs explains how these approaches within NAIITS suggest an alternate model of both indigenous and church governance that echo some of the visions for indigenous nationhood found in the work of anarchist and feminist indigenous scholars and activists. Mohawk scholar Taiaiake Alfred contends that while the term *sovereignty* is popular among Native scholars/activists, it is an inappropriate term to describe the political/spiritual/cultural aspirations of Native peoples. He contends that sovereignty is premised on the ability to exercise power through the state by means of coercion and domination. Traditional forms of indigenous governance, by contrast, are based on different understandings of power.

> The Native concept of governance is based on . . . the "primacy of conscience." There is no central or coercive authority and decision-making is collective. Leaders rely on their persuasive abilities to achieve a consensus that respects the autonomy of individuals, each of whom is free to dissent from and remain unaffected by the collective decision . . . A crucial feature of the indigenous concept of governance is its respect for individual autonomy. This respect precludes the notion of "sovereignty"—the idea that there can be a permanent transference of power or authority from the individual to an abstraction of the collective called "government." . . . In the indigenous tradition, . . . there is no coercion, only the compelling force of conscience based on those inherited and collectively refined principles that structure the society.[24]

As long as indigenous peoples frame their struggles in terms of sovereignty, Alfred argues, they inevitably find themselves co-opted by the state—reproducing forms of governance based on oppressive, Western models. In addition, the concept of sovereignty continues to affirm the legitimacy of the state: "To frame the struggle to achieve justice in terms of indigenous 'claims' against the state is implicitly to accept the fiction of state sovereignty."[25] He generally juxtaposes nationhood and nationalism as terms preferable to sovereignty.

> Sovereignty is an exclusionary concept rooted in an adversarial and coercive Western notion of power.[26]
>
> It is with indigenous notions of power such as these that contemporary Native nationalism seeks to replace the dividing, alienating, and exploitative notions, based on fear, that drive politics inside and outside Native communities today.[27]

Similarly, Adrian Jacob argues that both churches and society at large can model themselves over the principles of consensus and egalitarianism that Alfred outlines. He concurs that Iroquois leaders "derived their power from the people."[28] He then contends that this model is one that can be informative to all Christians.

> I am suggesting that one of the greatest contributions that Iroquoian people can make toward reformation among Aboriginal people is assisting the return to the value of consensus decision-making and the inherent respect of that process. Abusive people find it very hard to work in an environment of open heartedness, respect, trust, and group sharing. Hierarchical systems maintain their structures through the careful control of information. Closed-door meetings and in-camera sessions abound in this system emphasizing privileged information. Dictators know the value of propaganda.[29]

As I discuss in other work, the principles articulated by Jacobs resonate with Native feminist calls to envision nationhood based on principles of horizontal authority, interconnectedness with a larger global world, and mutual respect and responsibility. This vision contrasts sharply with nation-state forms of governance that are based on principles of domination, violence, and social hierarchy.[30] It also echoes many of the calls made by indigenous activists in Latin America who argue against statist forms of governance in favor of non-hierarchical models of organizing. Thus, what may be even more important than the specific positions various NAIITS members take on the issue of decolonization is the ways in which they attempt to decolonize the process of theologizing itself.

Native Evangelicalism and Disidentification

José Esteban Muñoz offers a model for political engagement he terms disidentification. According to Muñoz, whereas assimilationism seems to identify with the dominant society, and whereas counteridentification seeks to reject it completely, disidentification "is the third mode of dealing with dominant ideology, one that neither opts to assimilate within such a structure nor strictly opposes it; rather, disidentification is a strategy that works on and against dominant ideology."[31] Muñoz explains that disidentification neither fully accepts nor rejects dominant cultural logics, but internally subverts them, using the logic against itself. Muñoz clarifies that disidentification is not a middle ground between assimilationist and contestatory politics; rather, it is a strategy that recognizes the shifting terrain of resistances.[32] Disidentification is a helpful analytic by which to assess the unexpected discourses of decolonization within Native evangelicalism because it challenges the dichotomy of positioning Native peoples as either complicit with or resistant to imperialism (which itself becomes another expectation for Native peoples—they are simple rather than complex and sometimes contradictory). Thus, the rest of this essay will focus on the complexity of evangelical decolonization, which, while not a politics of pure resistance, still includes significant kinds of opposition.

Evangelical Mission

Within the discursive economy of NAIITS, we can see a strategy of disidentification with evangelical missions whereby Christian missionization is simultaneously presumed and contested within a politics of decolonization. Robert Francis (Mid-American Indian Fellowships), began his 2007 NAIITS conference keynote address, centering on the need for decolonization, with an adaption of Mark 5:1–20:

> One day Jesus got into a fishing boat with his twelve disciples, and they all sailed out onto Lake Gennesaret, intending to picnic on the opposite shore. As they were about halfway across the lake, a sudden storm swept in. In keeping with his usual behavior during inclement weather, Jesus was fast asleep in the stern of the boat when a huge twister or whirlwind swept up the little craft, transporting the boat, along with all thirteen passengers through space and time to twenty-first-century North America. When the wind abated, Jesus and his disciples found themselves on dry land, somewhere in the midst of an Indian reservation. Jumping down from the boat, John and Peter looked around, shrugged their shoulders, and spread a cloth on the ground for the picnic. . .
>
> Just then an automobile came roaring down the paved road not far from where the group sat eating . . . The car slowed but did not stop, the passenger door flew open, and a woman, pushed by a hairy, masculine hand, tumbled out into the roadside ditch. She lay there for a moment, a seemingly lifeless heap of rags and flesh. Then leaping to her feet, the woman began to scream and cry in an alarming manner . . . The woman stood there, hesitating, a hideously twisted expression on her face, but her astonished silence did not last long. "Jesus! What are you doing here?" screamed a voice from within the woman. "You're the last person I'd expect to see here!" This statement was followed with maniacal laughter.

> Looking deeply into the woman's eyes, Jesus asked, "What is your name?"
> "My name?" asked the voice. "What is my name? My name is . . . Cavalry . . . Infantry . . . Military Mega-Complex. My name is Trading Company . . . Border-Town Liquor Store . . . Multinational Corporation. My name is Proselytizing Missionary . . . Religious Order . . . Denominational Mission Board. My name is White Man's School . . . Historical Misrepresentation . . . Hollywood Stereotype. We are many. We are organized. We are in control. Our intentions are always and only for the very best."
> "Get out of here," Jesus said. . . . "There remains no place for you in this land. There remains no place for you in any land. Get out! Get the Hell Out!"

In this parable, Robert Francis specifically names the many facets of colonization: capitalism, militarism, and racism. However, he situates the Christian church as a colonizing institution on par with the military. Consequently, he ends the parable with a call to divest not only from the settler state, but from the Christian church as well.

> With one last shriek, the evil spirits left the woman. The disciples and Jesus took her to a nearby house . . . This was the home of the woman's aunt, who began calling people on her phone . . . Finally, Jesus stood up and said, "I appreciate your hospitality, but we have to be going now if we're to catch the next twister back to Galilee."
> The woman who had been healed also stood. "Jesus," she said, "may I go with you? I want to become a Christian."
> With a weary smile and a shake of his head, Jesus replied, "No child; this is not my intent for you. Stay here, with your own people, and tell them what Creator has done."[33]

This last paragraph seems to suggest that for Native peoples to follow Jesus, they can best do so, not by becoming Christian, but by following their traditional ways. This implication was corroborated further by Francis's analysis of religion as a tool of colonization. Here, he echoes Vine Deloria's critique of Christianity, claiming that any religion that is based on exclusivist notions of salvation necessarily becomes a religion tied to conquest and empire. "When a people develops the idea that they have exclusive possession of communication from God and exclusive control of the means of salvation, all peoples of earth stand in peril."[34] He then went on to denounce "the combination of public school, Sunday school, and Vacation Bible School" as tools of colonialism, "especially when followed up with Bible College and seminary."[35]

Francis then calls for a project of decolonization—of total divestment from all colonial structures, including churches. If one must engage these colonial institutions, one should do so as a warrior going to battle, but one should never become invested in them.

> Even so, it is not for us to somehow share power with the colonizers. Can you imagine Jesus saying this to his disciples? "Here's good news: I had a positive meeting with Lucifer in the wilderness. He shed light on several issues. Afterward, the two of us met with Caesar, Pilate, Herod, and Caiaphas. They are expressing a willingness to share some of their power with us. All we have to do is, ahem, submit to their superior authority. What do you say, guys? 'If you can't beat 'em, join 'em!' Right?"
>
> If we are called into church, into the economic system, into the military, into school, college, or seminary, it is proper that we go in the way of a warrior entering the camp of the enemy, knowing the dangers that are there, knowing that we risk captivity and death at the hands of cannibals, knowing that at the very least we will sustain grievous wounds, the scars of which we will bear all our lives.
>
> Jesus entered the seat of the colonizing power. He rode into Jerusalem. He stormed into the temple. He walked into the governor's own mansion and out of the city to the place of the skull. He will forever bear the scars. That is what Jesus did, and as surely as we choose to call ourselves Jesus' followers, we may do no less. We must live our lives and give our lives for the purpose of decolonization, that the People may live.[36]

Francis seems to suggest that evangelicals may even need to leave the church to follow a truly decolonized Christianity. Ironically, Native peoples can follow Jesus more effectively by NOT becoming Christian.

Others also argue for decolonization while not calling for a complete abandonment of Christianity. The Vacation Bible School (VBS) curriculum of My People International (a collaborating organization with NAIITS that recently merged with it) addresses one of the tensions Native evangelicals address: "For many Native people nothing good came of colonization. For others, only one good thing came—the news about God's son Jesus which came to us with the Bible . . . We realized we are part of this plan of God from the beginning as all people everywhere."[37] Native evangelicals address the entanglement of colonization and Christianization in a number of complex ways. In the VBS curriculum, we see an interesting departure from Robert Warrior's famous critique of the Exodus narrative in "Canaanites, Cowboys, and Indians." In this essay, Warrior argues that the Bible is not a liberatory text for Native peoples, especially considering the fact that the liberation motif commonly adopted by liberation theologians—the Exodus—is premised on the genocide of the indigenous people occupying the Promised Land—the Canaanites. Warrior does not argue for the historical veracity of the conquest of the Canaanites. Rather, the Exodus operates as a *narrative* of conquest—a narrative that was foundational to the European conquest of the Americas. Warrior's essay points not only to the problems with the Exodus motif, but also to liberation theology's conceptualization of a God of deliverance. He contends that "as long as people believe in the Yahweh of deliverance, the world will not be safe from the

Yahweh the conqueror."[38] That is, by conceptualizing ourselves as oppressed peoples who are to be delivered at all costs, we necessarily become complicit in oppressing those who stand in the way of our deliverance. Instead, Warrior argues, we need to reconceptualize ourselves as "a society of people delivered from oppression who are not so afraid of becoming victims again that they become oppressors themselves."[39]

The VBS curriculum, by contrast, seems to demonstrate a shift in narrative sympathy. At first, this curriculum similarly likens Native peoples to the Canaanites about to be destroyed at Jericho. "Native North Americans, like many others, have been victims of war that came with colonization . . . Like the people in the city of Jericho, our defenses were destroyed, our villages stripped and torn down . . . This colonization of North and South America is an example of ungodly, selfish, and sinful patterns of people."[40] However, the narrative sympathy then switches to the Israelites who destroy Jericho because "Joshua had to fight with these people to take control of the land as God has asked."[41] At this point, the curriculum does not critique the conquest of the Canaanites who had previously been likened to Native peoples because "the people of Israel trusted in God. That is why they received the new land and the city."[42]

The curriculum resolves this tension by now likening Native peoples to Rahab. Rahab is described as a Canaanite/"indigenous" believer who recognizes that God is on the side of the Israelites, sides with them, and hence earns God's protection. "As we trust in God he will take care of us, just like God took care of Rahab."[43] The Native student is asked to ponder the following question: "Would you be found in Rahab's house willing to get to know and to follow the God of the Bible or would you be found within the walls of the city of Jericho where the people chose not to believe in the power of God?"[44] So it is implied that the godly response of Native peoples to colonization was to have sided with Christian colonizers against Native communities.

Ironically, the text then points to four Black Seminole fighters who sided with the U.S. army and won a Medal of Honor, only to find that their people would be relocated west of the Mississippi. This text intervenes in anti-Black racism in Native communities by pointing to the joint histories of Native and African Americans. But it also demonstrates that when Native peoples assume the role of Rahab, they are in fact not protected from their colonizers by God. By contrast, the *NAIITS Journal* published an article by Jonathan Dyck and Cornelius Buller that calls into question the notion of a promised land, which they contend "is always also a vigorous ideological assertion of entitlement without regard for other inhabitants. Land may be given by promise but it is taken by violence."[45]

Adrian Jacobs, a NAIITS speaker, similarly addresses this theme. He argues that God uses nations to judge other nations. So, he suggests that colonization may have been a judgment against Native nations. For instance, he considers the possibility that the colonization of the Iroquois may be a judgment for their role in the destruction of the Huron. He also postulates that the destruction of the Aztec was a judgment against its human sacrifices.[46] He does not think all Native nations are equally "guilty," but that Native nations that were less sinful may have escaped the harsher forms of genocide. However, Jacobs does not place colonizers on the side of God. Rather, he contends that they too may face the same judgment. He evokes Saul's broken treaty with the Gibeonites in the Bible to say "God really does care about broken treaties and will bring judgment eventually."[47] He suggests that the billion-dollar damage to Hydro Quebec during an ice storm in January 1998 was perhaps a consequence of its destroying Cree lands by constructing a dam that flooded their territory. Jacobs states that he is not a prophet and thus cannot "declare the state of affairs in North America to be His judgment on broken treaties," but concludes that "when there is a recounting concerning broken treaties, I do not want to be on the side of the violators."[48]

Another approach to addressing these tensions is found in a leaflet for a "Memorial Prayer for Reconciliation" developed by the Healing for the Native Ministry handed out at one of the NAIITS events. It says in part:

For the policy of genocide and for the ongoing unjust policies of the United States government, we ask your forgiveness . . .

> For the destruction of the Native family structure through the demoralization of Native American men, for placing your children in foster homes and boarding schools, and for the subservient positions forced on your women, we ask for your forgiveness.
>
> For over three-hundred broken treaties, for the myth of "Manifest Destiny," and for the notion that Native people stood in the way of progress, we ask your forgiveness.
>
> For the sins of the church, for withholding the true gospel, for misrepresenting Jesus Christ, and for using religion in an attempt to "civilize the Natives," we ask your forgiveness . . .
>
> We ask for . . .
>
> Forgiveness for taking your land at gunpoint and for forcing you on to barren reservations . . .
>
> Forgiveness for the policy of our government of genocide toward the Native Americans . . .
>
> Forgiveness for the broken treaties . . .
>
> Forgiveness for the ongoing policies of the government . . .

> Forgiveness for misrepresenting the gospel to our Native American forefathers. When your fathers asked us for truth we gave them white man's religions. When your fathers asked for God we withheld the true gospel of Jesus Christ.

This prayer seems to suggest that the Christianity that came with colonization is not "true" Christianity. While colonization is responsible for a false and imperialist Christianity, colonization is also the necessary precondition for Native peoples to have a relationship with Jesus in the first place. Consequently, Native evangelicals disidentify with the Christian mission—they cannot reject it completely, but they reject the version of Christianity that emerges from it. Jesus and the Bible become disarticulated from Christianization and colonization.

Decolonization and Its Unintended Consequences

If the relationship between Native evangelicalism and decolonization is one of disidentification, then the social and political ramifications of this work will also not follow set expectations. As the work of Native feminist scholar Jennifer Denetdale makes clear, one cannot always anticipate the kinds of politics that will emerge from decolonization projects. In her critique of anti-Black racism, homophobia, and U.S. patriotism within Native communities, Denetdale argues that Native communities often support colonialist and imperialist ideologies under the names of tradition and decolonization.[49] She calls for a continued interrogation of these terms and the politics mobilized under them.

Similarly, evangelicals were split when Gene Robinson was elected as bishop of the Episcopal Diocese of New Hampshire in 2003. He was the first openly gay person to be ordained as a bishop in a major Christian denomination. Many of the churches that most vociferously opposed his ordination were churches in the third world who articulated their stance against homosexuality as a stance against colonization from the Western church. Some of the most outspoken critics have been Peter Jasper Akinola from Nigeria, Henry Luke Orombi from Uganda, Gregory Venables of the Southern Cone representing South American countries, Drexel Gomez in the West Indies, Emmanuel Kolini in Rwanda, and Datuk Yong Ping Chung representing Southeast Asia. According to Akinola: "The church that we inherited was a church that was vastly dependent on Western aid and what we now call handouts . . . No more."[50] Now, many of the conservative Episcopalian congregations are seeking to have their oversight transferred to these bishops in the third world. Several U.S. ministers were ordained by ministers in Uganda, Rwanda, and Nigeria.[51] According to Martyn Minns of Virginia Truro church: "In a real sense we are learning what it means to be a global community, learning from folks we've been thinking need our church. What God is doing is getting our attention and moving us out of our narrow parochialism and cultural ghetto."[52] Conservative Christian *World* magazine argued that to support homosexuality is to support "white theology" against "Third World" theology.[53] Meanwhile some of the more liberal church members have articulated what Jasbir Puar calls a "homonationalism,"[54] tying gay rights to U.S. exceptionalism. "Here we have the faith of the Founding Fathers, the religion that is the purest representation of old-line American power and money, tearing itself apart before our very eyes."[55]

Within NAIITS, on the one hand, the embrace of Native traditionalism, in combination with the fact that many members seem to be involved in charismatic churches that are often more supportive of women's ordination than noncharismatic evangelical/fundamentalist denominations, appears to contribute to an overall support for gender equality. On the other hand, however, some participants support male headship (the position that men should be the spiritual and decision-making head of the household and/or that only men should be pastors of the church). States one participant:

> I don't want to use the word submissive, but I think that as a husband and wife they are working together, but ultimately, it comes to him to make the decision. If you are behind the husband and saying, I believe you and I believe that you will make the right decision for our family, the best decision, then I think it takes some weight off his shoulders and makes him stand up as a man, to do what's best. I really think that's where God's Scripture comes in. There's so much about humbling ourselves and unique to him and I think, what if men had that in their head, they are submitting to Christ and living up as he did for others. When people hear about wives submit to their husbands, that's a hard one for people because they have all this other stuff they are thinking about—not what Christ is like. So if we had our minds on what Christ is like and that's what husbands should be, I think it's really comforting and that you know there is a man that is going to protect you and that he is going to be there for you.

But most seem to call for women's equality in the home and church—linking their thinking to both precolonial gender roles in Native communities and their understanding of Scripture.

As Cheryl Bear, NAIITS board member, explains,

> And way back, originally, women and men had much more of a partnership with our people historically, and so I think that part of the colonization effect is that women have been subjected to the same things that they have in Western culture, and our Native women

> have been oppressed in our situation and sort of rules popped that women are not equal or welcome in certain places or whatever, and I don't think it was historically so. In some instances, I was told by some elders that women were treated better and where I am from it's a matrilineal society, so women tend to have a bit more of a voice in the tribe. We don't have anything like [male headship] in the marriage.

Most participants however, do contend that homosexuality was a sin, even as they are careful to argue that it should not be elevated as a sin above other sins:

> Ray Aldred: Inevitably, evangelicals tend to reduce morality to abortion and gay marriage, but there are all these other moral issues they say nothing about, like unemployment.
>
> David Bird: Homosexuality, we always try to be very respectful of the person who has that lifestyle. I know there is some debate about how homosexual lifestyle begins. Even in Native traditions, these individuals like this would rise up every now and then, and they were considered people who walked in two worlds. So they were treated with a lot of respect and treated with a lot of hesitancy. I believe the Bible defines homosexuality as sin. But it also defines murder as sin. But we don't shun murderers as much as we would to a homosexual, which is just so not right.

There were some exceptions to this rule, however. One participant argues:

> There is a verse that pretty bluntly states that homosexuality is wrong. For most fundamentalists, this is very wrong, but for my people, we call it "half man half woman." They can see a male and female side. They are blessings to our people; they are our medicine people.
>
> The problem is, Christianity has influenced our people in a fundamentalist way that this is very wrong. There is an elder woman who pouring her heart out on how hard it is her for her to accept that her son is gay. She bluntly told me that she knows that he'll burn in hell but while she is here with him she wants to love him and know him. So she can't turn her back. I'm like, what motivates you to form this conclusion about your son? Obviously you're not following traditional ways. This is a woman who is full-blood and fluent speaking, raised at the ceremonial ground. But her grandmother said you have to pick, the ground or the church, and she chose the church, but her sister chose the ground. And I just feel for her so much. She's been lied to, people took Scripture and they manipulated it to socially control the people how they felt was appropriate, and now it's created domestic problems. And this will affect his whole life psychologically. She couldn't accept him as a Muskogee, and he will never know his responsibility as a gay man in Muskogee society, because the only teaching he's been exposed to is Christianity. He doesn't even know that to be a gay person is a blessing.

In this case, traditional spirituality is employed to critique Christian homophobia.

Another controversy emerged with the involvement of NAIITS in the World Conference Gathering on Indigenous Peoples (WCGIP). This gathering brings together indigenous peoples from around the world to "enable indigenous believers of Jesus Christ to meet, and express themselves to God and to each other in ways which affirm godly indigenous worship, teaching, prophecy, pasturing, evangelism, and discussion."[56] The gatherings of the WCGIP have taken place in Rotoroa, New Zealand (1996); Rapid City, South Dakota (1998); Sydney, Australia (2000); Hawai'i (2002); Sweden (2005); and Davao City, Philippines (2006). In 2007, the conference was held in Jerusalem and was hosted not by Palestinians but by Messianic Jews. The *NAIITS Journal* also published an article by Gavriel Gefen that articulates Messianic Judaism as an "indigenous ministry." Gefen uncritically holds that the state of Israel has a covenant with God while neglecting to mention the oppression of Palestinian peoples at all.[57] Some participants at the 2009 conference expressed some critique of what seemed to be an investment in Christian Zionism and called for the development of solidarity between indigenous peoples in North America and Palestinian peoples who are facing similar conditions of colonialism. How this work will develop remains to be seen.

In addition, as the history of the race reconciliation with Christian evangelicalism demonstrates, situating justice struggles within the context of evangelicalism often has the impact of spiritualizing and depoliticizing them. For instance, racism is generally articulated as a personal or "spiritual" problem,[58] possibly resulting from faulty biblical analysis,[59] and its remedy lies in changing individual attitudes and behaviors rather than in a fundamental reweaving of the social fabric. As former Ku Klux Klan *cum* racial reconcilist Tom Tarrants states: "[Racism] is an issue of the lordship of Jesus Christ; it is not a sociological issue."[60] Or as Promise Keepers' speaker Wellington Boone states, "we don't have a 'skin problem,' we have a 'sin problem.'"[61] It is thus important to ask if situating decolonization within Native evangelicalism spiritualizes it in ways that distance Christianity from concrete political struggles against settler colonialism. Again, this relationship is complex. Certainly this tendency exists among some participants at NAIITS conferences. According to one participant:

> Jesus himself was under the dominant Roman society, and the people who were part of his people group desperately wanted out from under that oppressive government, and they thought he might be king and take them out of that. And they were looking for a revolution, and it's interesting to me that Jesus was more interested in a revolution of their hearts than society, and I think that's what he's on about today as well.

By contrast, however, many peoples involved in NAIITS make internal critiques of the tendency to spiritualize responses to colonization. States staff person for My People International, Ray Aldred:

> If you have a relationship with Christ, it should make you less of an ass. I just think you can't take people's land and somehow justify that. That's just wrong. I try not to spiritualize stuff too much. There are specific land claims dealing with this land right here. They need to give it back. When it comes to those reconciliation gatherings, the ones that have really been effective in helping the relationship move forward are talking about specific things. They aren't just talking airy fairy, it's about specific things.

Hence we may also find evangelicalism an "unexpected" place to also critique radical movements for change. NAIITS speaker and founder of Wiconi International, Richard Twiss, for instance, offers an implicit gender critique of the American Indian Movement from his evangelical vantage point.

> And during that time AIM was going strong and I joined the American Indian Movement and went to Washington, D.C., to participate in the takeover of the Bureau of Indian Affairs office building with that whole eight days of occupation and all that. And during that time . . . there would be times when I would watch our highly respected spiritual leaders, our medicine men, who were very much espousing a kind of lifestyle, a set of values—respect and honor and all of that. And yet, there would be times during the height of the whole focus on spirituality that these men would come out of the bar drunk as a skunk with a woman under each arm. And there was this whole phenomenon of this stud complex, and so many of those guys have children all over the country today. Some guys a couple dozen babies. But there was this sort of hypocrisy, they would be espousing these values and holding us young guys to it, but meanwhile it was about drugs, it was about promiscuity, it was about drinking and carousing. So it created a bit of a disillusionment.

Randy Woodley similarly ties a belief in Jesus to a political commitment to social justice:

> God has a preference for the poor and justice and so anything that reeks of corporate greed or anti-environmentalism, I would use the Bible to support and say, you can't say you follow Creator and follow the policies of George Bush, like war. I wouldn't say I'm a pacifist, I guess I'm a wannabe pacifist, but I really do believe in peace. The Evangelical church has used the Bible to make it into the opposite of what it says and that's very sick.

Besides these critiques of colonization, some evangelicals proffer visions of sovereignty based on biblical principles that echo some feminist and other more radical perspectives. NAIITS board member Terry LeBlanc ties Native nationalism to an implicit critique of capitalism:

> The gap between rich and poor still exists. In fact, it's widening at an increasing rate—despite the assurances of the World Bank and the G7 that there is overall improvement in the human condition worldwide. Sadly, those of us in the indigenous community seem to be buying it hook, line, and sinker! MBAs are being churned out in Indian country faster than the social work and legal degrees . . . The battle against assimilation is being conceded on a selective front. We are buying into an economic worldview so foreign that it didn't even register as a remote possibility to our ancestor . . . When, under the rubric of development, we disguise unchecked greed for bigger and better and more of Western free enterprise and big business, we do a grave disservice to our fellow human beings.[62]

Thus, decolonization is articulated as a political project that is not simply about cultural revitalization, but that also transforms the current political and economic world order. In assessing the tendency to spiritualize decolonization within evangelicalism, it is important to not lose sight of those sectors that very much connect Christianity to concrete political struggles against white supremacy, capitalism, and settler colonialism.

Decolonization in Unexpected Places

Decolonization as a political project within Native studies and Native activism signifies diverse and often contradictory positions. Glen Coulthard notes that Native struggles articulate their claims under a rubric of decolonization when their actual campaigns focus on seeking recognition from the settler state rather than dismantling the state itself. In some contexts, decolonization can also be mobilized to support notions of cultural authenticity in abstraction from concrete political struggles; in other words, Native peoples must demonstrate their decolonization by rejecting Christianity, not eating fry bread, living on reservations, and so on. But by looking at decolonization in unexpected places, the point is not simply to challenge notions of cultural authenticity, but to remind us again that ultimately, as Waziyatawin argues, decolonization is a political project designed to dismantle white supremacy, settler colonialism, and capitalism. As such, it requires seeking alliances with all those who have an interest in decolonization. To build the political power necessary to effectively decolonize indigenous nations, and indeed the world, our political imperative is not to foreclose possible alliances with Native peoples who seem to be assimilationist or conservative, but to identify possible nodal points of connection that can lead to global transformation.

While Native decolonization within the United States often centers the colonial relationship between the U.S. settler state and Native nations, this political agenda is informed by decolonization struggles on a global scale.

Some key sites for such global solidarity include the involvement of Native peoples within in the United Nations Permanent Forum on Indigenous Issues and the Working Group on Indigenous Affairs that provide a space for Native peoples in the United States to coalesce with indigenous groups around the world. More nonstatist global sites include the World Social Fora that have provided an opportunity for indigenous peoples to strategize with each other and with peoples from radical social movements around the world. At the 2008 World Social Forum, an entire day was dedicated to highlighting the struggles of indigenous peoples, who called on *all* peoples to resist the nation-state form of governance in favor of indigenous models of radical participatory democracy. However, as this article has demonstrated, sites for global dialogue and exchange between Native peoples in North America, indigenous peoples around the world, and other third world decolonization movements can exist in unexpected places. One such place is the Christian mission field, which has brought Native evangelicals into conversation with evangelicals from colonized nations around the world. In what would seem to be purely a site of religious and cultural imperialism, a politics of decolonization has emerged that threatens to reshape the boundaries of Christianity itself. How decolonization discourse within Native evangelicalism will develop and to what effect remains to be seen. But the emergence of decolonization within what would seem to be an intrinsically colonial evangelical discourse perhaps speaks to the inherent instability of colonization itself. To quote African theologian Emmanuel Martey: "Unlike Audre Lorde, who might be wondering whether the master's tools could indeed be used to dismantle the master's house, African theologians are fully convinced that the gun, in efficient hands, could well kill its owner."[63]

Notes

1. Waziyatawin Angela Wilson and Michael Yellow Bird, *For Indigenous Eyes Only* (Santa Fe: School for Advanced Research, 2005), 5. The second opening quote is from Robert Francis (Keynote Address, NAIITS Conference, Rapid City, South Dakota, November 29, 2007).
2. Devon Mihesuah and Angela Cavendar Wilson, eds., *Indigenizing the Academy* (Lincoln: University of Nebraska Press, 2004).
3. Linda Tuhiwai Smith, *Decolonizing Methodologies* (London: Zed, 1999).
4. Francis, keynote address.
5. Philip Deloria, *Indians in Unexpected Places* (Lawrence: University of Kansas Press, 2004).
6. Anne McClintock, *Imperial Leather* (New York: Routledge, 1995).
7. Deloria, *Indians in Unexpected Places,* 11.
8. Ibid., 14.
9. Ibid.

10. Dick Bernal, *American Spirituality Mapped* (San Jose, Calif.: Jubilee Center Press, n.d.), 92.
11. See also NAIITS Web site at http://www.firstnationsmonday.com/NAIITS/about.htm.
12. Jeanine LeBlanc, "Walking 'The Good Red Road': NAIITS, the Obstacles It Faces and How They Are Being Overcome," *NAIITS Journal* 6 (2005).
13. For a longer discussion of intellectual ethnography, see Andrea Smith, *Native Americans and the Christian Right: The Gendered Politics of Unlikely Alliances* (Durham, N.C.: Duke University Press, 2008).
14. Smith, *Native Americans and the Christian Right.*
15. Tony Evans, *America's Only Hope* (Chicago: Moody Press, 1990).
16. Smith, *Native Americans and the Christian Right.*
17. Craig Smith, *Whiteman's Gospel* (Winnipeg: Indian Life Books, 1997), 106.
18. Charles Amjad-Ali, "Redemption, Reconciliation, Restoration: Journeys toward Wholeness," *NAIITS Journal* 5 (2007): 6.
19. Ibid., 12.
20. Ibid., 5.
21. Tite Tiénou, "Indigenous Theologizing from the Margins to the Center," *NAIITS Journal* 3 (2005): 114.
22. Ibid.
23. Ibid., 116–17.
24. Taiaiake Alfred, *Peace, Power, Righteousness* (Oxford: Oxford University Press, 1999), 25.
25. Ibid., 57.
26. Ibid., 59.
27. Ibid., 53.
28. Adrian Jacobs, *Aboriginal Christianity: The Way It Was Meant to Be* (Rapid City, S.D.: Self-published, 1998), 69.
29. Adrian Jacobs, *Pagan Prophets and Heathen Believers* (Rapid City, S.D.: Self-published, 1999), 25.
30. Smith, *Native Americans and the Christian Right.*
31. José Esteban Muñoz, *Disidentifications* (Minneapolis: University of Minnesota Press, 1999), 11–12.
32. Ibid., 18.
33. Francis, keynote address.
34. Ibid.
35. Ibid.
36. The text of Robert Francis's talk can be found on Our Daily Frybread. http://www.injesus.com/index.php?module=message&task=view&MID=RB007DPI&GroupID=VB0060SI&label=&paging=all (accessed April 29, 2010).
37. My People International, *Vacation Bible School Curriculum,* year 1, book 1 (Evansburg, Alberta: My People International, 2000), 35.
38. Robert Warrior, "Canaanites, Cowboys, and Indians," in *Natives and Christians,* ed. James Treat (New York: Routledge, 1996), 99.
39. Ibid.
40. My People International, *Vacation Bible School Curriculum,* year 5, book 5 (Evansburg, Alberta: My People International, 2000), 35.
41. Ibid.
42. Ibid., 39.
43. Ibid.
44. Ibid., n.p.
45. Jonathan Dyck and Cornelius Buller, "Mapping the Land," *NAIITS Journal* 2 (2004): 66.
46. Jacobs, *Aboriginal Christianity,* 64.
47. Ibid.
48. Ibid., 66.
49. Jennifer Denetdale, "Carving Navajo National Boundaries: Patriotism, Tradition, and the Diné Marriage Act of 2005," *American Quarterly* 60.2 (June 2008): 289–94.
50. Marvin Olasky, "Left Behind?" *World* 21 (December 16, 2006): 20.
51. John Draper and Adrienne Gaines, "U.S. Anglicans Form Conservative Council," *Charisma* 33 (December 2007): 26.
52. Olasky, "Left Behind?" 20.

53. Ibid.
54. Jasbir Puar, *Terrorist Assemblages* (Durham, N.C.: Duke University Press, 2007).
55. Lisa Miller, "Family Feud," *Newsweek*, August 19, 2009, http://www.newsweek.com/id/212713?from=rss (accessed June 5, 2010).
56. See WCGIP Web site: http://www.wcgip.org/wcgip/aboutus/index.cfm?Handler=Default.
57. Gabriel Gefen, "Re-Contextualization: Restoring the Biblical Message to a Jewish-Israeli Context," *NAIITS Journal* 6 (2008): 192.
58. Randy Frame, "Dues-Paying Time for Black Christians," *Christianity Today* 34 (August 20, 1990): 51.
59. "Loving People Who Are Different?" *Alliance Witness* 121 (February 12, 1986): 31; William Baker, "Equal Before God," *Moody Monthly* 87 (January 1987): 18–20; Karen Mains, "Finally Listening," *Moody Monthly* 94 (May 1994): 28.
60. In Joe Maxwell, "Racial Healing in the Land of Lynching," *Christianity Today* 39 (January 10, 1994): 24–26, quote on 26. See also Kenneth Kantzer, "Has the Melting Pot Stopped Melting?" *Christianity Today* 33 (March 3, 1989): 42.
61. Wellington Boone, *Breaking Through* (Nashville: Broadman & Holman, 1996), 85.
62. Terry LeBlanc, "Compassionate Community—or Unchecked Greed?" *Mission Frontiers* 22 (September 2000): 21.
63. Emmanuel Martey, *African Theology* (Maryknoll, N.Y.: Orbis, 1994), 46.

Transnational Indigenous Exchange: Rethinking Global Interactions of Indigenous Peoples at the 1904 St. Louis Exposition

Danika Medak-Saltzman

A remarkable photograph taken at the 1904 Louisiana Purchase Exposition in St. Louis provides a glimpse into the lives of people on display at the fair, capturing in this case two Native women from opposite sides of the globe, in an unstaged and revealing moment (see fig. 1). This photograph, titled "Ainu and Patagonian Women Getting Acquainted" does not fit the archetypical representations of Indigenous peoples at the turn of the twentieth century; it is neither a posed anthropological portrait, nor is it intended to capture these "primitive" women in their "modern" surroundings. Instead it is a candid and unscripted moment between two women that requires a new lens of analysis to reveal its significance. On the left we see an Ainu woman wearing warm layers over her traditional embroidered *attus*; underneath this she wears leggings and Western-style shoes. Her hands are on her knees as she leans toward the Patagonian woman, who is looking toward the Ainu woman as she sits on the ground in front of a building, bundled against the cold with her dog in her lap.[1] That this transnational Indigenous encounter was made possible in this instance is striking for a number of reasons. Most readily evident, perhaps, is that it occurred at the 1904 exposition—a context that foregrounds imperial desires to display technological and racial progress at the turn of the century—yet the goals of empire are neither the subject of the photograph, nor are they necessarily relevant to the interactions of these Native women. Even though this image raises many questions, using it as a starting point for examining the experiences of these women at the fair might seem an impossible task. But the fact remains that the historical moment this photograph evidences, the women's interest in each other, and the manner in which they made meaning of their experiences while at the fair are very real. This article engages the questions the image poses and offers an analysis that might recover Indigenous perspectives. Previous means of analysis relegate

Figure 1.
"Ainu and Patagonian Women Getting Acquainted." Papers of Carlton Stevens Coon (neg. 98-10290), National Anthropological Archives, Smithsonian Institution. Reprinted by permission.

these women and their experiences—and thus the experiences of all Indigenous peoples—to the realm of unknowable, unimportant, and powerless positions in history. By contrast, this essay seeks to provide a theoretical space where explorations of transnational Indigenous encounters can be undertaken to illuminate their significances and to highlight the intellectual possibilities opened up in the process. By interrogating the encounter captured in this photograph and reading against the colonialist discourse embedded in selected archival materials and contemporary scholarship, this article demonstrates both the challenges presented by an incomplete and colonialist record and the possibilities for exploring historical Indigenous consciousness.

Revealing the many ways that Indigenous peoples have always been active actors on the global stage is a contemporary scholarly challenge. It requires us to look at the archives more carefully and to read against the colonialist narratives that cloak experiences such as those portrayed in the photograph at hand. To do otherwise would be to perpetuate historical silences. For as Michel Rolph Trouillot outlines in *Silencing the Past,* these silences are not only produced in the compilation and selection of materials that become an archive.[2] More precisely, it is in the scholarly act of reading, interpreting, and constructing narratives from the archive that these silences become even more deeply entrenched. Without question, there have been many instances when Native peoples saw that strategic negotiating power could be garnered by uniting toward common goals, and some of these instances are regularly acknowledged in standard historical narratives, albeit in sanitized versions that are most often removed from their political contexts and are defined as ultimately unsuccessful and surprising moments in history.[3] As Shari Huhndorf tells us, "anti-colonial indigenous alliances have a long history."[4] Yet the prevalence of such events suggests that rather than being anomalies, these historical moments are evidence of an ever emerging and expanding Indigenous consciousness, similar to the way colonial nation-states were trading in knowledge of colonial processes, as I have argued extensively elsewhere.[5] To be clear, examining the historical record to shed light on transnational Indigenous encounters is not about seeking a continuous resistance movement where there is none. It is about recognizing Indigenous resistance as a continual part of Native negotiations with colonial regimes and about considering how moments of colonial celebrations of empire may have inadvertently served anticolonial purposes by presenting the Indigenous participants with opportunities to interact across larger distances than had been practical or possible in the past.

Attempting to view the image presented here through the lenses more commonly used in world's fair studies—those focused on the original intent of the fair organizers, expressions of empire, and the display of pseudo-scientific racial hierarchies—might cause us to see this photograph and the circumstances of its production from a vantage point that claims the experiences of Indigenous peoples are irrecoverable. This, however, is a standpoint that provides the rationale for leaving questions about Native experiences unexamined, in spite of the fact that there is much we do know. In the case of this photograph, we know that two women, one Ainu and one Tzoneca,[6] began this journey to the St. Louis fair at a time when transcontinental and trans-Pacific travel was still a new possibility and an even rarer opportunity for Indigenous peoples. In the cold months that followed the dawn of 1904, these women and members of their communities were presented the opportunity to travel to St. Louis to be part of a grand exposition. Once there, they would be expected to live and to perform their traditional lifeways for visitors for the good part of a year, as if they had never left home. Thus, even at world's fairs, Indigenous peoples built communities and interacted with each other and their colonizers in ways that have yet to be critically examined. This article is an attempt to excavate such interactions and to consider how these encounters and interactions may have informed later decisions to bring Indigenous concerns to global audiences.

The subject of transnational Indigenous encounters, particularly at world's fairs, with rare exception, has not been addressed in contemporary scholarship.[7] For example, the recent book *Anthropology Goes to the Fair* by Nancy Parezo and Don Fowler offers a comprehensive account of the fair, clearly intended to demonstrate that the 1904 fair came as the discipline of anthropology was becoming an academic and increasingly Boasian pursuit rather than the purview of hobbyists, even though it was primarily hobbyists, particularly W. J. McGee, who were in charge of representing anthropology at the fair. The authors go to great lengths to recover the names of as many of the Native participants in the fair as they can and work to piece together how the participants "were assembled, cared for, treated, displayed, and interpreted."[8] But in the end, the development of the field of anthropology and the fair's role in it becomes the focus of this text, despite the authors' declared intentions to reinsert Native presence into narratives about the fair. To avoid such a pitfall, I would like to follow the lead of Ngugi wa Thiong'o and *move the center*[9] away from its usual hegemonic focus and toward the experience of the people who found themselves "on display."

Historical Silences, "Moving the Center," and Speculative Scholarship

To take up this call to "move the center" one must proceed with the understanding that archival materials—however collected, assembled, and reproduced as fact—are repositories of colonial privilege. As Trouillot tells us, "the ultimate mark of power may be its invisibility; the ultimate challenge, the exposition of its roots."[10] Being aware that this vantage point is evident in archival materials (photographic and otherwise) on an intellectual level is one thing; seeing it within archival materials and interrogating the sources to lay bare the colonial desires embedded within them, is another. When examining archival materials for echoes of Indigenous experiences—mediated/interpreted by colonial agents though they may be—one must consciously read such texts as much for what they do say as for what they do not. Exposing the roots and residue of colonial power as exerted in the process of recording and making meaning of that which is observed is part of the challenge faced by contemporary scholars of Indigenous studies. The necessarily speculative nature of such work does not make it somehow less important. After all, much of what has made it into the historical record as "fact" about Native people is equally, if not more, speculative—in that colonial lenses were used to judge and interpret Indigenous cultures against "civilized" conventions of the era—and yet the colonial vantage point goes unchallenged and remains intact when reproduced in contemporary scholarship.[11] Simply because colonial suppositions have become part of the archival record, privileging them and allowing them to be endlessly cited as "fact" does not make it the case. Rather than basing the speculation in this research on imperialist assumptions about Native peoples or allowing the speculative "facts" from archival materials to have the final say, I intend to raise alternative readings of these events that privilege the possibility that Native peoples at the fairs were thoughtfully engaged with their surroundings. This should not be a radical assertion, yet precisely because the experiences this article discusses—when illuminating moments of transnational Indigenous exchange that complicate spaces of encounter—run counter to more familiar narratives about Indigenous pasts, it becomes so.

Thus this article uses a grounding in particular Indigenous traditions, cultures, and histories to interrogate the colonial assumptions that permeate both archival records and scholarship about the 1904 fair.[12] To begin to answer some of the questions raised by the image "Ainu and Patagonian Women Getting Acquainted," I will first examine the treatment of this photograph when it appeared in the public domain on two recent occasions. Then using a journal kept, published, and sold at the fair by Frederick Starr—the man charged with "collecting" the Ainu group for exhibit—the analysis moves toward considering what the experiences of the Ainu group were like en route to and after arrival at the fairgrounds. Then the focus moves from the specific cases of Ainu and Tzoneca experiences to the geography of the fair to illustrate more broadly how transnational Indigenous encounters, interactions, and exchange were unintended consequences of the fair's design. And finally the article returns to the Ainu group, this time focusing briefly on the youngest members of the fair group, to raise the possibility that the turn Ainu political activism takes in the 1960s and 1970s, from assimilationist leanings to a move toward a global Indigenous rights movement, may have been partly informed by precisely the sorts of transnational Indigenous encounters and exchange made possible for the first time on a broad scale at the 1904 exposition. I thus raise the possibility that seeds of a global anticolonial movement may have been collected at the fair, remaining nascent for decades until the fertile grounds of the late twentieth century made themselves available for Indigenous rights movements on a global scale to begin to take root.

Photographic Evidence

When I first embarked on this project, the image of these two Indigenous women together at the fair quelled lingering suspicions that my investigations into transnational Indigenous encounters were more of a historical hope than a reality. How this image has appeared recently in the public domain reveals how the significance of the transnational Indigenous exchange it evidences has been overshadowed in its presentation. This photograph, although relatively obscure, has appeared twice in the last decade in widely available media. The most recent was as a part of the St. Louis Public Library's online exhibit, commemorating the centennial anniversary of the 1904 fair, called "Celebrating the Louisiana Purchase."[13] The other was in a large volume published by the Smithsonian Institution in 1999, as part of a renewed global interest in Ainu people, titled *Ainu: The Spirit of a Northern People.* This publication coincided with a large exhibit by the same name for the Smithsonian's National Museum of Natural History. The key difference between the way the St. Louis Public Library and the Smithsonian represent this image is visible in the text that accompanies the image in each instance.

In the case of the St. Louis Public Library exhibit, the caption for this picture refers to the women not by their individual names but simply in the manner established by the photo's title, calling them "Ainu woman" and "Patagonian woman." But these women are not unnamed in the library's exhibit because they are unknown. Their names actually appear elsewhere on the library's Web site, handwritten on the individual photographs of them taken by fair documenters. Using these and other records, it is not difficult to find their names. Santukno Hiramura is the name of the Ainu woman, and the Tzoneca woman's name is Lorenza. Even Lorenza's dog—which is always in Lorenza's arms in photos of her—had its name, "Kik," recorded by the fair's records keepers. Yet, despite the availability of this information, by not explicitly naming these women, the implication and "take home" message to the viewers of the St. Louis library's online exhibit is that it did not, and does not, matter who these women were—beyond their presence at the fair, their gender, and ethnic designations. This is further reinforced by text that accompanies this image on the Web site: "It is interesting to speculate about conversations these women had when they met on the Fairgrounds. Would a Patagonian woman ask an Ainu woman about raising her children?"[14]

To be fair, this text acknowledges that the women were historical actors engaging each other, but what is concerning is the fact that the question is posed rhetorically, allowing readers to accept the implication that "we will never know," or perhaps—and this would be of greater concern—"we do not care to know."[15] In part due to the diligence of the fair documenters, who saw themselves as preserving images of "dying races," there are starting points for exploring the experiences of these women. This fact underscores that the textual laments that allow readers and scholars alike to be comfortable with dismissing the importance of Indigenous experiences effectively reinscribe the "vanishing Native" archetype that still plagues contemporary representations of Native peoples. Part of the insidiousness of this narrative of Native disappearance is that it is much easier to maintain than it is to write Native actors and experiences into public consciousness.

Although the St. Louis library's use of this photograph is more recent than the Smithsonian's, its caption seems more in line with thinking about Native peoples from an earlier era. In contrast, the 1999 Smithsonian exhibit was curated by Native and non-Native scholars who focus their work on Ainu people. This broader and more inclusive range of viewpoints is evident throughout the volume. This can be seen in the caption associated with the Smithsonian's publication of this photograph of Santukno and Lorenza:

> Comparing Notes: The 1904 St. Louis Exposition must have been remarkable for the native participants; it brought people from the far corners of the world into contact with each other and with Americans. In this unusually candid snapshot by Jesse Tarbox Beals, Sangtukno [*sic*], an Ainu woman, shares a moment with Lorenza, a Patagonian woman, and her dog.[16]

By providing this accompanying text, the Smithsonian presents this photograph in a manner that takes the perspective of those being photographed into consideration (surprisingly uncommon in the framing accompanying images of Indigenous peoples). This caption also credits the photographic style of the photographer who "captured" this image as a candid shot, as opposed to the often staged scenes or studio portraits that are markers of other photographs of the fair. The work of Jessie Tarbox Beals was aimed at capturing the unstaged moments of the fair, whether they fit into W. J. McGee's narrative of racial and developmental progress or not. The fact that Jessie Tarbox Beals (not Jesse, as the Smithsonian text claims) sought out alternative views of the fair seems somehow less surprising when we consider her position as one of a few women professional photographers at the fair. Beals aimed to capture images of the fair as she saw it, rather than as she was supposed to have seen it. Thanks, in part, to George Eastman's marketing of Kodak cameras to "ladies," photography was becoming an increasingly accessible medium for women, like Beals, with the means to support such an interest. As Laura Wexler explains in *Tender Violence*, "to the photographing woman, the fairs and expositions offered congenial stimulation and a way to gain recognition and make some money selling photographs. . . . The fairs encouraged them to emerge from domestic confinement and to test just how far the designation 'lady with a camera' would let them go."[17] Official fair photographers spent their time taking photographs of what they were expected to document, from staged photographs of Native peoples in profile, to scenes that portrayed the progress of the civilized world. "Beals played the woman's angle for all it was worth, which was considerable. She made many sets of 'sympathetic' pictures of domestic life on the anthropology exhibits."[18] Her interests at the fair are memorialized in a biography of her life that explains that Beals focused on "the scenes of the daily lives of exotic, little-known peoples in their native habitats. She took pictures of the Igorots, the Bogobos, the Zulus, the Hottentots, the Eskimos, the Filipinos and other defenseless recipients of missionary barrels."[19] Due in part to Beals's characteristic assertiveness and her interest in the Indigenous peoples at the fair, a variety of photographs like the one of Santukno, Lorenza, and Kik were taken at the fair. Thus, in the process of taking advantage of the power to document the world she saw through the viewfinder, Beals has also provided contemporary scholars with candid photographs of some of the daily interactions taking place in the anthropology section of the fair and, importantly, a repository of evidence of transnational Indigenous encounters at the 1904 St. Louis exposition. Beals managed to take many of the few existing photographs of the Tzonecas upon their arrival, since she had been first on the scene. "By the time the other photographers arrived, Beals had already made her interpretation of the event."[20] It is unclear whether the photo of Santukno, Lorenza, and Kik was taken shortly after the arrival of the Tzonecas or not. What is clear is that when the Tzonecas arrived at the fair after their long journey, they were not keen on having photographs taken. Having been told while en route to the fair, both in Liverpool and in New York, that they would receive copies of photographs taken of them—copies that never materialized—the Tzonecas were understandably tired of having cameras pointed at them.[21] This is in part what led to the report that shortly after their arrival in St. Louis "an old Patagonian woman issued an edict that no black boxes were to be pointed at her people and she chased the camera men over a barbed wire fence. But Jessie had already made her images and they were exclusives."[22] Characterizing

Lorenza's assertion that no more photographs could be taken at that time as the issuance of "an edict," and describing her as "old"[23] indicates that a familiar way of thinking about American Indian women—as either young, beautiful, and helpful to the colonizer or as old domineering hags who remained loyal to their people—is being employed to construct Lorenza in a particular light.[24] Although they miss mentioning the inextricable linkage of Native women with their perceived colonial or tribal loyalties, Parezo and Fowler assert that Lorenza was often portrayed in the media as "sullen," and that the Tzonecas were not particularly happy during their time at the fair. Parezo and Fowler also recount occasions when the Tzonecas report being lied to about various things—in addition to not receiving copies of photographs as promised, the group had agreed to come to St. Louis when they were promised white horses that also never materialized—an issue that would surely have left any group of people disenchanted and reluctant to fulfill the whims of fairgoers, the organizers, and the media.

While on one hand we can look at the body of work that Beals produced at the fair to find alternative narratives of fair experiences, we must remember that for Beals, as much as she may have been interested in the "exotic" and "little-known" peoples at the anthropology exhibit, fair photography was largely an economic endeavor. More to the point, much of her best-selling work supported the narratives that fair organizers were constructing for visitors, elements that were not necessarily evident in the more candid moments of Indigenous life at the fair. Perhaps to ameliorate this, Beals also asked members from different Indigenous nations to pose together in manners that more clearly supported the larger narratives of racial hierarchy, colonial progress, and the United States' role in aiding in the racial uplift of many of the Indigenous groups on display. The most famous example of one of Beals's posed pieces is also her best-selling photograph, titled "Pygmy and Patagonian Giant." This juxtaposition—which mirrored the physical layout of the anthropology exhibit that began with "pygmies" and ended with "Patagonian Giants"—made a spectacle of human difference and supported the lessons of human progress portrayed in the exhibit.[25]

Photographs can provide powerful evidence, yet they cannot tell the whole story, and the stories they tell are not created equal. As Wexler explains,

> photography has always been a constitutive force, not merely reflecting but actively determining the social spaces in which lives are lived. . . . As a social institution, American domestic photography commemorates a popular struggle to envision—and the struggle to be visible in—a modus vivendi for American lives. The right to see and be seen, in one's own way and under one's own terms, has been the point of contention.[26]

Thus attempts to re-view the photograph of Santukno and Lorenza in a manner that places Indigenous peoples at the center must take into consideration that these women had unique lived experiences that brought them together very far from home and that had bearing on their interactions and how they understood them. Lorenza and Santukno had traveled great distances with their families, young children, and perfect strangers, to be a part of the anthropology exhibit at the 1904 fair. Once there, these women were expected to set up homes, produce food and clothing, and exhibit tribal arts and musics, so that fairgoers might have a traditional and "authentic" experience from the safety of their figurative American backyards. In the case of Lorenza, she was the only adult woman member of the six-member Tzoneca group who traveled to the fair. "The Telehueche contingent consisted of an extended family from the province of Santa Cruz, Argentina. There were five adult men, one adult woman (Lorenza), an eight year old girl named Gigi."[27] According to photographic evidence, the Tzoneca group also had two dogs with them, a fact that brings us to an aspect of the photograph in question that has been overlooked. The curators of the library's online exhibit and the editors of the Smithsonian collection seem to have missed what is holding Santukno's interest in this image. Namely, that Santukno—whose family was not allowed to bring its dogs, even though dogs were considered important members of Ainu families—is looking most intently at Lorenza's dog, Kik. Most Ainu families included dogs, which traditionally served important roles in Ainu survival. Some used dogs for hunting, some to pull dogsleds, and others to breed for income. When discussing the place dogs hold in Ainu life one scholar writes that "the treatment and spiritual station of dogs often reflect their unusual place as domestic animals that straddle both human and natural worlds."[28] The significance of dogs to Ainu communities was well known and is evident in the fact that in order to subdue Ainu resistance, Japanese colonial agents often threatened to "bind the legs of their prized hunting dogs and toss them in the rivers to drown."[29] And yet, it did not occur to those sent to "collect" a group of Ainu for the fair to bring the family dogs. Knowing the important role that dogs played in Ainu society at this time allows us to recognize that Santukno's gaze is focused rather than casual, invoking a longing rather than a simple curiosity.[30] Reading the photograph this way moves the center away from the intentions of the collectors and toward the experiences of the people who themselves were the objects of interest. Thus, this photograph has presented another entry point to accessing the histories and hidden narratives of Native experiences.

Considering the windows on Indigenous experience that this one photograph has opened suggests that the archives and the records of fairgoers and fair chroniclers contain embedded information that can further nuance our understanding of transnational Indigenous exchange. To do this we must look more closely at the circumstances surrounding how these women were selected for the fair. This is easier in the case of the Ainu woman, largely due to the fact that the man charged with "collecting" the Ainu group for the fair kept a record of the journey to gather the Ainu and bring them to St. Louis. While I have yet to find comparable records in the Tzoneca case, the fact remains that the interactions of individuals such as Santukno and Lorenza have been long overlooked, and we must work to illuminate such spaces of encounter.

Transnational Indigenous Exchange and Encounters

On his journey in January of 1904 to "collect" Ainu people and items of cultural production for exhibition, Fredrick Starr—who had been appointed by anthropology exhibit organizer W. J. McGee—took extensive notes to document this experience. Starr's journal was published upon his return under the title *The Ainu Group at the St. Louis Exposition* and sold at the Ainu "exhibit" for $0.75 per copy.[31] In this firsthand account many aspects of the Ainu group's experiences are evident, if not directly stated, or fully understood, by Starr. And it is fair to say that he is not alone in missing the significance of some of what he shares in this journal. While Starr's published journal has been utilized in other recent scholarship, much of the information within it that reveals what Native peoples were doing and saying at the time of "collection," and at the fair, has gone largely unexamined. When interrogating this text in the manner described above, it becomes clear that Starr's journal provides ample evidence of transnational Indigenous encounters. Some of the encounters evident in this text begin even before the Ainu group arrives at the fair. For example, while discussing their journey to the United States, Starr mentions that American Indians traveled to train stations to watch as trains, loaded with Ainu people and exhibit materials, traveled through American Indian homelands on their way to St. Louis. He writes, "both at stations and in the cars meetings with Indians took place and it was curious to see the mutual close inspection. On the whole the Ainu took the inspection well and sometimes reciprocated fully."[32] Starr also writes, "At Seattle . . . the men were much interested in the totem pole set up in the city and inquired about its use and the Indians who made it."[33] Although it does not fully reveal what the Ainu group may have thought about the Native peoples they met, Starr's colonialist narrative nevertheless documents that the Ainu people were curious about the Indigenous peoples they saw evidence of and encountered along the way. These experiences are also presented in a way that illustrates that there was interest on the part of all parties involved, with the groups in some cases "reciprocating fully." That American Indian peoples traveled to train stations to see the Ainu visitors indicates a level of awareness not often attributed to Native peoples in this era. Moreover, rather than viewing this mutual interest as a historical anomaly, it seems worth considering how the parties in each case made meaning of these interactions. In other words, when we recognize the theoretical spaces that encounters and exchanges such as these occupy in the minds of the participants, this mutual interest ceases to be merely anecdotal. Instead, it becomes an indisputable example of a transnational Indigenous encounter that occurred at the beginning of the twentieth century. It is entirely possible that stories about these experiences would have been shared for a long time after such an event. That we might not be able to trace what these experiences meant to Ainu and American Indian peoples at the time—let alone follow the transmittal of such stories to the present—should not erase or overshadow these moments of exchange and the meaning people ascribed to them. Moreover, when viewed this way, the Ainu interest in totem poles foreshadows the cross-cultural explorations of Bikky Sunazawa, an Ainu artist—and son of Ainu rights activists discussed in the conclusion of this article—whose interest in totem poles led him to befriend Haida artist Bill Reid in the 1980s.[34]

In their important intervention into world's fair studies, Parezo and Fowler still miss many opportunities to interrogate the colonial assumptions embedded in their sources. Their use of Starr's published journal is a prime example. Citing Starr, they state as fact that Ainu people had to obtain Japanese passports to travel to St. Louis; in doing so, they missed the opportunity to examine how race and nation informed this decision. Glossing over this fact is an example of a historical blindness that obscures a Native perspective by placing Indigenous people naturally into the nation-state that colonized them. To adopt an Indigenous perspective demands that scholars fully interrogate the archive as a repository of colonial privilege. When we fail to examine transnational Indigenous encounters as the experiences of people having nuanced engagement with their surroundings that include political, economic, diplomatic, and other sophisticated thought processes, our representations remain in lockstep with the original intent of anthropology displays of the 1904 exposition.

Details from Starr's journal coupled with McGee's articulations of meaning have elsewhere been used with little consideration of the Indigenous perspective, particularly assertions that the clean-shaven faces of the young Ainu men at the time of "collection" were the result of their effort to look more "Japanese." While it is likely that these young men were indeed clean shaven due to temporal pressures in Japan to appear less Ainu, reproducing this detail with little analysis obscures the lived reality of Ainu people in the winter of 1904. Such an assertion—in the original case and each time it is repeated in contemporary scholarship—quietly erases the enforcement of Japanese assimilation policies forbidding the practice of cultural beliefs that were manifested physically on Ainu bodies: in the forms of wearing earrings, tattoos, or beards. Ironically, when it came to choosing members of the Ainu group, it was precisely bearded older men and women with facial tattoos who were high on Starr's list of desirable "acquisitions." While is possible that Starr instructed the young Ainu men to regrow their beards while at the fair to look more Ainu, the only thing we know with certainty comes from the photographic archives (see fig. 2). Photos taken before the group departs from Japan show the young Ainu men clean shaven, and the photographs of the group from the months that follow show the young men's beards becoming consistently longer. This is something both Starr and McGee describe—and Parezo and Fowler reproduce—as the young Ainu men's attempt to fulfill the desires of the onlookers who came to see "traditional" Ainu people. Despite such implications, it is highly unlikely that the average American attendee in 1904 had much, if any, information about what Ainu people were "supposed" to look like—other than what fair publicity and signage declared. Although the Ainu people were continuously referred to at the fair as the "hairy Ainu," as they had been for centuries in Japan, there was little directly linking this reference to hirsuteness to beards specifically. Moreover, beards were common enough among European and American men that it is highly unlikely that beards would be viewed as an "oddity" in the way they had been in Asia. In fact, many fair visitors commented in postcards home and to fair officials that they were surprised to find the Ainu called the "Hairy Ainu" and as a result began to interpret Ainu women's facial tattoos as facial hair.[35]

Consideration of the motives behind the young Ainu men's decision to regrow their beards requires that we give careful thought to how being on display in a foreign country and seeing and interacting with other Indigenous people—also on display—affected Ainu people in this situation. It is entirely possible that Ainus on display at the 1904 fair saw the existence and continued survival of other Indigenous populations from around the world as a reason for renewed pride in their own culture. Furthermore, being in St. Louis provided a temporary reprieve from Japanese colonial regulation, and this allowed the men to grow out their beards in the traditional Ainu way without suffering consequences. Thus, while it is possible the young men chose to grow their beards out for the benefit of the visitors, such a reading—that privileges the expectations of fair visitors and the visions for the fair articulated by fair organizers—forecloses the possibility of alternative readings. Breaking away from conventions that privilege hegemonic interpretations of Indigenous decisions allows for the equally possible reading of this beard regrowth, as an expression of cultural pride, to emerge. Contemplating the motivations of the young Ainu men, and allowing for the possibility that they saw their role in the world as not solely focused on pleasing a white audience and fulfilling the desires of fair organizers, reconstitutes their vantage point with historical agency. Although a reading of Ainu decision making at the fair must foreground their colonized status, this should not mean that their actions are always interpreted as accommodating colonial desires, in a vacuum. If we consider how witnessing dozens of Indigenous cultures and peoples on display, and the crowds they were drawing, might have been understood by the Native participants, the possibilities for interpreting their decisions expand to include more complicated human motivations. When considered this way, interpreting Ainu beard re-growth at the fair as an expression of cultural pride and Indigenous identity becomes a distinct possibility.

While at the fair, Native peoples garnered attention and monies from onlookers and each other by making crafts, performing dances or songs, and charging for photographs to supplement their meager pay as fair participants. This caused a problem for fair organizers, who lamented that participants from different groups were purchasing items from each other and "contaminating" the ethnographic display by having items created by others in their homes. This exchange led McGee to request, after more stringent guidelines were resisted, that Native peoples be authentic during performance hours (from 9 to 11 a.m. and 2 to 4 p.m.), asking that all objects and possession that were not culturally appropriate be out of the sight of visitors.[36] And it is here that we also see evidence of both cross-cultural curiosity and transnational Indigenous exchange occurring at the fair more broadly. This exchange and the act of charging visitors for items of cultural production, photographs, and other cultural commodities make it clear that Native peoples were interested in each other and saw performing Indigeneity as a valuable commodity. That these practices were encouraged by fair organizers should not undermine the fact that Native peoples were negotiating these experiences with their own motivations.

Figure 2.
"The Ainu Group in St. Louis." Papers of Carlton Stevens Coon (neg. 98-10290), National Anthropological Archives, Smithsonian Institution. Reprinted by permission.

Rereading colonial records with the goal of revealing rather than obscuring Native experiences is challenging, but narrative history provides one tool for doing so. For the Ainu group, sharing their experiences with their home communities would have been even more memorable to their home audience than has—to date—been considered in examinations of the 1904 fair. Most of the nine Ainu people[37] who were in St. Louis in 1904 had been prepared for departure by their communities in a very public and telling manner; their communities held funerary rights for them. Starr wrote in his journal that the Ainu group "reported that, at their leaving, there was a gathering of the village and much weeping, since they were looked upon as dead men never again to be seen in the old home."[38] This largely overlooked historical detail reveals a great deal about the home community's concerns for the traveling members and the collective recognition of the very real possibility that the travelers might never return home. The Ainu participants from the Saru River region of Hokkaido were each prepared so that if any one of them were to die while en route, they would be able to make their way to the next world and meet their ancestors properly. Both the travelers themselves and their home community members knew that even if they did return, they would come home changed by the experiences that awaited them, and would therefore come home as different people. The simple scholarly recognition that the majority of group members had been ceremoniously prepared for death before they left strongly suggests that the return of the Ainu group to their homes in Ainu Mosir—quite literally from the dead—would have been uniquely memorable. Starr even considers this himself when he provides culturally specific details about rituals of return:

> In [Hokkaido], when an Ainu has been away from the village and returns, his homecoming is made a public occasion. All the people gather, someone being their spokesman. He and the traveler seat themselves facing. He who has been away begins to sing, narrating his adventures, telling where he has been and what he has seen and done. Presently he stops and the other begins to sing the happenings of the village during the traveller's absence from home. So they sing, alternating until both stories are completed. When our Ainu group returns, they will be received as those who were dead and have returned; what a many things the poor fellows will have to sing of the people and places they seen so far away from their home villages in the Saru River valley.[39]

That Starr considers what a momentous occasion their return would be makes it even more striking that this aspect of the Ainu group's experience has gone unnoted in narratives that use the journal to construct their histories of the fair. Lest the impression be given that the impending departure was an entirely morose occasion for the Ainu group, and to offer as comprehensive a narrative of Ainu experience regarding travel to the fair as possible, it should be noted that at least one member of the group was excited about, and looking forward to, the trip. Starr documents this with an obvious level of satisfaction when he writes, "Goro was lively and happy and anxious to go. That was something, and we believed his influence would do much to cheer the somewhat morose Yazo, the timid Shirake, and the group that were mourned as dead."[40] It is clear however, that even as Starr shares this, he acknowledges that for most of the group, this was not a joyous occasion. In fact, from the very beginning of his attempts to gather a group of Ainu for the St. Louis fair, he recognizes a reluctance on the part of potential group members, and his endeavor proved successful only after he obtained the assistance of John Batchelor, a British citizen whose decades of missionary work among Ainu communities was influential and earned the respect of many Ainu people. As I have explained elsewhere, the Japanese government sought Americans to advise the Colonization Commission (開拓使) in its endeavors to colonize and develop Hokkaido in the 1870s. This international exchange of colonial practices involved the employ of a former Indian agent, Horace Capron, as the main advisor to the commission. And the influence of American Indian and U.S. land policies are evident in the 1899 law that Japan issued to regulate its interactions with Ainu people, the Former Natives Protection Policy (北海道旧土人保護法). While U.S. agents were more concerned with seeing the territory settled and making the land productive, the few British subjects in Hokkaido at the time, most notably Reverend John Batchelor, were more concerned with Ainu welfare and the introduction of Christianity among them. As Starr tells it, Batchelor was known for offering his home as a safe haven for Ainu who needed a place to stay for whatever reason. So, for these reasons, when Batchelor made requests of individual Ainus on behalf of Starr, it was difficult for those who felt they owed Batchelor a debt of gratitude to say no. In fact, as Starr writes, "Mr. Batchelor told [an Ainu man] that we wished him, with his wife and child, to go with us to the United States; that he would be gone nine months; that he should go. A look of blank helplessness came over [the Ainu man's] face, but he replied that he would have to go, of course, if *he* said so."[41] Starr's use of italics for the word *he* in the original indicates that the Ainu man's reluctance to accept the offer was only overcome because Batchelor was making the request.

Amid the joy, reluctance, mourning, and manipulation—some might even argue coercion—that marked the departure of the Ainu group to the St. Louis exposition, few at home in Ainu Mosir expected the group to return. While the Ainu group had been selected to participate in the fair as a colonized and vanishing race, this experience was far from a death march. As the "Ainu and Patagonian Women Getting Acquainted" photograph and brief analysis of portions of Starr's text has made clear, the Ainus were headed to a place where they would meet other Indigenous peoples with whom they would forge new relationships.

Stages of Empire

As Robert Rydell explains in *All the World's a Fair*, the print media saw and reported that the 1904 fair would have long-lasting effects on visitors. *Harper's Magazine* reported, "Remember that such a fair as this that St. Louis offers leaves no intelligent visitor where it found him. It fills him full of pictures and of knowledge that keep coming up in his mind for years afterwards. It gives him new standards, new means of comparison, new insight into the conditions of life in the world he is living in."[42] That such effects are predicted on behalf of the "intelligent" visitor is not only not a surprise; it is accepted as undoubtedly the case. And yet, an equivalent assertion about the lasting effects of transnational Indigenous encounters on Native participants at the fair is most likely to be met with skepticism. Such skepticism betrays precisely how deeply entrenched the pseudo-science of racial hierarchies and primitivist discourses are to this day.

World's fairs—as a growing scholarly literature contends—were stages upon which ideas of empire and progress were publicly displayed. But at the 1904 Louisiana Purchase Exposition in St. Louis, exhibitions of non-Western people and cultures reached a pinnacle. Indeed, organizers constructed exhibits to educate the public about racial progress and hierarchy, and they selected self-made American geologist, anthropologist, and ethnologist W. J. McGee to be in charge of the anthropological portion of the fair. As Parezo and Fowler detail, McGee intended to exhibit his understanding of racial hierarchies "so that both white American visitors and Native participants would understand and accept it as truth."[43] McGee selected participants for the anthropology exhibit "so that every known stage of industrial and social development [were] typified among the peoples on the exposition grounds."[44] Here he describes these people in organizational order: "The selection . . . is devoted to types of both race and culture (or development). The race-types include the pygmies of Central Africa . . . Patagonian Giants; the Ainu people, or hairy folk, of whom little is known beyond the fact that they are white, rather than brown."[45] The "race-types" that McGee mentions were thus exhibited as part of a spectrum that began with the "pygmies" in the darkness of Africa and moved toward the Ainu, whom he indicates were "white." McGee's word choice and use of parentheses around the phrase "(or development)" is intended to explain the inclusion of the "white" Ainu in this display; that is, Ainu "whiteness" was a whiteness of difference, rooted in their perceived lack of "development." McGee's uses of "white" and "development" highlight the racial anxiety that existed at the time regarding the classification of Ainus as a racially "white" people. This concern was largely rooted in the fact that the Ainu, by virtue of themselves being colonized, represented a branch of the white race that had not mastered surrounding territories, peoples, and resources. The fact that the Ainu people had not been colonized by other, more developed white people, but rather by the decidedly nonwhite Japanese, raised anxieties that the fair's narrative sought to soothe.[46] Moreover, at the time of the 1904 fair, these racial anxieties with regard to Japan were even more heightened, because Japan was at war with Russia, a Western imperial nation. Thus, "(or development)" here distinguishes between levels of whiteness, allowing for Ainu "whiteness" to still fit neatly within the "scientific" ideology of the evolution of racial hierarchies.

In re-creating the Native "homes" at the fair, the preferences and perspectives of the Indigenous participants were not considered. That reproducing the flora and fauna necessary for people's subsistence was not possible seems to have been of little concern to McGee, despite the fact that he hoped the participants would do exactly that. Moreover, as Parezo and Fowler make clear, little thought was given to how peoples from various parts of the world would handle the climate of St. Louis, let alone how appropriate their traditional houses and clothing would be for nine consecutive months of midwestern weather.

The "ethnology exhibit" described above stood out in stark relief in the midst of exhibitions of the developmental "success" of the nation-states also represented at the fair. The message of progress and stages of civilization were underscored by the geographical layout of the fairgrounds. Each of the main nations, such as Japan, Great Britain, and the Republic of Mexico, had their own exhibits in the main section of the fair. In contrast, Native peoples on display were situated near each other in a separate area of the fair, where each group was limited, during performance hours to their respective onsite "reservations."[47] Outside of these hours Native people were free to visit other exhibits, and it was not uncommon for Native peoples to spend time together; there is even a photograph from the fair showing Navajos visiting the Igorot village on a "Sunday outing."[48] While some might be tempted to claim that language barriers would have prevented communication during moments of such transnational Indigenous exchange, and while this likely posed a barrier in some cases, we should not underestimate Indigenous ingenuity. For evidence of this we need only look to a statement by Maria Martinez, a Tewa Pueblo woman, who mentions, when asked about her conversations with Geronimo, that "we talked Spanish because we didn't know each other's Indian."

Yet, even while able to overcome some obstacles presented at the fair, Native peoples had little say about the design and layout of their exhibits, and found it difficult to negotiate various aspects of their lives at the fair. For example, Parezo and Fowler note that "the Ainus continuously protested that visitors were peering through their windows even though they had said that they had agreed to interact only with visitors outside their home."[49] The exhibits of the world's nations, on the other hand, were a different story. For example, Japan's was situated with the exhibits of other developed nations, and had been designed by Japanese officials.[50] It would have been difficult for anyone, Indigenous or otherwise, to miss the fact that the colonial and developed nations of the world were on display in one area while tribal peoples were in another.[51]

On the Power of Naming

To conclude, I offer a story about the two youngest members of the Ainu group, two little girls known as Kiku and Kin, ages three and six, respectively, when they arrived at the fair.[52] These names are particularly symbolic, and may not have been the girls' original names. Kin is often referred to in primary materials as Kettle—a distinctly Ainu and not Japanese name. In Japanese, Kiku (菊) means "chrysanthemum" and Kin (金) means "gold."[53] Since the thirteenth century the Japanese royal family has used a golden chrysanthemum as its crest, and it remains to this day a literal and visual signifier of Japan. Naming the children after the colonial nation-state might have been a choice their Ainu families made as an outward expression of assimilation to garner favor from–or avoid the wrath of—the colonizer and to avoid having the children become the targets of discrimination. However, if the choice to change the girls' Ainu names to Kiku and Kin was made when the Ainu group's passports were issued by the Japanese government, this would have been a symbolic claiming of Ainu people as Japanese citizens by naming them for the colonial state.

Kiku and Kin were not the only Native children at the fair. Most of the groups of Native people present at the fair included one or more children, and the fair organizers planned for this, building community playgrounds and organizing "Children of All Nations" events to bring the children together—both for the sake of fairgoers and the enjoyment of the children. Children "from all nations" played together and observed each other, their families, and their cultures. Kiku and Kin and their cohort of other Native children in St. Louis lived together for months, thousands of miles away from home and their regular playmates. This set of interactions represents yet another point for investigation into moments of transnational Indigenous exchange that has escaped much consideration in the field to this point.

While this particular history is yet to be done, we must recall that as Starr's journal states, stories about the fair would have been shared upon the group's return. Being so young at the time of the fair, Kiku and Kin were poised to see dramatic changes in Ainu-Japanese governmental relationships. The girls were part of the first generation to grow up under the Former Native Protection Policy, which was passed only five years before the fair. But they likely also grew up hearing stories about their time at the fair. It is interesting to consider how stories about interactions at the fair might have been shared beyond the individual villages the Ainu returned to. And even how they may have informed later Ainu resistance movements. The trajectory of Ainu social movements is very similar to that of American Indians, with many in the 1920s and '30s urging assimilation to ensure survival. While it might be tempting to think of assimilationism as the antithesis of resistance, we must bear in mind that under such circumstances, the very act of survival is resistant. As elsewhere, Indigenous resistance movements took several forms, and as Richard Siddle underscores, in 1932 the Alliance for the Abolition of the Protection Act (Kyuudojin Hogoho Teppei Domei) was formed by the same group who had formed an Ainu welfare reform group led by Ichitaro Sunazawa in 1926.[54] Siddle, further exhibiting a similarity with the timing and political trajectory of other Indigenous rights movements, calls the change seen in Ainu groups toward the end of the 1960s as a move from welfare politics to Indigenous rights. These new Ainu rights movements were pro-Ainu identity and culture reclamation and anti-assimilation. "The Ainu, as an indigenous people, were not just another disadvantaged social group in need of state welfare but a 'nation' desirous of decolonization."[55] In Ainu Mosir, North America, and elsewhere, the Native resistance movements of the 1970s are often pointed to as the moment a global Indigenous consciousness began to travel along a path that led contemporary Indigenous people to seek audiences at the United Nations and organize in many ways to work against oppression. Yet, it seems worth considering that the seeds for a global Indigenous rights movements might have been gathered much earlier and were kept safe until the political ground was thought to be appropriately fertile. As Siddle writes,

> Ainu nationhood was greatly stimulated by contacts with indigenous peoples in other countries. Yoshimi Hiramura, the young founder of the Ainu newspaper *Anutari Ainu*, consciously identified with Native Americans after a trip to the United States in 1972, and the first issue of the paper devoted a page to the confrontation at Wounded Knee between activists of the American Indian Movement and federal authorities. Ainu began to travel and actively seek out other Native peoples, from China to Alaska.[56]

In 1992, during the inaugural activities for what the United Nations had declared was the "International Year for the Indigenous People," an Ainu man named Giichi Nomura took the stage and declared himself and his fellow Ainu people Indigenous to what is now northern Japan. While this may not seem like a statement that would garner tremendous international attention, it did. Until then, the Japanese government had publicly maintained that it was a homogenous nation with no racial or ethnic minority groups.[57] Such national assertions had long precluded the possibility that there were any Indigenous populations in Japan, and thus Nomura's statement was a public shaming of sorts, proclaiming, as it did, that the origin story of Japan as a one-race nation was simply myth. Shortly after this event, Japan declared it did not acknowledge the Ainu people as indigenous to northern Japan, but instead as an ethnic group within Japan. In a country whose textbooks had long taught that Ainu people were essentially extinct, where sameness is valued and individuality shunned, the government's statement was truly shocking. In 2008, more than fifteen years later, Japan officially declared that Ainu people are Indigenous to northern Japan.

I have sought to show throughout this article that Indigenous experiences at the 1904 Louisiana Purchase Exposition and the decisions individual Native peoples made while there are significant in their own right. Their actions—the young Ainu men regrowing their beards, for example—may have been made with the new knowledge that there were many, many people around the world in similar political and colonial situations. Given the conventions of Ainu culture, specifically, we know that stories of these encounters would have been shared with their communities and friends when they returned home. Seeing how much attention was garnered by simply performing everyday Ainu lifeways—in a historical moment in which expressions of Ainu-ness were banned and belittled by the Japanese assimilationist government—may well have suggested to the Ainu group that there were people in other parts of the world who were interested in Native traditions. While we know that this "interest" stemmed from a desire to preserve these "primitive" and "vanishing" people, how might the narratives we construct about these experiences change if we consider that the motives behind this "interest" might have been understood and interpreted differently by the Native participants at the time? This question and the answers presented here are far from complete. But this discussion is offered as a means of moving Native experience, perceptions, and peoples from silenced and marginalized positions within these histories to the center of intellectual exploration, one that seeks out and critically engages with instances of transnational Indigenous exchange.

Notes

I am grateful to the editor, editorial board, and guest editors for their comments and suggestions. I also appreciate the generous insights offered by my friends and colleagues Daryl Maeda, Dory Nason, Antonio T. Tiongson Jr., and Phoebe S. K. Young.

1. Ainu people are indigenous to what is now northern Japan, the coast of Siberia, and nearby islands. Tzoneca people, more often referred to as the "Tehuelche" or "the Patagonians" in fair materials are indigenous to what is now Argentina.
2. Michel Rolph Trouillot, *Silencing the Past: Power and the Production of History* (Boston: Beacon Press, 1995), xix.

3. Tecumseh's attempt to unite certain American Indian tribes against the invaders is one of the most well known examples, although Metacomet's War is often considered the first such event.
4. Shari Huhndorf, *Mapping the Americas: The Transnational Politics of Contemporary Native Culture* (Ithaca, N.Y.: Cornell University Press, 2009), 14.
5. In the 1870s Japan sought advice from the United States on the "opening of new lands" that Ainu territories represented. That the main American advisor to the 開拓使 (Kaitakushi) Japanese Colonization Commission served as an Indian agent prior to his time in Japan should not be overlooked; see D. Medak-Saltzman, "Staging Empire: The Display and Erasure of Indigenous Peoples in Japanese and American Nation Building Projects (1860–1904)" (PhD diss., University of California, Berkeley, 2008).
6. Nancy J. Parezo and Don. D. Fowler, *Anthropology Goes to the Fair: The 1904 Louisiana Purchase Exposition* (Lincoln: Nebraska University Press, 2007), 195. Despite noting the preference of the Tzoneca to be referred to as Tzoneca, not as "Tehuelche," a term used by their neighbors, meaning "southerners," Parezo and Fowler use the terms "Patagonian" and "Tehuelche" throughout their text.
7. A rare exception is Sharon Delmendo's consideration of the paradox of Filipinos at the 1889 Paris Exposition being inspired to frame their resistance to American empire after witnessing American Indian performances in the Wild West shows—themselves displays of empire and Indian "authenticity"—in *The Star Entangled Banner: One Hundred Years of America in the Philippines* (Newark, N.J.: Rutgers University Press), 17, 29–36.
8. Parezo and Fowler, *Anthropology Goes to the Fair*, 3.
9. Ngugi wa Thiong'o, *Moving the Centre: The Struggle for Cultural Freedoms* (Oxford: James Currey Ltd., 1993).
10. Trouillot, *Silencing the Past*, xix.
11. A prime example is calling *ikupasuy*, Ainu prayer sticks, "mustache lifters." To the nineteenth-century European eye, Ainu use of *ikupasuy* was similar to the European use of devices to keep mustaches clean while eating and drinking. Ainus have long contested this as derogatory; see Fosco Maraini, "Ikupasuy: It's Not a Mustache Lifter!" in *Ainu: Spirit of a Northern People*, ed. William W. Fitzhugh and Chisato O. Dubreuil, 327–34 (Los Angeles: Perpetua Press, 1999).
12. The reader will notice that while complicating the spaces of encounter where the Ainus are concerned, only bits and pieces of the Tzonecas' experiences have been illuminated. This treatment is not intended to undermine or diminish the experiences of the Tzonecas at the fair but is due to the limited availability of resources in the Tzoneca case.
13. See http://exhibits.slpl.org/lpe/intro.asp (accessed October 8, 2007).
14. Text appears next to the image in the library's online exhibit. See http://exhibits.slpl.org/lpe/data/LPE240023178.asp?thread=240029402 (accessed October 10, 2007).
15. This exchange is imagined using a Western conceptualization of gender, and women's roles in world society, a point that is underscored by the fact that while this image is of two women and a dog, the hypothetical question posed in the caption is about child rearing.
16. Fitzhugh and Dubreuil, *Ainu*, 141.
17. Laura Wexler, *Tender Violence: Domestic Visions in an Age of U.S. Imperialism* (Chapel Hill: University of North Carolina Press, 2000), 265.
18. Ibid., 279.
19. Ibid., 43.
20. Ibid., 276.
21. Anonymous, "Patagonian Giants Here: Ask for Diet of Horse Meat," no source, April 15, 1904, n.p., W. J. McGee Papers, box 16, Library of Congress. Quoted in Parezo and Fowler, *Anthropology Goes to the Fair*, 197.
22. Alexander Alland Sr., *Jessie Tarbox Beals: First Woman News Photographer* (New York: Camera/Graphic Press, 1978), 43.
23. Lorenza is listed as forty-five years old in archival materials.
24. Rayna Green, "The Pocahontas Perplex: Images of American Indian Women in American Culture," *Massachusetts Review* 16 (1975): 698–714.
25. Here I am echoing Wexler's argument (*Tender Violence*, 277) yet departing from it by underscoring that it is Beals's candid photographs that may serve future endeavors in exploring transnational Indigenous exchange.
26. Ibid., 299.

27. Parezo and Fowler, *Anthropology Goes to the Fair*, 195.
28. Fitzhugh and Dubreuil, *Ainu*, 252.
29. Brett L. Walker, *The Conquest of Ainu Lands : Ecology and Culture in Japanese Expansion, 1590–1800* (Berkeley: University of California Press, 2001), 160.
30. This reference to the position of dogs in Ainu society is not based on the long-held and pejorative belief—initiated by Wa-jin (ethnic Japanese) and perpetuated by others—that Ainu are "hairy" because they trace their origin to a union between humans and dogs. While this belief was ostensibly based on a portion of an Ainu origin story, the story itself was about transformation, not about bestiality, as the colonial narrative implies, but it was nevertheless misused to justify inhumane treatment of Ainu people.
31. Parezo and Fowler, *Anthropology Goes to the Fair*, 210.
32. Frederick Starr, *The Ainu Group at the Saint Louis Exposition* (Chicago: Open Court Publishing Company, 1904), 104.
33. Ibid.
34. Chisato O. Dubreuil's recent biography of Sunazawa, *From the Playground of the Gods: The Life and Art of Bikky Sunazawa* (Washington, D.C.: Arctic Studies Center, National Museum of Natural History, Smithsonian Institution, 2004) documents this aspect of his artistic interest.
35. Parezo and Fowler, *Anthropology Goes to the Fair*, 214.
36. Ibid., 100.
37. The people living with John Batchelor at the time of "collection" were not part of the ceremonies.
38. Starr, *Ainu Group*, 76.
39. Ibid., 116–18.
40. Ibid., 76.
41. Ibid., 56.
42. Robert Rydell, *All the World's a Fair* (Chicago: University of Chicago Press, 1984), 155.
43. Parezo and Fowler, *Anthropology Goes to the Fair*, 50. McGee wanted anthropology classes to use exhibits as sites for fieldwork and as classrooms. McGee refers to the anthropology exhibit as a "university" in his article "Anthropology," in the *World's Fair Bulletin* 5.5 (1904): 4.
44. W. J. McGee, "Opportunities for Anthropology at the World's Fair," *Science* 20.503 (August 19, 1904): 253.
45. W. J. McGee, "The Anthropology Exhibit," *Harper's Weekly*, April 30, 1904, 683.
46. Japanese colonization of the "white" Ainu also actually called their racial designation into question among European and American scientists. See Rotem Kowner, "'Lighter Than Yellow, But Not Enough': Western Discourse of the Japanese 'Race,' 1854–1904," *The Historical Journal* 43.1 (March 2000): 103–31.
47. The names provide primitive allusions for visitors. Some of these living displays were referred to as "reservations" and the body of water near the "Philippine reservation" was named "Arrowhead Lake."
48. Parezo and Fowler, *Anthropology Goes to the Fair*, 279, fig. 10.4.
49. Ibid., 272.
50. Japan sent national exhibits to almost every fair after 1873. The 1904 exhibition, however, was the first time Ainu people were part of exhibitions outside of Japan.
51. There is significant evidence (archival, photographic, etc.) that Native peoples interacted with each other at the fair. The first Olympic games held in the United States coincided with this fair and while nation-state representatives competed with each other in the "Olympic Games," Native peoples were made to compete in "Anthropology Days" against their "own kind," in "primitive" skills—all had to participate in bow and arrow contests even though these were foreign tools to some Native participants.
52. Ages are approximate due to differences in how children's ages were calculated in Japanese, and perhaps even Ainu, customs.
53. Although these names have been published with the English translations in reverse order, and then repeatedly published uncorrected, it is an error. My translations are accurate to the Japanese definition of these names.
54. Father of the late great artist Bikky Sunazawa. Bikky's mother, Peramonkoro, was also an important Ainu rights activist.

55. Richard Siddle, "From Assimilation to Indigenous Rights: Ainu Resistance Since 1869," in *Ainu: Spirit of a Northern People*, ed. Fitzhugh and Dubreuil, 108–15.
56. Ibid., 114–15.
57. Much of the work published in Japanese studies argued the case of Japanese exceptionalism and cultural homogeneity until the early 1990s when a large body of work began arguing otherwise. These efforts occurred on the heels of Ainu efforts that were under way in the 1970s and 1980s (largely as an undertaking of the Ainu Association of Hokkaido 北海道アイヌウタリ協会), in attempts to repeal the Former Native Protection Policy that had been in effect since 1899, a policy containing elements similar to the U.S. General Allotment Act of 1887.

"Sioux Yells" in the Dawes Era: Lakota "Indian Play," the Wild West, and the Literatures of Luther Standing Bear

Ryan E. Burt

In 1902 Luther Standing Bear decided to join William "Buffalo Bill" Cody's Wild West show as it traveled across the Atlantic and toured England. A shift in federal Indian policy made it difficult for Standing Bear, as with many Lakota, to support his family at Pine Ridge reservation, and Cody's show promised gainful employment, mobility, and perhaps a sense of adventure. Initially hired as an interpreter for the Lakota, the nation from which most Wild West "Indian" performers came, and upon whom Cody's fortunes largely relied, Standing Bear soon found himself "playing Indian" in Cody's show as well.[1] He quickly became a savvy performer, so much so that Buffalo Bill approached him before the troupe's weighty debut in front of King Edward the Seventh. As Standing Bear later recalled in his autobiography *My People the Sioux* (1928), Cody told him: "'We must please the King at this performance . . . when the King attends the show, I want you to do an Indian dance in front of his box. Will you do this for me?'"[2] Standing Bear agreed to the request. When the day of the show arrived, he was up for the challenge:

> I had a beautiful lance, and as the dance proceeded I worked over toward the King's box. There I shook the lance in his face and danced my very prettiest, you may be sure. The King had been very dignified thus far and had not even smiled. But when I got down to doing my fancy steps and gave a few Sioux yells, he had to smile in spite of himself. I saw that I had made a hit with him, and was very happy.[3]

Such an amusing anecdote is remarkable and profoundly insightful. The story underscores the keen sense of awareness Standing Bear, like many American Indian performers and writers at the turn of the century, developed in relationship to the model of "Indian" identity a non-Native audience wanted to see. Standing Bear had a nuanced understanding of "Indian expectations," a phrase Philip Deloria uses to suggest the "dense economies of meaning, representation, and act" that produce "the body of accepted knowledge about Indian people" and, consequently, shape U.S. colonial power relations.[4] For more than thirty years, from 1883 to 1916, Buffalo Bill's Wild West produced "Indian expectations" for millions of audience members in the United States and Europe.

King Edward's presence also points to the particularity of Cody's self-consciously constructed American frontier narrative. While the Wild West was originally little more than a rodeo saddled on theatrical melodrama, Cody recast it in 1886, perhaps in anticipation of its first English tour, as a uniquely American epic.[5] The show paraded American exceptionalism as Cody, unlike Edward the Seventh, rose from humble frontier origins to become "King of the Border Men" in the vanguard of American civilization. Moreover, the Plainsmen's heroism, and the possibility of available western land for an Edenic, "egalitarian" society, relied upon a strangely inverted colonial narrative. Somehow white colonizers always found themselves surrounded by attacking Indians. By 1902 Standing Bear's "Sioux yells" were a Wild West signature as the show made "Custer's Last Stand" a climactic set piece, hence offering the Lakota a most villainous role in U.S. history. Rejecting the word *show*, Buffalo Bill promoted this historical account as "realist," a claim authenticated by the fact that many performers, such as Sitting Bull, actually lived through the events the Wild West portrayed.

Although he traveled with Cody's troupe for only one year, Standing Bear moved to California a decade later and "played Indian" in a variety of Westerns, such as *Cyclone of the Saddle* and *Miracle Rider*, until his death in 1939 during the filming of *Union Pacific*.[6] In Hollywood, near the end of his career, Standing Bear finally sat down to write four books that offered accounts of his life and the history and customs of the Lakota: *My People the Sioux* (1928), *My Indian Boyhood* (1931), *Land of the Spotted Eagle* (1933), and *Stories of the Sioux* (1934).[7] By the time he picked up his pen, Standing Bear was well aware of the persistence and ubiquity of the Wild West's "Indian." Buffalo Bill translated Native violence—long disseminated in the nineteenth century via "blood and thunder" dime novels—into a visual language readily adapted by an emergent film industry in the twentieth century.

However brief Luther Standing Bear's time with Cody, the Wild West provided an experience that transformed his life and his life's work. In an era when the federal government endeavored to immobilize and disband the Lakota, the show helped him, as with previous performers like the Oglala holy man Black Elk, leave Pine Ridge, as Standing Bear wrote, to "better the conditions of my people" rather than "fight the [reservation] agent all the time."[8] In this regard he was one of "hundreds of Indian people [who] took advantage of Wild West tours in order to adventure around the world, producing the modern through their mobility and their works of representation."[9] More than this, as I argue in what follows, Standing Bear's own work of representation, in particular his autobiography *My People the Sioux*, was necessarily and dynamically conversant with both Cody's and filmic narratives that relied on Lakota violence. The Wild West provided Standing Bear intimate, behind-the-scenes contact with this powerfully spectacular frontier story and the "authentic" techniques used to stage U.S. history. As evinced by *My People the Sioux*, Standing Bear learned these lessons well. While he dismantled accounts of the Battle at Little Big Horn and the "battle" at Wounded Knee popularized by Cody, he also grounded the veracity of *My People* in a Cody-esque rhetoric of "authenticity."

But the Wild West was not the only popular American developmental narrative Luther Standing Bear had to address. Born in the late 1860s, Standing Bear was part of the first generation of American Indians to experience the full force of the Dawes General Allotment Act (1887) and its attendant boarding school project, both of which aimed to dissolve indigenous sovereignty, transform Native subjectivity, and assimilate tribes into the body of the nation-state through citizenship.[10] Such policies were born on the wings of reformers, mostly white middle-class Protestants from the East, who believed social and racial "uplift" was a one-way street leading to private-property-owning American citizenship. Standing Bear, like a number of Native writers and intellectuals in the early twentieth century, was influenced by and repurposed such reformist rhetoric in *My People the Sioux* and *Land of the Spotted Eagle*, the other book this essay considers.[11] He was as dynamically conversant with this rhetoric as he was with the Western's visual rhetoric. As *Land of the Spotted Eagle* makes clear, Standing Bear considered the address of both discourses a linked task. Written on the eve of the Indian New Deal, the work blasted the arrogance of a "progressive" ideology that threatened to destroy, because it failed to understand, the sophistication and value of Lakota society.

"Reality Eclipsing Romance": The Wild West, or History as Inverted Conquest

Shortly after the Civil War, a young William Cody found gainful employment serving as a guide for the U.S. Army, where he was appointed chief scout of the Fifth Cavalry. The plainsman's accomplishments soon began to capture the public eye as he engaged in horse races and shooting contests, which, according to Joy Kasson, "mingled business with pleasure, compounded feats of skill with acts of self-promotion, and made frontier life inseparable from its embodiment as a spectacle."[12] Cody's spectacle spread, with surprising rapidity, from West to East. In 1869 William "Buffalo Bill" Cody met the dime novelist Ned Buntline, who used the frontiersman as the protagonist for the serialized and wildly successful novel *Buffalo Bill, the King of the Border Men.*[13] Three years later Cody traveled to Chicago and performed in his first theatrical drama, also written by Buntline, titled *The Scouts of the Prairie.* For the next decade the "King of the Border Men" alternated between summer employment as a military scout and winter employment in eastern theaters. "The plays themselves were trivial and the acting amateurish," notes Richard Slotkin, "but [their] success . . . was evidence of the public's deep and uncritical enthusiasm for 'the West,' which could best be addressed through a combination of dime-novel plots and characters with 'authentic' costumes and personages identified as 'the real thing.'"[14]

By 1883 Cody left the theater and started down a career path that defined his contribution to the mass public's interpretation of the American frontier experience: he created the Wild West.[15] Initially the show was a mash-up of sorts, combining elements from rodeo, such as horse racing and marksmanship, with melodramatic scenes of "western" life that were largely gleaned from dime novels: the attack on the Deadwood Stage, a raid on a settler's cabin, and a Pony Express display.[16] However, in 1886 this program was recast as "America's National Entertainment." While the content of the show had not really changed, the Wild West now sold itself as "an exemplification of the entire course of American history."[17] Promotional material promised the audience would see "many types of the Pioneers and Vanguards of Civilization. Celebrated Scouts, Veritable Cow-Boys, Mexican Vaqueros. Representatives of THE RUGGED LIFE OF PRIMITIVE MAN."[18] The advertisement suggested that all these characters' "lives have been passed in REALITY ECLIPSING ROMANCE." This final phrase effectively distilled the larger cultural work the revamped show tried to accomplish: it presented romanticized frontier mythology as realist history. A popular midwestern journalist, in a review that was soon incorporated into the Wild West's program (distributed to audience members), proclaimed the exhibition a "Wild West Reality . . . a correct representation of life on the plains . . . brought to the East for the inspection and education of the public."[19] Another newspaper reporter enthused: "The whole thing is real . . . It is the picture of frontier life painted in intense realism . . . No, not painted, but acted as it is being acted along the entire frontier."[20]

The shift to the Wild West's purported pedagogical function, tellingly, may have been in anticipation of the show's first European tour (1887–89).[21] Perhaps it is for this reason that the "picture of frontier life painted in intense realism" was dyed in the deepest shades of red, white, and blue American exceptionalism. As Jonathan Martin points out, unlike its dime novel predecessors, which frequently foregrounded a labor-vs.-capital theme, issues "of class were conspicuously absent from the show, a tacit affirmation that such issues were not American concerns."[22] Cody was cast as the archetypal, self-reliant American frontier hero whose rise in social rank affirmed "the bourgeois success story of individualism and hard work."[23]

However, the most dramatic example of the Wild West's historical exceptionalism was the show's depiction of American Indians. Cody's heroism, and ticket sales, depended on a particularly savage, war-bonneted villainy. Indeed, Cody established the visual grammar, embraced by Hollywood only decades later, for one of the most entrenched colonial myths in American popular cultural history: white victimhood at the hands of Plains Indians. Historian Richard White labels this Buffalo Bill's "inverted conquest," writing that

> the role of these Indians in the show was to attack whites. Many of the great set pieces of the Wild West—"A Prairie Emigrant Train Crossing the Plains," the "Capture of the Deadwood Mail Coach by the Indians," and, the most famous of all, "The Battle of the Little Big Horn, Showing with Historical Accuracy the Scene of Custer's Last Charge"—featured Indian attacks.
>
> Buffalo Bill offered what to a modern historian seems an odd story of conquest: everything is inverted. His spectacles presented an account of Indian aggression and white defense; of Indian killers and white victims; of, in effect, badly abused conquerors . . . Americans had to transform conquerors into victims. The great military icons of westward expansion are not victories, they are defeats: the Alamo and the Battle of Little Big Horn. We, these stories say, do not plan our conquests . . . We just retaliate against barbaric massacre.[24]

While the story of "inverted conquest" may originally have been a history lesson intended for European audiences, the Wild West's rationalization of U.S. colonial expansion reached enormous, enthusiastic crowds upon returning to the United States in 1893. Thus the show came to represent what Cody's business associate, Nate Salsbury, called "the grandest and most cosmopolitan Object Teacher" American audiences had seen.[25] In an era (1870–1920) in which 26 million immigrants entered the United States, the Wild West could put "inverted conquest" to a particularly domestic educative role.[26] One of the show's selling points throughout this period was that it introduced new European immigrants, "the blond, blue-eyed Norseman, the swarthy Italian," to "the people whose place they have taken," the American Indian.[27] Because the most famous set piece in the Wild West was "The Battle of the Little Big Horn, Showing with Historical Accuracy the Scene of Custer's Last Charge," white American identity was measured, most explicitly, in hostile relationship to the Lakota.

To a degree, this was a result of the relative contemporaneity of the highly publicized U.S. military conflict with the tribe. About ten years before the Wild West's first tour, on June 25, 1876, George Armstrong Custer, with the 7th Cavalry under his command, attacked an encamped village of seven thousand Lakota and allied Cheyenne along the banks of the Little Big Horn. Custer was tasked with moving Native "hostiles" onto reservations in Dakota Territory, yet, after repeated treaty violations by the U.S. government, the tribes were hesitant to relocate. When Custer charged into the northern end of the village leading two hundred soldiers, Lakota and Cheyenne warriors defended their people, killing all the cavalrymen.[28] For many Lakota, the Battle at Little Big Horn was one in a series of conflicts catalyzed by the abrogation of the Ft. Laramie treaty, a treaty that secured their beloved Black Hills from white settlement. Custer himself was implicated in the treaty violations as he had, two years prior, led a military expedition into the Hills, facilitated the "discovery" of gold, and fanned the publicity flames that sparked the Black Hills gold rush.[29]

But Wild West audiences would not catch a glimpse of the Lakota's historical perspective. Instead, the show abstracted the violence at Little Big Horn and Buffalo Bill made the "image of Custer's defeat and the slaughter of most of his command the chief icon of this theme of the conquering victim."[30] Starting in the 1880s this iconography marked the performative apex of Cody's shows around the country and world; was plastered, thanks to an Anheuser-Busch campaign, across thousand of barrooms in the United States in the 1890s; and, at the dawn of the twentieth century, was translated to the silver screen in some of the earliest motion pictures.[31]

One of the most important early films for Thomas Ince, a director who influenced the development of the cinematic Western, and for whom Luther Standing Bear later worked, was titled *Custer's Last Stand*, released in 1912.[32] A year later, a bankrupt Cody, hoping for celluloid gold, founded the Cody Historical Pictures Company and went to work on an epic Western titled *The Last Indian Wars*. Eventually released in 1914 as *The Indian Wars*, the film staged a reenactment of the Ghost Dance revival and the ensuing Massacre at Wounded Knee.[33] The movie was not a commercial success, but one reviewer's comments reveal a great deal about the continuity between the Wild West's frontier narrative and its translation to film. In the words of a writer from the Omaha *World Herald*, "there is nothing to be learned from the pictures as to the causes of these Indian wars."[34]

If audience members were left guessing at the causes of the "Indian wars," the Lakota were nevertheless left to deal with their aftermath. More accurately, they faced an altogether different type of warfare that aimed to immobilize, disband,

and disinherit them. "The logic of events demands," stated the commissioner of Indian Affairs, Thomas Morgan, in 1889, "the absorption of the Indians into our national life, not as Indians, but as American citizens."[35] While the Wild West reaped huge profits narrating a history of inverted conquest from 1883 to 1916, in reality it was the Lakota who were surrounded in this period.

"We all got busy fencing ourselves in": Pine Ridge, the General Allotment Act, and Lakota "Indian Play"

While Standing Bear's performance in front of King Edward was indeed remarkable, it was far from unique. Cody's Wild West had been literally banking on Sioux performers since the summer of 1885, a year when Sitting Bull helped the show play to a million audience members, earning one hundred thousand dollars and clearing Cody's remaining debts from previous seasons.[36] Although Cody initially employed Pawnee actors, in the wake of Sitting Bull's popularity the Wild West hired nearly all Sioux, most of whom were enrolled at Pine Ridge agency (later, reservation).[37]

One of the early employees from Pine Ridge was the Oglala holy man Black Elk. Roughly twenty years prior to Luther Standing Bear's own royal performance, a contingent of nearly one hundred Lakota performers, including Black Elk and warriors like Kills Plenty, Rocky Bear, and the soon to be celebrity Red Shirt, accompanied Cody on his first trip to England.[38] Although they performed in front of a young Edward, then Albert Edward Prince of Wales, the occasion for this first tour in England was the celebration of Queen Victoria's Golden Jubilee. The performers thus soon found themselves in front of Victoria herself. Black Elk later recalled: "We danced and sang, and I was one of the dancers chosen to do this for the Grandmother [Queen Victoria], because I was young and limber then and could dance in many ways."[39] The Sioux performers, in Black Elk's estimation, enjoyed their encounter with the queen. "Maybe," he mused, "if she had been our Grandmother, it would have been better for our people."[40]

To be sure, the Oglala holy man hoped learning from his travels might help him to help the Lakota. While Black Elk's rationale for traveling with the Wild West may have been unique to his calling, the material conditions he responded to at home surely motivated many Lakota performers to seek employment with Cody:

> Hunger was among us often now, for much of what the Great Father in Washington sent us must have been stolen by Wasichus [whites] who were crazy to get money . . . [I joined the Wild West hoping] I might learn some secret of the Wasichu that would help my people

> somehow . . . Maybe if I could see the great world of the Wasichu, I could understand how to bring the sacred hoop together and make the tree bloom again at the center of it.[41]

When Black Elk finally returned to Pine Ridge, however, he found conditions worse than when he had left. Drought, failed crops, and the federal government's inability to provide treaty provisions, such as cattle, created starving conditions. Clearly the allure of the Wild West, the promise of indigenous mobility, and the reasons for Lakota "Indian Play" in this era must be understood in relation to late nineteenth- and early twentieth-century federal Indian policy.

Like Black Elk before him, Luther Standing Bear's reason for joining Cody's troupe was directly linked to the local conditions on the Pine Ridge and Rose Bud reservations, conditions closely tied to the policies of the General Allotment Act of 1887. Also known as the Dawes Act, this legislation radically transformed Native communities and their relationship to the federal government. According to the policy, reservations were to be divided by allotting each head of a family 160 acres (with lesser amounts to other individuals) and the land was to be held in trust by the United States for twenty-five years (to protect new owners from unscrupulous whites). Any "surplus" land remaining after all allotments were made was opened to white settlement. Finally, with allotment came American citizenship.[42] The Dawes Act realized the ideals of eastern reformers such as the Friends of the Indian, the Indian Rights Association, and the Boston Indian Citizenship Committee.[43] Like the eponymous Senator Henry Dawes, these organizations believed citizenship would eliminate racial barriers and secure justice for the tribes. Moreover, an appreciation of private property and the capitalist mode of production would, in their estimation, "rescue" Native peoples. While reformers were convinced that enfranchisement and liberal capitalist democracy was the "Indian problem's" salve, the historical effects of allotment legislation demonstrate the markedly less altruistic drive behind the policy.

Labeling the Dawes Act "a historical catastrophe for the American Indian," Louis Owens describes a policy aimed at undermining tribal sovereignty, landholdings, and communal relations.[44] Within forty-five years of its passage, tribes lost 90 million acres of land. This was accomplished via a combination of both legal and bureaucratic control, working in concert with vocational education at off-reservation boarding schools. Taken as a whole, this allotment matrix proved a powerful form of colonial domination for indigenous communities across the United States. The situation at Pine Ridge was no exception. From the 1880s to the 1930s the Lakota encountered new colonial techniques that sought to subject them to the authority of the United States. The primary modes of subjection, according to Thomas Biolosi, included empropertiment, the creation of the liminal "wardship" status, the practice of blood-quantum calculation, and the recording of family genealogical records by the Office of Indian Affairs.[45] All these practices were intended to facilitate the assimilationist thrust of allotment policy and the government's desire to transform indigenous subjectivity. "The Lakota," Biolosi notes, "had to be forced to conform to a certain minimum definition of modern individuality. In this way, they would be constituted as social persons who could fit into the American nation-state and the market system of metropolitan capitalism."[46]

Even before allotment became official policy at Pine Ridge, Standing Bear was encouraged, from a young age, to "conform to a certain definition of modern individuality." As one of the first group of Native students to attend the Carlisle Indian School in Pennsylvania, Standing Bear, following his father's wishes, left Rosebud for the school conceptualized and directed by the military man Richard Henry Pratt.[47] An unapologetic assimilationist, Pratt enforced an English-only curriculum, pushed students to learn a trade, and stressed the importance of acquiring discipline.[48] He also hoped an "outing system," a summer program that arranged for Native students to work and live with white families, would discourage students from returning to the reservation.

Standing Bear excelled in his studies but eventually, after four years in the east and to Pratt's displeasure, returned to Rosebud. He later wrote, "There came the battle of my life—the battle with agents to retain my individuality and my life as a Lakota."[49] Efforts to reshape Lakota identity on the reservation were well under way as paternalism, restrictions on cultural traditions, and insistence on the market economy ruled the day. Standing Bear recalled:

> A rule would come out forbidding something to be done, and in a short while another order would be issued forbidding something to be done, until gradually and slowly rights began to disappear . . . there one day appeared a printed notice, by order of the agent, that no returned student would thereafter be permitted to attend any tribal dance. This was done to make young people turn away from things traditional . . . Soon another rule followed, stating that whenever a horse or present was given away, it must be done silently.[50]

Presumably Lakota models of material distribution, in this instance gift giving and the celebration of it, threatened the "progressive" Office of Indian Affairs' understanding of commodity exchange and needed to be rendered clandestine.

Labor practices, in the estimation of the Interior Department, also needed to be transformed, even if, and likely because, this transformation meant a movement away from treaty obligations. As the tinsmithing trade Standing Bear learned at Carlisle proved useless at home, he worked a variety of odd jobs around the reservation. Shortly before joining the Wild West, he was enjoying working on his own ranch when, "like a thunderbolt from a clear sky came an order from the Interior Department that all rations and annuity goods which had been issued to all able-bodied Indians were to be cut off unless the Indians were willing to work for them."[51] As an able-bodied man, Standing Bear now, as he put it, "had to get out and hustle."[52] The irony of "free labor" in the allotment period, as employment itself was now linked to the federal government's effort to control the Lakota, was not lost on Standing Bear, who described the "hustle" he was forced to undertake:

> When the agent called for more men, I went to him, and was assigned to help build a fence around the entire Indian reservation. This seemed like a funny proposition to us—fencing us in like a lot of wild animals—and the Interior Department had approved such an order!
>
> However, we all got busy fencing ourselves in, at $2.50 per day for a man and his team. It seemed like a positive disgrace to construct this fence around a race of people who had always been free to roam where they chose.[53]

This sense of physical entrapment was paralleled by the sense of financial entrapment movement into the market economy produced. After a season of work, Lakota men were indebted to the storekeeper from whom they bought groceries and horse feed. With little cash to prepare for winter, the men took on more debt, which meant they would have to work the following summer to pay their loans off. "This working out one year put me back two years," Standing Bear recalled. "There was no encouragement in such an arrangement for any of us. We were in the clutches of the white man—and the Interior Department was behind it!"[54]

In the midst of impoverishment and agency surveillance, the possibility of travel and employment with Buffalo Bill allured hundreds of Lakota. For Standing Bear it surely seemed more attractive to freely roam the streets in New York City and London rather than beg an agent for permission to leave reservation territory. And while the Wild West relied on the clichéd images of Indian barbarity, it also provided a chance to wear traditional clothing, demonstrate equestrian mastery, and perform tribal dances in an era when these practices were condemned and outlawed on the reservation.[55]

It is, perhaps, for this very reason that reformers were widely opposed to Native participation in traveling shows like the Wild West. Despite the fact that American Indians were legally entitled to join them, reformers actively tried to check the practice, arguing the "shows encouraged unsettled habits and brought Indians into contact with disreputable characters."[56] In 1889 the new Indian commissioner Thomas Morgan began an active campaign, in spite of the law, to check the performance of "the lowest type of Indian, with his war dances, paint and blanket."[57] To discourage Indians from joining the show, he threatened the loss of their allotments, tribal status, and annuities.

But join the Wild West the Lakota did. Between 1887 and 1906 nearly one hundred performers a year, mostly from Pine Ridge, signed up with the show. In fact, the most significant flow of money onto the reservation in this period may have come from Lakota performers touring nationally and internationally.[58] In 1902, three days after he was offered the job of interpreter for the Lakota, Standing Bear packed his family's bags and inaugurated a career in cultural production that would ultimately position him as one of the harshest critics of America's mythologized frontier past and the arrogance of progressive reformers. Perhaps the best forecast of Standing Bear's future cultural work came from his disheartened former schoolmaster, Richard Henry Pratt. "Luther Standing Bear," he later wrote, "went off with 'Buffalo Bill' and lost his character . . . There [was] no better [boy] in [his] time at Carlisle than Luther Standing Bear."[59]

With Buffalo Bill, however, Standing Bear immediately received a hands-on education in the acting profession that proved far more consequential to his future than the tinsmithing he learned at Carlisle. Soon after arriving in London he began to work, and witness, the behind-the-scenes orchestration of a Wild West extravaganza. In rehearsals, the Lakota learned to "play Indian," acting the part of tribes like the Cheyenne as well. "While all the Indians belonged to the Sioux tribe," Standing Bear later recalled, "we were supposed to represent four different tribes, each tribe to ride animals of one color."[60] Even though his own horse initially "knew more about the show business at that time than I did myself," Standing Bear was a quick study.[61] When the show finally opened, his acting proved good enough for him to "play cowboy" as well. While in England, Standing Bear acted, translated, advocated for the working conditions of his people, and encouraged them to save wages for their families at home. He impressed and befriended Buffalo Bill, who hired him for the following year's tour. Unfortunately, in April 1903, en route to join Cody in New York City, Standing Bear and other Lakota performers were involved in a catastrophic train wreck that left several dead and Standing Bear severely injured and unable to travel. He returned to Pine Ridge after the accident and spent another decade struggling against Indian Office bureaucracy and agent authoritarianism. "With all my title of chieftain, and with all my education and travels," he wrote, "I discovered that as long as I was on the reservation I was only a helpless Indian . . . that is, according to the views of the white agent in charge."[62] Standing Bear once again packed his bags and left. In 1912 he arrived in California to work for film producer Thomas Ince.

"I told him that none of the Indian pictures were made right": *My People the Sioux* and *Land of the Spotted Eagle*

Standing Bear was certainly not the only Native performer turning to film as the Wild West was on the decline. Many Native actors worked in California's young film industry: from the Nebraska Ho-Chunk actress Lillian St. Cyr and her husband-director James Young Dear, to the Carlisle graduate and Cheyenne actor Richard David Thunderbird.[63] By 1916 Thomas Ince alone employed 121 American Indians, including a contingent of "Inceville Sioux." But Standing Bear was unique, as he eventually moved beyond acting and directly engaged the cultural politics of representation through his literature.

Like the autobiographical writing of his Sioux contemporaries, Charles Eastman (Santee) and Zitkala-Sa (Yankton), published earlier in the twentieth century, Standing Bear's works *My People the Sioux* (1928) and *Land of the Spotted Eagle* (1933) can be productively read in relation to the "progressive" discourses shaping Indian policy in this period.[64] Standing Bear was not, like Eastman and Zitkala-Sa, an active member of the Society of American Indians, a pan-Indian organization formed in 1911 with the goal of shaping public opinion to facilitate "the uplift of Indian people."[65] But to a degree his writing was, as Lucy Maddox notes, resonant with objectives of the SAI, which recognized "the need for Native spokespersons to communicate with white audiences" and for "the creation of an Indian public opinion—as well as an Indian influence on the formation of state and federal policies."[66]

Standing Bear initially turned to Thomas Ince himself in an effort to shape public opinion. "I told him," he wrote, "that none of the Indian pictures were made right."[67] Ince listened to this criticism, astonished. At least for a brief period, Standing Bear hoped Native writers might be able to actually transform the work of the culture industry: "I [told] Mr. Ince that I was willing to work for my people and help him, if he would accept my ideas and my stories. I waited for a reply, but none came."[68] *My People the Sioux*, then, was Standing Bear's first attempt to conduct his own ideas and stories directly to a larger white audience. When he turned to this project he was well prepared.

Buffalo Bill had done more than help Standing Bear off the reservation and offer a skill set adaptable to the movie business. The Wild West provided the actor prolonged contact with, and a sophisticated understanding of, the story of "inverted conquest" that now targeted the Lakota in motion pictures. Standing Bear also recognized the way Cody "authenticated" his melodramatic plots and enveloped them in the discourse of realism. By the time he worked at Inceville, both of these conventions had come to define the Western. The films produced at Inceville relied not only on former Wild West actors and props; they adopted the show's focus on action scenes featuring Indians.[69] Like Cody before him, Ince sold his films as true to life. The promotional poster for Ince's *Custer's Last Fight* (1912) underscores this point. The film is described as "EDUCATIONAL!" and "TRUE AND AUTHENTIC" as it depicts "the dashing Custer and his command . . . [who] were led into ambush by thousands of Bloodthirsty Indians under Sitting Bull and slain to the last man."[70]

One clear task of *My People,* then, was to disassemble the "Lakota expectations" cinema now capitalized on. Perhaps more surprising was the way Standing Bear approached this task. While he questioned the Western's romanticized colonial violence, his story drew on the same argument for fidelity promoted by the Wild West and, later, Ince Films. On this point the promotional poster for *Custer's Last Fight* serves as rich counterpoint to the opening pages of *My People the Sioux.* Standing Bear's preface asserts that he aspired, in a phrase saturated with performative awareness and Wild West "realism," to "bring my people before [the] eyes [of the white 'race'] in a *true and authentic* manner."[71] While grounding his authority, the preface also forecasts an objection to the dominant misrepresentations of native communities. "The American Indian," he wrote, "has been written about by hundreds of authors of white blood or possibly by an Indian of mixed blood who has spent the greater part of his life away from the reservation . . . White men who have tried to write stories about the Indian have either foisted on the public some *blood curdling, impossible 'thriller'*; or, if they have been in sympathy with the Indian, have written from knowledge which was not *accurate and reliable.* No one is able to understand the Indian race like an Indian."[72] Standing Bear secured the accuracy of his own "true and authentic" account, which would soon dismiss the Lakota from "blood curdling" thrillers, by elevating his role as witness and participant. Unlike "white" or "mixed blood" writers who had not, in this figuration, lived with Indian people, Standing Bear frames his knowledge as "accurate and reliable" because his stories came from actual historical agents.

In this regard his father played a tremendously significant role in *My People.* Certainly the fact that the accuracy of Standing Bear's autobiography has been questioned, as he supposedly inflated his father's importance, might speak less to the author's "failed" memory than to his awareness of the necessary claims to "authenticity" a white reader might expect. "Written late in his life," Richard

Ellis suggests, "it is not surprising *My People the Sioux* . . . contains some errors and perhaps an inflated sense of family and self-importance."[73] There is "the possibility that Standing Bear overemphasized the importance of his father, who is described as a major political figure among the Sioux."[74] Rather than reading this purported overemphasis as "factual error," we might note that Standing Bear's account may simply display a profound awareness of the way participation/observation authorized, as with the Wild West, history.[75]

The simultaneous conversation (or claim for historical realism) and contest (overturning the "blood curdling" thriller) with the Wild West characterizes Standing Bear's autobiography. This narrative strategy is particularly effective and poignant in the report of two conflicts that defined the Lakota in white America's imagination: the Battle of Little Big Horn and the "conflict" at Wounded Knee. In sharp counterpoint to Cody's near deification of Custer and his command, Standing Bear minimized the cavalryman's significance in Lakota history. While he dedicated a chapter to "Custer's Last Fight and the Death of Crazy Horse," the chapter itself is one of the shortest in the book. In an autobiography approaching three hundred pages, the "last fight" receives barely two. And in his terse account, Standing Bear repeatedly stresses the relative insignificance of the battle. Legitimating his account through his father's historical witness, he describes "the story of Custer's last fight, *as my father related it to me*": "after he had returned from the north, he told about killing the 'Long Hair.' This was the name given to General Custer by the Sioux. I asked him to tell me about it. He did not care to talk much about this, as it was considered a disgrace for us to kill a white man."[76] What Standing Bear does divulge about the conflict, notably, upends the gallant portrayal of the U.S. Cavalry and the depiction of Lakota aggression. According to his father, "when we rode into these soldiers I really felt sorry for them, they looked so frightened. They did not shoot at us. They seemed so panic-stricken that they shot up in the air. Many of them lay on the ground, with their blue eyes open, waiting to be killed . . . We men got off the field [after the battle], as it was no honor to be seen on a battle-field with these weak victims as our adversaries."[77] Standing Bear ends his story of Custer's "last stand" writing: "This was all that [my father] ever mentioned about Custer being killed. In all the years I was at home, I never heard this battle spoken of in a bragging way."[78]

The subsequent description of the massacre at Wounded Knee offered a similar inversion. Cody's motion picture debut, *The Indian Wars,* was shot on location at Wounded Knee in 1913.[79] The U.S. Army actually participated in the filming of the movie, and the primary military officer in command during the massacre, General Nelson Miles, was on location. While Cody apparently hoped to present Wounded Knee "as a massacre down to the last detail," General Miles balked at the idea.[80] Women and children were, consequently, removed from the filming of the "battle" scenes. Against this rendering of Wounded Knee, Standing Bear noted that his brother was "present at the Killing of all of Big Foot's Band, and was a witness to everything that happened."[81] Here was a radically different story than *The Indian Wars*:

> Men, women, and children—even babies were killed in their mother's arms! This was done by the soldiers. According to white man's history this was known as the "battle" of Wounded Knee, but it was not a battle—it was a slaughter, a massacre. Those soldiers had been sent to protect these men, women, and children who had not joined the ghost dancers, but they had shot them down without even a chance to defend themselves.[82]

Standing Bear centered the innocents in his account, and he did not mince words. Wounded Knee was no battle; it was a "massacre." For the Lakota, in these renderings, both the Little Big Horn and Wounded Knee were characterized by the U.S. Cavalry's failure to participate in actual battles. In the former, soldiers "waited to be killed," and in the latter, there was never any actual battle, just "slaughter."

In its strategic, direct engagement with the old, constantly retold stories of Lakota villainy, *My People the Sioux* was unique among American Indian autobiographies written during the allotment period. Yet Standing Bear's conclusion locates him squarely in the company of the Society of American Indians, who thought citizenship would help ameliorate the problems of Native communities. In the final chapter, "American Citizenship," he pictures an American modernity that includes American Indians and measures their value in relation to white citizens. "The Indian has just as many ounces of brains as his white brother," he wrote, "and with education and learning he will make a real American citizen of whom the white race will be justly proud."[83] As with the SAI, Standing Bear likely understood citizenship, not as a vehicle for assimilation, but as a mechanism for liberation from the paternalism of the Indian Office and reservation agents.[84] This outcome differed from white reformers', like the Friends of the Indian, assimilationist ideology, but Standing Bear still deployed the rhetoric of uplift to his own ends, beseeching his white readers, as he put it, "to help my people, the Sioux, by giving them full citizenship."[85]

Only five years passed between the publication of *My People* and Standing Bear's next major work, *Land of the Spotted Eagle* (1933), but those five years weighed heavy on the writer. After a fifteen-year absence he returned for a visit to Pine Ridge Reservation and found that conditions remained deplorable for the Lakota: their land base destroyed, culture under assault, economy faltering, and again facing starvation.[86] This was the case even after the Indian Citizenship Act (1924) ostensibly secured universal citizenship for all American Indians.[87] And the material realities of the Lakota were the rule rather than the exception for Indian peoples in this period. As the influential Merriam Report (1928), bellwether for the impending radical shift in Indian policy, stated: "the poverty of the Indians and their lack of adjustment to the dominant economic and social systems produce [a] vicious cycle."[88] Having witnessed the effects of the Dawes Act in Lakota country, Standing Bear now dismissed outright the "promise" of liberal capitalist democracy and the type of individuality demanded by it.

To a degree the differences between *My People* and *Land of the Spotted Eagle* serve as indexes in the sea change in Indian policy between their publication dates. Policy criticisms had grown throughout the 1920s, culminating in the passage of the Indian Reorganization Act, or the "Indian New Deal," in 1934. The act prohibited further land allotment, recognized Indians' right to develop their own governments, and empowered tribes to organize their own businesses.[89] John Collier, new commissioner of Indian Affairs and the bill's primary advocate, also opposed the pedagogy of assimilation and called for the retention and development of tribal cultural practices. Published in 1933 at the beginning of this Indian New Deal, *Land of the Spotted Eagle*, as it emphasized the values within Lakota society while blasting past Indian policy, found both favorable reviews and a receptive audience.[90]

While *My People* was written through and against the Western's depiction of Lakota and U.S. relations, *Land of the Spotted Eagle* acknowledged a much broader discursive network that undergirded American exceptionalism. "Books, paintings, and pictures," Standing Bear wrote, "have all joined together in glorifying the pioneer . . . in their course of conquest across the country" while "lurid fiction, cheap magazines, motion pictures, and newspapers help to impart the wrong idea that a scalp and a war dance are counterparts of native American life."[91] In the face of ubiquitous misinformation, Standing Bear ventured an "attempt to tell my readers just how we lived as Lakotans," detailing his people's customs and cultural traditions.[92]

The rich, loving detail with which Standing Bear describes Lakota society in *Land of the Spotted Eagle* is made even more pronounced by his palpable hostility for post-allotment America. For Standing Bear the reality at Pine Ridge demonstrated both the failures and arrogance of the policies of so-called progressives.[93] In a section titled "VIRTUES," for instance, he repurposes and interrogates the way terms such as "industrious" and "enterprising" circulated in relationship to the Lakota:

> The Lakota was [naturally] industrious, his whole life's necessity tending to make him so . . . [Yet], no matter what his spiritual conception of his humane consideration of life or animal life, never could he arrive at that superior status of the white man's world called "enterprising" until he changed his whole idea of human evaluation. To the Lakota every other individual in the tribe was as important as himself and it was his duty to protect the identity of the tribe. In opposition was the European concept of "glory to the conqueror—every man for himself and the devil take the hindmost."[94]

Against this model of Western individualism, Standing Bear explained individuality from the perspective of the Lakota, who were "self-governors" yet could not consider themselves "as separate from the band or nation."[95] Ultimately, Standing Bear refused to associate with the term "progressive" altogether. "I did not come home [from Carlisle] so 'progressive' that I could not speak the language of my father and mother . . . I have never, in fact, 'progressed' that far."[96]

This rejection of "progress" was, paradoxically, an argument for a new model of subjectivity for both Native and non-Native communities. Standing Bear's intended white readership needed to get comfortable with the fact that, as he prefaced *Land*, "people who live differently from themselves still might be traveling the upward and progressive road of life."[97] Americans needed to abandon the vanishing race nostalgia that registered Native cultural production "as curios" and recognize indigenous art as a "timeless art" of enduring peoples.[98] They needed to acknowledge how their "lack of vision" precipitated the "situation now alluded to as the 'Indian Problem,'" and how the perpetuation of the "savage" myth masked "a sore and troubled conscience" regarding U.S. colonialism; to incorporate a "fair and correct history of the native American" in public schools; and, perhaps most important, when they considered questions regarding American Indians and the U.S. social order, to realize that none "but the Indian [should] answer!"[99]

For Native communities Standing Bear envisioned a hybrid modernity. At the dawn of the Indian New Deal, he began to theorize new modes of indigenous subjectivity and new forms of self-determination. Youngsters would be doubly educated to "appreciate both traditional life and modern life," and antagonisms between older and younger generations would be reconciled through a bilingual curriculum that respected "ancestral teaching."[100] Problems on the reservation would, therefore, be solved by Native peoples themselves, young and old alike. Reservations would be well staffed with a host of Native professionals, not only doctors and engineers but instructors in tribal ritual, dance, and lore. And while these models, in their hybridity, acknowledged a relationship with non-Native communities, *Land of the Spotted Eagle* fundamentally advocated for the future of the Lakotas to be decided by Lakotas, grounded in Lakota community, and nurtured by a Lakota value system.

Standing Bear traveled a long way to arrive at these conclusions: from Rose Bud and Pine Ridge to Carlisle Indian School, New York City, London, and Los Angeles. As with many from his generation, this mobility meant many things: a plucky journey to an unknown boarding school, freedom from a reservation overseer, and the promise of secure, even enjoyable, employment. But one journey in particular initiated a lifetime of calculated "Indian play" for the future writer. And as much as he enjoyed his contact with king and country across the Atlantic, it was the contact with Buffalo Bill Cody's spectacle itself that most profoundly shaped his future. This interpreter's ultimate fluency in the bombastic rhetoric of the Wild West left him with an important realization and task. To facilitate a vital future for the Lakota, he moved to write them out of an upturned colonialist romance. While his writing may never have reached audiences as large as an Ince film's, Standing Bear left a rich legacy for posterity, potentially a "new ghost dance literature," as Gerald Vizenor puts it, a "shadow literature of liberation that enlivens tribal survivance."[101]

Notes

This essay is dedicated to the memory of my grandmother Mary Louise Burt.

1. Philip Deloria describes the various ways, from the colonial period to the present, white Americans appropriated Native identities, or "played Indian," to negotiate dilemmas regarding American identity. He also suggests that Native peoples themselves co-opted "white people's Indian play." Philip J. Deloria, *Playing Indian* (New Haven, Conn.: Yale University Press, 1998), 8.
2. Luther Standing Bear, *My People the Sioux* (Lincoln: University of Nebraska Press, 1975), 254–55.
3. Ibid., 256.
4. Philip Deloria, *Indians in Unexpected Places* (Lawrence: University Press of Kansas, 2004), 11.
5. Richard Slotkin, "Buffalo Bill's 'Wild West' and the Mythologization of the American Empire," in *Cultures of United States Imperialism*, ed. Amy Kaplan and Donald Pease (Durham, N.C.: Duke University Press, 1993), 169.
6. *Cyclone of the Saddle*, directed by Elmer Clifton (1934; Yuma, Ariz.: Argosy); *Miracle Rider*, directed by B. Reeves Eason (1935; Burbank, Calif.); *Union Pacific*, directed by Cecil B. DeMille (1939; Burbank, Calif.: Paramount).
7. Luther Standing Bear, *My Indian Boyhood* (1931; Lincoln: University of Nebraska Press, 1988); Standing Bear, *Land of the Spotted Eagle* (1933; Lincoln: University of Nebraska Press, 1978); Standing Bear, *Stories of the Sioux* (Lincoln: Bison Books, 1988).
8. Standing Bear, *My People*, 277.
9. Deloria, *Indians*, 68.

10. I address the details of the Dawes General Allotment Act (1887) below.
11. Lucy Maddox, *Citizen Indians: Native American Intellectuals, Race, and Reform* (Ithaca, N.Y.: Cornell University Press, 2005), 11. Standing Bear also wrote two books for children, *My Indian Boyhood* and *Stories of the Sioux.*
12. Joy Kasson, *Buffalo Bill's Wild West: Celebrity, Memory, and Popular History* (New York: Hill and Wang, 2000), 13.
13. Ibid., 20–21.
14. Slotkin, "Buffalo Bill's Wild West," 167.
15. Kasson, *Buffalo Bill's Wild West,* 44.
16. Slotkin, "Buffalo Bill's Wild West," 168–69.
17. Ibid., 169.
18. As quoted in Kasson, *Buffalo Bill's Wild West,* 55.
19. Quoted in Richard White, "Frederick Jackson Turner and Buffalo Bill," in *The Frontier in American Culture,* ed. James Grossman (Berkeley: University of California Press, 1994), 7.
20. As quoted in Kasson, *Buffalo Bill's Wild West,* 61.
21. Slotkin, "Buffalo Bill's Wild West," 169.
22. Jonathan D. Martin, "'The Grandest and Most Cosmopolitan Object Teacher': *Buffalo Bill's Wild West* and the Politics of American Identity, 1883–1899," *Radical History Review* 66 (Fall 1996): 97. On the cultural politics of the dime novel, see Michael Denning, *Mechanic Accents: Dime Novels and Working-Class Culture in America* (New York: Verso, 1987); and Shelley Streeby, *American Sensations: Class, Empire, and the Production of Popular Culture* (Berkeley: University of California Press, 2002).
23. Martin, "Grandest and Most Cosmopolitan," 107.
24. White, "Frederick Jackson Turner," 27.
25. Martin, "Grandest and Most Cosmopolitan," 112.
26. Matthew Frye Jacobsen, *Barbarian Virtues: The United States Encounters Foreign Peoples at Home and Abroad, 1817–1917* (New York: Hill and Wang, 2000), 61.
27. As quoted in Martin, "Grandest and Most Cosmopolitan," 108.
28. Michael Elliot, "Indian Patriots on Last Stand Hill," *American Quarterly* 58.4 (December 2006): 992–93.
29. Edward Lazarus, *Black Hills, White Justice: The Sioux Nation Versus the United States, 1775 to the Present* (New York: HarperCollins, 1991), 71–95.
30. White, "Frederick Jackson Turner," 12.
31. Elliot, "Indian Patriots," 993.
32. L. G. Moses, *Wild West Shows and the Images of American Indians, 1883–1933* (Albuquerque: University of New Mexico Press, 1996), 227–28.
33. Ibid., 228–51. Deloria, *Indians,* 80–90.
34. As quoted in Moses, *Wild West Shows,* 246.
35. Thomas J. Morgan, "Statement on Indian Policy," in *Americanizing the American Indians: Writings by the "Friends of the Indian," 1880–1900,* ed. Francis Paul Prucha (Lincoln: University of Nebraska Press, 1973), 75.
36. Moses, *Wild West Shows,* 30.
37. Ibid., 25.
38. Jacquelyn Kilpatrick, *Celluloid Indians: Native Americans and Film* (Lincoln: University of Nebraska Press, 1999), 12–15.
39. John G. Neihardt, *Black Elk Speaks: Being the Life Story of a Holy Man of the Oglala Sioux* (Lincoln: University of Nebraska Press, 1988), 221.
40. Ibid., 223.
41. Ibid., 214–15.
42. Francis Paul Prucha, ed., *Americanizing the American Indians: Writings by the "Friends of the Indian," 1880–1900* (Lincoln: University of Nebraska Press, 1973), 6–7.
43. Frederick E. Hoxie, "The Curious Story of Reformers and American Indians," in *Indians in American History: An Introduction,* ed. Frederick Hoxie and Peter Iverson (Wheeling, Ill.: Harlan Davidson, 1998), 184.
44. Louis Owens, *Other Destinies: Understanding the American Indian Novel* (Norman: University of Oklahoma Press, 1992), 40.

45. Thomas Biolosi, "The Birth of the Reservation: Making the Modern Individual among the Lakota," *American Ethnologist* 22.1 (February 1995): 30.
46. Ibid.
47. Richard N. Ellis, "Luther Standing Bear: 'I would raise him to be an Indian,'" in *Indian Lives: Essays on Nineteenth- and Twentieth-Century Native American Leaders*, ed. L. G. Moses and Ramond Wilson (Albuquerque: University of New Mexico Press, 1985), 144–45.
48. Ellis, "Luther Standing Bear," 145.
49. Standing Bear, *Land*, 236.
50. Ibid., 237.
51. Standing Bear, *My People*, 241.
52. Ibid., 242.
53. Ibid.
54. Ibid., 242–43.
55. Moses, *Wild West Shows*, 253.
56. Ibid., 63.
57. Quoted in ibid., 73.
58. Deloria, *Indians*, 69.
59. Quoted in Moses, *Wild West Shows*, 182.
60. Standing Bear, *My People*, 252.
61. Ibid., 253.
62. Ibid., 277.
63. Deloria, *Indians*, 78–81.
64. See, for example, Charles Eastman, *From the Deep Woods to Civilization* (1902; Lincoln: University of Nebraska Press, 1977). See also Zitkala-Sa's autobiographical stories, originally serialized in the *Atlantic Monthly* in 1900, collected in *American Indian Stories* (Lincoln: University of Nebraska Press, 1985).
65. Maddox, *Citizen Indians*, 4.
66. Ibid., 8–9.
67. Standing Bear, *My People*, 283.
68. Ibid., 285.
69. Deloria, *Indians*, 81.
70. Ibid., 82.
71. Standing Bear, preface to *My People*, emphasis added.
72. Ibid., emphasis added.
73. Ellis, "Luther Standing Bear," 141.
74. Richard Ellis, preface to *My People the Sioux*, xv.
75. Ibid., xiv.
76. Standing Bear, *My People*, 82, emphasis added.
77. Ibid., 83.
78. Ibid.
79. Moses, *Wild West Shows*, 229.
80. Ibid., 232.
81. Standing Bear, *My People*, 231.
82. Standing Bear, 223–24.
83. Ibid., 288.
84. Carlos Montezuma, a prominent and founding member of the SAI, demanded American Indians "be freed from the bondage of the Indian Office" and "made citizens" before serving in World War One. Carlos Montezuma, "Carlos Montezuma on the Draft," in *Talking Back to Civilization: Indian Voices from the Progressive Era*, ed. Frederick E. Hoxie (Boston: Bedford/St. Martins, 2001), 125–27.
85. Maddox, *Citizen Indians*, 14–15; Standing Bear, *My People*, 288.
86. Richard Ellis, foreword to *Land of the Spotted Eagle*, vii. Ellis, "Luther Standing Bear," 152–53.
87. Standing Bear, *Land*, 245.
88. Quoted in Vine Deloria Jr. and Clifford M. Lytle, *The Nations Within: The Past and Future of American Indian Sovereignty* (Austin: University of Texas Press, 1998), 44.
89. Ibid., 140–53.

90. Ellis, "Luther Standing Bear," 152.
91. Standing Bear, *Land*, 227–28.
92. Ibid., xv.
93. Maddox, *Citizen Indians*, 163–64.
94. Standing Bear, *Land*, 66–67.
95. Ibid., 124.
96. Ibid., 235.
97. Ibid., xv.
98. Ibid., 258.
99. Ibid., 248–54.
100. Ibid., 252–55.
101. Gerald Vizenor, *Manifest Manners: Postindian Warriors of Survivance* (Hanover, N.H.: Wesleyan University Press, 1994), 106.

Mexican Indigenismo, Choctaw Self-Determination, and Todd Downing's Detective Novels

James H. Cox

Todd Downing, one of the most prolific and most neglected American Indian writers of the twentieth century, began his career as an author of detective fiction after working as a tour guide in Mexico during the summer months of the late 1920s and early 1930s. Downing traveled, like his contemporaries Will Rogers (Cherokee), John Joseph Mathews (Osage), Lynn Riggs (Cherokee), and D'Arcy McNickle (Confederated Salish and Kootenai), in a postrevolutionary Mexico that was in the process of incorporating indigeneity into a unified national identity. In eight of the ten novels that he published between 1933 and 1945, Downing appropriates and refigures this *indigenismo*—the official celebration of Mexico's indigenous history and culture—to reveal evidence of the modern indigenous people obscured by *indigenismo* discourse. These indigenous people thrive in a world in which two postcolonial settler governments, the United States and Mexico, are in conflict with each other while also maintaining against indigenous populations within their borders the colonial practices of the European empires from which they secured their own independence.[1] In his novels, Downing makes three extraordinary discoveries in the context of mid-twentieth-century American Indian literary and activist histories. He detects a persistent though enervated European colonial presence and a more potent neocolonial invasion of Mexico by U.S. tourists, academics, journalists, smugglers, drug addicts, kidnappers, and criminal venture capitalists. He also identifies a contested yet successful indigenous Mexican resistance to this invasion, as well as to the oppressive policies of the Mexican state. Finally, Downing's literary model of self-determination in novels such as *The Cat Screams* anticipates the anticolonial discourses of the American Indian civil rights movement of the late 1960s and early 1970s and the literary renaissance that attended it.

Atoka, Norman, Ardmore: The Local Roots of Downing's Mexican Mysteries

George Todd Downing was born in 1902 in Atoka in the Choctaw Nation, Indian Territory, to Maude (Miller) Downing and Samuel Downing. In "A Choctaw's Autobiography," published in 1926 in a Tulsa periodical called *The American Indian*, Downing observes:

> My father has always been a power among the Choctaws. During the Spanish-American war he was a member of Theodore Roosevelt's Rough Riders, serving the incomparable "Teddy" as interpreter with the Choctaw and Chickasaw members of this organization. He was a member of the statehood delegation to Washington that secured statehood for Oklahoma. At present he is a member of the Choctaw Tribal Council and is taking a leading part in the efforts to wrest from the United States government the fulfillment of promises which have never been fulfilled and to prevent further encroachment upon the rights of the Indians.[2]

Downing published this autobiography almost twenty years after the final stages of allotment culminated in Oklahoma statehood in 1907 and during an era characterized by what Choctaw anthropologist Valerie Lambert calls "the very high level of attenuation of Choctaw tribal relations and structures."[3] Downing presents his father as a political activist working as a member of an official Choctaw government body to maintain those Choctaw tribal relations and structures and to defend all American Indians from a settler colonial government.

Downing took the legacy of his father's political activities quite seriously. "A Choctaw's Autobiography" includes the outline of a political platform that Downing develops in greater detail first in his novels and then in a history of Mexico called *The Mexican Earth* (1940). Downing begins the autobiography by providing what he calls a "brief summary of the history of the tribe of American Indians in which I am proud to claim membership—the Choctaws."[4] After asserting himself as a Choctaw, Downing argues that American Indians should adopt a pan-Indian, anticolonial politics:

> Their fatal fault and weakness in the past has been this inability to cement an effective union on racial, instead of tribal grounds, a consistent weakness which rendered unavailing their efforts to resist the encroachments of the white man. This still remains the hardest single obstacle in the path of those Indians who are not [*sic*] attempting to hold the United States government—a government dedicated to liberty and the proposition that all men are created equal—to the promises made to their fathers. It seems to the writer that it is indeed high time we Indians thought more of ourselves as Indians and less as representatives of a single tribe.[5]

Though Downing rejects tribal specificity as a political position in his autobiography, he still calls it a Choctaw's, rather than an American Indian's, life story and publishes it in a magazine edited by Lee F. Harkins, a Choctaw writer, printer, editor, publisher, and rare book collector.[6] He continues, too, to identify himself to a broad audience as Choctaw throughout his life.

Downing wrote "A Choctaw's Autobiography" while he was a twenty-four-year-old MA student at the University of Oklahoma in Norman. After graduating from high school in Atoka, he entered the university in 1920, earned his BA in 1924, and continued as a graduate student with his work in indigenous and colonial Latin American literature and history. By the time he completed a master's thesis on Florencio Sánchez, a Uruguayan dramatist, Downing was an accomplished intellectual who spoke five languages (Choctaw, English, French, Italian, and Spanish). After completing his graduate degree, he remained at the university as a Spanish instructor in the Department of Modern Languages. He was also a reviewer of books in French, Italian, and Spanish for *Books Abroad*, the forerunner of *World Literature Today*, for which he also served as advertising and then business manager from 1928 to 1934; a voracious reader of U.S., English, Mexican, and Latin American history and literature; and an equally avid reader of mystery novels by Agatha Christie, Sir Arthur Conan Doyle, Dashiell Hammett, Dorothy Sayers, Ellery Queen, and Wilkie Collins, whose collected works are part of the library of more than fifteen hundred volumes that Downing donated to Southeastern Oklahoma State University.

Organized crime and murder in Mexico became Downing's specialties, but he began to write his first detective novel following a local act of violence that threatened the diplomatic ties between the United States and Mexico: the murder of two young Mexican college students by deputy sheriffs in Ardmore, Oklahoma, about seventy miles from Atoka, on June 8, 1931.[7] Emilio Cortes Rubio and Salvatore Cortes Rubio, both relatives of Mexico's president, and Manuel Garcia Gomez were traveling together from colleges in Atchison, Kansas, and Rolla, Missouri, to Mexico City when they stopped in Ardmore. The conflicting testimonies of the survivor, Salvatore Cortes Rubio, the law enforcement officers, and the eyewitnesses frustrate attempts to reconstruct the sequence of events that culminated in the murders. The men with badges had, however, the legal and cultural sanction to tell the most authoritative, if perhaps not the most plausible, narrative. After stopping to question the men, Deputy Sheriffs William E. Guess and Cecil Crosby claimed "that the shooting occurred after the two youths had drawn guns, although they did not fire;

that Crosby disarmed one youth; that the other emerged from the car with a gun protruding from a blanket thrown about his shoulders; that thereupon Guess fired, killing the student; that the first youth, who had been disarmed, produced a small pistol, and Guess fired on him."[8] Representatives at the highest levels of the Oklahoma, U.S., and Mexican governments corresponded in a diplomatic language of earnest regret as opaque as the specific circumstances of the fatal confrontation that early summer morning.[9]

Following the murders in Ardmore, Downing wrote his first novel, *Murder on Tour* (1933). After its publication, Downing resigned from the university and moved to New York to become a professional writer. While he lived in New York and then Philadelphia in the 1930s and 1940s and worked for several advertising agencies, including the famous firm N. W. Ayer and Son, Inc., Downing achieved, as an American Indian fiction writer, a level of success matched only at the end of the twentieth century by writers such as Louise Erdrich (Turtle Mountain Ojibwe) and Sherman Alexie (Spokane and Coeur d'Alene).[10] Downing had the powerful New York publisher Doubleday Doran promoting him as a Choctaw author to a broad, international audience that appears to have relished his novels.[11] Doubleday Doran published eight of his ten mysteries for its Crime Club and advertised his novels in the *New York Times.* The same newspaper reviewed at least eight of those novels and made announcements about Downing's career.[12] Four of those novels were reprinted at least once in the United States, and at least thirteen editions or translations of Downing's novels were published in European countries.[13]

Three novels were also reproduced in other popular or mass culture formats. Downing's second novel, *The Cat Screams* (1934), was published in England by Methuen, translated into Italian, reprinted in the United States by the Popular Library, and adapted by Basil Beyea into a Broadway play, also called *The Cat Screams,* in 1942.[14] The *New York Times* reported on the play during every step from pre-production to its opening on June 16, 1942, at the Martin Beck Theatre and its closing on June 20, 1942, after seven shows.[15] Downing's third novel, *Vultures in the Sky,* was printed in 1935 in four successive issues of *Short Stories Twice a Month,* a pulp magazine published by Doubleday Doran, then printed in its entirety on December 15, 1935, in newspapers such as the *Detroit Free Press* and the *Philadelphia Inquirer* as the featured Sunday novel of the week. It was then reprinted in England by Methuen (1936), in *2 Detective Mystery Novels* magazine in the spring of 1950, and in translation in Finnish, Spanish, and Italian. The Italian translation was reprinted as late as 1977. Downing's fifth novel, *The Case of the Unconquered Sisters,* was reprinted in

Detective Novel magazine in August of 1943. Three of Downing's other novels were reprinted, and *The Lazy Lawrence Murders* earned mention in *Time.*[16]

Downing maintained a presence in local histories, such as Mary Marable and Elaine Boylen's *Handbook of Oklahoma Writers* (1939), fellow Choctaw Muriel Wright's *A Guide to the Indian Tribes of Oklahoma* (1951), and *Tales of Atoka County Heritage* (1983); national publications such as Marion E. Gridley's *Indians of Today* (1936; 1947); and reference guides such as Bill Pronzini and Marcia Muller's *1001 Midnights: The Aficionado's Guide to Mystery and Detective Fiction* (1986). A. S. Burack even included an essay by Downing, along with contributions by such luminaries as Dorothy L. Sayers and S. S. Van Dine, in the edited collection *Writing Detective and Mystery Fiction* (1945). Following the reprinting of Downing's *The Mexican Earth* in 1996 by the University of Oklahoma Press, however, we have not assessed the place of his mystery novels in twentieth-century American Indian literary history. The scholarly neglect of Downing is at least curious in light of the critical scrutiny of popular culture productions about indigenous people by nonindigenous artists.

Downing's novels show an author interested in much more than mining incidents of lethal force by the local police for plot material.[17] The indictment of a culture of U.S. violence in these novels includes an unwavering indignation at the treatment of Mexican citizens, especially the indigenous population, and an incisive critique of the sustained, criminal abuse of Mexico by a U.S. neocolonizing force that augments and, Downing suggests, rivals the already present settler colonialism at work in Mexico for sheer brutality and contempt for indigenous life.[18] By also engaging Mexican national discourses of *indigenismo,* Downing sustains in his novels a two-pronged, binational reproach to settler-colonial aggression.

Postrevolutionary *Indigenismo*: The Mexican Context of Downing's Mysteries

The family politics that Downing inherited from his father shaped his appropriation of these Mexican national discourses as well as indigenous Mexican history and culture. Following the end of the Mexican revolution in 1920, *indigenismo* made indigeneity a much more significant feature of national identity in Mexico than in the United States. Though according to most commentators the contribution of indigenous people to *indigenismo* was negligible, *indigenismo* as a Mexican national discourse provided Downing with a public space in which he could imagine indigenous people as modern political and cultural actors.[19] Historians Mary Kay Vaughan and Stephen E. Lewis describe the origins of *indigenismo*: "In 1921, on the heels of the twentieth century's first social revolution, the Mexican government launched a nationalist movement celebrating the culture of Mexico's *mestizo* and indigenous peoples and recasting national history as a popular struggle against invasion, subjugation, and want."[20] While American Indians in the United States continued in the early twentieth century to experience the rejection of their place both in history and modernity, "the revolutionary version of history" in Mexico, assert Vaughan and Lewis, "placed great emphasis on Mexico's indigenous foundations and contemporary cultures."[21] In his study of two celebrations of independent Mexico's centennial in 1921, Rick López provides a more dramatic reading of this context: "According to the emerging nationalist rhetoric first articulated by Manuel Gamio in 1916, to be truly Mexican, one had to be part indigenous or at least to embrace the idea that indigenousness was vital to the national consciousness. Rejection of Mexico's contemporary indigenous peoples and cultures, de rigueur before the revolution, was now criticized as a mark of unpatriotic xenophilia."[22]

By contrast, during the era of the Society of American Indians from 1911 to 1924, American Indians had a much more uncertain place in national U.S. discourses. At that time, explains Phil Deloria, "according to most American narratives, Indian people, corralled on isolated and impoverished reservations, missed out on modernity—indeed, almost dropped out of history itself. In such narratives, Native Americans would reemerge as largely insignificant political and cultural actors in the reform efforts of the 1920s and 1930s."[23] In the United States, as Shari Huhndorf demonstrates in her analysis of the racial politics of the 1893 World's Columbian Exposition in Chicago and the 1909 Alaska-Yukon-Pacific Exposition in Seattle, the national ideal was white racial purity. Huhndorf assesses Chicago's White City and Seattle's Cascade Court as the spatial and material expressions of the whiteness that indigenous racial difference threatened to attenuate.[24] Postrevolutionary Mexico offered, therefore, an attractive alternative for American Indian authors such as Downing. Neither history nor modernity in Mexico had been settled, as it had according to dominant narratives in the United States, so decisively in favor of non-Native people.

Yet *indigenismo* in Mexico had U.S. roots. López argues of the centennial celebrations that "both reveal the extent to which the turn toward an 'ethnicized' or 'Indianized' definition of Mexico's national culture did not flow inevitably out of Mexico's historical experience, as is generally assumed, but instead resulted from a distinct movement led by cosmopolitan nationalists inside and outside the government . . . in a profoundly transnational context."[25] Two cosmopolitan nationalists, Adolfo Best Maugard and Manuel Gamio, were principal organizers of these celebrations: Best of the Noche Mexicana in Chapultepec Park and Gamio of the Exhibition of Popular Arts. Best and Gamio were influenced by the time they spent in the United States with Franz Boas, the anthropologist who launched a critique of evolutionary anthropology in the 1880s and 1890s while arguing that "race, language, and culture were not now and probably never had been closely correlated."[26] In addition to his long affiliation with Columbia University and his influence on such American Indian intellectual-activists as Arthur C. Parker (Seneca), Archie Phinney (Nez Perce), and Ella Deloria (Yankton Dakota), Boas served in 1910 as the first director of the Escuela Internacional de Antropología in Mexico. Boas's former student Gamio was "the founder of postrevolutionary *indigenismo*" and one of the leading *indigenistas*—a non-Native promoter of *indigenismo*.[27]

These centennial celebrations, the federal policies, and the national discourse of *indigenismo* were symptoms of the non-Native and *mestizo*-identified dominance of Mexico. Nonindigenous Mexican people were the primary actors in the creation of a postrevolutionary national identity. Put another way by historian Alan Knight: "The Indians themselves were the objects, not the authors, of *indigenismo*."[28] The *indigenistas* argued among themselves about how to incorporate indigeneity into a unified Mexican national identity. For example, Best and the prominent intellectual and bureaucrat José Vasconcelos thought that Native material culture required interpretation and improvement by nonindigenous artists, while Gamio and Gerald Murillo, the painter, writer, and centennial celebration organizer known as Dr. Atl, wanted to maintain the "authenticity" of indigenous arts. Dr. Atl saw, observes López, "indigenous artisans as primitive producers isolated from modern commercialization."[29] In this context, characterized by postrevolutionary nationalism and *indigenismo*, López explains, "the masses can contribute only passively to the nation, through their instincts and intuition, not through their self-determined cultural or political genius."[30] In López's assessment of the Mexican context, there is an echo of Deloria's observation that Native people in the United States were "largely insignificant political and cultural actors" in the 1920s and '30s.

Downing was most interested, however, in the distinct indigenous contexts in Mexico that *indigenismo* made part of public conversation. In Mexico, the Zapotec leader Benito Juárez was a national—Mexican—hero. Popular and official histories asserted that the Yaquis in Sonora, who are separated from

Yaquis in Arizona by the Mexico-U.S. border, had never been conquered. Though the Yaquis had experienced removal to Yucatan in 1908, a year after Oklahoma statehood, they were still resisting militarily in the 1920s. This history of military resistance led to the creation of an anomaly in indigenous Mexican life. There were no reservations in Mexico, but in the late 1930s President Cárdenas "recognized the authority of Yaqui governors and set aside 450,000 hectares as Mexico's only tribal land grant."[31] Cárdenas had also started his land reform program that involved the redistribution of land owned by the large haciendas to indigenous communities. Indigenous people were not silent in this era, either. Jan Rus describes assertive Maya politics and cultural revitalization in Chiapas in the late 1930s and early 1940s. He observes that, to distinguish this era from the revolution of the 1910s, "the years from 1936 to the beginning of the 1940s are sometimes referred to in Chiapas as 'la revolución de los indios.'"[32] Thus, *indigenismo*, particularly in its most radical formulations in the 1930s, created a public space for indigenous Mexicans to make some political demands.[33] That public space was also available for appropriation by American Indian writers who witnessed the brief, less dramatic reform era in the U.S. that began with the passage of the Indian Reorganization Act in 1934.

White Villains and Red Herrings: Indigenous Mexico in Todd Downing's Novels

From within the context of a politicized Choctaw history, Downing claims in his novels this public space created by indigenous Mexican history and culture and official Mexican *indigenismo*. A detective novel such as *The Cat Screams* becomes in Downing's hands an investigation into both the disregard for Mexican lives represented by the deputy sheriffs of Ardmore and the strategies that indigenous Mexicans develop to resist or evade similar acts of state-sponsored violence. Many of Downing's characters view indigenous Mexican people as superstitious and latently violent, even as frequently on the threshold of armed revolution, but Downing consistently exposes this figuration of indigenous people as a colonial red herring, as an alibi for non-Native people that draws the attention of readers away from the crimes that non-Natives are committing. Downing only once in his ten novels delivers to readers an indigenous criminal, a young man in "The Shadowless Hour" (1945) named Jesus, who kills both his mother's drug dealer and a zealous Christian missionary who discovers evidence of his guilt. Instead, indigenous and nonindigenous Mexicans are the frequent victims of crimes committed by visitors, immigrants, and expatriates from various European countries and north of the border; crime is the primary export to, rather than a product of, Mexico in Downing's novels.

In an era in the United States of menacing cinematic Indians, indigenous Mexican peons obstructing modernization, and anti-Mexican hysteria fed by the Great Depression, the novels represent an extraordinary public challenge to the dominant U.S. views of indigenous Americans and indigenous and nonindigenous Mexican nationals as well as to the contemporary (and still prevailing) narrative about the flow of violent crime in North America from the south toward the United States.[34] As two postcolonial settler nations vie for power—economically, politically, narratively—and the neocolonial agents of the United States descend on Mexico, Downing finds indigenous people in a vulnerable position but with resources available that help them to escape the fray. *Indigenismo* made indigenous Mexico part of a daily conversation in which indigenous Mexicans had a limited role. By identifying in a novel such as *The Cat Screams* the strategies that contemporary indigenous Mexicans use to maintain their communities as the battle rages around and against them, Downing appropriates *indigenismo* and forces Native voices, beliefs, and bodies into that conversation. This reconstituted Mexican national discourse, a Choctaw's *indigenismo*, anticipates the program of Choctaw self-determination that Downing embraces near the end of his life.

Criminality in *The Cat Screams* has the same European and U.S. origins as it does in his first and third novels, *Murder on Tour* (1933) and *Vultures in the Sky* (1935). In *Murder*, a U.S. couple smuggle indigenous Mexican artifacts into the United States and commit murders to hide their illicit business. This theft of indigenous Mexican cultural productions by U.S. criminals is an apt metaphor for *indigenismo*, the intellectual and bureaucratic theft of Mexican indigeneity by a predominantly nonindigenous and *mestizo* Mexican elite. In *Vultures*, a kidnapper flees south Texas on a train to Mexico in disguise as a businessman interested in purchasing mining leases from indigenous people. He hopes to escape prosecution in south Texas by participating in the sanctioned criminal activity of dispossessing Native people. The kidnapper murders several passengers and an indigenous porter to avoid detection, and he finds unexpected cover when a French citizen and dangerous Catholic militant also traveling to Mexico City consumes the attention of the authorities. A Yaqui platoon of soldiers eventually captures the militant, a Cristero aligned with the Catholic counterrevolutionaries who, in the Cristero War from 1926 to 1929, fought the Mexican government's efforts to curtail the Church's power. To any members of a U.S. audience predisposed to see either dangerous Mexican immigrants undermining the U.S. economy or childlike Mexican peons, the image of Yaqui soldiers marching with a Catholic Cristero as their prisoner would likely have been disconcerting. It also might have pleased some American Indian readers experiencing the legacy of what Osage-Cherokee author George Tinker calls in his book of the same name the "missionary conquest" of North America. The image is a surprising reversal of the dominant representations of indigenous Mexicans in the United States and Mexico as well as an assertion that indigenous Mexicans have an active role to play in a modernizing Mexico.

Downing writes a detailed story of a modern—and revolutionary—indigenous Mexico in *The Cat Screams*. In the novel, the suicides of several women haunt the U.S. colony in Taxco in the southwestern Mexican state of Guerrero. The deaths can be traced to the drug dealing of Madame Céleste Fournier, the daughter of French immigrants, including a father who was an administrator in Maximilian's court during the French occupation of Mexico from 1862 to 1867.[35] Fournier's home is an alien colonial space: "Madame Fournier during her occupancy installed modern plumbing and called the house a pension, so that the discriminating tourist might distinguish it from the many native *casas de huéspedes* in the town."[36] Downing then confirms that we should read Fournier, one of the few non-U.S. villains in his canon, as the sign of an unassimilated European presence in Mexico, for "on Bastille Day she always hung out the Tricolor and invited her guests to drink champagne with her."[37] Her current guests comprise a rogue's gallery of U.S. citizens that includes Donald Shaul, a predatory tabloid journalist from New York; Dr. R. L. Parkyn, an archaeologist from Chicago looking for potentially lucrative jade deposits; and Gwendolyn Noon, a New York stage actress and drug addict. These visitors are the privileged beneficiaries of a caste system that structures a colonized indigenous Mexico dominated by Europeans and their descendants. While the guests at the pension are all non-Native visitors from the United States, the members of the staff are all indigenous Mexicans: Esteban, the *mozo*, or servant; Micaela Guerrero, the cook, who shares a name with the Mexican state in which she lives and works; and Maria, the *criada*, or waitress.

Yet Fournier is an infirm sign of French colonial aggression and European or nonindigenous dominance, and the recognition of her vulnerability is crucial to Downing's search for possible sites of indigenous resistance. Benito Juárez, the Zapotec land reformer and president of Mexico, led the successful fight against the French and had Maximilian executed. Though the nonindigenous residents of Fournier's fragile world fear indigenous Mexicans, they do not take seriously the possibility of a similar assault on them by indigenous revolutionaries. *The Cat Screams* begins with a translation from the Spanish of an article from the Mexico City *Mundial*. The introductory headings to the newspaper article, which has a dateline of June 18, 193–, from Taxco, announce "FOREIGNERS IN PANIC" and link the aforementioned suicides of U.S. citizens to a "*Revival of Primitive Practices*." The author of the article foments anti-indigenous hysteria that could be read as a refraction of the anti-Mexican hysteria in the United States in the 1930s: "Queer rumors were current about the plaza. That native witch doctors still ply their trade among the ignorant persons of Taxco is a well-established fact, and one of these, a woman famous in her trade, is being sought by the police. These *curanderas*, the ignorant ones believe, can injure or drive insane any person, provided they possess an article of his clothing."[38] As in *Murder on Tour* and *Vultures*, Downing uses indigenous Mexican beliefs and practices in *The Cat Screams* to imbue the atmosphere with fear and to suggest a possible source of the crimes.[39] Readers soon learn that Micaela Guerrero, the aforementioned cook, is the "woman famous in her trade," but the close proximity of these "primitive practices" to the colonial center never manifests as a dramatic display of anticolonial or domestic revolution. Instead, again as in *Murder on Tour* and *Vultures*, the threat of indigenous violence with origins in those revived "primitive practices" is a red herring, and the gravest threat to Fournier is her own involvement in the criminal underworld sustained by visiting U.S. nationals.

Indigeneity, however, does threaten Fournier's world, though less sensationally and more strategically than the newspaper article suggests. The novel's title alludes to the practice of *nagualism* by many indigenous groups in Mesoamerica. Antonio de Herrera and Bernardino de Sahagún refer to nagualism in their sixteenth-century *historias*, while Daniel G. Brinton's *Nagualism: A Study in Native American Folk-lore and History* (1894) is the first attempt to produce a comprehensive study.[40] The *nanahualtin* (singular *naualli* with alternate spellings such as *nagual*, *nahual*, *naual*, and *nawal*) are either animal guardians or "masters of mystic knowledge, dealers in the black arts, wizards or sorcerers" who have the power to transform into animals.[41] Though often brutally suppressed by the Catholic Church, *nagualism* was still common when Brinton wrote his study.

Indigenous revolution is a real possibility in *The Cat Screams*, though the simulation of hysteria in the discourse of sensational journalism about a revival of primitive magic helps to keep *nagualism*, the potential driving force of the revolution, hidden in plain sight. The newspaper article foments anxiety while disparaging the source of it and discouraging critical investigation. Downing introduces *nagualism* as part of the narrative thread about Esteban, the *mozo* who begins the novel bedridden and hidden from the view of readers and the other characters. Madame Fournier describes Esteban's mysterious illness to Hugh Rennert, a customs agent for the Department of the Treasury and the primary detective in eight of Downing's ten novels. In her description of the illness, Fournier mentions that the screaming of the titular Siamese cat, Mura, frightens Esteban. She tells Rennert that after the cat screamed, "He said something in a low voice, something that I could not understand. Then he turned his face to the wall."[42] When the local government places the pension under quarantine in response to Esteban's undiagnosed illness, the novel begins to function as a pseudo-captivity narrative with Esteban and his mysterious illness as the figurative captors of the visitors from the United States. Throughout the novel, Esteban's illness then shadows the central mystery: the deaths that start at the pension soon after Rennert's arrival.

The solution to the mystery of what Esteban says to himself requires knowledge of indigenous languages that only Professor Parkyn has. Parkyn represents a recurring character type in Downing's novels: an academic with some appreciation for indigenous history and culture but with a concomitant belief in his superiority. He is not overtly villainous, but he is a U.S. *indigenista*: he values indigenous history and material culture rather than indigenous people. Parkyn consults Aztec manuscripts for clues that will lead him to jade deposits, but he views indigenous religious beliefs as superstition. Downing's cast of academics from the United States studying and at times exploiting indigenous Mexico includes Dr. Xavier Radisson, a linguist of indigenous languages and the murderer in Downing's sixth novel, *The Last Trumpet: Murder in a Mexican Bull Ring* (1937).[43] Radisson's Mexican counterpart is the drug dealer and former university professor of Mesoamerican studies Don Evaristo Montellano in "The Shadowless Hour." The representations of Radisson, the linguist-cum-murderer, and Montellano, the professor-cum–drug dealer, make legible the violence of intellectual *indigenismo*.

As he fights his illness, Esteban refuses to speak in Spanish and, therefore, constantly reminds readers of the indigenous presence at the spatial center of the pension. Strategic linguistic separatism and bilingualism are the primary tools of cultural preservation and anticolonial resistance in the novel: the indigenous characters speak colonial languages, Spanish, English, and French, but only one nonindigenous character speaks Nahuatl. Fournier finally identifies the word—*nagual*—that she failed to hear earlier but that Esteban repeats frequently in his conversations with Micaela. Fournier shares the information with Rennert, who plans to take the word to Parkyn for translation. Downing defers for many chapters the meeting between Rennert and Parkyn, but in those chapters he consistently references *nagualism* and the connection between *nagualism* and the screaming cat. Rennert attempts, for example, to secure the guests' fingerprints by writing *nagual* on a sheet of paper then asking each guest about the word with the expectation that they will hold the paper while they ponder his question. Downing stages two mysteries simultaneously in this scene: as Rennert tries to solve the overt mystery of who is killing the guests, Downing considers the covert mystery of how indigenous people can survive and thrive in the twentieth century. They can thrive, Downing proposes, by exploiting the settler colonial state's inability to control indigenous knowledge. As the only character who can translate the word *nagual* or understand the implications of Esteban's use of it, Parkyn is also the only character whom the settler colonial state could use to infiltrate the indigenous world. He is, however, interested only in jade.

To extend the life of the mystery, Downing obstructs Rennert's attempts to discuss *nagualism* with Parkyn until two-thirds of the way through the novel. At that point, Parkyn gives Rennert a lecture that reads like a condensed version of Brinton's study and provides an authoritative guide for reading the indigenous knowledge—and the indigenous resistance to linguistic and religious domination—that structures the novel. Parker concludes his history of the levitating, shape-shifting *naualli* who protect their communities from sorcerers and natural disasters by observing: "Under torture, many of the natives confessed to such practices and the Spaniards had great difficulty in stamping out the cult, which had for its avowed object the elimination of Christianity in Mexico."[44] Like an orthodox *indigenista*, Parkyn dismisses these indigenous beliefs as superstition and indigenous people as primitive. Yet the three members of the indigenous staff seize upon the possibility that a malevolent *nagual* has attacked Esteban after the doctor who practices Western medicine fails to diagnose his illness accurately. Despite Parkyn and Rennert's doubts about *nagualism*, the failure of Western medicine creates a fissure in the empirical and rational foundation of the detective novel genre and opens a space for the application of indigenous religious knowledge to the mystery.[45]

Through that fissure emerges the covert mystery that Downing is investigating: the status of internally colonized indigenous people in the twentieth century and the strategies available to them to maintain or revitalize their communities. Esteban's ravaged body represents the state of this dominated indigenous world; to identify the disease, however, is to begin the process of finding a cure. Left with the mystery of why Esteban is dying, Micaela, a healer or *curandera*, applies her religio-medico knowledge to the case and offers a diagnosis of witchcraft.[46] This diagnosis introduces other mysteries: has a *nagual* transformed into Mura to attack Esteban, and what are the motives for the attack? The violence directed against Esteban initially appears to have indigenous origins: the native witch doctors to which the journalist refers in the prologue are *nanahualtin*, practitioners of *nagualism*, and, therefore, the most obvious suspects. Yet the possibility of indigenous against indigenous violence is another red herring; the indigenous characters are too marginal to be the villains. As S. S. Van Dine insists in his influential essay "Twenty Rules for Writing Detective Stories," one of the rules that govern modern detective novels requires that the culprit plays a prominent role in the story.[47] Downing cites Van Dine in his own essay about writing detective novels and suggests to beginning authors that "there is a premium for originality in tales of crime . . . [b]ut this originality must lie within certain prescribed bounds, and until the writer is familiar with these he is venturing among pitfalls if he gets off the beaten path."[48] Charles Rzepka elaborates on this unique characteristic of detective fiction: "The concept of fairness is alien to nearly every other form of literary realism, where we rarely assume the author to be ethically delinquent when he or she withholds certain facts, feeds us misinformation, or is mistaken him- or herself."[49] Downing strategically leaves the *nanahualtin* at the margins of the narrative; they are not the practitioners of the mystic arts that have attacked Esteban and threaten to destroy Fournier's carefully arranged domestic colonial space.

Downing provides many suspects who might be the witch attacking Esteban and the indigenous world that he embodies. The most obvious suspects include the drug-dealing Fournier, who murders to cover her tracks, or the neglectful doctor who misdiagnoses Esteban, or even Parkyn, the condescending, opportunistic archaeologist. However, Downing most explicitly connects Gwendolyn Noon to the cat, the *nagual*'s familiar in the context of Micaela's diagnosis of Esteban's illness. Noon sets the violence in motion by deciding not to marry Stephen Riddle, the son of an Oklahoma oil man, and instead comes to Taxco to get a quick divorce from her secret first husband, and her drug use leads to two murders. She also shares physical characteristics with her familiar. Downing describes Noon as explicitly white—her fingers, dress, face—offset only with the red of her fingernails. When Rennert approaches Noon with the intention of confronting her about a chloroform attack on Fournier, he watches her carefully: "As if conscious of his scrutiny she quickly let her hand fall to her side and her fingers clenched themselves with a febrile movement. Their crimson nails seemed to be digging into the white skin. *Curiously*, he thought, *like the painted claws of a cat*."[50] When he finally confronts Noon, her eyes begin to twitch like a cat, and, "incredibly, her white face seemed to have grown whiter."[51] The screaming cat is a *nagual*, the avatar of malevolent magic—the tabloid journalism and celebrity obsession that worships whiteness, the morphine addiction that leads to suicide and murder—that originates with and is most clearly exemplified by Noon.[52]

Fournier's illicit drug trade and the rampant drug addiction fed by her dealing reinforce *nagualism* as a key to a covert mystery and to Downing's search for evidence of indigenous Mexican resistance. Brinton's study includes an overview of the intoxicants used by practitioners for spiritual insights: *peyotl* or peyote; the seeds of the *ololiuhqui* or *coaxihuitl*; and the bark of the *baal-che* that makes a drink called by the Mayas *yax ha*, first water, and by the Spanish *pitarilla*. While the use of intoxicants can produce spiritual insight, the potential abuse of the power gained from these insights makes *nanahualtin* dangerous. The drug use by bourgeois Anglo American and French Mexican women is, too, an abuse of privilege that makes them dangerous to themselves as well as to others: Fournier murders Shaul and Riddle to prevent them from exposing her other criminal activities; Noon chloroforms Fournier and leaves her to suffocate to death while she searches desperately for Fournier's morphine stash, and then she pulls a gun on Rennert; and drug addicts continue to commit suicide when the quarantine on Fournier's pension obstructs access to their supply. Most dramatically, a young indigenous man of the Mexican class of working poor lies dying throughout the novel while members of the U.S. privileged class self-destruct.

A scene in which Downing parodies what Phil Deloria calls "playing Indian" in his study of the same name confirms the connection that Downing encourages readers to draw between Noon and the neocolonial U.S. presence in Mexico figured as a dangerous supernatural power. After Noon chloroforms Fournier but fails to find the morphine, she disguises herself behind a jade mask of the Aztec god Xipe as she returns to her room. Parkyn identifies Xipe as "the god of sacrifice by flaying," which, in turn, explains the fright of the waitress, Maria, when she witnesses Noon holding the mask in front of her face.[53] Noon's travesty of indigenous religious belief is a compelling representation of a long history of colonial criminality that in *The Cat Screams* culminates in the absurdity of a drug addict disguising her identity behind a tiny mask.

The mask carries another meaning equally germane to the mystery of Esteban's illness and revelatory of the anticolonial resistance at the heart of the mystery. Parkyn explains that "those who were suffering from diseases of the skin were believed to be under the protection of Xipe."[54] Prior to Noon's appropriation of Xipe in order to hide her criminal activities, Micaela takes the mask in an effort to draw on Xipe's power to protect Esteban. Micaela's theft of the mask potentially implicates her in the murders. As he summarizes the case, however, Rennert exonerates her: "The cook had nothing to do with these deaths. . . . She escaped at the first opportunity, knowing that she would be under surveillance and not wanting to run the risk of another encounter with the police. Further than this, however, she has no connection with this case."[55] Micaela Guerrero, whose last name translates as "warrior" and who takes her first name from the archangel who leads the Christian heaven's armies, evades the authorities like one of her *curandera* ancestors, Maria Candelaria, described by Brinton as a famous *nagual* who led an indigenous revolution in Chiapas in 1713 and escaped after the revolution failed.[56] This indigenous woman is not a suspect in the murders at the pension, though the police consider her responsible for several deaths linked to her medical practice as a *curandera.* Downing suggests that indigenous people and their cultural beliefs and practices are always under surveillance. In the case of *The Cat Screams*, however, a powerful indigenous woman whose name invokes sacred warfare maintains those beliefs and practices while Western medicine surveys the repercussions of its failures: Esteban's death and the other deaths made possible by the misdiagnosis that trapped Fournier's guests in a quarantine.

Downing does not foreground indigenous epistemologies, as many of his literary descendants do, but *nagualism* becomes for him a means of conveying an anticolonial critique of the U.S. presence in Mexico and identifying indigenous languages and spiritual traditions as a resource for resisting that presence. Downing asks readers to recognize *nagualism*'s crucial presence in his literary practice and in indigenous Mexican communities; *nagualism* as Downing presents it in the novel has unequivocal literary, ideological, and political value. *Nagualism* is a sign of untranslatable indigenous difference and a separatist indigenous cultural and political position. When Esteban first whispers the word *nagual* to Micaela, Downing reveals a separate indigenous religious world still inaccessible to colonial, neocolonial, and settler colonial authorities. Fournier overhears but cannot understand. This indigenous difference is inflected by modernity: Downing presents Micaela, Maria, and Esteban as members of a servant class that uses indigenous Mexican spiritual traditions to navigate an international tourist industry. The adaptation of *nagualism* to this world is unsuccessful in the case of Esteban, who dies of acute appendicitis. Yet as the nonindigenous world feeds on itself with drug abuse, suicide, and murder, and the infirm colonial agent, Madame Fournier, kills herself with arsenic to avoid arrest, the indigenous archangel warrior, Micaela Guerrero, escapes, survives, and lives to continue her fight. She is an unfamiliar figure in the discourse of *indigenismo*: an indigenous actor adapted to the modern world as well as living in and interpreting it through an indigenous religious worldview.

Downing's focus on Mexico is unusual but not anomalous in American Indian literary history. Will Rogers, who was born into a prominent Cherokee family in 1879, was the most famous celebrity in the world in the 1920s and 1930s. He traveled frequently to Mexico, too. Though he rarely mentions indigenous Mexicans, he consistently condemned the United States for interfering in the affairs of its southern neighbor. John Joseph Mathews and D'Arcy McNickle also visited Mexico. From October 1939 to August 1940, Mathews spent a year in Mexico on a Guggenheim Fellowship, and Mathews and McNickle attended the first Inter-American Congress on Indian Life in Patzcuaro, Michoacán, Mexico, in 1940. McNickle's 1954 novel *Runner in the Sun* is a reimagined Inter-American Congress on Indian Life with indigenous people exclusively as the actors. In addition to a narrative model of the peaceful establishment of new, healthy American Indian nations, it is an emphatic appropriation of *indigenismo* and an equally emphatic assertion of autonomous indigenous political expression. Cherokee dramatist Lynn Riggs, also a frequent traveler to Mexico, stages in *The Year of Pilar* (c. 1935–1938) the contemporary indigenous Mexican, or, more specifically, Mayan revolution that exists as a covert but real threat in Downing's *The Cat Screams.* His satire of a failed counterrevolution by *hacendados* in *A World Elsewhere* (c. 1935–1939), a companion play or sequel to *Pilar*, confirms that the possibility of armed anticolonial resistance and dramatic social change for indigenous peoples in Mexico was quite real for Riggs.[57]

Todd Downing sustained in his writing, with the exception of his eighth and ninth novels, an explicit condemnation of colonial and neocolonial practices in Mexico. For American Indian writers, the 1930s immediately preceded what Chad Allen characterizes as "an important preparatory period of indirect opposition to dominant discourses that attempted to direct an indigenous minority 'self-determination' on nonindigenous terms." Of the authors deploying these "relatively quiet" narrative strategies, Allen asserts that "they questioned the assimilationist orthodoxy of the day and prepared the way for the more explosive tactics of the indigenous minority renaissance of the late 1960s and 1970s."[58] Like the narrative strategies used by the authors under Allen's consideration, such as Ruth Muskrat Bronson (Cherokee) and Ella Deloria, the challenges to colonial dominance in Downing's novels are quiet and indirect. Yet between his ninth and tenth novels, he published *The Mexican Earth*, a well-reviewed history that celebrates Mexico as an unconquered collection of indigenous nations, posits explicit connections between those nations, the Choctaws, and other indigenous nations in the United States, and makes frequent and far more direct assertions of indigenous Mexican strength in the present.[59] By writing the history of Mexico as a statement of the continuous centrality of indigenous people to the life of that nation, Downing produces another articulation of Native-centric writing that clearly anticipates the work of civil rights–era writers.

Downing Detected

The investigation of the murders on June 8, 1931, yielded conflicting testimony about what happened between the moment that Deputy Sheriffs Guess and Crosby emerged from their car and the fatal shooting of Emilio Rubio and Manual Gomez. The newspaper articles conveyed the details of an enduring mystery to the reading public: the deputy sheriffs claimed to have identified themselves as officers of the law and even to have displayed their badges, while the survivor, Salvatore Rubio, asserted that they did not; the young men were reported to have mistaken the deputy sheriffs for bandits, while Deputy Sheriff Guess, according to an Associated Press story on the front page of the *New York Times*, "believed he had encountered desperadoes";[60] an eyewitness gave testimony that Deputy Sheriff Crosby pointed to Emilio Rubio and said, "I got that boy," while Crosby called the accusation a "falsehood."[61] The trial did not reconcile any of these discrepancies, but the basic outline of events remains clear: the deputy sheriffs killed two men and were arrested, charged, tried, and acquitted. The United States then sent thirty thousand dollars as reparation to the victims' families in Mexico. This dissatisfying but perhaps unsurprising outcome motivated Todd Downing to write novels in which he investigates the place of indigenous people in a world in which the international relationship of two postcolonial settler nations evokes the long history of conflict between the U.S. settler government and the indigenous domestic dependent nations within its borders. Downing's detective, however, always reconstructs the specific details of the mystery, and the U.S. citizens who perpetrate crimes against Mexican nationals—indigenous and nonindigenous—always face punishment.[62]

During this difficult era for the Choctaw Nation, Downing followed what Lambert identifies as one of four typical patterns of Choctaw urban migration: following birth in the Choctaw Nation, this type of migrant goes to an urban area or a series of urban areas before returning permanently to the Nation.[63] While Downing lived abroad from the Choctaw homeland, he looked to Mexico for examples of indigenous strategies to resist settler governments as well as to maintain and revitalize tribal nation traditions. He was still thinking of the murders in Ardmore when he wrote *Murder on the Tropic* (1935), in which a young man named Esteban Flores returns to his family's old hacienda in Mexico from the college that he attends in Kansas. In the same novel, an indigenous mother, Maria Montemayor, covertly uses the hacienda's water supply to sustain the flowers in the plaza under which her son has been buried. As he contemplates Montemayor's devotion to the flowers and her son, Hugh Rennert thoughtfully observes:

> The flowers . . . were here before men. . . . [Maria] stood, the embodiment of the Mexico that stands self-sufficient by the side of the road while conquering armies pass by, to be replaced in days or years or centuries (it doesn't matter) by other armies under other banners. *Along the paved highway to the east,* Rennert thought, *will come another, more dreadful army, with billboards and refreshment stands and blatant automobile horns, but Maria and her kind will stand when they have passed by.*[64]

The Mexican Earth is a celebration of this self-sufficient and explicitly indigenous Mexico. Downing was also a model of this patient self-sufficiency, which N. Scott Momaday (Kiowa) characterizes in *House Made of Dawn* (1968), the novel that initiated the American Indian literary renaissance, as the "long outwaiting" of the residents of the Jemez Pueblo.[65]

His detection of this indigenous world in Mexico had a strong impact on his own contributions to the Choctaw Nation of Oklahoma. Downing returned permanently to his homeland in 1951 after teaching one year as an assistant professor of Spanish at Washington College in Chestertown, Maryland.[66] He cared for his parents and lived with his fellow Choctaw citizens more than a decade under the threat of the termination of their tribal nation.[67] In the early 1970s, Downing published his last two works: *Chahta Anompa: An Introduction to the Choctaw Language* (1971) and *Cultural Traits of the Choctaws* (1973). Both works were assigned as part of the Choctaw Bilingual Education Program (CBEP) to which Downing devoted the last years of his life. This program was in part the product of his ability to see through the many strata of internal and U.S. neocolonial oppression in Mexico and to detect a thriving indigenous world there. The goals of the program were:

> (1) to help each child to develop a positive self-concept—to be proud of himself and his heritage, and to have a positive attitude toward the language or languages familiar to him; (2) to help each child to progress rapidly toward mastering standard English as well as the other tool subjects; (3) to encourage teachers to learn to recognize individual differences, particularly those rooted in language and culture, and to make these differences contribute to the total learning process.[68]

Downing's participation in the CBEP as an administrative assistant and "writer, translator, and professor" coincided with a moment of activism that galvanized the resurgence of the Choctaw Nation.[69] The federal government responded to the resistance of culturally and politically invigorated Choctaws by repealing the Choctaw termination act one day before it would have ended the federal trust relationship between the United States and the Choctaw Nation on August 25, 1970.[70]

Notes

1. The United States and Mexico are postcolonial in the most orthodox use of the term by first-generation postcolonial theorists such as Bill Ashcroft, Gareth Griffiths, and Helen Tiffin, the coauthors of *The Empire Writes Back* (New York: Routledge, 1989). See Chadwick Allen, *Blood Narrative* (Durham, N.C.: Duke University Press, 2002), 28–36, for a critique of orthodox postcolonial theory's failure to account for indigenous people.
2. Todd Downing, "A Choctaw's Autobiography," in *The American Indian*, December 1926, 10, in *The American Indian, 1926–1931*, ed. J. M. Carroll and Lee F. Harkins (New York: Liveright, 1970).
3. Valerie Lambert, *Choctaw Nation: A Story of American Indian Resurgence* (Lincoln: University of Nebraska Press, 2007), 60.
4. Downing, "Choctaw's Autobiography."
5. Ibid. "Not" is a troubling word in the context of what Downing is saying. "Now" is more consistent with the message of this passage and the entire text.
6. *The American Indian* also had a predominantly American Indian staff.
7. Charles J. Rzepka makes a distinction between detective fiction, "any story that contains a major character undertaking the investigation of a mysterious crime or similar transgression," and a story of detection, "in which the puzzle element directly engages the reader's attention and powers of inference." Downing's mysteries are both detective novels and novels of detection. This genre, Rzepka explains, "[dominated] . . . the interwar best-seller lists." See Rzepka, *Detective Fiction* (Cambridge, U.K.: Polity, 2005), 12 and 154.
8. L. H. Woolsey, "The Shooting of Two Mexican Students," *American Journal of International Law* 25.3 (1931): 514.
9. For documents from the Hoover administration related to the case, see *The American Presidency Project*, http://www.presidency.ucsb.edu/ws/index.php?pid=22701 and http://www.presidency.ucsb.edu/ws/index.php?pid=23149 (accessed February 25, 2010).

10. After his stint at N. W. Ayer and Son, Inc., Downing took a position in 1947 on the copy staff of the advertising firm Gray and Rogers. The *New York Times* reported in 1949 that Downing then secured an appointment as a "special consultant on Latin American advertising" at Weightman Advertising in Philadelphia. He was, simultaneously, the editor of *Panamericanismo*, which was published by the Pan American Association in the same city. See "Advertising News and Notes," *New York Times*, Mar. 28, 1947, 39; and "Advertising News and Notes," *New York Times*, June 8, 1949, 44.
11. The *New York Times* mentions that Downing was Choctaw at least three times. See "Books-Authors," *New York Times*, Mar. 5, 1940, 26; "Napoleon's Letters," *New York Times*, Nov. 4, 1934, BR17; "Book Notes," *New York Times*, Aug. 18, 1934, 7. The Popular Library reprint of *The Cat Screams* (New York: Popular Library, 1945) also identifies him as Choctaw on the back cover.
12. See "Book Notes," *New York Times*, May 4, 1935, 11.
13. The translations of Downing's work include Dutch, Finnish, Italian, and Spanish editions. The British publisher Methuen published editions of six Downing novels.
14. Wolfgang Hochbruck indicates that *The Cat Screams* was also translated into Swedish and German. I have not been able to find these editions of the novel. See Hochbruck, "Mystery Novels to Choctaw Pageant: Todd Downing and Native American Literature(s)" in *New Voices in Native American Literary Criticism*, ed. Arnold Krupat, 205–21 (Washington, D.C.: Smithsonian Institution, 1993).
15. For a review of *The Cat Screams*, see Gerald Bordman, *American Theatre: A Chronicle of Comedy and Drama, 1930–1969* (New York: Oxford University Press, 1996), 215.
16. "Murder in May," *Time*, June 9, 1941, http://www.time.com/time/magazine/article/0,9171,795384,00.html (accessed February 25, 2010).
17. This cursory view is reproduced in Marion Gridley, ed., *Indians of Today* (Chicago: Millar, 1936), 43, and *New York Times*, March 17, 1940, 95.
18. See Allen, *Blood Narrative*, 7–10, for a discussion of the distinctions among kinds of indigeneity and colonial practice.
19. See Lucy Maddox, *Citizen Indians: Native American Intellectuals, Race and Reform* (Ithaca, N.Y.: Cornell University Press, 2005), for the main influence on this argument about Downing claiming a public space from which to speak.
20. Mary Kay Vaughan and Stephen E. Lewis, introduction to *The Eagle and the Virgin: Nation and Cultural Revolution in Mexico, 1920–1940*, ed. Vaughan and Lewis (Durham, N.C.: Duke University Press, 2006), 1. *Mestizo/as* are people of indigenous and Spanish heritage. The identification has specific social and political connotations in Mexico, too.
21. Vaughan and Lewis, *Eagle and the Virgin*, 8. As Maureen Konkle demonstrates in *Writing Indian Nations: Native Intellectuals and the Politics of Historiography, 1827–1863* (Chapel Hill: University of North Carolina Press, 2004), nineteenth-century American Indian leaders were already challenging the exile of their people from history by writing American Indians into it.
22. Rick A. López, "The Noche Mexicana and the Exhibition of Popular Arts: Two Ways of Exalting Indianness," in *The Eagle and the Virgin*, ed. Vaughan and Lewis, 36.
23. Deloria, *Indians in Unexpected Places*, 6. The SAI was the first reform organization founded and run by American Indians.
24. See Shari M. Huhndorf, *Mapping the Americas: The Transnational Politics of Contemporary Native Culture* (Ithaca, N.Y.: Cornell University Press, 2009), 46–70.
25. López, *Noche Mexicana*, 23–24.
26. George W. Stocking Jr., ed., *The Shaping of American Anthropology, 1883–1911: A Franz Boas Reader* (New York: Basic Books, 1974), 4.
27. Stephen E. Lewis, "The Nation, Education, and the 'Indian Problem' in Mexico, 1920–1940," in *The Eagle and the Virgin*, ed. Vaughan and Lewis, 177.
28. Alan Knight, "Racism, Revolution, and *Indigenismo*: Mexico, 1910–1940," in *The Idea of Race ni Latin America, 1870–1940*, ed. Richard Graham (Austin: University of Texas Press, 1990), 77. Ashcroft, Griffiths, and Tiffin discuss the appropriation of indigeneity by settler colonists in *The Empire Writes Back*.
29. López, *Noche Mexicana*, 38.
30. Ibid., 41.
31. Lewis, "Nation, Education," 190.
32. Jan Rus, "The 'Comunidad Revolucionaria Institucional': The Subversion of Native Government in Highland Chiapas, 1936–1968," in *Everyday Forms of State Formation: Revolution and the Negotiation of Rule in Modern Mexico*, ed. Gilbert M. Joseph and Daniel Nugent (Durham, N.C.: Duke University

Press, 1994), 266–67. However, Rus argues that the policies of the Cárdenas administration ultimately "led to a more intimate form of domination" (267). See also Rus, 270–72, for a description of some of the cultural revitalization efforts and for specific examples of Maya resistance to interference by outsiders.

33. See Knight, "Racism, Revolution," 85 and 92.
34. See Francisco E. Balderrama and Raymond Rodriguez, *Decade of Betrayal: Mexican Repatriation in the 1930s* (Albuquerque: University of New Mexico Press, 1995), for an account of the hysteria and deportations. Gilbert G. González explains that the peon was for U.S. authors "synonymous for Indian," and the peon as an obstacle to modernization became "conventional wisdom" by 1930. See González, *Culture of Empire: American Writers, Mexico, and Mexican Immigrants, 1880–1930* (Austin: University of Texas Press, 2004), 80–81.
35. See Michael C. Meyer and William L. Sherman, *The Course of Mexican History*, 5th ed. (New York: Oxford University Press, 1995), 387–401.
36. *The Cat Screams*, 12. A *casa de huésped* (guest house) consists of a room in a private home.
37. Ibid., 12.
38. Ibid., 3.
39. See, for example, *Murder on Tour* (New York: Putnam's, 1933), 73; and *Vultures in the Sky* (Garden City, N.Y.: Doubleday, 1935), 66–67.
40. Downing owned *Rig Veda Americanus: Sacred Songs of the Ancient Mexicans, with a Gloss in Nahuatl* (1890). For the references in Herrera and Sahagun, see Daniel G. Brinton, *Nagualism: A Study in Native American Folk-lore and History* (Philadelphia: MacCalla & Company, 1894), 4–5 and 5–6.
41. Brinton, *Nagualism*, 5.
42. Downing, *The Cat Screams*, 20.
43. Other academics include Professor Horace Starns Bymaster in *Murder on Tour;* Professor Garnett Voice, Professor Fogarty, and the archaeological students Karl Weikel and John Clay Biggerstaff in *The Case of the Unconquered Sisters* (Garden City, N.Y.: Doubleday, 1936); and Professor Gulliver Damson in *Night Over Mexico* (Garden City, N.Y.: Doubleday, 1937).
44. Downing, *The Cat Screams*, 210.
45. See Rzepka, *Detective Fiction*, specifically 15, for an assessment of the detective genre's debt to the modern sciences.
46. The assessment of colonialism as witchcraft anticipates Leslie Marmon Silko's novel *Ceremony* (New York: Penguin, 1977) in which a contest between witches leads to the creation of brutal European colonizers.
47. S. S. Van Dine, "Twenty Rules for Writing Detective Stories," in *Writing Detective and Mystery Fiction*, ed. A. S. Burack (Boston: The Writer, 1945), 198.
48. Downing, "Murder Is a Rather Serious Business," in *Writing Detective and Mystery Fiction*, 182.
49. Rzepka, *Detective Fiction*, 15.
50. Downing, *The Cat Screams*, 251 (italics in original).
51. Ibid., 252.
52. While Noon is the primary locus of *nagualism*, the colonial avarice that motivates Parkyn's attempted pillaging of indigenous Mexican wealth also feeds the malevolent magic that is attacking Esteban. Indeed, *The Cat Screams* was inspired by Wilkie Collins's *The Moonstone* (1868), a detective novel that is, according to John R. Reed, an indictment of the crimes of British imperialism. Reed, "English Imperialism and the Unacknowledged Crime of *The Moonstone*," *Clio* 2.3 (1973): 281–90.
53. Downing, *The Cat Screams*, 206.
54. Ibid., 207.
55. Ibid., 294.
56. Brinton, *Nagualism*, 35–36.
57. D'Arcy McNickle, *Runner in the Sun: A Story of Indian Maize* (Philadelphia: John C. Winston, 1954); for *The Year of Pilar* and *A World Elsewhere*, see Lynn Riggs, *4 Plays* (New York: Samuel French, 1947).
58. Allen, *Blood Narrative*, 42.
59. See James H. Cox, "Indigenous Nationhood and Intertribal Kinship in Todd Downing's *The Mexican Earth*," *MELUS* 33.1 (Spring 2008): 75–92, and the laudatory review of Downing's book by the archaeologist and historian Philip Ainsworth Means, "Mexico, Its Land and Its People: A Notable History from Earliest Times with a Sympathetic and Convincing Analysis of the Problems of Today," *New York Times*, March 31, 1940, 89.

60. "Oklahoma Deputy Kills Two Mexican Students, One Kin of Ortiz Rubio; Hoover Sends Regret," *New York Times*, June 9, 1931, 1.
61. "Two Held for Trial in Mexican Deaths," *New York Times*, June 11, 1931, 16.
62. The detective's reconstruction of the crime by analepsis is a convention of classical detective fiction of the 1920s and 1930s. See Rzepka, *Detective Fiction*, 19.
63. See Lambert, *Choctaw Nation*, 137–38.
64. Downing, *Murder on the Tropic* (Garden City, N.Y.: Doubleday, 1935), 191–92 (italics in original).
65. N. Scott Momaday, *House Made of Dawn* (New York: Harper and Row, 1968), 58.
66. Thank you to Maria Rose Hynson, executive secretary to the provost and dean of the college, for finding Todd Downing in the 1950–1951 *Washington College Catalog* and the 1951 Washington College yearbook, *Pegasus*.
67. See Hochbruck, "Mystery Novels," 212, for the explanation that Downing returned to Atoka to take care of his mother and father.
68. The quoted passage is from a pamphlet titled "Choctaw Bilingual Education Program." My gratitude belongs to Charles Rzepka for sharing these materials.
69. Ibid.
70. See Lambert, *Choctaw Nation*, 3.

Maori Cowboys, Maori Indians

Alice Te Punga Somerville

> When we came out of the theatre Willie Boy and I saw ourselves as white, aligning ourselves with our heroes and heroines of the technicolour screen. Although we were really brown, we would beat up on each other just to play the hero.
> Neither of us wanted to be an Indian.
>
> —Witi Ihimaera, "Short Features"

In the contemporary critical, scholarly, artistic, and political moment, Maori are most often understood as "Indigenous" and, in turn, Maori are expected to most closely resemble other groups also understood as "Indigenous." The moment in which the Maori boys in Witi Ihimaera's "Short Features" simultaneously desire to be "heroes and heroines" and desire to *not* be "Indian" interrupts assumptions we might be used to making in comparative Indigenous studies: we are surprised to hear the Maori boys identify with "white . . . heroes" instead of "Indian[s]"; and this surprise points to our expectation that they will identify with Indians.[1] Focusing on moments of *dis*identification with "Indian[s]" does not, in my view, paralyze or contradict the work of comparative Indigenous studies or the potential of the term "Indigenous." Rather, it demands that we grapple with the place of specificity in Indigenous identifications and with the complexities of local, regional, and national particularities. Disidentification is countered not by "correcting" identification but by exploring its terms. A methodology that merely identifies instances of resemblance between communities and experiences can both struggle to analyze specific examples, such as that elaborated in Ihimaera's story, and obscure the complicated foundations of connection upon which any conception of Indigeneity depends. Tracing the range and stakes of various Indigenous-Indigenous connections not as a stocktaking of similarities but as a historicized matrix of self-recognition, mutual recognition, and misrecognition is more productive and, ultimately, more useful. This more nuanced articulation of Indigeneity will, rather than undermine the value of comparative work, enable us to more confidently, productively, and ethically elaborate its possibilities.

"Short Features," a four-part short story by Witi Ihimaera, recalls Maori consumption of U.S. and British popular culture in the mid-twentieth century.

The four short vignettes each focus on film, and one section, titled "Nobody wanted to be Indians," focuses on Maori engagement with "westerns." For these two Maori boys in the story, the conventions of the "cowboys and Indians" film genre turns their attention back onto themselves. The narrator cannot "remember" this particular pop cultural form without also remembering specific anxieties around race ("[we] saw ourselves as white . . . although we were really brown"). The literary text "Short Features" articulates a recollection of coming into awareness of a racialized position ("we were really brown") by turning to another, very particular, kind of text that represents encounters between Indigenous and non-Indigenous people: the film western. Importantly, "Short Features" suggests that the narrator and his friend produce a (youthful, historicized) Maori reading of the western film genre in which two mutually exclusive categories are produced: "Willie boy and I" (Maori), "brown," "Indian" on the one hand; and "white," "heroes and heroines" on the other. While we might be used to, in comparative Indigenous studies, exploring the complexities of a connection—or indeed slippage—between, for example, "Maori" and "Indian," which sit alongside each other on one side of this configuration, Ihimaera's text interrupts this connection with an expression of desire on the part of these two Maori boys to cross the line. Why do "neither of [them] want to be an Indian"? And what might this mean for comparative Indigenous studies?

"I really was looking at myself": Maori Indians

On what basis might a Maori narrative of colonial history begin with Columbus in the Americas? Some Maori articulations of Indigeneity gesture toward a five-hundred-year-old history of imperialism and thereby include the two centuries of colonialism in Aotearoa in the much longer story of the Western Hemisphere. In her *Decolonizing Methodologies*, for example, Linda Tuhiwai Smith writes that "for most of the past 500 years the indigenous people's project has had one major priority: survival."[2] Similarly, in his "Research and the Colonisation of Maori Knowledge," Moana Jackson identifies the relationship between Indigeneity ("the indigenous world") and the specific chronology of European occupation of the Americas:

> From the moment that Christopher Columbus first drafted the ethic of contact between the world of western Europe and the indigenous world, those scriptwriters began to create a fantasy in which the colonisers were the heroes and Indigenous Peoples were either the villains, or irrelevant to the telling of the story.[3]

This rhetorical move mobilizes five centuries of European presence in the Americas as an appropriate and strategic context for the local Indigenous situation in Aotearoa, New Zealand, even when European presence in these islands has been significantly shorter. Linda Tuhiwai Smith and Moana Jackson are both Maori scholars, and Maori had no contact with Europeans until 1642 when Dutch explorer Abel Tasman sailed by; it was not until 1769 that Cook actually came on shore. Why, then, do Smith and Jackson place themselves within an imperial history of much longer duration? If "the indigenous peoples' project" and "the indigenous world" and "indigenous peoples" have been around for at least five hundred years, when and how did Maori (and indeed "Indians") become Indigenous?

A connection between Maori and American Indians depends on our cooperative huddling under the umbrella term "Indigenous." Although there are other bases for connection—such as our similar positions as minority groups in large white settler nations—the primary connection between Maori and American Indian communities is our shared Indigenousness. Maori have connected and articulated a relationship with other Indigenous communities through creative, activist, political, organizational, and historic alliances: through anthologies of creative or scholarly writing;[4] through political configurations such as the WCIP and various UN groups;[5] through scholarly networks and spaces such as WINHEC, WIPCE, and NAISA;[6] through sporting and cultural festivals, events, and exchanges;[7] and so on. These connections are often long-standing and there are countless deeper histories and moments of Indigenous-Indigenous encounters that await scholarly treatment. Certainly Maori have elaborated relationships with Indigenous communities in Australia, Hawai'i, and elsewhere in the Pacific. For the purposes of this article, however, this specific moment in Ihimaera's short story in which "neither" of the Maori boys "wanted to be an Indian" turns our attention to the relationship between Maori and Indigenous communities in the Americas.

It is difficult to avoid reaching a theoretical dead-end trying to unpack the multiple uses of the term *Indigenous.* After all, as I have written elsewhere, how can a term stand in both for the name of any Indigenous group as well as for the umbrella under which all Indigenous groups sit? How do you find things you "share" when the basis of your connection is your insistence on uniqueness?[8] There is a proliferation of definitions in scholarly, activist, and political spaces, and most of them contain some combination of connection to land, colonial histories, particular (familial, communal, holistic, ecological) values, unique cultural and linguistic features, and a present context of marginalization. When

"Indigenous" is used as a prescriptive rather than descriptive term, the exciting possibilities of recognizing connections across vast distances and differences can be dulled by becoming yet another authenticity test for communities and individuals who have already suffered from such tests. Because it is impossible for all members of any Indigenous community to ever completely satisfy all requirements of any one definition, the most useful definitions of the word are those that allow space for contingency, flexibility, and negotiation. Because the term has real political valence and utility, it is tempting to attempt to theorize into being some abstract bridges over these troubled waters, and certainly this is an important thread in the growing body of scholarly work that grapples with the question of comparative Indigenous studies.

Sometimes Maori identify specifically as, or at least with, Indians: Ihimaera's story would not ring true if the boys claimed to fight because "neither of [them] wanted to be [Indigenous]." Despite the seductiveness of the "Indigenous" umbrella, which promises to produce an exhaustive list of things shared among all it gathers together, often the meaning and parameters of the term are figured out through nation-to-nation (or perhaps context-to-context) relationships, as with specific instances of Maori identification not with the abstract global category "Indigenous" but with the category "Indian," which is specific to North America and, usually, to the United States. Elsewhere in Ihimaera's own oeuvre, Maori affiliation with American Indians is explored in two rather distinct ways: as symbolic figures, and as real people. In his 1994 novel *Bulibasha*, the protagonist Himiona invokes the dualism of the U.S. frontier when he laments to his mother that their immediate family is marginalized in their extended family structure:

> It's the way it's meant to be, isn't it? We're here because in this life there are chiefs and there are Indians. We're the Indians.[9]

Himiona refers to "Indians" here because they are readily available as a symbol of subjugation rather than because he identifies with them on the basis of shared perspectives of experiences as Indigenous peoples. This mode of identifying with "Indians" is entirely dependent on the circulation of popular non-Indigenous representations and has little to do with any relationships with actual "Indians" at all. A very different kind of identification is explored in a later Ihimaera novel, *The Uncle's Story*, in which an elaboration of connections between Maori and American Indians is an overt part of the narrative when some of the Maori characters travel to take part in an "Indigenous" conference in North America.[10] Unlike in *Bulibasha*, in this novel the "Indians" are "actual" people as opposed to symbolic figures.[11]

In her 2009 short story "Sugar-coated," Maori writer Charlie Holland deals explicitly with the need to disentangle these two kinds of "Indians": the "Indians" as encountered through non-Indigenous cultural forms, and "actual" Indigenous people from the United States.[12] The protagonist in "Sugar-coated," Miria, travels to New Mexico for an Indigenous literary conference, and she secures funding for her trip from a group of middle-class white women, one of whom introduces a link between Miria and the Indigenous people of the Southwest:

> But the people! You'll swear you were looking at yourself . . . You know: the locals, look just like your people: Maori. You'll swear you were looking at yourself. You really must go down and have a look.

That the white woman is the first in the story to suggest a connection between Maori and American Indians (despite Miria's presumed prior awareness of this connection as evidenced by her desire to attend the conference in the first place) echoes the place of Europeans in the production of the transnational category "Indigenous." Importantly, although the connection is described by the woman as merely physical and dependent on the act of "looking," the doubled meaning of "look" leaves room for the "locals" to share both physical appearance ("look") and perspective ("look") with "Maori." Furthermore, the white woman presumes that her own recognition of similarity ("the locals, look just like your people") will be shared by Miria: "you'll swear you were looking at yourself." Indeed, she assumes that this recognition of similarity will be such that Miria herself will be unable to distinguish herself from "the locals."

When Miria arrives in Albuquerque she admits to being curious about whether the white woman is right:

> I followed close behind, pretending to be interested, while clandestinely checking out the people. They looked nothing like me, and I suddenly felt stupid for suspecting that they would.

Miria recognizes that adopting the European expectation of identification between Indigenous people on superficial bases ("the locals, look just like your people") is "stupid" and her first encounter with the Indigenous people in New Mexico focuses on difference: "they looked nothing like me." The doubled meaning of "look" is repeated here and suggests that "the people" resemble Miria neither in appearance nor in perspective. This sequence critiques unthoughtful Maori adoption of European representations of "Indians"—of which Himiona's claim "we're the Indians" is a rich and complex example—

and neatly points to the ultimately white (and colonizing) source of such a simplistic identification.

"Sugar-coated" does not end with a disavowal of connection, however: instead, it shifts the basis for connection between Maori and American Indians from immediate and superficial resemblance to historicized and multilayered resonance. After "clandestinely checking out the people" selling local art to tourists, Miria goes to the museum, a space that similarly provides Miria with an opportunity to "look" at American Indians. When she sees an exhibition of woven blankets, she recognizes the community of people behind the construction of the pieces, commenting, "Wow . . . imagine all the korero that these weavers had when these blankets were being produced." Miria finds a point of connection not in the forms themselves but in her understanding and recognition of communal weaving in a Maori context, and she imaginatively brings her knowledge of Maori weaving, Maori language ("korero"), and communication ("korero") into the American Southwest. This connection in turn reframes the nearby photographic display about the colonial history of the region:

> I normally find these sorts of displays pretty boring, but there was something about the stagnant faces of these Native Americans that was intriguing.

Again Miria is "checking out the people," but these "Native Americans" are in photographs (with "stagnant faces"), and from the past. She notes the small inscriptions with a bare minimum of details: "Local Native with Horse," "Local Women Preparing Food." Like the white woman in New Zealand who spoke about "the local people," the museum captions describe the people merely as "local," whereas Miria has named them (albeit broadly): "Native American."

When Miria happens upon a particular photograph of "local people" that resonates with home, she is struck immediately: "suddenly I stopped and couldn't move." In this way she mimics the people represented in the image, her inability to "move" paralleling the "stagnant faces" of the "Native Americans." Her proximity to the image itself is restricted—it is "wedged behind a thick layer of glass"—but she recognizes and elaborates a connection nonetheless. Her first reaction to the image is disbelief—"at first I thought my eyes were deceiving me so I looked closer"—which again centers the place and limits of "looking." Unlike her earlier unsuccessful act of "looking" at the market, however, while Miria distrusts her eyes at first, she then confirms after a "closer" examination that she had been "right." The photograph depicts "a group of men standing outside a low wall that enclosed an empty courtyard" and Miria both engages with the overt detail of the image and recognizes the extent to which she brings her familiarity with its subject matter through the highly mediated genre of western films: "I imagined that their uniforms were dark blue and white like in old western movies." However, Miria only imports the representation of *white* men from the "western movies"—unlike Himiona, or the boys in "Short Features," she refuses to "check out the locals" through the same frame of reference.

The photograph is captioned "Public Execution," and along with the soldiers it depicts three men, one of whom is lying on the ground, one of whom is still standing, and one of whom is "another man, knees bent and head collapsed backwards. Smoke or dust was suspended around the middle of his torso." It is possible to imagine that Miria's reaction to such a photograph would not be restricted to Indigenous people: the subject matter is horrific and the viewer is forced to be the voyeur on an intimately violent scene. While Miria looks at the photograph, a curator leads a tour past and intones: "Oh, yes. There were literally thousands killed." The photograph—which is described as hanging "like a prize"—both represents and enacts the violence of a specific colonial encounter, but Miria extends its meaning beyond the "local" to the "Indigenous":

> These men were Indigenous. Did someone tell their whanau . . . ?

The shift of the photographic subjects from "Native American" to "Indigenous" opens space for Miria to connect this specific experience with the global and, in turn, with another specific experience. Importantly, the word *Indigenous* enables the concept of "whanau" to travel as well as the experience of colonial violence, although just as importantly the colonial violence has the capacity (through being represented by a visual image) to travel across linguistic borders, whereas the word "whanau," while able to be guessed at, travels with rather more constraint. Once the men are identified as "Indigenous," their broader family relationships ("whanau") become important. Although "whanau" might refer to the blood relatives and communities of the men, it is tempting to read "whanau" more broadly as an articulation of an extended network of "Indigenous" people. When read in this way, the matter of informing "whanau" relates not only to notifying the spatial and temporal as well as genealogical context of these specific men but also to "tell[ing]" the wider "Indigenous" "whanau" of their experiences and plight. In this way the photograph, despite being "wedged behind thick glass" and displayed like a "prize," performs the important function of "tell[ing]" Miria and, in turn, Maori.

At this point, Miria offers something in return: another kind of "tell[ing]." Inserted into the story is an excerpt from a New Zealand newspaper account of a Waitangi Tribunal[13] finding that, in one specific series of incidents in the nineteenth century,

> Crown forces acted mercilessly, killing non-combatants intentionally and summarily executing some prisoners.

This extract interrupts the story both visually (it is indented) and narratively and recalls an example of extreme violence enacted on Indigenous people by the State, which resonates with the scene depicted in the photograph. The parallel between the photograph and the newspaper snippet is layered: both present narratively similar predicaments; photographs and newspapers are both popularly understood to be "real" or "factual" and thereby a truth claim is inferred by their very forms; and the word "executing" in the newspaper echoes the caption of the photograph, "Public execution." While the comparison with "old western movies" provides Miria with a way to understand the soldiers in the photograph, the coding of "Native Americans" as "Indigenous" provides space for Miria to explore another kind of connection on the basis of shared colonial experiences but also shared cultural values ("whanau").

In a story that is all about "looking," and the limits of trusting one's "eyes," Miria's response to recognizing the depth of connection between Maori and American Indians has a profound effect on her vision:

> My vision blurred, and I quickly looked up to prevent any tears. Within the photo I saw eyes staring. She was right—I really was looking at myself.

At first unable to see clearly at all ("my vision blurred"), Miria realizes there are "eyes staring" in the photograph. It is possible that Miria recognizes something in the eyes of the men in the photograph—"within the photo I saw eyes staring"—and in this way her "looking" has been returned by the men from a previous century, producing a moment of mutual "looking" and, in turn, mutual recognition ("I really was looking at myself"). Alternatively, considering the photograph is behind a "thick wedge of glass," Miria could be seeing her own reflection superimposed on the photograph of the men ("I really was looking at myself") and so in this act of "looking" at the "Native Americans" Miria, like the boys in "Short Features," comes ultimately to a moment of self-awareness or self-recognition. It could be her own "eyes staring" that Miria can finally see: she is now able to recognize her own perspective and modes of "looking" and to turn that view back on herself so that she becomes an object in her own exploration of Indigenous connection. Finally, recalling Chadwick Allen's discussion of Momaday's "Carnegie, Oklahoma, 1919," the "eyes" could also be a pun on the plural of the word "I."[14] The "I[s] staring" could be an inclusive us/we "staring" from the photograph, and Miria could thereby be being looked at by a collective "I" made up of "Native Americans" *and* Maori: she claims the "Native Americans" as an "I" as well, both bringing them into her own genealogy and claiming the situation depicted in the photograph as her own. In this reading, Miria is claiming a productive slippage between "I" of her own Maori community and an "I" of a broader Indigenous community: the "eyes" become an expression of Indigenous "whanau." The "staring" here is a heightened version of the "looking" that has occurred over the course of the rest of the story, reinforcing this point of mutual and self-recognition as the narrative, symbolic, and political center of the story.

The place of the colonial gaze in this moment of connection is worth noting: the white woman who had confidently assured Miria "you'll swear you were looking at yourself" haunts this moment of connection: "she was right—I really was looking at myself." The story suggests, however, that the woman was both "right" and not right about what Miria would see in New Mexico. On the one hand, she sets up the possibility of connection and the terms of engagement, introducing the superficial and self-centered practice of "looking," which is central to the story and beyond which Miria never extends her modes of connection with Indians, even though she attends a conference at which Indigenous scholars are present and is in close proximity to Indian people at the market. That the point of recognition occurs for Miria at a museum, and with a group of Indians from historical rather than present time, could suggest that her mode of connection cuts out the possibility of recognizing herself in people who have engaged more deeply with modernity and the "now" or, indeed, that her recognition of connection ("I really was looking at myself") is entirely self-directed and can only be articulated in spite—or perhaps because—of her avoidance of discussions with "actual" Indians in the present day.

However, another reading of this is possible: Miria undermines the white woman's mode of "looking" after realizing that "looking" for resemblances is "stupid" and, although her act of "looking" at the market may appear to merely extend her "looking" at the museum, and her words at the point of recognition echo exactly the words of the prediction ("she was right—I really was looking at myself"), Miria's connection with "Native Americans" on the basis of resonance is rather different from the predicted connection on the basis of superficial resemblance.[15] So then, we might, like Miria in "Sugar-coated," expect the boys in "Short Features" to identify with Indians because they're Indigenous. But they don't: "neither of [them] wanted to be an Indian." Instead, they identify with cowboys.

"Those varmint injuns": Maori cowboys

Maori visual artists Michael Parekowhai and Nathan Pohio have produced numerous pieces that engage with the western genre, and specifically subvert the figure of the cowboy. A description of a recent Pohio piece explicitly notes that Maori manipulation of the cowboy image undermines the expected connection between Maori and "Indians":

> Scenes of a Maori rodeo champion and a panoramic view of whanau dressed in Western costume illustrates that "indians" can indeed become cowboys under certain circumstances.[16]

Certainly Indigenous communities and individuals engage in "cowboy" cultures in North America, and it would be misleading to suggest that the categories "Indian" and "cowboy" are always mutually exclusive. When Robert Leonard discusses Parekowhai's use of "dominant" cultural images, he explicitly ties contemporary artistic appropriation—including of cowboy culture—into much longer histories of cultural appropriation for pro-Indigenous purposes:

> Rather than wearing Maoriness on his sleeve, Parekowhai appropriated images from the dominant Pakeha culture, subtly recoding them to speak of Maori concerns. In this they recalled the way Maori had long drawn on the colonising culture for their own needs, for instance taking the Old Testament as a blueprint for resistance.[17]

Maori participation in rodeos can thus be simultaneously read, at its furthest reaches, as an act of imperialism and an act of resistance; Maori cowboys are neither fully victims of a specific project of global imperialism nor completely independent agents in a discourse-free sports arena. Just as American Indian individuals and communities have long histories of engagement with "cowboy culture," Maori engagement in rodeo culture (like Indigenous cowboy cultures in other sites such as Australia and Hawai'i)[18] cannot be read as a simple or singular act of cultural cross-dressing.

Maori have identified with cowboys over a long period of time and in many spaces. Certainly there is a vibrant Maori presence in New Zealand's rodeo scene, which draws heavily on aesthetics as well as practices of cowboy culture; a popular weekly show called *Rodeo Kaupoai*, combining the English term *rodeo* and the Maori transliteration for *cowboy* in its title and making visible the world of Maori participants in rodeo circuits, has screened on Maori TV.

In the 1950s, Johnny Cooper was a popular musician and entertainer known as "the Maori Cowboy," and Maori people have actively participated in New Zealand's small but vibrant country music scene as entertainers and audiences. "Westerns" have circulated widely in New Zealand, and before the widespread arrival of television in the 1960s films were a particularly important part of social life in small rural Maori communities. The discourse of "cowboys and Indians" is thoroughly present in New Zealand to the extent that Ihimaera's protagonists in "Short Features" (and in *Bulibasha* and in Holland's "Sugar-coated") are fully aware of the conventions of the genre. In the context of comparative Indigenous studies, one might argue that the U.S. western film, and especially its repeated inscription of the "frontier," provides a framework for talking about Indigenous–non-Indigenous relationships. Whether the film western is a map to be overlaid on all Indigenous contexts everywhere, or a map we might notice is ill fitting in the land of its birth, let alone in the places to which it has been transported, is in some ways secondary to the fact of the map's wide circulation.

Ihimaera's "Short Features" explores the relationship between Maori attendance at—and valorization of—the movies, and the depictions of non-Europeans available to them through the screen. The narration of each section is from the perspective of what Maori writer Patricia Grace calls "now time," a knowledgeable present, and the sections are framed as reflections on four separate but related memories. The second of the four parts, "Nobody wanted to be Indians," is sandwiched between other short episodes that explore racialized perspectives on beauty ("But I'm supposed to look like this"), sexualized roles between Indigenous women and white men ("a pattern as old as Fletcher Christian himself"), and the example of the movie star Merle Oberon, who obscured her brown (including Maori) ancestry in order to maintain her "white image" on the silver screen. Each of the four segments recalls Maori consumption of film and in each of them collective multigenerational consumption is foregrounded. The memories of watching movies are peopled by relatives ("my cousin Georgia," "our grandmother," "Nani Miro"), as well as by the names of twenty-six British and American film stars. These two communities—film stars and family—come together in the final section, "Merle Oberon was a Maori," which describes the Maori family's reaction to the news that the famous "British" screen actress had Maori ancestry. The story ends with the narrator "start[ing] to grin at the subversiveness of somebody playing white and getting away with it, who had a mother who was one of us," a moment that knits the film star into the family tree ("a mother who was one of us") and in turn delights in the figure of one person bringing together these two communities.

The connection between race and gender is elaborated in each of these other sections, and this foregrounds the place of gender in the piece "Nobody wanted to be Indians." For the narrator and his friends, the masculinity epitomized by the cowboys is particularly appealing:

> Our husky cowboy idols were laughing Burt Lancaster, Kirk Douglas, Alan Ladd and Audie Murphy. Willie Boy and I would toss each other for who would play the hero and who would play the villain like Jack Palance or Richard Widmark.

The masculinity of the leading white actors, all of whom are known by name to the narrator, is secured by their "husk[iness]" as well as by the fact the two boys spend time outside the movie theater attempting to emulate them. The humorous recognition in the previous section of the story that the narrator's cousin Georgina "always wanted to play the heroine parts and she wasn't exactly what we had in mind" does not produce any self-reflexive awareness about the similar—and perhaps similarly humorous because similarly impossible—identification with the white "heroes" on the part of these young brown boys.

Paralleling the formula of western movies themselves, the "Indians" are barely present in the discussion until near the end—the vanishing Indians indeed—and the battles are, at least for the first section of the narrative in which identifications are being established, all between white men as goodies and white men as baddies. When Indians are finally introduced into the narrative, they introduce the first division between the two friends:

> Willie Boy and I always had our hardest battles over who would play who when we wanted to re-enact those westerns in which the cavalry fought the Red Indians.

The term "Red Indians" highlights that the boys are not only familiar with, but also consent to, the terms of identification expected by the genre itself. Furthermore, these terms that are set up in the film extend beyond the space in which the film is consumed when the boys reinscribe the distinctions between "cavalry" and "Red Indians" in their own "re-enact[ments]" outside of the theater. The boys "re-enact" the texts they "love . . . the most" in their home space—presumably Maori space—and the terms of engagement between "cavalry" and "Red Indians," as set by the films, are therefore infinitely replicated across Indigenous spaces. In this way, the boys "re-enact" not just the form of the "westerns" but also "re-enact" the violence of colonialism they portray.

Despite Maori engagement with cowboy culture, the comment about Pohio's art, that "'indians' can indeed become cowboys under certain circumstances," exploits a rhetorical, even if not "actual," dualism of "cowboys" versus "indians," which in turn crafts a broader dualism in which "western costume" and "cowboys" are on one side and "whanau" and "indians" are on the other. In the film audiences of "Short Features," despite the resonances between Maori and American Indian experiences identified by Miria in "Sugar-coated," Maori viewers ally themselves with the "cavalry" rather than the "Red Indians:"

> How we would cheer and yell and throw peanuts when, at the last reel, the cavalry would appear to save the fort! . . . just before the last attack by those varmint injuns you'd hear a bugle and on they would come, the cavalry.

Despite—or indeed because of—the colonial context in Aotearoa, New Zealand, the audience appears to identify wholly with "the cavalry" against the "varmint injuns," and the description of Indians "attack[ing]" and Europeans "sav[ing]" the fort underscores this identification. The reference to "the last reel" makes visible the constructedness of the display—the "cheer[ing] and yell[ing]" is interrupted by explicit reference to the artificial and literally projected nature of this form—and yet this does not undermine the ability of the genre to demand, and receive, engagement by the Maori audience.

Finally, the narrator outlines his perceptions of "the Indians," letting out a long line of stereotypes and observations:

> The white man was always right in the Westerns and only in a very few were the Indians anything other than wrong. The Indians smoked peace pipes, but you knew they were as mean as snakes. Not only that, but they were an illiterate lot. All they could say was "How" or "Heap big medicine" and they communicated by smoke signals instead of by telephone. They were mean sons of a bitch.

The narrator betrays his knowledge of the genre at the same time as he undermines his ability to critically analyze the images of Indians with which he has been confronted. The recognition that the "cowboys" operate in a particular historical context is not also afforded the Indians. Their conduct and technologies are (humorously) judged according to the contemporary norms enjoyed by Maori: "litera[cy]," "telephone." Interestingly, this renders the "white man" timeless (the usual position of "the native") and sets the Indians in a specific, albeit historical, time.

The narrator of the story is not incapable of distinguishing between "real" Indians and those represented on screen: "Even when they were played sympathetically, they weren't really Indians at all but simply Rock Hudson all browned up as Tara." The bodies on the screen are distinguished from "real Indians" because they are played by white actors "all browned up," and the narrator admits that a "sympathetic" representation of "Indians" does not make the representation any more "real." Indeed, the only people who have the capacity to "be an Indian" in this story are the Maori boys who consume the western film genre on the other side of the world from "real Indians." In this way, echoing Himiona's comment "we're the Indians" in *Bulibasha*, "real Indians" are exploited as a representational shortcut for something other than themselves because (despite their desire to be the "heroes") the boys take up the place of "be[ing] an Indian" in a story which therefore still has no room for "real Indians." Ultimately, this medium of the western film, the genre the narrator and his friend "love . . . the most," simultaneously represents and "re-enact[s]" the work of the colonial project.

In the final sequence, there is an admission of the wider racist colonial context in which the disidentification with "Indians" takes place, although the reminiscent mode of the narrative suggests that this insight comes from the voice of a matured perspective, looking back. After describing the practice of white actors and actresses "playing Indian,"[19] the possibilities of "playing white" are considered:

> When we came out of the theatre Willie Boy and I saw ourselves as white, aligning ourselves with our heroes and heroines of the technicolour screen. Although we were really brown, we would beat up on each other just to play the hero.

The boys are merely seeking to "play" white in the same way that the white actors are playing Indian. Although the narrator, even from the perspective of his boyhood, was able to recognize the whiteness of the actors, the boys attempt to override their "real brown[ness]" by their own imaginative identification with white "heroes." As in Pohio's art, in which Maori "dressed in Western costume" are still ultimately "whanau" and "indians," and only able to be cowboys "under certain circumstances," while the boys claim to have partially achieved this racial transformation ("Willie Boy and I saw ourselves as white") this is undermined almost immediately by the recognition that they are "really brown."

The final line "neither of us wanted to be an Indian" paradoxically suggests a deeper recognition of the connection between Maori and "Indians" at the very moment that connection is disavowed. The difference between the boys wanting to "*play* the hero" and wanting to "*be* an Indian" suggests that the default for the boys is to be understood as "an Indian" rather than as "the hero." Unlike the white actors who are not "really Indians," these Maori boys do not need to be "browned up" because they are already "really brown." To extend this acknowledgment of "be[ing] an Indian," if being "really brown" enables the boys to "be an Indian," a slippage is produced between being "really brown" ("really" Maori) and "be[ing] an Indian." The boys' stated desire to *not* be "an Indian" is, through their rejection of being "brown," a form of disidentification not just with "Indians" but also with themselves. To clarify, we might imagine a chain of slippages in which "neither of us wanted to be an Indian" becomes "neither of us wanted to be brown" and, finally, "neither of us wanted to be Maori." Further, this hysterical disidentification with "an Indian" and the implied disidentification with themselves, is reinforced by the introduction of intracommunity violence: "[we] always had our hardest battles over who would play who"; "we would beat up on each other just to play the hero." Indeed, at the very point that a connection between Maori and Indians is hysterically and categorically avoided ("we would beat up on each other just to play the hero") the finishing phrase "neither of us wanted to be an Indian" might be read as the moment at which identification with Indians is most acute.[20]

"Yet made different": When Natives Won't Act Like Natives

Sometimes Maori identify with Indians and sometimes Maori identify with cowboys. Despite the colonial frames of Holland's photograph and Ihimaera's film that literally foreground the act of visual representation even as Maori viewers engage with them ("an image framed with a bold, constricting black edge and wedged behind a thick layer of glass," "at the last reel"), we hope—Indigenous studies hopes—that Maori will identify something about the Indians that is familiar and even, perhaps, familial. We want the boys in "Short Features" to identify with Indians in the same way that Miria does. If only the Native boys would behave as proper Natives: if only they would identify with the Native characters in the film! What, indeed, can we make of Maori boys who fight each other to avoid "be[ing] an Indian"?

In various "national" contexts we have struggled with the question of how to treat those Indigenous individuals (and communities) who do not appear to perform an explicitly anticolonial, pro-Indigenous stance. We grapple with how we might account for behavior and positions that feel like contradictions: the temptation is to explain, reframe, and perhaps absolve Indigenes who seem to participate in anti-Indigenous projects. Due to the hard work of Indigenous and non-Indigenous scholars, Indigenous studies scholarship has preferred complex narratives of negotiation over simple narratives of loyalty/disloyalty: we point to the impact of specific histories, pressures or pragmatisms that enable us to understand the choices people have made. Indigenous figures (Charles Eastman, Peter Buck, James Carroll) who have been held up by the colonial project as icons of assimilation (indeed civilization) are reclaimed by Indigenous scholars and communities as people who were consciously committed to undermining those very structures that have held them up. These projects of reclamation and reframing are significant and profound, and I myself am engaged in such projects elsewhere, but it is perhaps worth reflecting on the strategies by which we reclaim them.

Early in her exploration of Indians in film, *Wiping the War Paint off the Lens*, Beverly Singer writes about specific Indian people who have participated in the American film industry and she wrestles with the place of seemingly "problem" Indians in her overarching narrative about "solution" Indians in the film world. Before outlining the Native filmmakers who have been engaged in wiping the war paint off the lens, she needs to deal with those Native actors who wore the war paint in the first place. How might such Natives fit into a story of Native filmmaking as Natives, if a prerequisite of Natives is that they are committed to wiping the paint *off*? An attempt to reclaim them in the history of Native film requires a focus on aspects that confirm their consciously pro-Indian and anti-imperial stance. For example, despite the possibility that Harold Preston Smith (Jay Silverheels) could attract critique for playing Tonto in the television series *The Lone Ranger*, which arguably reinforced an image of stoic, silent helpful sidekick Indians in white America, Singer prefers a redemptive narrative in which she emphasizes his self-conscious participation in the film industry in order to achieve specific pro-Indian ends. She describes Silverheels as "a striking reminder that many Native people are drawn to movie careers to change the perception of Indians."[21] Singer goes on to describe the rather more difficult job of reconciling the Hollywood work of Russell Means and Dennis Banks with their highly visible activist work:

> Their acting performances in the 1990s are the antithesis of their original message as AIM leaders who were caustically critical of Hollywood movie portrayals of Indians. Their roles are based on the old stereotypes of Indians; the plot of each movie remains rooted in the defeat of Indians in American history.[22]

In order to reframe the work of these latter two men, Singer turns to a historical configuration of compromised Indigenous agency in a context of "humiliat[ion]":

> Buffalo Bill's Wild West Show exploited these Indian leaders in humiliating demonstrations that reenacted the cultural genocide they had fought to prevent. We now hope to remember them as historic Native leaders, not actors.[23]

Interestingly, Singer finds it necessary to move these figures outside of the realm of representation ("historic Native leaders, not actors") in order to recuperate them; this enables her to step aside from questions of Indigenous political infidelity and restore the men to a rightful place in Indigenous memory. This is a worthy, timely, and important move, but I cannot help but wonder what would happen if we engaged with the risk of discussing these men as "actors" in an industry that was itself all about the acting out ("reenact[ment]") of "genocide"? How indeed can we write about Natives who won't act like Natives?

Which brings us back to our boys. In order to explore Maori (dis)identification with American Indians further, it is instructive to depart from that particular relationship and turn to a text that explores another kind of Indigenous-Indigenous connection in order to consider more carefully the impact of historical and ongoing colonialism. Chantal Spitz's *L'Ile Des Reves Ecrases* was the first novel by an Indigenous writer from French Polynesia, and sixteen years later, in 2007, the Maori publishing company Huia launched Jean Anderson's translation of the novel *Island of Shattered Dreams.*[24] Of the several characters in the novel, Tetiare is the most creative and least easily shaped by the colonial institutions of schooling and patriotism. She drifts for some time before leaving Tahiti, and later returns with new perspectives and a more complex sense of connection to place. The section describing her return is worth quoting at length:

> Tetiare has finally come home, after years of wandering round the Pacific, in a vain attempt to heal the wound in her soul. She has met the cousins who came with them long ago in their big canoes, born of the same dream of freedom, but who stopped where the wind had blown them on tiny hopeful islands, over the centuries forgetting the ones who journeyed further. She has found them again, so similar in body and soul, yet made different by the various foreign governments that have been squatting on their land. She has discovered them, peoples of the first people, attempting through little disorganised movements to shake off the Foreigner and immerse themselves again in their origins, to be themselves, the lost children of this huge family in search of one another.[25]

Tetiare's decision to "wander[] round the Pacific" is an attempt to grapple with the violence and loss of colonialism. On an individual level she "attempt[s] to heal the wound in her soul," but on a regional level her travels fit into a broader context of movement as well. Tetiare's mobility has two distinct genealogies: a distant historical series of migrations ("long ago in their big canoes . . . stopp[ing] on tiny hopeful islands"), and more recent attempts to travel in order to reconnect ("the lost children of this huge family in search of one another").

Tetiare's travels around the Pacific enable her to reconnect with various "cousins," many of whom are themselves engaged in projects of reconnection: "the lost children of this huge family in search of one another." The basis of connection for these "cousins" is also doubled, on the one hand articulated as familial ("the cousins who came with them," "so similar in body and soul") and on the other hand articulated as a shared political project: "attempting through little disorganised movements to shake off the Foreigner and immerse themselves again in their origins, to be themselves." Given the "forgetting" that has occurred "over the centuries" in the various specific locations of the Pacific, as communities have shifted their focuses from the explicitly regional context of migration to the rather more local contexts in which they are immediately involved, one of the important issues is mutual recognition: how does one remember someone whom one has already forgotten? The mode of recognition is multilayered: there are shared physical and cultural characteristics ("so similar in body and soul"), shared political positions ("peoples of the first people"), shared political predicaments ("attempting . . . to shake off the Foreigner"), and shared *kaupapa* and aspirations ("to be themselves," "in search of one another"). All of these provide a matrix by which the various "cousins" can be recognized.

Importantly, though, while the "cousins" may be "members of this huge family," they are deeply inflected by their various and specific experiences of colonialism: "made different by the various foreign governments that have been squatting on their land." Perhaps it is difficult to clearly articulate a definition of "Indigeneity" because we risk either demanding a refusal of real difference or paying attention to differences that might be a barrier to meaningful (or indeed any) engagement. The "wound" Tetiare seeks to "heal" is intimately tied to memory. The "cousins [of the] big canoes" have been separated over time and space and this separation is tied closely to forgetting and recollection: "over the centuries forgetting the ones who journeyed further"; "she has found them again"; "she has discovered them." Spitz identifies two layers of forgetting: historical amnesias about "the ones who journeyed further," but also more contemporary disconnection from cultural memory that is implied by resisting the "Foreigner" by "immers[ing] themselves in their origins."

We might note that despite the "cousins" being deeply inflected by the colonial process ("made different by the various foreign governments that have been squatting on their land"), they are ultimately compelled by the same desires: "the lost children of this huge family in search of one another." This detail perhaps suggests that the "forgetting" that took place around the earlier migrations—the "forgetting" of a regional perspective—was never complete because otherwise the deep familial pull ("this huge family in search of one another") would surely be less strong. Indeed the ability of the various "cousins"—"peoples of the first people"—to "shake off the Foreigner" in any one context is linked to a deeper compulsion to "be themselves" by reconnecting not only to their previous configurations but also to "their origins" in terms of "long ago" regional migrations and genealogical networks. Certainly *Island of Shattered Dreams* makes visible the need for regional and hemispheric commitments as well as "global Indigenous" movements. Additionally, though, the novel foregrounds the extent to which Indigenous peoples may be so used to competing for the attention of our respective occupying nation-states that we may lose sight of the ways those State-Indigene relationships shape the ways in which articulations of Indigeneity take place even in the moment of Indigenous-Indigenous encounter. Our various colonial experiences have not only shaped us but they have also jealously claimed our attention. In this way, perhaps, we want to be "heroes" rather than "Indian[s]"—to "see ourselves as white"—to unconsciously identify with and through colonizing frameworks rather than to diligently seek other connections.

The perspective of the Maori boys in Ihimaera's story emphasizes the extent to which representation of Indigenous people travels along the same economic and cultural trade routes that underpin colonialism.[26] Indeed, relationships between Indigenous communities are dependent on particular linguistic and economic factors that determine the parameters of Indigenous-Indigenous connection, especially when the lands of those communities are under the control of different settler nations. Specifically, the circulation of the westerns that Ihimaera's narrator "love[s] . . . the most" is inseparable from the well-rehearsed histories of hegemonic U.S. influence over cultural (as well as other) forms through the twentieth century, an influence that was reinforced and extended by the presence of American soldiers in New Zealand during World War II. The inverse of this circulation is also significant: because of established paths of circulation and related issues of funding, relative size, and global hegemony, young Maori boys have seen more films "about" "Indians" than young American Indian boys (or indeed Maori boys) have seen films "about" Maori. Indeed, this recognized connection with "an Indian" on the basis of being "really brown" is exacerbated by disparities between the New Zealand and American film industries and the distribution of their films. The representation of *Maori* people onscreen was, and continues to be, far less accessible to Maori communities than representation—in whatever form—of American Indians.

Returning to Singer's stated desire to "remember [certain figures] as historic Native leaders, not actors," and reading this alongside Tetiare's attempts to remedy a legacy of "forgetting," the place of memory becomes key. Laying aside the discursive problems of an opposition between the "real" ("historic Native leaders") and the "represented"/performed ("actors"), it seems Singer is also relying on another kind of opposition: the possibility of remembering these figures as laudable/honorable/loyal ("historic Native leaders") or as shameful/disloyal/dishonorable ("actors"). Simply refusing to resuscitate these figures—deciding to leave them as not-Native or to deem their participation in ultimately anti-Native projects irredeemable—is neither an ethical nor a productive strategy. However, attempting to save Natives from their participation in the film industry as "actors" too closely approximates, even in its inversion, killing the Indian to save the man. We have, I argue, a responsibility to find conceptions of Indigeneity that do not insist that Natives act like Natives, but that instead provide space for Natives to act like themselves and our analyses to flexibly work around them.

Like Ihimaera's story, Singer's project is ultimately a project of hope ("we now hope to remember them"). Ihimaera does not leave us with "Willie Boy and I" but places them alongside a series of Maori engagement with and in film culture. Finishing "Short Features" with the case of Merle Oberon both secures Maori as participants as well as consumers of popular film culture and unsettles assumptions about historical relations between "historic Native leaders" and "actors." Like the boys, and unlike Silverheels, Means, and Banks, "although [she was] really brown" Merle Oberon did not "want[] to be an Indian." Her fame as an actress came as a result of passing for white and we have the option of deciding whether her whitening makeup or her Maoriness is the "war paint" on the lens in her case. There is no redemption for Oberon, who died before her Maoriness was revealed; no subterfuge, no undercover mission to make things right for Maori representation. Oberon's refusal to explicitly engage in the representation of race (other than whiteness) makes her recuperation trickier than Silverheels's, and yet her place at the end of Ihimaera's story enables a different articulation of Maori participation in film than if she had remained absent. The stakes of remembering and forgetting are inextricably tied in "Short Features" to racialization, Indigeneity, and desire: neither the boys nor Oberon act like the Natives we would like them to. And yet, when the narrator expresses pleasure at "the subversiveness of somebody playing white and getting away with it," he also in that very moment reclaims his "brown" self who "saw [him]self as white."

"We were really brown": Maori Cowboys, Maori Indians

Does this mean that Indigeneity is an impossible dream? Does Ihimaera's narrative about Maori rejection of "be[ing] an Indian," and Spitz's reflection on the ways in which Indigenous people are "made different," not only by Indigenous but also colonial forces, provide sufficient caution to the comparatist who seeks to work with a global view of Indigenous communities? While comparative Indigenous studies has the analytical machinery to read Holland's story of Indigenous-Indigenous connection, it is hard to know what to do with a short story by a Maori writer in which young Maori boys do not "want to be an Indian." How might we envision and practice a way of recognizing these differences (historical, inherited, and contemporary) and yet remain committed to the possibilities of comparative work?

Each of these texts is about the possibilities of *looking* and, ultimately, the act of recognition: recognition of other Indigenous communities and recognition of selves. While Miria realizes "[she] really was looking at [her]self" and the boys "saw [them]selves as white," they both encounter a visual text that produces a kind of self-recognition even where, in the case of the boys, this comes in the form of misrecognition or a desire to misrecognize. The politics of recognition are central to Indigenous claims because, arguably, a central claim of Indigenous communities is for recognition. Acknowledging that respective colonial experiences deeply inflect the ways in which various Indigenous communities "look" at one another need not recenter the colonizer in the Indigenous story, and yet decentering is a more complex project than a pretense of invisibility and valorization of things shared outside of colonialism. Seeking similarities is an easy but unsatisfying game, and Indigenous studies can surely only strive for—unlike the superficial *resemblance* championed by the white woman in "Sugar-coated"—Indigenous-Indigenous recognition on the basis of *resonance.*

Maori articulation of identification with other Indigenous groups is multifaceted, but it is not absolute. Our position as Indigenous people is inseparable from our existence within a context of colonialism, and so particular configurations of power, proximity, racial self-hatred, and so on may well shape how we choose whom we identify with at any given moment. This means that comparative Indigenous scholarship cannot help but be inflected by historic and ongoing patterns of circulation and mobility, many of which will be historically colonial. When a Maori text articulates an affiliation with "cowboys" more than with "Indians," however, it does not suggest a simplistic identification with colonizers as much it foregrounds the global circulations of representation and power that impact all Indigenous communities, albeit differently. Our inability to be extricated entirely from the operations of colonial power does not mean that colonial maps cannot be challenged and reframed but, instead, that careful and critical consideration of the ongoing processes of colonialism, and paying attention to our own specificities, is essential to that process.

Notes

I would like to acknowledge the editors of *American Quarterly*, and especially the editors of this special issue. Thanks to the anonymous reviewers who provided feedback, and friends and colleagues who discussed this topic with me. Versions of this article have been shared at the Pacific History Association and Harvard University, and I thank the audiences in both spaces for the feedback provided. Nga mihi nui ki a koutou.

1. Witi Ihimaera, "Short Features," in *Te Ao Marama 5: Te Torino*, ed. Witi Ihimaera et al., (Auckland: Reed, 1996), epigraph from 221–24.
2. Linda Tuhiwai Smith, *Decolonizing Methodologies: Research and Indigenous Peoples.* (Dunedin, N.Z.: University of Otago Press, 1999), 107.
3. Moana Jackson, "Research and the Colonization of Maori Knowledge," in *Te Oru Rangahau: Maori Research and Development Conference*, ed. Te Pumanawa Hauora (Palmerston North, N.Z.: Massey University Te Putahi-a-Toi, 1998), 71.
4. Creative anthologies that bring together Indigenous writing from more than one nation-state include Kateri Akiwenzie-Damm, ed., *Without Reservation : Indigenous Erotica* (Wiarton, N.Z.: Kegedonce Press; Wellington: Huia Publishers, 2003); Kateri Akiwenzie-Damm and Josie Douglas, eds, *Skins: Contemporary Indigenous Writing* (Alice Springs, Aus.: Jukurrpa Books; Wiarton, N.Z.: Kegedonce Press, 2000); L. Maracle and S. Laronde, eds., *My Home as I Remember* (Toronto: Natural Heritage Books, 2000); Trixie Te Aroha Menzies, ed., *He Wai : A Song: First Nation's Women's Writing* (Auckland: Waiata Koa, 1996).
5. Chad Allen's work on the WCIP is significant here. Chadwick Allen, *Blood Narrative: Indigenous Identity in American Indian and Maori Literary and Activist Texts.* (Durham, N.C.: Duke University Press, 2003).
6. WINHEC is the World Indigenous Nations Higher Education Consortium. WIPCE is the World Indigenous People's Conference on Education. NAISA is the Native American and Indigenous Studies Association.
7. For example, The Dreaming (Queensland, Australia), Planet IndigenUs (Toronto, Canada), the Denver Indigenous Film and Arts Festival (Colorado, USA), Wairoa Maori and Indigenous Film Festival (Aotearoa, New Zealand).
8. Alice Te Punga Somerville, "The Lingering War Captain: Maori texts, Indigenous Contexts," *Journal of New Zealand Literature* 24.2 (2006): 20–43.
9. Witi Ihimaera, *Bulibasha* (Auckland: Penguin Books, 1994), 56. Ihimaera has described *Bulibasha* as his attempt to write a Maori western.
10. Witi Ihimaera, *The Uncle's Story* (Auckland: Penguin Books, 2000).
11. Ihimaera does not only pay attention to Maori-American Indian connections. In *The Whale Rider* (the novella, not the film) he explores Indigenous bases of connection between Maori and Papua New

Guineans; in his most recent novel he extends his interest in Indigenous-Indigenous connections to specific historical links between Maori and Indigenous Tasmanians. Witi Ihimaera, *The Whale Rider* (Auckland: Reed, 1987); Witi Ihimaera, *The Trowenna Sea* (Auckland: Penguin, 2009).

12. Charlie Holland, "Sugar-coated," in *Huia Short Fiction 8* (Wellington: Huia, 2009).
13. The Waitangi Tribunal is the Crown agency created under the Treaty of Waitangi Act 1975; the tribunal is tasked with investigating and producing reports on claims brought by Maori against the Crown that allege the Crown has breached the Treaty of Waitangi, the 1840 agreement that provided the foundation for British colonization in New Zealand. Many of the tribunal reports on historical breaches become the primary written accounts of specific incidents and places.
14. Chadwick Allen, "Engaging the Politics and Pleasures of Indigenous Aesthetics," *Western American Literature* 41.2 (Summer 2006): 155.
15. Several other Maori writers articulate connections between Maori and Indians, and Hinewirangi Kohu focuses on the experiences of colonialism as she elaborates specific reasons that Maori and American Indian people might gravitate toward one another in her poem "Sisters," from her collection *Kanohi ki te Kanohi,* which explores Maori connections with Indigenous peoples of the Americas, Australia, and the Pacific. The speaker in "Sisters" is clear about her physical place ("Here / on the shores / of the Great Turtle") and points to a number of connections between Maori and American Indian women. Hinewirangi Kohu, *Kanohi ki te kanohi* (Wellington: Moana Press, 1990).
16. "Exhibition brings together Maori narratives on landscape, history and people," www.comsdev.canterbury.ac.nz/news/2002/02083001.shmtl (accessed September 14, 2009).
17. Robert Leonard, "Michael Parekowhai," in *Nine Lives: The 2003 Chartwell Exhibition,* ed. Robert Leonard with Michael Bifkins (Auckland: Auckland Art Gallery Toi o Tamaki, 2003), http://www.aucklandartgallery.govt.nz/exhibitions/docs/ninelivescatalogue.pdf (accessed February 9, 2010).
18. Indigenous Australians have a strong tradition of participating in rodeos. For example, see Kate Hunter, "Rough Riding: Aboriginal Participation in Rodeos and Travelling Shows to the 1950s," *Aboriginal History* 32 (2008): 83–96. In Hawai'i, there is a long-established culture of cowboys and cattle culture. Paniolo (Hawaiian cowboys) are regularly present at Maori-dominated rodeos.
19. Look to Deloria and Huhndorf for more on this. Philip Joseph Deloria, *Playing Indian* (New Haven, Conn.: Yale University Press, 1998); Shari M. Huhndorf, *Going Native: Indians in the American Cultural Imagination* (Ithaca, N.Y.: Cornell University Press, 2001).
20. This hysterical disidentification with other Indigenous communities finds one expression in the form of discrimination that some Indigenous communities (or, at least, some members of some Indigenous communities) will visit on other Indigenous communities. This, however, is a very complex topic and falls outside the scope of this essay.
21. Beverly R. Singer, *Wiping the War Paint off the Lens: Native American Film and Video* (Minneapolis: Minnesota, 2001), 21.
22. Ibid., 22–23.
23. Ibid., 23.
24. Jean Anderson, trans., *Island of Shattered Dreams* (Wellington: Huia Publishers, 2007).
25. Ibid., 121.
26. These trade routes and networks of connection deeply inflect why, for example, I have tended to work within the English-language Indigenous scholarly communities of North America, for example, rather than those who speak Japanese, Spanish, or French.

A Dying West?
Reimagining the Frontier in Frank Matsura's Photography, 1903–1913

Glen M. Mimura

Other echoes
Inhabit the garden. Shall we follow?

—T. S. Eliot, *Four Quartets*

How differently might United States history appear today were it not told from the standpoint of its victors? A good deal of contemporary historical scholarship has been devoted to diminishing the hegemony implied in that question by revising the once-standard accounts to include the perspectives of a much wider range of historical agents. In part, this intellectual project relies on the discovery and recovery of neglected sources that have challenged or disputed the reigning point of view all along. Contributing to that effort, this essay examines the largely overlooked photography of Frank Matsura, a turn-of-century Japanese immigrant who recorded the transformations in latter-day frontier society and continuing Indian presence in Washington's Okanogan County. My interest lies not in the strict documentary value of Matsura's photographs but, rather, in their status as cultural-historical representations. His work is remarkable for its striking departure from the dominant understanding of frontier life that prevailed during the early twentieth century and that persists to this day in the enduring, popular genres of the Western in literature, film, and mass culture.[1] Predating recent efforts to rethink visual representations of the West by seventy years and more, Matsura imagined the frontier neither as the one-way street of Manifest Destiny nor as the unilateral proving ground of white American manhood, but as a multivalent space constituted by the uneven, overlapping histories of indigenous adaptation and white settlement.

To be sure, Matsura was not alone in this effort. Like many others in the western territories and states, he set up shop out of equal passions for photographic technology and the recording of local life, probably with little or no sense of the stirring debates to the east regarding the ostensibly "dying frontier" and its "vanishing Indians." Yet the work of photographers such as Matsura remains largely unexamined, dormant in local museums and professional and personal collections scattered across the American West, displaced by the enduring pastoral romance popularized by urban, eastern seaboard tourists and professionals seeking an Edenic frontier soon to be vanquished by the advance of Progress. These melancholic travelers took what would become iconic or emblematic photographs of western places and their Native inhabitants usually within a short span of time—vacation, tour, mission—capturing for posterity what they regarded as fundamentally different, tragic, and redemptive about them. In contrast, small-town amateur and professional photographers like Matsura recorded life in one place over years, not days or weeks; hence their respective locales become so richly "local" in their photographs because they cumulatively record historical change, not prelapsarian innocence or timelessness, in meticulous detail. Moreover, these local photographers developed long-term relationships with their subjects and participated in the daily life of their regions.

Given the paucity of research on these collections, the degree to which Matsura's body of work resonates with this revisionist archive-in-the-making is difficult to assess. Still, what little we know of his unique biography suggests that his work is more likely exceptional or exemplary rather than typical. Matsura was keenly aware, and time and again made aware, of his peculiar, contradictory status as local and outsider: an outsider who, however beloved, could not become local in quite the same way as white settlers due to his racialization, which provided occasion for his affinity with the region's Native peoples. Such awareness is evident in his photographs and other available evidence. This essay, then, offers a critical introduction to Matsura's work and life as a representational foil against the nostalgic mythos of the frontier and its vanishing Indians—toward a more democratic, inclusive account of its history.

Not a Typical Immigration Story

In 1903, a well-dressed, well-mannered Japanese American man named Frank Matsura arrived in Conconully, a recently settled town in Okanogan County, north-central Washington state.[2] Hired from Seattle to work as a cook's helper and a laundryman at the town's Hotel Elliot, Matsura pursued his passion for photography in his free time. Over the next ten years, he photographed the region's landscapes, growing farming and agricultural economy, social life, significant events, and—most richly—its citizens. In early 1906, Matsura began selling some of his pictures as postcards to supplement his part-time work at the hotel. In two years, he opened a studio that contained a workroom for developing photographs, a gallery for shooting portraits, and a small shop up front from which he sold his postcards and small Japanese gift items purchased during trips to Seattle.

Locally, Matsura enjoyed unrivaled popularity due as much to his high spirits, good humor, and intelligence as to his photographs, admired for the formal dignity with which they recorded their subjects. Matsura's work also gained serious recognition beyond the county when several of his pictures of Okanogan's industries, resources, and scenery were displayed as part of the 1909 Alaska-Yukon-Pacific Exposition held in Seattle. The summerlong event boasted such esteemed visitors as William Jennings Bryan, Henry Ford, and newly elected President William H. Taft. The event's official photographer, J. A. McCormick, praised Matsura's pictures in a personal letter as the best contributions to the exposition's exhibit among the entire pool of images received not only from throughout the state but from throughout the nation.

Matsura's business was unsteady but modestly successful by 1911, as the region's population gradually grew. Early in 1912, however, Matsura contracted a severe cold that persisted throughout the year and worsened to the point that he closed his studio temporarily from October until the Christmas holiday season. Suffering from chronic pain, he sold most of his store's belongings in February 1913 to devote his full energies to documenting the region's developing railroad system and rapidly expanding orchards. Given Matsura's characteristic liveliness and humor, many assumed that his health was gradually improving. However, on the evening of June 13, 1913, while assisting the city marshal with a routine patrol, Matsura died from a sudden, violent fit of coughing and choking brought on by tuberculosis. He was thirty-nine years old.

According to the few available accounts, Matsura befriended virtually everyone he met among the region's sparse but culturally diverse population. Historian JoAnn Roe notes, "His funeral was held in the town's large auditorium because the mourners could not crowd into the church. More than three hundred people came to pay their respects—both whites and Indians, the Northwest people among whom he had chosen to make his home and seek his fortune."[3] It was easily the largest funeral held in the county till that time. The friendships and public respect reflected by this turnout are confirmed by the photographs, distinguished not only by the remarkable breadth of their content but by the clearly evident intimacy between Matsura and his subjects. Several family portraits of local Indians, for example, were taken at their homes

Figure 1.
Portrait of four Wenatchee Indians, reprinted from JoAnn Roe, *Frank Matsura: Frontier Photographer* (Seattle: Madrona Publishers, 1981), 134. Unless otherwise stated, illustrations for this chapter are reprinted by permission from Roe's book (cited here).

by Matsura, who was invited as a guest. Other pictures show friends engaged in horseplay or otherwise casually carrying on, clearly at ease with a photographer with whom they were personally acquainted (figs. 1 and 2).

Predicated on these close relations and a familiarity with the local environment and developing society, Matsura's work provides an extraordinary visual record of a turn-of-century Northwest region in transition. Taken over a ten-year period, these photographs are noteworthy both for their comprehensiveness as a collection and for their formal attention to details to which only a participant in the society they documented would be sensitive. Remarkably, several hundred glass plates have survived. After Matsura's death, they were stored safely by a friend, Judge William Compton Brown, who donated part of the collection in 1954 with his own papers to the archives at Washington State University, Pullman.[4] After Brown's death, the part of the collection that he retained—the majority of Matsura's work—eventually found its way into

Figure 2.
Portrait of Billy Collins and two friends, 140.

the archives of the Okanogan County Historical Society. There, they were rediscovered and seriously examined for the first time in 1975 by JoAnn Roe, who was conducting research for another book. Impressed by the depth and quality of the collection, Roe later returned to it, intending to have several of the images processed and published in book form. In 1981, Madrona Publishers, a small Seattle-based company, released *Frank Matsura: Frontier Photographer*, edited by Roe, a selection of more than 150 photographs drawn from the glass plates preserved by the Okanogan County Historical Society. The book received several awards, including the Governor's Award of Washington. However, published only in one edition, it soon went out of print.

This essay examines the photographs collected in this book as well as the historical and biographical information that it provides. Roe's preface sheds light on her early, detective-like research involved in tracking down the few, then-inconclusive details of Matsura's life prior to his arrival in Okanogan County. Roe also explains the history of the glass plates from their storage by Judge Brown to their current possession by the Okanogan County Historical

Society. Murray Morgan's introduction illuminates the region's history and Roe's biographical essay, "Frank Matsura," cogently summarizes the photographer's life and work in the county. It is composed mainly of reminiscences by the few surviving members of the region's early twentieth-century community, colorful anecdotes passed down through family histories, and the handful of accounts of Matsura's life and work recorded in the local press. Besides these sources, probably the most significant published writing on Matsura's work is Rayna Green's short but important essay, "Rosebuds of the Plateau," an insightful, witty, and moving interpretation of a photograph of two Indian girls in Victorian dress, casually draped across a fainting couch.[5] These few yet rich writings remain the most substantial information and perspectives on Matsura's works and days.

Matsura's Epistemological Difference

To be sure, the turn-of-century understanding of "frontier life" and its ostensible decay was more mythical than empirical. Indeed, the frontier is better understood as a chronotope of the national imaginary: an abstract synthesis of particular temporal and spatial relations, the symbolic divide between imperfect Society and ideal Garden, historical time and natural time.[6] Its continuing existence justified and gave moral compass to the constitutive exercise of national expansion. Yet this utopia could not last forever and, toward the close of the century, the great celebrators of the liminal frontier would mourn its destruction by the mass expansion and settlement it had incited. In 1890, the United States Census officially declared the frontier "closed" as a geographic and demographic category.

In response to this closure, historian Frederick Jackson Turner articulated his enduring "frontier thesis," which characterized the difficult, violent, transformative encounter between wilderness and westward expansion as the distinctively American experience through which American democracy had been forged.[7] All men were made equal, argued Turner, in their confrontation with this uniquely American environment. His repertoire of frontier subjects—trappers, ranchers, farmers, miners, adventurous businessmen who planned the railroads—excluded people of color and women, who were imagined in Turner's narrative logic as either servants or enemies of the expansionist spirit. Nor did he consider the ways in which the concrete experience of territorial accumulation exhibited forms of capitalist aggression, social stratification, violence, and mechanization of human labor similar to the corrosive realities he attributed to the eastern seaboard cities and regions.[8] Rather, the eventual disappearance of "virgin land" meant the loss of a way of life; in other words, the loss of the material conditions for the persistent renewal of American democracy and freedom. For Turner, if empire building was therapeutic and edifying for the American character, its eventual completion was tragically ossifying.[9]

In the photographic canon, similar sentiments find their refrain most famously in the contemporaneous work of Edward Sheriff Curtis. Supported by wealthy financier and industrialist John Pierpont Morgan, as well as Theodore Roosevelt during and after his presidency, Curtis was dedicated to recording and cataloging the cultures of Native North Americans. Beginning in 1896, his research resulted in one of the most extensive projects in the history of photography: publication of *The North American Indian* (1907–1930), a twenty-volume series amounting to more than 40,000 photographs.[10] With Turner's frontier thesis, Curtis's photographs popularized the melancholic vision of a mythic American West disappearing before the advance of industrialization. But the two men's views of Native peoples differed significantly. Turner, without devoting serious thought to the matter, conceived of Native Americans mostly as obstacles, like rugged terrain, to be tamed or eliminated in the interests of expansion. Curtis shared Turner's nostalgia for the American wilderness as recuperative proving ground and his anxiety over its disappearance. But for Curtis, the decline of frontier innocence was most poignantly associated with the fate of the Indians. Hence he tirelessly dedicated his energies to documenting the lives of Native Americans before they ostensibly "vanished," with the frontier, into the past.

Contrary to this uniform pronouncement on the "death" of the frontier and its Native peoples, Frank Matsura's photography offers far more complex images of a frontier society in transition. Okanogan of the early twentieth century certainly evidenced the consequences of modernization: the local Indians were moved onto reservations as their former territories were cleared for white settlement, agricultural development, irrigation, city planning, and the arrival of modern transportation and communications technologies. But through Matsura's lens, these changes were not unilateral in direction, nor were their futures as inevitably fatal as Turner and Curtis anxiously believed. In Matsura's pictures, Okanogan's Native peoples did not resign themselves to the irreversible process of cultural and biological extinction wistfully represented by Curtis. Rather, we witness them—and white settlers—surviving and adapting in ways unimaginable and inexplicable in the dominant cultural-historical discourse. While we see some Native peoples living amid traditional arrangements with tepees, we see others living in modest houses. And while most resided on the nearby Colville Reservation, Indians routinely interacted with whites and participated in the daily life of the local towns (fig. 3). Such normative relations are recorded nowhere in Curtis's massive body of work, in which these daily scenes would have appeared aberrant or less authentic to the movement of history. By contrast, Matsura's work is replete with pictures of Indian cowboys, ranchers, and lawmen equally "at home" on the plains or riding down the street. Neither stoically traditional nor fatally assimilated, the Indians in Matsura's photographs comfortably mix traditional Native and modern Western garments. Rayna Green poignantly assesses their epistemological break from the prevailing representational codes:

> What [Matsura] shows of Indians, however, what he shows of this frontier world, is not deviance and heartbreak and isolation. There is a rather startling integration of himself, of Indians, of others who might have been strange and alien and enemies elsewhere. Matsura's Okanogan world cheers the hell out of me. Yes, the land settlements were a mess, and yes, the homesteaders and the Army Corps of Engineers and the lumber mills and fruit companies took it all. But somewhere, in this world he shows us, Indians aren't weird, heartbroken exiles, or zoo animals for the expositions, endangered species preserved forever in photographic gelatin. . . . [T]hey are changed, but in control.[11]

As Green sensitively suggests, Matsura's work opens up or initiates a narrative perspective in which the survival of Native Americans is not a freak accident of history. If the transformations experienced by Okanogan were motivated not solely by the mythical engine of Progress but by a variety of historical forces and social actors, then the same should hold true for U.S. history—or our interpretation of it—in general. Matsura gives us a way out of mythical history.

Although popular cinematic and literary representation mostly continues to reproduce the dominant perspectives codified by Turner and Curtis, an extensive body of more sophisticated, critically imaginative works has displaced their authority in scholarship and artistic production. Historians since Henry Nash Smith, following World War II, have critiqued the elegiac view of a decaying frontier nostalgically marking the decline of national innocence.[12] In the wake of the new social movements for civil rights, feminism, Native self-determination, and environmental justice, the so-called New Western history has issued sobering, more balanced revisions of westward nation building, bringing into view the struggles of women, Native Americans, and other people of color, and a more complex understanding of the environment—all occluded from Turner's influential vision.[13] Similarly, several books have been

Figure 3.
Photograph of Indian and white horsemen, 32.

published in the past twenty years that expand and reinterpret the photographic history of the American West. Particularly noteworthy are *Crossing the Frontier*, published in conjunction with an exhibition organized by the San Francisco Museum of Modern Art, September 26, 1996–January 28, 1997, which dramatizes the encounter between the environment and expanding industry and technology since the mid-nineteenth century, and Geoffrey Ward's *The West: An Illustrated History*, companion volume to the highly acclaimed eight-part documentary for public television *The West*, produced by Stephen Ives and Ken Burns, that richly complicates the expansionist myth by bringing into view the participation of women, Native Americans, and racial-ethnic immigrants and laborers, as well as white male settlers.[14] Not surprisingly, the latter volume includes essays by several of the New Western historians. Other prominent titles have made visible the contemporary work of particular groups, including *Hopi Photographers, Hopi Images* and *From the West: Chicano Narrative Photography*.[15]

The recovery of work by Frank Matsura and other small-town frontier photographers will provide historical precursors and a salient archive for these contemporary scholarly and artistic projects, in their efforts to displace the dominant point of view. Ironically, however, this discursive struggle circumscribes the publication of Matsura's work, as the introductions provided by JoAnn Roe and Murray Morgan reproduce the historiographical perspective that Matsura's photographs refuse and exceed. Hence we turn to Roe's book, by which Matsura's work has been recuperated.

Representing Okanogan's Settlement

The southern edge of Okanogan County begins about ninety miles east of Seattle, at the base of the towering North Cascade Mountains and including the start of the Columbia River. Its western boundary follows the Cascades north and formally ends at the forty-ninth parallel—the U.S.-Canadian border. Crisscrossed by several rivers that feed into the great Columbia, Okanogan County continues east more than sixty miles, encircling the western territories of the Colville Indian Reservation.

Geographically isolated from the rapid economic, social, and cultural transformations taking place in urban Seattle, Okanogan County experienced the effects of modernization slowly and less dramatically.[16] Its story, as narrated by JoAnn Roe and Murray Morgan, nonetheless follows a familiar pattern of Progress and development. In the early 1810s, white explorers representing commercial interests from the eastern United States and Britain inaugurated and negotiated a fur trade with the local Indians. By the mid-nineteenth century, a complex trade route over land and waterways was established; in other words, the valley was "regarded not as a place to settle but as a pathway to somewhere else."[17] Soon thereafter, unsuccessful and desperate ex–California gold rushers quickly arrived in the region, lured by speculations (fueled by newspapers and through word of mouth) about the discovery of gold and other rare minerals. With few exceptions, the short-lived rumors turned out to be a bust but nevertheless attracted white prospectors to the area, some of whom decided to stay. One such man was H. F. "Okanogan" Smith, the valley's first white settler, who ambitiously initiated its permanent political incorporation into the territorial government as well as its future economic development. After building his cabin in 1860, Smith appointed himself the region's first representative to the territorial legislature and planted an orchard of 1,200 seedling apples, as well as some peach trees. Motivated by the promising growth of eastern and central Washington, the federal government redrew the boundaries of Indian territories to increase the areas for white settlement, establishing the Colville Reservation by executive order in 1872. Experiencing slow but steady white settlement and the nascent expansion of an agricultural economy, Okanogan County was formally recognized by the territorial legislature in 1888, the year before Washington achieved statehood.

Frank Matsura arrived in Okanogan in 1903, just three years after the first telephone lines were wired into the county's larger towns and settlements and three years before the first railroad tracks were laid in its southernmost territories. In other words, his arrival coincided with the start of the region's concerted settlement and economic development by whites.

Roe goes on to provide richly investigated details of Matsura's life. However, Roe and Morgan's interpretive framework vacillates between two historiographical tendencies—Turnerian and "post-Turnerian"—that reassert a dominant historical view over the more complex representation of Okanogan life offered by Matsura himself. While the two tendencies may appear contradictory, they are better understood as two sides of the same epistemological coin. For example, Morgan writes with Turnerian nostalgia that Matsura arrived in an America that "would soon cease to exist"; yet he also characterizes the region at the time as "still a backwater" and celebrates its slow but vibrant growth.[18] Several of these ostensibly competing opinions can be found in Morgan's account. Yet the latter view simply represents the historiographical successor to Turner's elegiac frontier thesis, as its affirmation of "growth" tacitly and uncritically accepts the validity of the Progress narrative; it simply approves of what Turner rejected. Historian Donald Worster underscores the continuity with wit: "We might call it the mythic world of the Chamber of Commerce, for whom the West will be an unfinished frontier until it is one with Hoboken, New Jersey, until we Americans will have written a saga of industrial conquest from sea to shining sea."[19]

To be sure, much of Matsura's work was appropriated in the interest of celebrating this chamber-of-commerce myth of Progress, with the photographer's enthusiastic participation. Detailing Matsura's growing notoriety, JoAnn Roe writes:

> His more serious work was beginning to gain recognition outside of Okanogan County. The Okanogan Commercial Club had photos of orchards and ranches run in Eastern publications to tout the charms of the Okanogan region for homesteading. Matsura traveled to Spokane to photograph the prize-winning entries of Okanogan County in the apple expositions, the pictures later appearing in the *Okanogan Independent.*[20] (fig. 4)

Roe thereafter recounts the high praise Matsura received for the photographs of the county's "industries, resources, and scenery" he submitted for inclusion in the 1909 Alaska-Yukon-Pacific Exposition in Seattle. Following the Expo, about forty of Matsura's photographs were selected and used in a nationwide advertising campaign to promote the region, organized in 1911 by the Great Northern Railway Company. While this recognition represents a significant achievement, Roe appears to regard the photographs as "serious" precisely because they appealed to commercial interests and not vice versa. The pictures probably also sold well as postcards in Matsura's shop for similar reasons: Unlike his presumably "less serious" work, these photographs promoted an idealized image of regional Progress to attract visitors and investors—outsiders. In this respect, such images might be better understood as examples of a commercial aesthetic.

A significant portion of Matsura's work can be divided into active scenes of social change, on one hand, and images that suggest a timeless or unchanging nature, on the other. The collection edited by JoAnn Roe brings together pages of workers building a dam, laying railroad tracks, and building a town's waterworks, alongside still-life photographs of nature from panoramic views of mountains and valleys to intimate close-ups of regional plants and wildlife. Several of these pictures have been contextualized to represent commercial interests to attract tourism and capital, and some were evidently taken with this purpose in mind. But in the context of Matsura's body of work, they contribute to a composite portrait of the county that privileges or values no one aspect of its social or natural environment over the others. The images of social life, in particular, do not amount to a consistent, monumental endorsement or critique of the region's economic development per se. As a resident of the community who routinely took pictures as his time allowed, Matsura recorded Okanogan's "dailiness," its quotidian social realities, and not primarily those exceptional moments that may have been noteworthy beyond the local population. He did capture such events as the visits of a delegation from the Great Northern Railway Company in 1910 and of Governor M. E. Hay in 1911; but they are simply overwhelmed by the diverse pictures of everyday working life and leisure. Considered together, given the sheer heterogeneity of their subjects, these images fail to support such abstract, uniform views as the Turnerian myth or the myth of industrial progress.

Matsura's photographs of regional forms of leisure may best exemplify this attention to local details that cannot easily translate into the idealizing, universalizing rhetoric of advertising. He recorded home theatrical performances, high school football games, potato-sack races, Fourth of July celebrations, and similar events (fig. 5). Such expressions of regional culture likely would

Figure 4. Photograph of an apricot orchard, 66.

have held little interest to outsiders for whom images of uninhabited nature or burgeoning industry would have been more appealing. These photographs of local residents enjoying themselves among their neighbors, or staging performances for their own community, offered dignified representations of the county to itself. Equally, however, Matsura's work also includes several scenes of inebriated men drinking and simply loitering in public (fig. 6). The range of behaviors, lifestyles, and ordinary social contexts depicted in the collection delivers a much broader representation of a regional society in transition than one determined by the prevailing cultural logic or by official political or business interests.

Representing Okanogan's Indians

For its striking contrast to the conventions of modern ethnographic representation, Matsura's photography of local Native peoples may be the most remarkable aspect of his work. As noted before, the dominant view of historical change imagined Indians either as obstacles to or victims of Progress if they were not occluded from the story entirely. Roe's and Morgan's accounts of Native

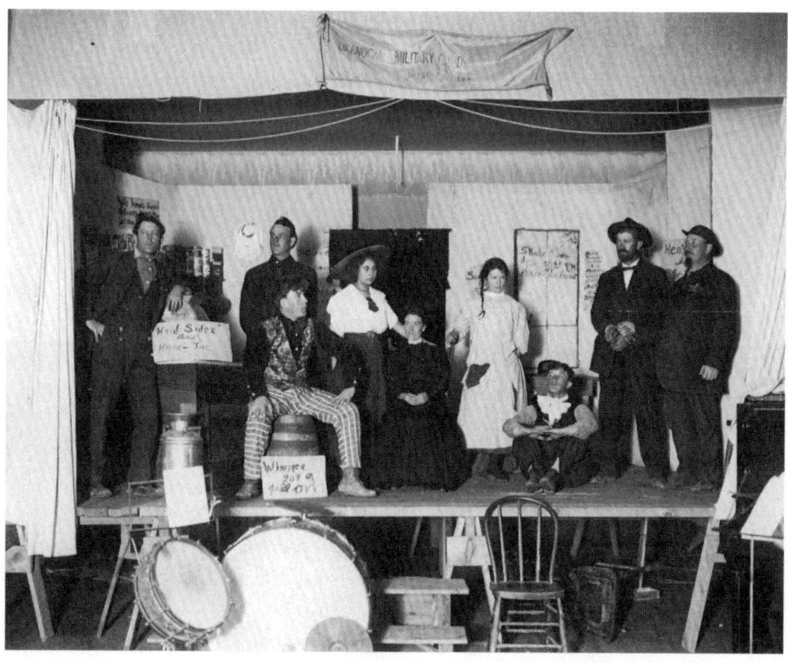

Figure 5.
Photograph of a home talent show, 84.

peoples' histories in Okanogan exemplify the problems built into their narrative logic, even as they also offer clues that might point the way out of this representational impasse. They essentially tell a story of a region sparsely inhabited by a handful of Native American tribes transformed into a county settled by former California forty-niners and others. Their narrative begins with the arrival of white men and centers their activities in the making of the region's history. Yet the prevalence of Indian place names throughout the county intimates a prior Indian presence, a Native geography only partially mapped-over by the geography of white settlement. As a dynamic, expanding economy and society benefiting from recent strides in transportation and communications technologies, Okanogan's settlement did not turn out to be such a bad thing for the county's white citizens, after all, Roe and Morgan surmise. But all of the trapping, logging, clearing, mining, damming, and redirecting of rivers adversely transformed the environment, a natural and social ecosystem to which the local Indian communities had effectively adapted. While Roe and Morgan can shed the cynicism of the frontier thesis in narrating the experience of whites, however, they largely repeat the melancholy, terminal diagnosis of Curtis's Vanishing Indian mythos in writing of local Native peoples.

Figure 6.
Photograph of four inebriated men on horses, 102.

Of the Indians living in the bordering Colville lands, Roe summarizes their fate by noting that they were "gradually adopting the white man's ways of raising cattle and crops."[21]

To be sure, the tribes in the region suffered profound losses as the federal government seized land and the formal boundaries of Indian territories were reduced to the reservation lands. Following the forced removals and westward relocations of Indians in the late nineteenth century, the situation was exacerbated in eastern and central Washington. Diverse bands of Native peoples from throughout the northwest and northern plains, including, most famously, Chief Joseph and his Nez Perce, were essentially thrown together to negotiate their coexistence on the Colville lands. But rather than "vanish" by way of literal death or irreversible assimilation, the Indian communities demonstrated extraordinary versatility in adapting to the new, difficult historical circumstances. Furthermore, the social-cultural traffic was not unilateral. Most insightful here is Roe's rich description of the region's ranch and cattle industry, which hired Indian and white cowboys since its origins in the 1860s and 1870s. Characterized by its relative geographical isolation, the region

Figure 7.
Portrait of four Indian cowboys, 137.

developed unique styles of work and dress heavily influenced by Indian practices and cultures. The horse most highly prized by all cowboys, for example, was the Appaloosa, selectively bred by the Nez Perce for speed and strength. Perhaps the region's most distinct form of dress featured the brightly dyed angora chaps worn only by veteran or proven cowboys, evident in several of Matsura's photographs (fig. 7). This attention to the complexities of real cultural exchange largely appears out of place, structurally and rhetorically, in Morgan and Roe's introductory essays and more generally in the historical and representational logic they reiterate. This kind of adaptive versatility and hybridity was seen by Curtis, for example, as a sign of impending cultural death, the corrosive force of modernization on Indian life.

But signs of this cultural hybridity thrive everywhere in Matsura's work, animated by Native peoples and scenes alien to the recognized corpus of frontier photography and the nostalgic myth of the American West generally: Indian cowboys, ranchers, and deputies; Indian and white women on horseback; infants and children in fine Western and traditional dress; and white settlers and Native peoples negotiating a respectful if uneven, ambivalent coexistence,

Figure 8.
Photograph of Sam George and his family, 42.

to name only a few. Among Okanogan's residents were Sam George and his family, their expressions, postures and well-maintained wagon bearing the kind of ordinary dignity one might find in a Wyeth painting, but with dark-skinned faces (fig. 8). And there was Minnie McDonald, jailed for stealing horses not for economic gain but simply because she had a penchant for fine horses (fig. 9). In her portrait, Minnie is concerned not with her own dust-laden dress but with positioning and presenting her horse to the camera. A demonstration in contrasting fashions, perhaps, another portrait shows off two Indians, friends from Canada, dressed as a cowboy and a "city dude" (fig. 10).

Tellingly, these three outdoor portraits, like many others, appear to have been taken during chance encounters between acquaintances: crossing paths along a back road, by the riverbank, or while walking through town. The sense of informality and familiarity that saturates these images is one of the signature qualities of Matsura's work. This evidently casual relationship between photographer and subject also disturbs a key ethnographic code governing conventional frontier photography: that Native peoples and their documenters—and, by extension,

Figure 9.
Photograph of horse thief Minnie McDonald, 43.

the audience for whom the images are intended—exist in distinct, incommensurable worlds, in separate times and places.[22] Edward Curtis's work constituted an epistemological divide between tragic Indians fading into the past, on one side of the photographic frame, and sympathetic viewers, on the other side, mourning their demise while living in the industrializing present. The photograph was a window looking onto an extinct, or quickly dying, world. In contrast, Matsura's work implies no such epistemological conceit: the photographer and his subjects evidently share the same world; walk the same streets, fields, and riverbanks; live in the same historical time. While several of his pictures have elicited wider appeal—his commercial aesthetic, so to speak—Matsura's photography typically presumes some acquaintance between its viewers and subjects, or at least familiarity with their world. One of the most engaging qualities of his outdoor portraitures—expressed in the three pieces described above—is their rhetorical contrast between a consistently high degree of formal composition and the informal, unstaged settings in which his subjects are often situated. The meticulous formal execution conscientiously dignifies its subject at the same time that the random, casual setting promotes

Figure 10. Photograph of an Indian cowboy and city dude, 34.

a rhetorically "close," intimate relationship between viewer and subject as if the photograph were intended for a mutual friend or family member, or for the subject him- or herself.

Unlike pictures of famous persons or events, Matsura's images largely document ordinary lives, events, and contexts for which little or no other documentation exists. Precisely because they are representations of everyday realities in a relatively little-known region, many if not most of the details in the photographs are difficult or impossible to verify. We are left with little specific information beyond the frame of the photograph itself. Further, given the paucity of such images as Matsura's in the historical archive, and their departure from the more familiar codes established by the canon of frontier photography, these works incite analytical speculation to explain their details, fill in the blanks; hence Rayna Green's thoughtful, evocative reading of a Matsura photograph. So Matsura's photo-stories begin with, and depart from, the differences they register in relation to the prevailing codes and frames of reference. Reading their textual hybridity therefore is an exercise in illuminating their antagonistic relationship to the discourses that omit or repress their significance.

This struggle over representation can be detected even in an apparently simple photograph, such as the one taken of six girls posing before a tepee (fig. 11). At first glance, it may appear like a conventional picture of a group of Indian girls. The habitation and surroundings situate them outside the typical spatial boundaries of settler society, represented by Okanogan's more established towns. The tepee—easily collapsible and mobile as required during the summer months, with its open structure designed to allow in air and sunlight—suggests that these girls organize much of their daily routine according to natural time, adapting to the seasons and the shifting weather patterns. But other elements in the frame already begin to disrupt what might otherwise be a conventional depiction. For starters, why are the girls looking so prim and proper anyway, wearing their finest dresses? Moreover, they are dressed to go—perhaps even beyond the photograph's epistemological frame of reference, the formal boundaries of Indian country. The smallest one in front is too young for school, so it is possible that Matsura stopped them on their way to church. Or perhaps the parents asked their friend Frank to take the portrait. Edward Curtis, in any case, would not have photographed these girls unless, perhaps, they were standing in front of the Sunday School, looking oppressed and morose, resigned to their impending extinction. In that case, the girl on the far left would need to lose her inappropriate smile, stop being a girl, and become an Indian for a moment. Or, conversely, Curtis would have asked them to change into more traditional garments—their own, or the ones he brought—and perhaps squat rather than stand before the tepee. Even then, he would need to brush out that tin can in the foreground, and maybe the plaid blanket in the tepee's shadow just right of the girls, before printing the image for display in an exhibition or in one of his books.

But so much for Curtis's ethnographic wisdom. Certainly, these girls waiting before the tepee don't know any better. The smiling one is preoccupied; the one next to her appears impatient, while the others look bored. They share no uniform sentiment, refuse stereotypical categorization. The girl on the right scratches herself as the picture is taken, her discomfort perhaps becoming too much as she stands under the hot sun while the dogs get to lounge in the shade. Posing for their parents, or possibly for themselves—but not for anthropological posterity—they are not trying to be "Indians," they are simply being themselves and consequently fail to sustain anything so grave as the mandate to represent their own cultural demise. Rather, their varied expressions convey a different message, perhaps best elaborated by Rayna Green's affirming speculation in response to the girls in her Matsura photograph: "These ladies have no small

Figure 11.
Photograph of girls in front of a tepee, 40.

measure of bravado. And not the 'It's-a-good-day-to-die' kind. I appreciate that often necessary and brave machismo, given the circumstances, but there might have been other ways of weathering the storm. These girls have got it. Matsura saw it. What's more, he took its picture."[23]

Among the most intriguing studio portraits is of a pair of Indians, an unidentified federal officer on the right and Johnnie Louie, Colville Indian cowboy and interpreter for the chiefs when their presence was required in Washington, D.C. (fig. 12). Lacking any definable background or depth, the photograph emphasizes their relationship in itself, not situated in or against any particular context. The only referents to the external world are their immaculate clothes, finely displaying the style of cowboy dress that Roe identifies as typical of the region and distinct from the widely recognized style of the big Texas and Oklahoma ranch empires: straight-brimmed cavalry style hats instead of the ubiquitous ten-gallon hats; gauntlets with the floral bead or stitched patterns particular to the area; guns worn high on the belt or inside it, in contrast to the low-slung six-shooter; and, once again, the beautiful dyed angora chaps, unique to cowboys of the northwest ranching and cattle industry. Like other pictures in the collection, this one may be surprising enough for its depiction of the pair in occupations so antithetical to popular representations of Indian men, particularly given their youthful, boyish faces. Further underscoring this contrast is the homosocial intimacy the men share, their casual embrace and ease of manner. Given the restrained demeanor and rigid, masculine authority associated with their official appointments, their affectionate mutual regard seems doubly contrary. While rarely depicted in the frontier photographic canon, intimate male homosociality was commonly expressed in literary, autobiographical, and other written accounts of frontier life.[24] But the gentle friendship recorded by the portrait does not correspond to the prevalent, intimate male relations described by Blake Allmendinger; such frontier homosociality was predicated on the sharing of domestic responsibilities and leisure by men in the absence of women, far removed from settled communities. The difficult responsibilities that these two men intimately shared were rather different: as an Indian lawman and an Indian interpreter, they were intermediaries between white settlers and Native peoples, ambivalent embodiments of the structuring relations of the colonial encounter.

Edward Curtis and other prestigious documenters of Indian life did not bother to record such lively, three-dimensional characters or scenes. According to their melancholy worldview, these Indians could only be understood as deviations from the movement of Progress, not as acceptably self-conscious victims but as freaks of nature or history (it does not matter which), out of step with the time: they simply were not representative. Matsura, in contrast, did not seek to photograph those who were "representative" of anything but their distinct, idiosyncratic selves. Indeed, he may well not have been familiar with the cultural-discursive funeral arrangements announced for the frontier and its Indian subjects. Instead, he had a knack for capturing the seemingly arbitrary moments that betray the easy closure or coherence of a "master narrative" or reverse its point of view in unexpected ways. As Rayna Green eloquently puts it, "[Matsura] wasn't a death-bringer, an undertaker for the Indian past, a necrophiliac who wanted to photograph the 'last-of' anything. . . . Good, somehow, for this 'little Japanese' photographer to have gotten through the muck to see the possibilities."[25]

Seeing the possibilities? One of the most richly subversive images is a group photograph of Wenatchee and Chelan women and children on horseback—posing proudly or defiantly, or both?—in town for a Fourth of July celebration (fig. 13). Could anything be more ironic? The book's accompanying caption gives us some of their names—Josephine Camille, Monique Simon, Julianne

Figure 12.
Portrait of two Indian men, 36.

Loup Loup Dick, Martha Timentwa—but we would not know that from the photograph itself. Inside the frame, telling signs of Progress are everywhere: vibrantly waving American flag, electric lamp hanging over the entranceway. But examine also the receding distance off to the left. The photograph's perspectival space—its formal and semantic depth—is punctuated by exemplars of the new transportation and communications technologies: automobiles parked along the curb and, behind them, a telephone pole. This is Independence Day and the future is looking bright for America. Still, isn't it curious that all the white people are in the background, incidental to the scene, gathered on the porch of the hotel—that preeminent establishment for outsiders?

Conclusion: Intimate Friend or Mysterious Stranger?

Since the posthumous publication of Matsura's photographs in 1981, JoAnn Roe and others have meticulously reconstructed much of Matsura's biography, especially prior to his arrival in the United States. Yet many details of his life remain as intriguingly elusive as those of his photographic subjects—an

Figure 13. Photograph of Indian women and children at an Independence Day celebration, 115.

incomplete portrait composed of inconclusive fragments, speculations, and curiously conflicting perceptions and reminiscences. Indeed, the existential questions Roe posed in 1981, after diligently researching leads throughout the western states and in Japan, continue to resonate with alluring uncertainty. Roe's 1981 preface opens thus:

> Who was this man Matsura? Why did a fastidious Japanese man of apparent culture, rumored to be well-educated, come from his homeland to work as a cook's helper in a backwoods town three hundred miles from Seattle? Who sent him money periodically and why?
>
> One can speculate: He left Japan because he was a younger son in a family where the eldest gained the advantage. He had an unhappy love affair. He was a fugitive. But we don't know. Why didn't he go home to Japan when he became ill? Did he know he had tuberculosis in 1901? Did he come to the high, dry Okanogan country to try to recover?
>
> A few people who remember him from their childhood days in Conconully and Okanogan assert, nearly seventy years after his death, that he was in the newspaper business in Japan. Others believe he had been a pantomime artist attached to the Japanese armed forces . . . (My Japanese researcher says that the latter is inconsistent with Matsura's apparent social level.) Newspaper accounts from Okanogan papers and written reminiscences shed little light on Matsura's thirty-nine years of life.[26]

Following the book's publication, Roe's persistence since has yielded important facts of his life. Her research has confirmed, for example, her earlier speculations that "Frank," who signed his earliest photographs "Frank S. Matsuura," was indeed Sakae Matsuura, who was born in 1873 and emigrated in 1901 from

Japan—and, thus, was seven years younger than Okanogan residents believed him to be.[27] Highly knowledgeable about politics and culture—quoting John Stuart Mill in an article he had written, supporting women's equality, for the local Okanogan paper—Matsura was well educated. And this eccentric man who occasionally performed a traditional dance with a ceremonial sword at public gatherings also, as many believed, came from a former samurai family: the Matsuura, lords of Hirado Island and descendants of Saga, fifty-second emperor of Japan.[28] But Matsura apparently, according to Roe, "divulged little about his past to anyone."[29]

And why was Matsura so profoundly devoted to recording every aspect of Okanogan life? Again, no clear answer is available besides vague, if believable, references to his deep affection for the place and its people. While he established successful, if temporary, commercial relations with agencies beyond the region—the Seattle Expo and the railroad company—Matsura made most of his modest living in Okanogan County itself, selling portraits of its citizens to its citizens. His friendliness and generosity in reaching out to others was legendary. Besides his large portrait camera, Matsura also used a stamp-photo machine that produced relatively inexpensive, stamp-sized photographs affordable to virtually anyone in the community. Moreover, as Roe writes, "a friend of the neighborhood children, Matsura often photographed them and gave them a free stamp photo or two"; and "sometimes he gave surplus cameras to his friends."[30]

Otherwise, his biography characterizes him equally, and contradictorily, as a man of reserved demeanor and as a kind of impish trickster, often clowning around. In his first job in Okanogan as a cook's helper and laundryman, Matsura was described as "always showing the deference required of a person in his menial position at the hotel."[31] Similarly, following his death, the obituary in the local newspaper paternalistically memorialized him as an "unpretentious, unassuming, modest little Japanese."[32] Yet he was also remembered as an extrovert who attended all of the local dances and parties and as a good-humored man who sometimes displayed a wicked wit: "strangers who came to town sometimes addressed him in pidgin English. Straight-faced, Matsura would lapse into an outrageous flood of broken English. If the stranger stayed long enough, he learned to his dismay that Matsura—except for a slight accent—spoke flawlessly."[33] According to another story, in 1904 Matsura unexpectedly returned to town after being called away to military service in Japan. When queried he replied, "I missed the boat!"[34] Besides hinting at a rebellious streak beneath the surface of this "unpretentious, unassuming, modest little Japa-

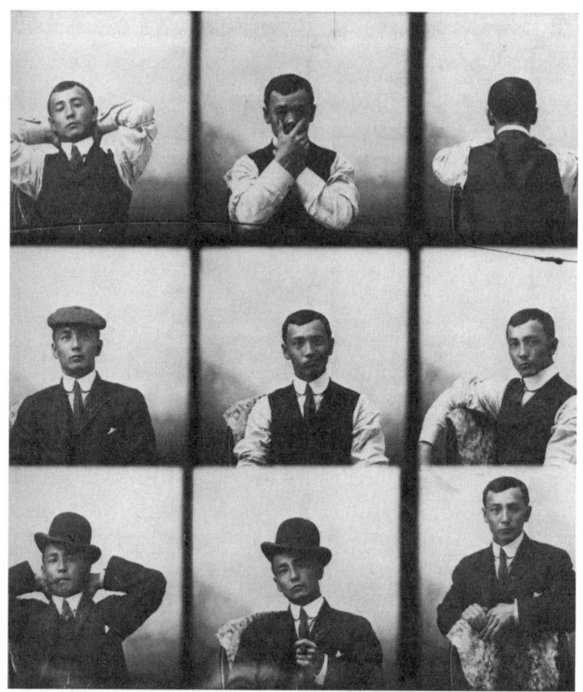

Figure 14. Self-portrait series, inside cover.

nese," both incidents—his mocking of an outsider who had mistaken him for an outsider, and his real or feigned military desertion—lend credence to the view that Matsura had deliberately chosen Okanogan as his home. Consequently, his activities over the brief ten years he lived and worked in the region have earned him a fond place in local memory. More than forty years after his death, Matsura's friend Judge William Compton Brown summed up his life concisely in a reminiscence written in 1954 for the *Okanogan Independent*: "Smiling Frank S. Matsura brought his wit, a style for winning friends and a brilliant talent for photography to the Okanogan from Japan."[35]

Perhaps Matsura should be best remembered, like his subjects, by his photographic representations—his self-portraits. Two in particular seem fitting images with which to close this essay. The first is a series of nine head-shots made with the stamp-photo machine (fig. 14). They show Matsura at turns relaxed, serious, elegant, wry, playful: who is the real Frank Matsura? Together, they wonderfully display the various personalities he apparently represented to different people and underscore the irreducibility of his biography to a coherent story. The scattered details of his life suggest an acute awareness on his

Figure 15. Self-portrait with surveyor, 23.

part of the potential stereotypical perceptions of his foreign otherness or oriental submissiveness; Matsura knew how to play the master's game and how to parody it, apparently. The stories both of his docility and his clowning find their visual refrain in these stamp-photos. His self-representation here textually works against the closure of a singular identity, ironically similar to the manner in which his photography refuses the historical endgame of frontier and Indian life wistfully narrated by Turner and Curtis.

The second photograph shows Matsura posing with federal and county surveyor Chelsea Woodward (fig. 15). The towering Woodward stands at ease, his rifle resting casually before him, pistol tucked into his gaiter, shells lining his vest. Standing beside a large portrait camera, Matsura appears the more aggressive of the two in expression and gesture, hardened gaze and hand ready to squeeze the shutter release. For Matsura this was probably just another local photograph, intended perhaps as a campy memento of two friends, white gentle giant and puckish "little Japanese." From our historical perspective, however, the striking contrast that it records also provocatively allegorizes the competing interpretations of frontier history examined in this essay. Gun and camera, government agent and commercial photographer: the technologies and historical subjects represented here share a long history of collusion in advancing material and symbolic violence in the interest of westward expansion. To be sure, many of Matsura's images were used to symbolically assimilate the region to the political-economic and ideological imperatives of nation-building: agricultural expansion, infrastructural development, tourism. But he dedicated his most sustained, creative efforts to represent Okanogan's diverse residents, places, and events to itself, over and above the hegemonic interests of industrial and consumer capitalism. In Matsura's commitment to valorize the local over the national, his camera also vibrantly documented an alternative vision of this corner of the American West that continues to unsettle the national imaginary. His photography opens up a critically rich, multiply authored historical narrative of Okanogan in contrast to the history of violent territorial acquisition and conquest represented by Woodward's rifle and surveying profession. In particular, by giving expression to the complex negotiation and continuing persistence of Indian life amid colonial displacement and dispossession, Matsura also anticipates the epistemological ground-clearing performed more recently by the New Western historians and revisionist photographers of the American West. I hope this cultural work will help galvanize the recovery of other local frontier photography toward the constitution of an alternative archive for reimagining diverse, ethical relations between the region's past, present, and future.

Still, dominant cultural representation—especially its most powerful, commercial forms—remains largely invested in the Adamic-Utopian story of the American West as a place of prelapsarian innocence.[36] But the Okanogan world that Matsura shows us is one from which there can be no mythic fall, for it is thoroughly steeped in historical experience from the start. Just as the Native peoples in his photographs continue to assert their presence, struggle to live not in the past but for the future, his own work remains dialogically engaged with the representational codes that would erase their persistent adaptations and survivals. Matsura's photographic imaginary delivers us not from a bleak, downward-spiraling present to a nostalgic past but from the teleology of mythical time to the contingent possibilities of historical time.

Notes

My thanks to *American Quarterly*'s editors and anonymous reviewers for their thoughtful comments, and grateful acknowledgment of the Okanogan County Historical Society, whose Matsura collection is the original source of the photographs examined here.

1. Will Wright, *Sixguns and Society: A Structural Study of the Western* (Berkeley: University of California Press, 1975); Jane Tompkins, *West of Everything: The Inner Life of Westerns* (New York: Oxford University Press, 1992); and Blake Allmendinger, *Ten Most Wanted: The New Western Literature* (New York: Routledge, 1998).
2. This introduction derives its biographical information from the account provided by the historian JoAnn Roe in her book *Frank Matsura: Frontier Photographer* (Seattle: Madrona Publishers, 1981).
3. Ibid., 13.
4. Although not examined in this essay, the WSU photographs largely square with and confirm the analysis and interpretation I pursue here. With the support of a Washington State Library grant, this outstanding collection has been digitized and made publicly available. See "The Frank S. Matsura Image Collection," http://content.wsulibs.wsu.edu/cdm-matsura/ (accessed February 25, 2010).
5. Rayna Green, "Rosebuds of the Plateau: Frank Matsura and the Fainting Couch Aesthetic," in *Partial Recall: Photographs of Native North Americans*, ed. Lucy Lippard (New York: The New Press, 1992).
6. My use of chronotope derives from Bakhtin's classic formulation: "In the literary artistic chronotope, spatial and temporal indicators are fused into one carefully thought-out, concrete whole. Time, as it were, thickens, takes on flesh, becomes artistically visible; likewise, space becomes charged and responsive to the movements of time, plot and history. This intersection of axes and fusion of indicators characterizes the artistic chronotope." Mikhail Bakhtin, *The Dialogic Imagination: Four Essays* (Austin: University of Texas Press, 1981), 84.
7. Frederick Jackson Turner, "The Significance of the Frontier in American History," *Annual Report, American Historical Association, 1893* (Washington, D.C.: Government Printing Office, 1894). The influence of Turner's thesis was felt far beyond the boundaries of scholarly debate. Of Turner and his two contemporaries, Charles A. Beard and V. L. Parrington, historian Richard Hofstadter writes: "Their work has to be seen as part of a general change in styles of thought that went on inside the academy in the years after 1890 and finally brought the work of academic scholars into a far more active and sympathetic relation to political and social change than it had ever had before." Hofstadter, *The Progressive Historians: Turner, Beard, Parrington* (New York: Vintage Press, 1970), 41.
8. More evocative and poetic than carefully supported by research, however, Turner's frontier thesis was not consciously malicious or insensitive. "Gentle and humane in his personal relations, Turner had no capacity to see the shameful side of the westward movement," explains historian Donald Worster. "In being so evasive he was not really lying about the past as much as he was omitting whatever interfered with what he regarded as the greater truth: the genesis of a free people." Worster, "Beyond the Agrarian Myth," in *Trails: Toward a New Western History*, ed. Patricia Nelson Limerick, Clyde A. Milner II, and Charles E. Rankin, 3–25 (Lawrence: University Press of Kansas, 1991), 10.
9. Hofstadter, *The Progressive Historians*; Ray Allen Billington, *The Genesis of the Frontier Thesis: A Study in Historical Creativity* (San Marino, Calif.: The Huntington Library, 1971).
10. Edward S. Curtis, *The North American Indian: Being a Series of Volumes Picturing and Describing the Indians of the United States, and Alaska*, with a foreword by Theodore Roosevelt, 20 vols. (Cambridge, Mass.: The University Press, 1907–1930).
11. Green, "Rosebuds of the Plateau," 52.
12. Henry Nash Smith, *Virgin Land: The American West as Symbol and Myth* (Cambridge, Mass.: Harvard University Press, 1950).
13. Limerick et al, eds., *Trails*; Patricia Nelson Limerick, *The Legacy of Conquest: The Unbroken Past of the American West* (New York: W. W. Norton, 1987).
14. Sandra S. Phillips, *Crossing the Frontier: Photographs of the Developing West, 1849–Present* (San Francisco: San Francisco Museum of Modern Art/Chronicle Books, 1996); Geoffrey Ward, *The West: An Illustrated History* (Boston: Little, Brown, 1996). Related to the Crossing the Frontier exhibit was an important symposium, Reframing the West, cosponsored by SFMOMA and San Francisco Camerawork, held on November 2, 1996.
15. Victor Masayesva Jr. and Erin Younger, eds., *Hopi Photographers, Hopi Images* (Tucson: University of Arizona Press, 1983); Chon Noriega, *From the West: Chicano Narrative Photography* (San Francisco:

The Mexican Museum, 1995). *Hopi Photographers, Hopi Images* originally accompanied the 1983 touring exhibition 7 Views of Hopi, organized by Northlight Gallery, Arizona State University. *From the West* was the catalog for a traveling exhibition that began at The Mexican Museum, San Francisco, December 9, 1995–March 3, 1996.

16. Although the interpretive framework here is mine, the historical facts of the region are drawn from Murray Morgan's introduction and JoAnn Roe's biographical essay "Frank Matsura," in Roe, *Frank Matsura.*
17. Ibid., 9.
18. Ibid., 12, 11.
19. Worster, "Beyond the Agrarian Myth," 13.
20. Roe, *Frank Matsura,* 19.
21. Ibid., 20.
22. Johannes Fabian, *Time and the Other: How Anthropology Makes Its Object* (New York: Columbia University Press, 1983).
23. Green, "Rosebuds of the Plateau," 50.
24. Allmendinger, *Ten Most Wanted,* chap. 4.
25. Green, "Rosebuds of the Plateau," 52.
26. Roe, *Frank Matsura,* 5.
27. Georgene Davis Fitzgerald, *Frank S. Matsura: A Scrapbook* (Okanogan, Wash.: Okanogan County Historical Society, 2007), 3.
28. Tatsuo Kurihara, "Matsura's Pre-Okanogan Days Remembered," *Omak-Okanogan County Chronicle,* October 24, 2007.
29. Roe, *Frank Matsura,* 15.
30. Ibid., 19, 14.
31. Ibid., 14.
32. Ibid., 19.
33. Ibid., 20.
34. Ibid., 15.
35. Ibid., 17.
36. R. W. B. Lewis, *American Adam: Innocence, Tragedy, and Tradition in the Nineteenth Century* (Chicago: University of Chicago Press, 1955); David W. Noble, *The Eternal Adam and the New World Garden: The Central Myth in the American Novel since 1830* (New York: George Braziller, 1967).

Between Dangerous Extremes: Victimization, Ultranationalism, and Identity Performance in Gerald Vizenor's *Hiroshima Bugi: Atomu 57*

Jeanne Sokolowski

Hiroshima Bugi: Atomu 57 (2003) constructs the story of Ronin Browne, the orphaned child of a Japanese prostitute (Okichi) and a Native American soldier (Orion Browne, a.k.a. Nightbreaker) who served as a translator in Japan during World War II and the subsequent occupation of Japan. The novel's episodic plot first focuses on Hiroshima, the Peace Memorial Museum, and the ground zero of the Atomic Bomb Dome to probe the role of victimhood in identity construction before moving into encounters between Ronin and the Japanese neonationalists. As the novel opens, readers learn that Ronin has made it his life's mission to protest the stance of aesthetic peace and victimhood that characterizes postwar Japan. His actions of protest include setting fire to the Peace Pond at the Hiroshima Peace Museum, burning the peace letters in the museum, and renaming the museum, using a large paper banner at its main entrance, the "Hiroshima Mon Amour Museum." Later, Ronin provides his own brand of critique of Japanese neonationalism by having sex with a Japanese woman selling souvenirs at the Yasukuni Shrine in Tokyo, initiating a spontaneous concert on the Ginza, and posing as a relative of Lafcadio Hearne, foreign teacher and later student of Japanese literature and culture. The episodes in the book are assembled and contextual information provided in alternating "envoy" chapters by a Native friend of Ronin's father who, together with the other Native veterans who live at the Hotel Manidoo in Arizona, takes on the project of turning boxes of Ronin's notes into the novel in its present form.

One of the most prolific of contemporary Native American writers, Gerald Vizenor is a poet, playwright, and novelist, as well as the author of short stories, newspaper articles, and critical theory essays. Vizenor's work is characterized by a playful yet serious deconstruction of the concept of the *indian*; his is an intellectual position that resists the ways in which false Native images (*indian* simulations) have led to absence rather than the assertions of presence that ensure survival. Vizenor's work advocates a strong, though not static, sense of individual and communal identity that will enable *survivance*, his term for an active presence that is "more than survival, more than endurance or mere response."[1]

Vizenor's textual forays into Asia began long ago: his earliest writings in the 1960s, inspired by his time stationed in Japan while in the military, were self-published volumes of haiku. And *Hiroshima Bugi* enters terrain similar to that traversed in Vizenor's 1987 novel *Griever: An American Monkey King in China*, in which a foreign (Native American) trickster protagonist protests and subverts conservative, oppressive social and political structures in an Asian location, while highlighting links between that culture and Native American (specifically Anishinaabeg) traditions and myths. *Hiroshima Bugi* reflects an ongoing interest in Asian culture, history, and society; Vizenor's choice to revisit, sixteen years later, narrative structures, settings, and themes similar to those in *Griever* also allows him the opportunity to demonstrate the evolution of his thinking on the topics of chance and native survivance.

Additionally, Vizenor engages in *Hiroshima Bugi* with recent debates within Native American studies about Native nationalism, providing a narrative that intervenes in these debates and thus has a more contemporary resonance for Native American studies than does *Griever*. Vizenor's narrative acknowledges the strong drive, present in nationalistic movements, to create a coherent identity. And *Hiroshima Bugi* creates an empathetic picture of the difficulties of identity construction.[2] Nevertheless, the novel refuses to validate an easy slide into the rigid extremity of either nationalism or victimization.

Vizenor's history of celebrating hybridity and cosmopolitanism continues in *Hiroshima Bugi* through a narrative identifying the historical and cultural links between Japan and Native America. This approach allows Vizenor a context in which to underscore the potential for chance encounters to compel a more dynamic construction of identity in a postnational, racially hybridized and hybridizing world. The novel's effect, consequently, is to infuse agency into a postmodern narrative through an emphasis on the role of performance. This essay will explore first those connections between the Japanese and Native American situations that allow Vizenor to imagine a narrative of chance, and then move into an analysis of Vizenor's use of music in service of an identity construction freed from the binary alternatives of victimization and nationalism. *Hiroshima Bugi* links Japanese history and identity construction to Native issues in the United States, triangulating the relationship among the United States, its Native peoples, and postwar, occupied Japan, and consequently requiring readers to think of power, victimization, history, and agency outside of the powerfully naturalized connections between nation and citizen.

Alternative Contact: Dependent Nations at Home and Abroad

The characters and events in *Hiroshima Bugi* demonstrate Vizenor's objection to two polarized postures of identification adopted by people who have experienced imbalances of power: victimization and ultranationalism. Vizenor's narrative coupling of occupation-era Japan with Native American populations draws on the unexpected parallel of their status as "dependents" of the United States. John Marshall's infamous opinion in the case of *Cherokee Nation v. Georgia*, 1831, proclaimed that American Indian societies are "nations" but not fully sovereign.[3] In Marshall's own words: "They may more correctly, perhaps, be denominated domestic dependent nations."[4] Likewise, the American occupation of Japan directly influenced the very nature and meaning of sovereignty in that nation through the U.S. government's role in the composition of the Japanese Constitution. Article Nine addresses one of the key claims of a sovereign nation, the right to declare war, stipulating that the "Japanese people forever renounce war as a sovereign right of the nation and the threat or use of force as means of settling international disputes."[5] Furthermore, the paternalism evident in the language of the Potsdam Treaty and in MacArthur's attitude toward the Japanese contains echoes of the paternalism that the U.S. government demonstrated toward Native Americans. One of MacArthur's reports even contained the following statement: "[I]n spite of their antiquity measured by time, [the Japanese] were in a very tuitionary condition. Measured by the standards of modern civilization, they would be like a boy of 12 as compared with our [Anglo-Saxon] development of 45 years."[6]

Though describing the status of these groups in relation to the United States as dependents captures something of the dynamic at work, the logic of colonialism also inheres in these relationships.[7] Critics within Native American studies analyze the ongoing state of internal colonialism of Native peoples, which is one reason there has been a general reluctance in the field to adopt the terminology and methodology of postcolonial studies.[8] And as Naoki Sakai writes, "the diplomatic relationship between Japan and the United States was unambiguously colonial, predicated on the fact of wartime victory and subsequent military occupation for one and defeat and subjugation for the other."[9] Additionally, the establishment and continuing presence of U.S. military bases in Japan reinforces the image of the United States as military protector of Japan; control of Okinawa was not returned to the Japanese government until 1972, and the implementation of a plan to rid Okinawa of all U.S. military bases by 2015 is incomplete. Sakai reminds us that "since Japan's independence in 1952, neither of these governments has ever openly characterized their relationship as colonial. . . . [T]he two countries are supposedly in equal partnership as two independent sovereign states, but the transnational reality that conditions their interaction far more resembles the unilateral domination of imperialism."[10] Intellectuals of both Japan studies and Native American studies make arguments for an ongoing colonial presence in these locations, suggesting that both Native American nationalists in the United States and Japanese neonationalists (especially during the turbulent 1990s) have struggled and continue to do so against the continuing colonial efforts of the U.S. government in their respective drives for autonomy and assertion of their sovereignty.

The irony in the creation of a modern Japanese identity rooted in victimization, and the dissonance between that context compared to the Native American, of course, lies in the fact that Japan's imperial projects, first through the creation of the Greater East Asia Co-Prosperity Sphere and later during World War II, victimized numerous countries and their citizens. The example of the Japanese undercuts the self-satisfaction of a stance of righteous victimhood by demonstrating how easy the slippage from dominating to being dominated is.[11] By emphasizing the ease with which the conqueror can become the conquered, Vizenor encourages optimism by indicating the rapidity with which power relations can shift. But the Japanese situation also speaks to the importance of maintaining a posture of vigilance toward projects and ideologies of dominance and oppression.

Both the Japanese and Native Americans have faced the task of identity reconstruction following experiences of military and political defeat, encountering in the process the lure of adopting an identity constructed around an internalized sense of victimization. Vizenor notes in the Native context that academic discussions tend to convert the "real sufferer" into a "pose of aesthetic victimhood," a posture that obfuscates the "tragic wisdom of [Native] survivance."[12] The sudden shift in fortune that Japan experienced with the bombings of Hiroshima and Nagasaki, its subsequent surrender and then occupation by U.S. troops, combined with the attendant changes in how the Japanese people conceptualized and reconstructed their identity as a nation—all this offers a fitting backdrop for Vizenor's meditations on nationalism and survival in the Native American context. As Japan's fate in the twentieth century demonstrates, ultranationalist ideologies, such as those exhibited by Japan prior to and during World War II, pose a threat to cultural and political survival, but so do national identities constructed around a history of victimization and rooted in what Vizenor sees as an unnatural pacifism.

The two extremes of victimization and ultranationalism represent positions especially pertinent in the context of contemporary Native American discourse and politics, making Vizenor's surprising linkage between the novel's two narrative strands more logical than it first seems. For both postwar Japan and contemporary Native American tribes, survivance necessitates creative resistance to domination and requires, as literary critic Linda Lizut Helstern writes, "striking a new balance with domination."[13] It does not, as one of the Native veterans in the novel discusses, "arise from separation, domination, or concession."[14] Nationalism and ultranationalism can encourage separatist attitudes or lead to a majority's ideological domination of the group; cultivating an identity as victimized, conversely, results in a consciousness of concession. In typical Vizenor fashion, the novel refuses the binary opposition between a surrender into victimhood and the aggressive stance of self-assertive nationalism; he demonstrates, rather, that victimization can motivate a reactionary nationalism.

Fake Peace and the Aesthetic of Victimhood

Ronin serves as an agent of transformation, modeling the means through which melancholia, disguised under a veneer of pacifism, morphs into an active and healthy anger that fuels survivance. Ronin's own identity as a mixed-blood orphan naturally aligns him with a group of other individuals who could be categorized as victims. First, the creation of a character such as Ronin gestures to the realities that undermine narratives of national cohesion and loyalty. *Hiroshima Bugi* meditates on the ways in which imperial projects forge transnational connections that may ultimately undermine national sovereignty. Despite prohibitive ordinances, fraternization between U.S. soldiers and Japanese women during the occupation of Japan resulted in a number of biracial children, the so-called GI babies. Exact numbers are difficult to come by, with estimates of 3,490 from the Japanese government contradicting claims that the actual numbers were between 150,000 and 200,000.[15] The existence of *hafu* (mixed-race, "half") children in Japan and elsewhere undermines the centrality of the geographically bounded nation to discussions of citizenship, as the very existence of these children implies a question of divided allegiance. The United States' formally legislated policy for citizenship blends concepts of jus sanguinis (law of blood) and jus soli (law of soil), making possible both citizenship by birth to an American parent and by birth on American soil. *Hafu* Japanese-American children born outside of America's physical boundaries still possess a link to the United States.

In the first chapter of *Hiroshima Bugi,* Vizenor stages a meeting between Ronin and Oshima, a leper who wanders the ruins of the Atomic Bomb Dome; the two form a bond because, in telling each other their histories, they recognize their common struggle against similar antagonistic forces. Oshima's father reported him as leprous to the authorities, and so Oshima was confined to an island leper colony for sixty years, "even after there was a cure for leprosy."[16] Parallels exist between the plight of the lepers like Oshima, orphans such as Ronin, the *hibakusha* (literally, "explosion-affected people"), the indigenous Ainu in contemporary Japan, and Native Americans in the United States. These groups all suffer from public attitudes (shaped and encouraged by governmental policy) that vacillate between fear and sympathy; all five groups, likewise, endure a peculiar type of memorialization that negates their present existence and survival.

Oshima describes a nightmare in which his fate as a leper merges with that of the *hibakusha*: "My bones were mounted in a museum," he tells Ronin, and "my remains were displayed in a diorama of victimry to promote peace."[17] For Native American readers, or those familiar with the history of Native-white relations, the references to museums and remains evokes the Native American Graves Protection and Repatriation Act, which helps tribes regain control over the sacred bones and relics of their ancestors.[18] Ronin recognizes Oshima's pain, but refuses to let him stagnate in victimhood; he transforms Oshima's tragic history and story into art. When creating a tattoo of chrysanthemums on the back of Miko (the Japanese shaman-painter who becomes Ronin's lover), he inserts a crippled leper's hand holding the flowers, in homage to Oshima. Additionally, through his association with Ronin and Miko, Oshima recovers his confidence and pride. Breakfasting with the two of them in the Anderson Bakery in the Hondori Shopping Arcade of Hiroshima, the leper is refused service by a clerk. Miko's compassion, as well as the decency of the other clerk, makes him "for the first time in sixty years . . . a free man."[19]

The agency Vizenor advocates in the novel uses the products and characteristics of the postnational world (including cultural hybrids and the flow of people and information across borders) to forge coalitions, alliances that undermine the fixity of national boundaries. Vizenor's novel dramatizes both the negative and the positive consequences of transnational contact. On the one hand, Ronin's biracial parentage marginalizes him within Japan while his father's ignorance of his birth and the U.S. military's bureaucracy complicate his status as an American.[20] On the other hand, this ambiguity is fundamental to Ronin's success as a protestor; he is able to insinuate himself into Japanese society in order to do his work, and the Japanese government is reluctant to directly accuse or punish him, as that would be an acknowledgment of Ronin's membership in Japanese society. And, as the above examples indicate, Ronin's status as marginal to Japanese society offers him the latitude to fraternize with Oshima, and thus fosters a sense of survivance in that character.

Ronin's actions and rhetoric also exhort onlookers to consider the constructedness of notions of "peace." Most people understand the concept of peace as a balance of power, but, as Vizenor writes in *Fugitive Poses*, "mythic peace is not a balance, but the cause of manifest manners and dominance."[21] For Vizenor, peace represents a relationship wherein one group holds power, and another group accedes to that imbalance. The more natural state of affairs consists of power struggles and shifting balances of power, a continual state of flux. Vizenor's narrative chastises the victims of the world, including, but not limited to, Native Americans and the Japanese, in part because victimhood incorporates a belief that the state of peace and the cessation of active warfare offer consolation for any loss of autonomy or identity. Vizenor has asserted that victimhood has become such a primary source of consciousness in America that "any other outcome" is simply "not believable."[22] *Hiroshima Bugi* specifically sets out to imagine alternative resolutions to identity construction in the wake of defeat and domination.

In the aftermath of World War II, a sense of victimization developed in Japan, partly in response to the bombing of Hiroshima and Nagasaki, and the genuine suffering of the *hibakusha*. But the intense debate over responsibility and repentance compounded the issue. Historian John Dower tracks the shifting sentiments in Japan in the period immediately after the war, noting that, following the surrender, Japanese leaders and governmental officials began to speak publicly about the need for collective responsibility (*ichioku souzange*, or "collective repentance of the hundred million").[23] Though most Japanese citizens felt that a greater degree of responsibility should fall on the shoulders of the wartime leaders and military commanders, the public also experienced substantial guilt about wartime atrocities, particularly as information about events such as the Nanjing Massacre became public knowledge in the months before the Tokyo war crimes trial. However, as Dower states, these sentiments "never developed into a truly widespread popular acknowledgment of Japan as victimizer rather than victim."[24]

The figure and fate of Emperor Hirohito himself served as a metonym for that of the nation. With General Douglas MacArthur's decision to maintain the institution of the emperor after the war in order to ensure continuity came the necessity to disassociate the person of Hirohito from blame. Japanese historian Takahashi Tetsuya insightfully analyzes the way in which the emperor's status as victim came to signify Japanese victimization in his 2003 article "The Emperor Showa Standing at Ground Zero: On the (Re-)configuration of a National 'Memory' of the Japanese People," in which he describes a junior high school history textbook produced by the neonational group *Atarashii Rekishi Kyokasho o Tsukuru Kai* (Society for History Textbook Reform). Takahashi's discussion focuses closely on the implications of the text's inclusion of the words of a sixty-eight-year-old female *hibakusha*, who is quoted as having said, on the occasion of the emperor's death: "I have a feeling that I have always been sharing hardships with the emperor."[25] The fact of a survivor of the atomic bombing expressing such a deep sense of empathy with Hirohito, a figure bearing a certain amount of responsibility for her suffering, testifies to the psychological confusion regarding war responsibility.

The transformation of Japanese memories of World War II from imperial victimizer to the victims of the first atomic bomb raises questions about the politics of memory. If, as Karl Kroeber writes of Native American history, Natives accept a designation as surviving victims, they "complete psychologically the not-quite-entirely successful physical genocide."[26] Violence and domination inevitably create victims, but there is much latitude in what use is made of the memories of victimization. Victims can choose to try to forget it completely (the route of repression), turn it into anger, transform it into a melancholy aesthetic form to linger over (the form Ronin so objects to in the Peace Museum), or turn it into the type of art that Vizenor is advocating—one that goes beyond the emphasis on mere endurance typical of victimhood to celebrate the active presence of survivors in today's world. Kroeber's recognition that "those who remained had almost to think of themselves as survivors and to feel a moral imperative to assert the special value of their traditional cultures that had been so savagely attacked" presents a formidable argument against Vizenor's attitude.[27] And yet it is not at all difficult to see how the "moral imperative to assert the special value" of a particular culture could develop into an ultranationalism with which Vizenor is equally uncomfortable.

Vizenor uses Ronin's acts of tricksterism protest to dismantle the less productive victim mentality, weakening the psychological hold of an identity born of historical trauma through a playful tease of the self-absorption that characterizes victims and renders them unable to take control of their lives. Ronin's disdain for the Peace Museum in Hiroshima stems from the manner in which victimization has been transformed into a consumerist enterprise, as well as for the ways in which politicians have used a rhetoric of peace to ensure their job security. But perhaps most significantly, Ronin's actions attack the passivity of a victim consciousness, and demonstrate the value of righteous anger.

Making constructive use of personal and historical memory then becomes a critical issue, and Vizenor's reclaiming of the term "survivance" demonstrates what Kroeber calls a "reorientation" instrumental in drawing on traditional cultural values in order to reinvent contemporary identities.[28] In chapter nine, Ronin narrates the scene from the movie *Hiroshima Mon Amour* in which the characters debate the representation of trauma in memory. Ronin asks: "What is remembrance, and how do we resist forgetting?" and juxtaposes this question with a list of image fragments, notably of morning glories and horseweed.[29] These images are significant for their symbolism, as these plants sprang up with surprising vigor in Hiroshima after the nuclear bombing. They recur later in the chapter as tattoos.

The tattoo serves as a particularly useful metaphor for memory in the hands of Vizenor, part of whose agenda, as Chadwick Allen has discussed, is "the location of adequate tropes for memory."[30] Allen characterizes Vizenor's employment of memory, like Momaday's, as "transitive," that is, it carries over elements of the past into the present, thus "producing a contemporary indigenous identity as text."[31] The tattoo is literally a scar, the body's mark of the memory of physical trauma. It is imprinted on the body, so it is permanent—a variation on Momaday's "memory in the blood." But rather than in the blood, the tattoo is on the skin, and blood is lost in its creation. These "invisible tattoos" which are, according to Ronin, the indigenous art form of the Ainu, a people native to Japan, alternate between being visible and invisible.[32] The image of the tattoo emerges when heat is applied—that is, when the body responds in excitement or embarrassment in a blush, or when the temperature of the external environment is greater than that of the body. The metaphor of the tattoo, an art form that transforms pain and trauma into an act of creation, a thing of beauty, and an aspect of identity, thus serves as a counterpoint to aesthetic victimhood. Additionally, the Japanese tradition of tattooing alters the significance of choosing to transform the body in this manner. As the Native veteran-narrator of the alternating "Manidoo Envoy" chapter explains, those who sport tattoos in Japan do so, not in order to express their individuality, but to offer proof of their membership in a group.[33] Getting a tattoo thus becomes both an act of individual marking and a sign of affiliation and connectivity.

By uniting Japanese history and culture with Native American locations and characters, Vizenor nods toward the chance connections, sometimes transnational, that can animate resistance and survivance. Ronin does, of course, "return" to the United States but undermines America's status as "center" by refusing to stay there permanently. Through his mobility, the novel invites thinking on how such figures both undermine and expand discussions of nation and sovereignty and, by extension, national dominance. Ronin's refusal to align himself unilaterally with any particular group gestures toward the flexibility and fluidity of trickster logic in the Native American literary tradition, but also indicates Vizenor's stance toward an issue-based politics, rather than one that is narrowly national, partisan, or identity-driven. His choice of a mixed-blood protagonist forces us to acknowledge that citizenship status premised on allegiance to a single, self-contained nation is already a faulty construct.

The Limitations of Nationalist Ideology

As Ronin's mixed-race identity indicates, the question of national allegiance in a transnational world is a vexed one; this problematic extends to the context of Native American nationalism. Though never mentioned explicitly in the book, current debates in Native American studies regarding nationalism versus more cosmopolitan (or lately, transnational) perspectives constitute part of the context for Vizenor's reservations about a Native nationalist agenda. An essay published in 1981 by Simon Ortiz stands as a seminal document in the articulation of a Native literary nationalism. In this essay, Ortiz emphasizes the resistance that characterizes the response of Native peoples to colonization and the importance of story as the means by which life is engendered, substantiated, continued, and created.[34] These claims do not seem so far removed from Vizenor's positions or from his art. Ortiz's assertion, however, that Native writers should assume the responsibility to "advocate for their people's self-government, sovereignty, and control of land and natural resources" demarcates the goals of literary nationalism, aims that Vizenor's writing does not always foreground.[35] Elizabeth Cook-Lynn, in the 1993 essay "The American Indian Fiction Writer: 'Cosmopolitanism, Nationalism, the Third World, and First Nation Sovereignty,'" identifies "tribal bonding with geography as the most persistent native nationalist sentiment," but, as Vizenor's novel demonstrates, for those individuals with links to multiple geographies, the issue of bonding, and therefore, nationalist sentiment, complicates the simplicity of Cook-Lynn's equation.[36] *Hiroshima Bugi* does convey the importance of land (specifically, that of Hiroshima) in shaping identity;[37] however, the fact that the land in question is "foreign" would render the novel's treatment of that topic less manifestly political and relevant for Native nationalists.

Vizenor maintains a decided reluctance to harness concepts of sovereignty (tribal or personal) to specific territory, though, as Krupat notes, Vizenor's writings "more or less resemble that of the cultural nationalist.[38] As Eric Cheyfitz points out in his essay "The (Post)Colonial Predicament of Native American Studies," Cook-Lynn's nationalist position, strongly rooted in the political, differs from the cosmopolitan or transnational position (of which Cheyfitz takes Arnold Krupat as exemplar) in that the cosmopolitan stance focuses much more on culture than on politics.[39] The intellectual sovereignty Vizenor advocates is devoted to a liberation of consciousness more than to the kinds of political activism that characterize Cook-Lynn's nationalism. Vizenor's depiction of Ronin's activism in the novel tends toward the ludicrous rather than the realistic; Ronin repeatedly plays the buffoon to avoid being identified as the culprit of these crimes. As a result, when interrogated by the Japanese police, Ronin comes to be regarded as a harmless eccentric, a "police maniac," and thus, ironically, freer to engage in his actions of protest.[40] Clearly, for Vizenor, resistance by tease and irony through imaginative, visionary acts of intellectual sovereignty possesses its own power in the war against domination and ongoing colonial practices. His attitude does not so much oppose Native nationalism and its tactics as treat it with the skepticism he holds toward most large, organized movements.[41]

Since Ortiz's foundational theorization of literary nationalism and Elizabeth Cook-Lynn's exhortations and admonishments for Native American studies, critics such as Jace Weaver, Craig Womack, Robert Warrior, Daniel Heath Justice, and, more recently, the Native Critics Collective, have been actively publishing criticism from a nationalist perspective.[42] Weaver, Womack, and Warrior, in the preface to *American Indian Literary Nationalism*, use Ortiz's theory to show that nationalism need not be isolationist. Jace Weaver, in particular, in his section of the book, states that the literary nationalism they advocate supports sovereignty in a broad, inclusive manner that extends to scholars such as Vizenor.[43] However, Vizenor himself may not want to be included under the umbrella term "Native nationalist," as *Hiroshima Bugi* demonstrates.

Vizenor's suspicion about Native or other types of nationalism stems from a concern that nationalism operates on the assumption of an unrealistically unified Native culture that is doomed to failure because it lacks the ability to represent the whole array of identity positions possible for contemporary Native Americans. Nationalism itself has a tendency to reify tradition and naturalize a myth of purity, and there exist, as Krupat asserts in his discussion of Native nationalisms, "dangers . . . in treating 'the people' or the 'nation' as a unitary force or indivisible essence."[44] Both of these tendencies can result in the perpetuation of static images and simulations of "Indian" identity, a topic about which Vizenor has written in depth.[45] His alternative approach builds on tribal and nationally specific cultural traditions, but emphasizes the urgency in creative adaptation of those traditions.

In Japan, debates over national identity have tended to divide into those who support "old nationalism" as opposed to the neonationalists. Rikki Kersten's work discusses the two camps, describing old nationalism as more hierarchical and rooted in the notion of a "family State," while neonationalists ardently work for a separation of nation and state.[46] Two of the contested issues in the debates over Japanese neonationalism are education and sovereignty. The question of sovereignty often involves discussions regarding Article Nine of the Japanese Constitution, military power, and Japan's ability to make decisions about self-defense, the last an issue that came to a head during the Gulf War in 1990–1991. The debates over the role of education crystallized in conflicts on the writing of history, as evidenced in Japan's textbook debates. Neonationalist groups felt that postwar democracy in Japan has been responsible for the "inhibition of a rehabilitated nationalism" and fought for the inclusion of material in textbooks that could encourage national pride, while downplaying elements of Japan's guilt and wartime crimes.[47] Both the topics of sovereignty and the writing of history reverberate for Native American nationalists, as well.

In addition to its response to the growth of nationalist impulses in Native American discourse, other elements also link *Hiroshima Bugi* to the larger tradition of Native American literature and render it less anomalous than it may appear. The antagonism between Vizenor's vision and that of other leading Native American writers appears in sharp relief when the novel is compared with two canonical Native American works. Vizenor's novel can be situated as a literary response to M. Scott Momaday's *House Made of Dawn* and Leslie Marmon Silko's *Ceremony*, novels that include protagonists who are World War II veterans returning to their families and homelands and looking for, as critic Arnold Krupat asserts, "a return to traditions," roots, and people.[48] These visions of reconstruction occur within the bounded United States and are nationalist to the extent that the authors direct their efforts to uncovering and articulating elements of Native tribal culture necessary for the process of healing their main characters.

Krupat argues that Momaday and Silko insist (at least in these early novels) on "the possibility of a recuperation of the traditional."[49] Vizenor states that he is "much more inspired by the works that reimagine the past with all its contradictions than [he is] with those literary artists who reimagine the past as a fundamental idea of tradition and value."[50] Consequently, he takes the same historical moment (the aftermath of World War II) as do Silko and Momaday as the point of departure for his novel, but directs his creative vision outside the boundaries of the United States. After the war ends, the Anishinaabe character Nightbreaker (Ronin's father) doesn't return home immediately; rather, his military service continues via his role as translator for Douglas MacArthur, and his exposure to the larger world extends to his romantic and sexual liaison with Okichi, the Japanese prostitute. And when he does return to the United States, Nightbreaker eventually seeks out a community of veterans off-reservation, at the Hotel Manidoo in Nogales, Arizona.

Ronin does travel to the United States (he is adopted by the Anishinaabe tribe when he is fourteen and spends time on the White Earth Reservation in Minnesota, later traveling to Arizona in an attempt to find his father), but it is important to note in this regard that Vizenor's novel is not structured so as to conclude with Ronin's immigration to the United States; that voyage is implanted within flashback sequences and retellings of stories about Ronin's time on the reservation in the explanatory Manidoo Envoy chapters. Thwarting expectations that the novel end with Ronin's trip "home" to the United States and Minnesota, the novel concludes with Miko coming to the White Earth Reservation and looking for ways to honor Ronin's memory. Through the novel, Vizenor aims to explore how people, places, and cultures outside of the United States can operate as potential sources for the creative energy needed for survival, rather than following the lead of Silko and Momaday in positing nation and reservation as the inevitable sources for inspiration and spiritual sustenance. Again, Vizenor demonstrates his ambivalence toward strict territorial allegiances.

Japanese postwar nationalism and neonationalism focus attention on the role of pride and guilt in cementing a relationship between the citizen and the state. Though the specific nuances are quite different in the Japanese and Native American forums, these emotional extremes present surprising similarities. In the Japanese context, prewar and wartime nationalism operated from an ideological position of cultural pride, infused with an implicit sense of cultural superiority, while a postwar nationalism based on guilt for wartime atrocities creates a sense of nationalism rooted in the past and buttressed by a fear of repeating the past in the future. It is the lack of cultural pride and patriotism in the postwar nationalism on which neonationalist movements seek to capitalize. In Native American nationalist rhetoric, cultural pride aims to combat a history of oppression based on a discourse of Native American tribes as savage and primitive. In addition to cultivating that sense of pride, certain

Native nationalists have injected guilt into the debate by suggesting that work within Native American studies and literature authored by Native Americans needs to take on an explicitly political, nation-centered focus; otherwise, it is of no use. The injection of guilt emerges, for instance, in Cook-Lynn's essay "The American Indian Fiction Writer," when she writes that Native authors must take responsibility for writing about the real world of Native American life or risk having Indians later ask, "Where were you when we sought clarification as Sovereigns in the modern world?"[51] In a more directed critique, Leslie Marmon Silko has criticized Louise Erdrich's novel *The Beet Queen* as a piece of postmodern writing in which "no history and politics intrudes" and in which the shared or communal life of Native Americans is, for Silko, inadequately reflected.[52]

Perhaps the most explicit connection between the neonationalism present in Japan in the 1990s and Native American nationalist organizations occurs in chapter ten, when Ronin visits Yasukuni Shrine. While there, he has sex with a "shrine maiden" who sells nationalistic war memorial souvenirs in her booth; the maiden asks Ronin if he knows Dennis Banks, with whom she is infatuated.[53] Banks and Vizenor both have real connections to Japan via their military service; Vizenor was stationed in Hokkaido in the early 1950s, while Banks, one of the leaders of the American Indian Movement (AIM), also served in the military in Japan in the mid-1950s and eventually married a Japanese woman. When the U.S. government would not allow him to bring his wife back to the United States with him when he was transferred, he went AWOL and was eventually given a dishonorable discharge from the service.[54] Vizenor has made no secret of his antipathy toward Banks. In *Manifest Manners: Postindian Warriors of Survivance*, he describes Banks's adoption of stereotypical Indian warrior clothing and rhetoric, calling him a "kitschyman of tribal manners."[55] Additionally, Vizenor's writing criticizes the ways in which the nationalist organization AIM achieved media publicity through its claims to be representatively Indian. Acknowledging some of the success of AIM, Vizenor nevertheless asserts that the leadership's recourse to violence and reluctance to negotiate prevented real, sustained institutional change.

Both Banks and AIM occupy positions of honor and respect within certain circles of Native activism. By contrast, chapter ten of *Hiroshima Bugi*, which takes place at the Yasukuni shrine honoring the memory of the war criminals, satirizes the deification of nationalist icons. Ronin's public performance at the shrine follows the prescribed rules for addressing the shrine deities. He rinses his mouth with water as part of the purification ritual and, at the altar, claps his hands, a gesture generally performed, along with ringing a bell, to get the attention of the gods.[56] Yet what superficially appears to be a prayer or supplication to the shrine deities, in recognition of their elevated position, actually becomes an act of rebuke. As war criminals during their lifetimes, these deities do not deserve the honor of being interred in and venerated at the shrine; rather, as Ronin says, "the atomu children deserve to be honored more than [them] or any emperor."[57]

Ronin's ironic mimicry of traditional shrine etiquette to chastise the war criminals, the shrine priests, and the Japanese tourists and neonationalists evolves (or devolves, depending on your perspective) into a sexual encounter with the shrine maiden infatuated with the romantic (but unreal) simulations of Indian identity on which Dennis Banks capitalized. Vizenor has elsewhere indicated that he understands the attraction of the radical politics represented by AIM and the particular brand of romanticized spirituality embraced by its leaders; in *The People Named the Chippewa*, he relates his temptation to succumb to such appeals.[58] However, in this episode, we see Ronin resist the attractions of the nationalist spirit so in evidence at Yasukuni Shrine. Rather, he accepts a charm from the shrine maiden, and gives in to her charms, resulting in a rambunctious act of fornication in the maiden's souvenir booth. The soundtrack to their sexual union is the "charm" or blended sounds of Ronin's patriotic American music broadcast over the loudspeaker of the booth and the maiden's lusty cries.[59] In typical Vizenor fashion, spontaneous, public intercourse at Yasukuni Shrine marginally avoids religious sacrilege (as the sex occurs, Ronin is careful to point out, in "a secular souvenir booth") and indirectly honors the spirit of the deceased "*atomu*" children, since, as the Manidoo Envoy narrator notes, "that erotic moment in the booth could have been the rise of a shrine *hafu* and the incredible start of another story."[60]

The Boogie/Bugi between Extremes: Performing Native Identity

If, on the one hand, Vizenor derides the aesthetics of fake peace and abhors the position of the tragically victimized, and yet seems equally critical of the aggressive pride that can push nationalism into a static ideology of dominance, what options remain in the struggle for cultural survival? Vizenor is not easy to pin down on this point, but therein lies the key. He rejects both extremes in favor of a stance of warrior tricksterism, an ironic sensibility, and an embracing of chance alliances that defend and support survivance. In the character of Ronin, for example, we see Vizenor's model of the individual who chooses to delight in chance connections and playfully embraces makeshift strategies for allied survival. The power of dominating forces is lessened in the face of these slippery, hard-to-predict tactics and elusive forms. Vizenor's novel suggests that recognizing and utilizing moments of chance connections, among individual stories, national histories, art and cultural forms, can be a central strategy and provide a model for survivance. Those connections can be between those who are similar to us, with whom we share a history, place, or features, but these affiliations can also be found in less obvious places. In both cases, the resulting stories, artwork, and consciousness gain increased strength from the hybrid melding of different sources.

These temporary and contingent linkages between people affect the construction of identity and occur through chance, an important concept for Vizenor. "Chance" refers not only to the unpredicted and unpredictable nature of these events and connections, but also to the chance or opportunity that they offer for re-creation. Though I have been referring to the novel in shorthand as *Hiroshima Bugi* for the sake of convenience, the subtitle, *Atomu 57*, holds great importance.[61] The specification of a particular date (the fifty-seventh year in Ronin's original calendar, which begins in the year of the atomic bombing) indicates that this *bugi* (either dance or type of warfare or both, i.e., military or strategic dance) is situated in the present time, but also suggests that this particular battle is only the current iteration in a long line of skirmishes. The modes of protest and subversion, of survival in the past and in the future, have been and will be different, contingent on the chance connections made between people and on our choices as performers of our own identities. The subtitle testifies to the fact that no boogie/bugi can exist that is not temporary and situational; the Hiroshima Bugis performed in Atomu 56 and yet to be performed in Atomu 58 possess their own forms and structures. The provisional nature of these performances, and the identities that they create, need not, however, undermine their efficacy. In fact, within that fluidity lies their power.

The power of such makeshift connections is suggested by the novel's title, which recalls the popular occupation-era song "Tokyo Boogie Woogie" (1948).[62] Jazz music had enjoyed a wide audience in Japan until the outbreak of World War II, when the government strongly discouraged jazz performances. With the arrival of the American occupation troops, however, jazz made a spirited reappearance. A *Time Magazine* article from June 1948 reporting on the boogie-woogie craze states that "Tokyo Boogie Woogie" could even be heard broadcast on the streets from loudspeakers.[63] The song's refrain goes: "Tokyo Bugi-ugi / ri-zu-mu uki uki / kokoro zuki zuki / waku waku." Translated, this could be rendered: "Tokyo boogie-woogie / the rhythm floating buoyantly / your heart madly pounding / thump thump."[64] However, this literal translation misses part of the fundamental pleasure of the song in the Japanese version.

One *Time Magazine* writer opined that the lyrics of Japanese jazz songs have a "strange poetic touch which knocks the Japanese for a loop, but leaves a Westerner vaguely feeling as if someone has been beating him over the head with a chrysanthemum petal."[65] The Japanese *gitaigo*, a "category of adverbs consisting of repetitive sounds," used in the lyrics of "Tokyo Boogie Woogie," like the compound word "boogie-woogie" itself, both simplify and enrich the utterance.[66] The repetition of the single syllable adverbs has, on the one hand, the effect of rendering them into a kind of childlike speech (such as when a toddler says "ma-ma" or "pee-pee") while simultaneously creating a stronger emotional emphasis, such as sometimes occurs with onomatopoeia in English, as well as a sense of pleasure and play with language. The Japanese adoption of the boogie-woogie musical style inspires the lyrical playfulness of *gitaigo* and effectively renders "Tokyo Boogie Woogie" a Japanese-American cultural hybrid.

If written in katakana (the syllabary used in Japanese for rendering foreign words), *bugi* most certainly refers to the style of music that I've been discussing. However, if written in hiragana (one of the other Japanese alphabets) or in kanji (Chinese characters), *bugi* takes on quite another meaning: that of military or combat skills, or martial arts. The translation of this term into English produces a semantic ambiguity that Vizenor intends, so that the title suggests a style of warrior combat that draws on diverse cultural traditions to effect its resistance and that refuses to be categorized as either serious or humorous, but rather partakes of both styles as the occasion suits. The lyrics of "Tokyo Boogie Woogie" similarly gesture toward a celebration of flexibility and movement. One verse includes the lyrics: "This Tokyo Boogie resounds and echoes all across the oceans / The boogie dance is the world's dance . . . / When you dance the boogie / the whole world is united as one / because the rhythm is the same / And the melody the same."[67]

The musical figure of boogie-woogie links Vizenor's fiction to the popular culture of occupation-era Japan and epitomizes Vizenor's advocacy of the playful irreverence of the culturally adaptable, transnationally flexible trickster tease. Boogie-woogie music arises from the blues tradition and is characterized by a steady, rhythmic base (played on piano by the left hand) accompanied by improvised melodic variations. Some early listeners didn't like that percussive monotony, but others felt that the "imposed limitation of the percussive touch proved to be a beneficial discipline."[68] If the title *Hiroshima Bugi* suggests a metaphoric connection between resistance to imperial and colonial projects (and the people who resist these forms of domination) and boogie-woogie—an unlikely connection, but, I would argue, par for the course of Vizenor's mind arrows—then the strength of that metaphor lies in its serving as a reminder that the forces of domination and oppression are pervasive and possess historical and cultural continuity despite surface differences.[69] It makes sense, therefore, that those who reject the stance of victimhood and strive for survivance can benefit from cross-cultural and transnational stories of successful activism. These stories become the contrapuntal melodies that tease the relentless bass poundings of hegemonic power, stories that are then transformed into performed identities for as long as they serve a purpose.[70]

The music of resistance permeates a scene that occurs near the end of the novel, in the penultimate chapter, "Ronin of the Ginza." After marching through Yasukuni Shrine (memorial to the warriors and soldiers who died in war), Ronin visits the war museum east of the shrine and meets a World War II veteran who calls himself Bogart. Ronin recognizes the veteran's warrior spirit in his recounting of "stories about war adventure, honor, courage, and loyalty, but never defeat."[71] Bogart has been hired by Japanese nationalists to drive a van around Tokyo, broadcasting patriotic, nationalist anthems and political speeches decrying liberal pacifists. Bogart, however, is not an ultranationalist, and acquiesces to Ronin's plan to play gospel music instead. From the huge black van with mirrored windows, normally used to disseminate Japanese nationalist propaganda, comes some of the mostly widely recognizable black vernacular expressive forms: gospel and blues music sung by the Queen of Gospel, Mahalia Jackson. What ensues is an ironic twist on the military occupation of Japan, a scene in which the "Ginza was truly liberated," and people "sing, dance, and move with the spirit of the music."[72] That black van becomes "the natural center of a gospel occupation, a new blue bugi on the Ginza."[73]

The first songs played include such classic spirituals as "Go Tell It on the Mountain," "Didn't It Rain?" and "Trouble of the World." The choice of these songs, sung by Jackson, in this scene signals Vizenor's conscious incorporation of blackness into the novel's exploration of cultural survival.[74] For while Vizenor clearly intends Jackson's music—which reaches and touches the hearts of those in the crowd—to be liberatory and inspirational, these musical forms function in a precarious relationship to a black nationalism founded on victimhood.[75] Forms of vernacular culture, like gospel and blues music, were actively promoted in the service of the Black Power movement and black nationalism, yet the church spirituals sung by gospel singers could be interpreted as operating in the service of an ideology of virtuous victimhood. Vizenor here acknowledges the delicate negotiation that must occur for art that seeks to memorialize a group's history while also imagining a collective future free from the oppression of the past. Jackson's gospel blues sensibility, as elaborated by Johari Jabir, makes her an excellent model for this: her singing contains a "tenacious hope" and songs such as "Didn't It Rain" both document disaster and reconstitute a vision of the community that will emerge.[76] Consequently, the scene functions as a gesture on Vizenor's part toward the resonance of his ideas for other minority communities.

The sound of the applause heard on the tape of Mahalia Jackson's singing inspires the crowd to clap their own hands, demonstrating the communal power of the performance. However, Ronin recounts how, after the first few days, the music no longer surprises or disrupts people's thinking or daily patterns. A cultural product like music that startles us out of our complacency (through pathos, sorrow, anger, energy, joy) can be productive, but continued for too long, it grows stale and useless. Change, evolution, survivance is the model.

What is the Hiroshima Bugi, then? It is place-specific but conjoins with other cultures; it is a song and dance that recognizes the persistent power and recurrent rhythms of imperialism, nationalism, and efforts at domination and oppression, but which refuses to let that noise dominate; it certainly has nothing to do with victimization. The Hiroshima Bugi is what is created when globalization puts resilient people in contact with one another, allowing them to draw inspiration from the survivance stories of others. The impromptu expression of joy in humans' ability and willingness to fight for their individual sovereignty is the Hiroshima Bugi. And the subversive quality of that joy is that, like boogie-woogie music, its enthusiasm and exuberance are contagious.

Notes

Many thanks to the audience members of the Alternative Contacts panel at the 2008 American Studies Association conference in Albuquerque for their comments on a shorter version of this essay, and to Paul Lai and Lindsey Claire Smith for arranging those panels and this special issue. My gratitude also to Chadwick Allen for reading a preliminary draft of this article, and to Stephen H. Sohn for his fine editorial eye, and to the *American Quarterly* editorial board.

1. Gerald Vizenor, *Fugitive Poses: Native American Indian Scenes of Absence and Presence* (Lincoln: University of Nebraska Press, 1998), 7.
2. Here, the empathetic treatment of Oshima is a case in point; Ronin takes steps to help Oshima reconstruct a sense of his own self-worth, which had been injured not just by his experience with leprosy itself, but by his family and his society's treatment of him as a leper.
3. Peter D'Errico, "American Indian Sovereignty: Now You See It, Now You Don't," in *American Indian Rhetorics of Survivance: Word Medicine, Word Magic*, ed. Ernest Stromberg (Pittsburgh: University of Pittsburgh Press, 2006), 242–43.
4. John Marshall, "*Cherokee Nation v. State of Georgia*, 1831," *AMDOCS: Documents for the Study of American History*, ed. George Laughead Jr., http://www.vlib.us/amdocs/texts/cherokee.htm (accessed August 21, 2008).

5. Gerald Vizenor, *Hiroshima Bugi: Atomu 57* (Lincoln: University of Nebraska Press, 2003), 136.
6. Eiji Takemae, *The Allied Occupation of Japan*, trans. Robert Ricketts and Sebastian Swann (New York: Continuum, 2002), 7.
7. The following discussion of Japan as a colonized nation in the wake of World War II is not intended to obscure or deny the country's own role as a colonizer in the era preceding its defeat. If anything, the contrast in roles for Japan before and after World War II exacerbates the shift required for the Japanese in terms of defining themselves as a people and a nation.
8. As Elizabeth Cook-Lynn has cogently argued in "Who Stole Native American Studies?": "In the past twenty or thirty years, postcolonial theories have been propounded by modern scholars as though Native populations in the United States were no longer trapped in the vise of twentieth-century colonialism but were freed of government hegemony and ready to become whatever they wanted, which, of course, they were not" (13), *Wicazo Sa Review* 12 (Spring 1997): 9–28.
9. Naoki Sakai, "Imperial Nationalism and the Comparative Perspective," *positions: east asia cultures critique* 17.1 (2009): 172.
10. Ibid.
11. Linda Lizut Helstern accurately points out that Japan is the place where "America stood staunchly against colonialism and racialist notions of purity," but this analysis of the United States' role in World War II seems to inadequately consider America's role in the occupation of postwar Japan, an occupation during which notions of American cultural and political superiority had pervasive effects on the reconstruction of the Japanese nation, and through which the United States established a strategic military base in Asia. See "Shifting the Ground: Theories of Survivance in *From Sand Creek* and *Hiroshima Bugi: Atomu 57*," in *Survivance: Narratives of Native Presence*, ed. Gerald Vizenor (Lincoln: University of Nebraska Press, 2008), 167.
12. Vizenor, *Fugitive Poses*, 21–22.
13. Helstern, "Shifting the Ground," 163.
14. Vizenor, *Hiroshima Bugi*, 9.
15. Miki Sawada of the Elizabeth Sanders Children's Home put the number at 200,000, while Takada Masami, chief of the Children's Bureau of the Welfare Ministry, put the figure closer to 150,000. See Yukiko Koshiro, *Trans-Pacific Racisms and the Occupation of Japan* (New York: Columbia University Press, 1999), 164.
16. Vizenor, *Hiroshima Bugi*, 4.
17. Ibid., 3.
18. The Native American Graves Protection and Repatriation (NAGPRA) Act was passed in 1990, and provides a process by which federal agencies and museums can return certain Native American remains and cultural artifacts to tribes. It has not been without controversy among the scientific community.
19. Vizenor, *Hiroshima Bugi*, 107.
20. Ibid., 107–20. Information provided in the second Manidoo Envoy chapter reveals that racial exclusion laws still in effect after World War II created obstacles to the immigration of half-Japanese children, in opposition to the social policy of *jus sanguinis* governing nationality and citizenship (Vizenor, *Hiroshima Bugi*, 23).
21. Vizenor, *Fugitive Poses*, 29.
22. John Purdy and Blake Hausman, "The Future of Print Narratives and Comic Holotropes: A Conversation with Gerard Vizenor," *American Indian Quarterly* 29.1–2 (2005): 215.
23. John Dower, *Embracing Defeat: Japan in the Wake of World War II* (New York: W. W. Norton, 1999), 496.
24. Ibid., 508.
25. Tetsuya Takahashi, "The Emperor Showa Standing at Ground Zero: On the (Re)configuration of a National 'Memory' of the Japanese People," *Japan Forum* 15.1 (2003): 3. Originally published as "Bakushinchi ni tatsu tenno" ("The Emperor Standing at Ground Zero"), in *Gendai Shiso* 16 (2001): 106–13.
26. Karl Kroeber, "Why It's a Good Thing Gerald Vizenor Is Not an Indian," in *Survivance*, ed. Vizenor, 25.
27. Ibid., 26.
28. The term *survivance* fell into disuse in the nineteenth century and carries the connotation of both survival and succession, that is, motion into the future. See Kroeber, "Why It's a Good Thing," 26.
29. Vizenor, *Hiroshima Bugi*, 120.

30. Chadwick Allen, "Blood (and) Memory," *American Literature* 71.1 (1999): 108.
31. Ibid.
32. The Ainu do have a history of tattooing, but the "invisible tattoos" that Ronin learns how to create are Vizenor's own fiction. These tattoos are made by pouring a mixture of beeswax and pollen into the design, rather than ink, so that "when the body is heated, the outline of the tattoo remains muted, only the natural color of the skin" (Vizenor, *Hiroshima Bugi*, 111).
33. Vizenor, *Hiroshima Bugi*, 104.
34. Simon J. Ortiz, "Toward a National Indian Literature: Cultural Authenticity in Nationalism," *Multi-Ethnic Literature in the United States (MELUS)* 8.2 (1981): 10.
35. Ibid.
36. Elizabeth Cook-Lynn, "The American Indian Fiction Writer: 'Cosmopolitanism, Nationalism, the Third World, and First Nation Sovereignty'," *Wicazo Sa Review* 9.2 (1993): 31.
37. Linda Lizut Helstern notes the importance of landscape and its linkage to history in "Shifting the Ground" (164).
38. Arnold Krupat, *Red Matters: Native American Studies* (Philadelphia: University of Pennsylvania Press, 2002), 4.
39. Eric Cheyfitz, "The (Post)Colonial Predicament of Native American Studies," *Interventions* 4.3 (2002): 419.
40. Vizenor, *Hiroshima Bugi*, 45.
41. This is not to argue that Vizenor avoids politics, social justice, and active participation as a Native American and citizen of the White Earth tribe of the Anishinaabe; on the contrary, his early career as a social worker in Minneapolis and his more current role as principal writer of the proposed Constitution of the White Earth Nation attest to his interest in political work.
42. The Native Critics Collection, which published the anthology *Reasoning Together* in 2008 (Norman: University of Oklahoma Press, 2008), includes Janice Acoose, Lisa Brooks, Tol Foster, LeAnne Howe, Daniel Heath Justice, Phillip Carroll Morgan, Kimberly Roppolo, Cheryl Suzack, Christopher B. Teuton, Sean Teuton, Robert Warrior, and Craig Womack.
43. Jace Weaver, Craig Womack, and Robert Warrior, *American Literary Nationalism* (Albuquerque: University of New Mexico Press, 2006), xvii, 73.
44. Krupat, *Red Matters*, 10.
45. See Gerald Vizenor, *Manifest Manners: Postindian Warriors of Survivance* (Hanover, N.H.: Wesleyan University Press, 1994).
46. Rikki Kersten, "Neo-Nationalism and the 'Liberal School of History'," in *Japan Forum* 11.2 (1999): 193.
47. Ibid.
48. Arnold Krupat, "Postcolonialism, Ideology, and Native American Literature," in *Postcolonial Theory and the United States: Race, Ethnicity, and Literature*, ed. Amritijit Singh and Peter Schmidt (Jackson: University of Mississippi Press, 2000), 81.
49. Ibid., 82.
50. Purdy and Hausman, "The Future of Print Narratives," 214.
51. Elizabeth Cook-Lynn, "Who Stole Native American Studies?" *Wicazo Sa Review* 12 (Spring 1997): 28.
52. Leslie Marmon Silko, "Here's an Odd Artifact for the Fairy-Tale Shelf," *Studies in American Indian Literature* 10.4 (1986): 180.
53. Vizenor, *Hiroshima Bugi*, 153.
54. See Dennis Banks, *Ojibwe Warrior: Dennis Banks and the Rise of the American Indian Movement* (Norman: University of Oklahoma Press, 2005).
55. Vizenor, *Manifest Manners*, 42.
56. Vizenor, *Hiroshima Bugi*, 150.
57. Ibid.
58. Gerald Vizenor, *The People Named the Chippewa* (Minneapolis: University of Minnesota Press, 1984), 235.
59. Vizenor, *Hiroshima Bugi*, 152–53.
60. Ibid., 155, 165.
61. The colon connecting the two parts of the title produces an interpretive ambiguity, and the reading

given here represents just one possible interpretation. Special thanks to Chadwick Allen for pushing me to incorporate a discussion of the significance of the second half of the title in relation to the first within my reading of the novel.

62. I am indebted here to Jonathan Arac's provocative suggestions in "Global and Babel: Language and Planet in American Literature," in *Shades of the Planet: American Literature as World Literature*, ed. Wai Chi Dimock and Lawrence Buell (Princeton, N.J.: Princeton University Press, 2007). Arac presents an argument for displacing American literature's frame from its usual "nationalist and monolingual enclosure" (20) to explore how literary texts negotiate between "America globalizing and the globe Americanizing" (25).
63. "Tokyo Boogie, *Time.com*, June 28, 1948, *Time Magazine*, http://www.time.com/time/magazine/article/0,9171,779890,00.html (accessed August 25, 2008).
64. My translation.
65. "Jazzy," *Time.com*, August 8, 1949, *Time Magazine*, http://www.time.com/time/magazine/article/0,9171,800536,00.html (accessed August 25, 2008).
66. Andrew Horvat, *Japanese Beyond Words: How to Walk and Talk Like a Native Speaker* (Berkeley, Calif.: Stone Bridge Press, 2000), 152.
67. Yukiko Koshiro, *Trans-Pacific Racisms and the U.S. Occupation of Japan* (New York: Columbia University Press, 1999), 125.
68. Max Harrison, "Boogie Woogie," in *Jazz: New Perspectives on the History of Jazz by Twelve of the World's Foremost Jazz Critics and Scholars*, ed. Nat Hentoff and Albert J. McCarthy (Cambridge, Mass.: Da Capo Press, 1974), 110.
69. The word *boogie* also bears a close resemblance to another type of dance, the Cherokee booger dance, which was a tool used by the Cherokee to cope with the stress of adversity by reducing their enemies through humor and mockery. As booger mask maker Will West Long told anthropologist Frank Speck, the booger dances were "spiritualistic aids in their struggle for life against . . . a menacing world of mankind." See William Douglas Powers, "Returning to the Sacred: An Eliadean Interpretation of Speck's Account of Cherokee Booger Dance," *Journal of Religion and Theatre* 1.1 (Fall 2002): 70.
70. The character of Ronin disappears at the end of the novel because there is "nothing more for [him] to tease," that is, his presence has served its purpose. Vizenor, *Hiroshima Bugi*, 202.
71. Vizenor, *Hiroshima Bugi*, 167.
72. Ibid., 171.
73. Ibid., 172.
74. I'm indebted to Curtis Marez, editor of *American Quarterly*, for urging me to consider the significance of blackness in this section of the novel.
75. Vizenor, *Hiroshima Bugi*, 170.
76. Johari Jabir, "On Conjuring Mahalia: Mahalia Jackson, New Orleans, and the Sanctified Swing," *American Quarterly* 61.3 (September 2009): 658.

Toward a U.S.-China Comparative Critique: Indigenous Rights and National Expansion in Alex Kuo's *Panda Diaries*

Wen Jin

In *Panda Diaries*, a novel published in 2006, Chinese American author Alex Kuo comments simultaneously on the effects of the Indian policies of the nineteenth-century United States and the experience of ethnic minorities in China since the mid-twentieth century under the state's campaigns to modernize and integrate the country. In an early part of the novel, the Oroqens, a small ethnic minority in northeast China, recount among themselves that when an ancestral clan of theirs crossed the "mythical linking land bridge" in the north, their name was forever changed to "Beiulup," likely a play on "Puyallup," a Native American tribe in Washington.[1] This detail can be read as an allusion to the theory that indigenous peoples in the Americas migrated from Asia tens of thousands of years ago, through the land bridge of Beringia. But it is also Kuo's way of suggesting that development programs in contemporary China have affected the country's minorities in a way reminiscent of the impact that U.S. westward expansion had on Native Americans. Both countries, for Kuo, have constructed a modernized, integrated national space at the expense of the livelihoods and cultural traditions of indigenous and minority communities. Kuo's comparison illuminates an important intersection between U.S. and Chinese histories that has started to draw critical attention. A recent news story in the *New York Times* on the Han settlers and migrants in Xinjiang, a province in northwest China that has received much U.S. media attention because of a series of ethnic riots and separatist activities, makes a similar comparison. It describes the Han Chinese in Urumqi, the capital of Xinjiang, as "sturdy and defiantly proud" people "who think of Xinjiang as China's version of Manifest Destiny, the doctrine undergirding the westward expansion of the United States in the 19th century."[2] The author, however, offers no further elaboration of this very suggestive analogy. This comparison has also been made in China, where intellectuals and policymakers cull from U.S. history what is usable for China. This effort is not without pitfalls. U.S. westward expansion often becomes, in complex ways, a model that justifies the Chinese government's policy toward economic development in minority areas. Kuo's *Panda Diaries* extends and refines the comparative insights that have been produced in both countries. It proposes a model of comparative critique that juxtaposes U.S. and Chinese histories, not to further entrench the ideology of development, but to contribute to a global perspective on the tensions between indigenous rights and majority nation formation.

There are no rigorous definitions of indigeneity. Current definitions emphasize that indigenous populations have "ancestral roots" deeply embedded in the lands they inhabit and are thus differentiated from the "more powerful sectors of society living on the same lands or in close proximity."[3] Some add that indigenous communities are also defined by their historical isolation from modernization and the modern process of state-formation.[4] In the context of contemporary China (the PRC, founded in 1949), ethnic minority groups are referred to as "minority nationalities" (*shaoshu minzu*), some of which fulfill the standard definitions of indigeneity. The system of regional autonomy for ethnic minorities in China offers the fifty-five officially recognized "minority nationalities" the rights to fair representation in local and national governments and to the continuation of traditional cultural practices, though these rights are highly circumscribed in practice.[5] Many of these minority nationalities are not "indigenous" in the strictest sense—while they have an ancestral claim to where they live, they had developed their own governments before being incorporated into imperial China and later Republican and Communist China.[6] There are a number of exceptions, however. The Oroqens, the group named in *Panda Diaries*, match the current definitions of indigeneity. One of the smallest minority nationalities in China, they were hunters in the Xingan Mountains (in northeast China) historically and did not develop a semi-agricultural lifestyle until after the founding of the PRC.[7]

Indigeneity has also been understood as an attitude toward place. In his article "Globalization, Indigenism, and the Politics of Place," Arif Dirlik reminds us that at the center of contemporary struggles against the simultaneously homogenizing and fragmentary forces of globalization is the effort to reclaim singular, and yet not isolated, places from these forces, often organized under the term "indigenism." It is important, Dirlik argues, to differentiate between the "indigenism" that simply reacts against the global and the "indigenism" that derives its meaning from "substantial autonomous claims" to "an almost absolute attachment to place understood concretely," in all its biosocial complexity.[8] The former sense of "indigenism" often takes the form of a nation-state, which in itself is "a colonial force that erases the local and the place-based in the name of its own universalistic claims."[9] The second sense of "indigenism," in contrast, "appears in its full critical significance against the colonialism not only of the global but also of the national."[10] More important, Dirlik interprets the place-consciousness that underlies the second sense of "indigenism" not as "localized parochialism," but as an ability to recognize the "interactions between the global and the local that cut across the boundaries of the nation, projecting the local into transnational spaces."[11] By troubling essentialist, static ideas of indigeneity, Dirlik's argument resonates with many recent voices in global indigenous studies. As Shari Huhndorf points out in a survey of the politics of Native American studies, the field's focus on the condition of colonialism that produced Native American literary and political articulations has led to an emerging, fruitful engagement with comparative studies of ongoing colonial patterns in the United States and other parts of the world, as one can see in the critical writings of Arnold Krupat, Eric Cheyfitz, and Chadwick Allen.[12] Outside of Native American studies, comparative and transnational perspectives on the indigenous condition have also flourished. Studies of the development of international norms for protecting indigenous rights and comparative indigenous studies, for example, speak specifically to and draw upon the Native American experience while placing it in a global framework.[13]

Not unlike these critical voices, Kuo works toward a comparative, transnational approach to the tensions between colonial and indigenous, anticolonial attitudes toward place. The interweaving of Chinese and U.S. histories in *Panda Diaries* enables an extended reflection on the contestations over space that have occurred in both countries, with contemporary China eager to repeat the stage of modernization realized in the United States during the nineteenth century. The U.S.-China comparison is crucial, as dominant conceptions of ethnoracial minorities in the two countries bear important parallels and have often intersected through various forms of cultural translation since the end of the cold war era. Since the mid-twentieth century, both countries have developed a version of multiculturalism that functions, without complete success, to mediate between official or civic nationalism and minority difference.[14] Since the collapse of the Soviet Union, the two countries have been compelled to burnish their international images by bolstering their multicultural credentials, often by using each other as foils.[15] These and other connections are often obscured by the ideological divide that customarily separates liberal democracies from a county like China. The history of Native Americans has hardly been understood in relation to that of ethnic minorities in China. Kuo's novel is part of an emerging cultural discourse that both constitutes and reflects upon these connections. Its juxtaposition and comparison of the two histories subject both countries—their governments and political cultures at large—to critical scrutiny. Against both cultural relativism and (Western-centric) moral universalism, Kuo argues that the Western world needs a stronger dose of self-criticism in decrying minority rights violations in the non-West and that developing countries cannot be exonerated from charges of such violations simply because they have been victimized by Western colonialism and imperialism. Reading Kuo does not show us what it is like to establish "actual" contact between Native Americans and indigenous or ethnic groups in China, and yet it lays an important conceptual basis for such contact. Kuo demonstrates, through his use of and commentaries on metaphor, how to draw conceptual linkages between the experiences of minority groups scattered in disparate, sometimes polarized, nations so as to stage a simultaneous critique of them. Entwined with the U.S.-China comparison, moreover, is a comparison along a different axis. For Kuo, the predicament of minority groups in a given national space should also be examined in relation to violence against animals and their natural environments. *Panda Diaries*, in other words, provides a comparative study of the impact of processes of national expansion on indigenous and ethno-racial groups while illuminating some of the ways in which, as David Alan Nibert puts it, "the devastation of other animals has been devastating for the cultural, spiritual, and economic well-being of the vast majority of humans."[16]

Rethinking Asian American Cultural Critique

Born in Boston in 1939, Alex Kuo spent his childhood and adolescence in Chongqing, Shanghai, and British Hong Kong. He moved to the United States with his family in 1955 and has spent most of his adult life in the Pacific Northwest. Between 1989 and 1998, he taught in Beijing, Changchun, and Hong Kong, as lecturer, Senior Fulbright Fellow, and Lingnan Fellow, respectively. He embarked on a literary career in 1971 as a poet, and has since published four collections of poetry.[17] His experiences in China and Hong Kong gave rise to a raft of stories and longer prose writings concerned with contemporary Chinese culture and individuals traveling or migrating between China and the United States. Not until 1998 did Asia 2000 Ltd., a Hong Kong–based small press (now defunct), publish Kuo's novel *Chinese Opera*, which was finished in 1989.[18] The same press published his collection *Lipstick and Other Stories* (2001), after it had been rejected by forty-six other publishers.[19] His *Panda Diaries* (2006) and *The White Jade and Other Stories* (2008) were both published by small presses, based on manuscripts composed in 1991–92 and

2003–4 respectively.[20] Although *Lipstick* won an American Book Award in 2002, Kuo's works have generated little discussion in Asian American literary and cultural studies.

The reasons for this neglect are many. When Alex Kuo was studying for his MFA at the Iowa Writers Workshop, he crossed paths with Frank Chin and Lawson Inada, who, along with Shawn Wong and Jeffery Paul Chan, edited the first anthology of Asian American literature, *Aiiieeeee!* published in 1974.[21] Although Kuo had published his first collection of poetry by 1971, his name did not appear in *Aiiieeeee!* or its updated version, *The Big Aiiieeeee!*[22] The circumstances for this omission were complicated, but the most important one involved the differences between Kuo's modernist poetics and the anti-assimilationist aesthetics advocated by the editors of the two *Aiiieeeee!* collections.[23] The exclusion of Kuo from Asian American literature is unfortunate, especially because the issues of race, immigration, and U.S. imperialism figure prominently in both his poetry and fiction. Like his poetry, his fiction has drawn a very limited audience. Although he has quite recently appeared in a few anthologies of Asian American literature, his offbeat, experimental style does not fit in with the lyrical realistic narratives about immigration and return that tend to dominate the market for ethnic narratives.[24] Crafting his narratives as poetry, Kuo does not provide vivid, detailed accounts of national histories or ethnic experiences, as readers have come to expect from Chinese American and other Asian American writers, preferring instead spare, pared-down narratives sprinkled with ambiguous vignettes and interludes as well as with political and cultural references that are usually left unexplained. The lack of scholarly interest has further narrowed the already limited market for Kuo's works.

A serious study of Kuo requires renegotiations of the structural limitations of Asian American literary and cultural critique, especially the diasporic paradigm. This paradigm has so far focused on the ways in which Asian American literature and culture articulate what David Eng has described as a state of "suspension" between different structures of citizenship and belonging, the impossibility of integration into the "host country" and the impossibility of returning to the "home country."[25] Kuo challenges this model by engaging both U.S. and Chinese histories directly, thus transforming the state of "suspension" that many Chinese Americans inhabit into a condition for critical comparativism. His writings call for a thoroughly transnational interpretive approach that bridges the gaps between Asian American studies, other fields in U.S. ethnic studies, and East Asian studies. This new approach, in turn, will allow us to consider the friction between minority rights and nation formation as a global phenomenon that perpetuates itself through translation and cultural borrowing.

A Panda Bear Is Not a Bear

In 1987, Native American (Anishinaabe) author Gerald Vizenor published *Griever: An American Monkey King in China*, a fictionalized memoir about his stint in Tianjing, China, as a foreign teacher. In the opening chapter, the author dreams about encountering a bear shaman on the southern Silk Road, who shows him cave paintings in the desert featuring images of bear shamans. The bear shaman then asks the author to pick a birch scroll to take with him, holding him responsible for the secrets "inscribed" on the scroll.[26] The subsequent narrative in the memoir is presented as the unfolding of what is prophesied in the scroll that the author receives in his dream. The author, in other words, merges with the bear shaman he sees in his dream and becomes a shaman with prophetic and healing powers. Throughout the novel, the narrator also dresses himself as or assumes some qualities of the Monkey King, a rebellious, powerful monkey in the classic Chinese fantasy *Journey to the West*, which figures as a Chinese analogue of the bear shaman in Native American myths. The bear and the monkey are among the many sacred and mundane animals that populate *Griever*, serving, along with the human beings connected to them, as mediums between everyday life and what lies beyond.

This essay is not about Vizenor, but the animal figures, especially the bear shaman, in *Griever* and the comparative vision it gestures toward are crucial for understanding the author that it does discuss. Kuo's *Panda Diaries* also germinated from the author's experiences in China as a foreign teacher. Although not published until 2006, it was written during 1991 and 1992, not long after the publication of Vizenor's book. While it claims to be a novel, *Panda Diaries* can hardly be properly designated as such. It offers a few snippets from protagonist Ge's life in China, including growing up separated from his parents during the Cultural Revolution and being demoted to the city of Changchun in northeast China after having presumably committed a political mistake as an intelligence officer in Beijing. The nonchronological narrative is further fragmented by various forms of authorial intrusion, including poetry, interpolated news stories, and critical commentaries on apparently unrelated historical events.

In the novel, Kuo weaves together the histories of small, endangered indigenous communities in both China and the United States, associating their precarious fate with the irresponsible killing of animals that have traditionally been endowed with mythical qualities in indigenous cultures, including wolves, horses, deer, and so on. He explicitly refers to the symbiotic relationship between Native Americans and bison as a parallel to the interdependence between the Oroqens in China and the animals that they worship and hunt. We can tease out at least two axes of comparison from Kuo's narrative. Vertically, animals and indigenous populations become metaphors for each other, occupying two interconnected worlds that are equally threatened by the process of modernization that nation-states propel. Horizontally, a metaphorical relationship is constructed between China's policy toward the Oroqens during the Cultural Revolution and the Indian policies of the nineteenth-century United States. In intertwining the vertical and horizontal metaphors, the novel reflects on the functions of metaphor as a rhetorical figure and conceptual model that grounds comparative studies. While metaphor predicates itself on the structuring of a "source domain" and a "target domain,"—two discreet units bound up in a static, sometimes hierarchized, relationship—it also implies the interdependence and interpenetration of the two domains that disrupt any given hierarchy imagined between them. Kuo demonstrates that as the different functions of metaphor cannot be easily disentangled from each other, metaphor is best understood in terms of irresolvable duality. Mediating between the restricting and liberating power of metaphor, *Panda Diaries* suggests a nuanced form of cultural critique that brings together the experiences of indigenous peoples, as well as species, from disparate time-space configurations.

The novel also features an animal character, the Panda mailman, presented as Ge's best friend in the beginning of the narrative. The Panda mailman talks and behaves just like human beings, except for some dietary peculiarities. He looks different from human beings, and yet the characters in the novel are not often alarmed by his presence outside the confines of a zoo. In many senses, the Panda mailman, representing an endangered animal species in China, figures as an animal double for Ge, a contemporary Chinese intellectual who feels beleaguered, or endangered, in a China soon to be engulfed by the 1989 student protests. The Ge-Panda duo is related to the metaphorical pairing of indigenous people and their sacred animals. Kuo invokes the latter kind of metaphorical pairing to comment on the simultaneous rise of species-based and race-based hierarchies, speciesism and racism, in the process of the modern nation's colonization of indigenous and minority space, and he uses the Ge-Panda duo to critique the state-centered, paternalistic approach toward environmental and ethnocultural justice that purports to remedy the ills of national expansion. As the panda does not figure in any traditional myth, one might say that Kuo's novel creates a new urban myth modeled upon, in an inverted manner, the oral traditions of indigenous communities on both sides of the Pacific. In other words, the panda bear in Kuo's narrative can be read as an inverted, modern, Chinese parallel of the powerful bear in Native American myth. The panda's utter vulnerability and dependence on humans' loving care forms a sharp contrast with the bear's command of fear and respect from human beings. One cannot understand the figure of the panda bear in Kuo's novel, then, without comparing it to the animal figures in Native American myth and cultures, as seen in such works as Vizenor's *Griever*. It is only fitting that we use a comparative mode of reading to understand a text that organizes itself around a series of comparisons.

Kuo's narrative presents the panda as a singular exception to other animals that have crossed paths with human beings since the advent of modernity. In an earlier part of the novel set in the Chinese city of Changchun, the Panda mailman and Ge drive to a California Noodle Company restaurant in the city, where Panda takes offense at the waitress who has addressed him as "Animal Ambassador," demanding that the waitress respect his "difference" rather than use the label attached to all pandas. The scene at the noodle company is then followed by the author's reflections on the history of various genocides in the New World that involve humans and animal species simultaneously. Kuo relates the destruction of the Plains Indians' bison commissary prior to the Battle of Little Big Horn "that was to change the colonial-native narrative forever" by eliminating the food source of the Indians.[27] He then turns to a more general critique of the history of "wanton killing" in the "new, new world" that stemmed from European colonists' espousal of "the right to expansion and the right to kill everything in its way."[28] The Panda mailman, then, represents an animal species that mysteriously escapes the modern human impulse to kill animals and other humans at whim. As an exception, however, he first and foremost proves the rule. Being constantly labeled as "Animal Ambassador," as Kuo suggests, constitutes a kind of character assassination—or, simply put, stereotyping—that, just as much as being physically annihilated, signifies a powerless position.

Kuo makes clear the metaphorical linkage between violence toward humans and violence toward animals in one of his explicitly intrusive passages: "Whose nightmare was it? Who had the ammunition, and who was the rifle pointed at? In the twinning of this metaphor, every half included another surrogate from the animal kingdom, always."[29]

On a specific level, Kuo is pointing out that the slaughtering of the American bison destroyed the livelihood of the Plains Indians, turning them into a historical analogue of the animals that they depended on. On a more general level, Kuo is arguing that the killing of animals naturalizes and logically facilitates the killing of people. In other words, the human practice of killing other human beings often arises from, or is motivated by, their experience of killing animals, whose characteristics are then mapped onto the human groups to be slaughtered. Zoltán Kövecses, a theorist of conceptual metaphor, argues that abstract ideas do not arise literally from experiences, but always through the mechanism of metaphorical mapping whereby abstract experiences in general are constituted on the analogy of more physical ones.[30] Kuo echoes Kövecses's view of metaphor by showing that it can serve as a conceptual basis for the transformation of one form of killing into another. Right before the quoted passage above, Kuo attributes to the Texas legislature that created a fellowship program to reward hunters of the Plain Indians' bison commissary a kind of "uncontrollable ambiguity" that "physically killed the body on both sides of the metaphor."[31] Kuo's remark on the "metaphorical twinning" of animals and humans suggests the historical entwining of speciesism and racism, the inseparability of environmental and ethno-cultural injustices committed during the era of expansion in U.S. history.

As Cary Wolfe points out (via a quote from Derrida), speciesism makes possible a symbolic economy in which we engage in a "noncriminal putting to death" of not only animals, but other humans as well "by marking them as animal."[32] Both speciesism and racism derived from the notion of the Great Chain of Being during the Enlightenment era, espoused by philosophers and writers as well as biologists and zoologists (such as Linnaeus and Buffon). The implication of natural science in the rise of modern racism has often been noted.[33] Kuo makes a similar point regarding natural scientists, quipping that their "specimen-gathering scientific rationality" is often "short-circuited by their anthropocentric will to kill."[34] But he goes further by placing the rise of both speciesism and racism against the background of European colonial endeavors in the New World. John James Audubon, for example, believed in "hunting and poisoning passenger pigeons," which led to the eventual extinction of pigeons on the U.S. continent.[35] The feat of putting an entire bird species to death echoes the slaughtering of bison herds and Indian populations, signaling that the expansion and homogenization of national space in the nineteenth-century United States were colonial processes with both a human and nonhuman cost. Kuo's emphasis on the colonial context situates the "metaphorical twinning" of speciesism and racism in a specific set of social arrangements. This move echoes Nibert's employment of a sociological, materialist approach to the conjoined fates of humans and "other animals" (Nibert's term) in various parts of the world throughout Western history, including the colonized areas of the

Americas, where "indigenous other animals were displaced and killed as land speculators and human settlers wreaked havoc on their lives and homelands," just as indigenous humans were regarded merely as "obstacles to maximum economic control" of the areas.[36]

As I mentioned earlier, the figure of the panda represents an intriguing complication to the extension of the twin phenomena of racism and speciesism into the contemporary era. Toward the end of the book, Ge starts to wonder whether the Panda mailman, the representative of the panda species in the novel, is a "message" he needs to heed and whether he should behave like some of the animal species that "have learned to make the adjustment between politics and environment."[37] Apparently, then, the panda comes to embody a kind of proximity to transcendent powers that resemble the status accorded to the mythical bear in the traditional cultures of Native Americans and other indigenous peoples. As David Rockwell argues, the bear is seen in these cultures as a "furry person, a relative."[38] Tribal people often model their lives upon the lives of bears, initiating their young into adulthood, for example, in an elaborate ritual during which the initiated dress up and act like bears.[39] According to Lydia T. Black, bears are seen in many indigenous cultures in the circumpolar North, among many other places, as inhabiting an "in-between" world that mediates between the human world and the "domain of deities and spirits."[40] The boundaries between the animal domain and the human domain remain porous, the crossing of which are often conceptualized as "death, birth, and sexual congress."[41] This observation echoes Joseph Epes Brown's point that bears are considered to have been created before human beings, closer to the Great Spirit in their anteriority.[42]

However, the panda in *Panda Diaries* can only be read as an *inverted* parallel of the bear shaman, representing a perverse extension of the premodern tradition of revering animals into our own times. Although the benevolence bestowed on the panda may seem to be a reversal of the human desire for territorial expansion that necessarily requires killing, it acts, at best, as a deceptive distraction from various forms of political and social violence. In fact, this benevolence is the flip side of speciesism, a manifestation of anthropocentrism, designating humans as benefactors of animals whose habitats are threatened by human practices in the first place.[43] *Panda Diaries* contains authorial comments and news inserts that satirize the ways in which pandas are cherished as national treasures in China and embraced all around the world. It opens with a preface that tells the story of Ruth Hackness, the U.S. fashion designer who, in 1936, brought back home wrapped in her arms the first live giant panda to be seen in the New World. The episode, for Kuo, inaugurated the ambassadorial role that the panda was to play from that time forward. As Kuo puts it,

> whenever a Nicolae Ceausescu is not losing his testicles in his own palace, or an Imelda Marcos is not counting her missing Parisian alligator shoes; or a Prince Charles is not traversing the remnants of the British commonwealth whining about the abuse of the English language; or the Palestinian and Israeli youths are not trying to kill each other with rubber bullets, stones, or more specific targeted killings; or another still-living *Enola Gay* airman or USS *Arizona* swabby is not saluting the flag; the world media focuses on the copulation effectiveness of these twenty-three zoo-bound pandas.[44]

Apparently capable of accomplishing the feat of uniting all countries on earth, the panda functions as a symbolic stand-in for what exceeds the symbolic, or human representational schemas, something that transcends the history of human strife. It provides human beings with a symbol of the sacredness of all creatures, an icon of the transcendent that, occasionally at least, elevates and cleanses the profane, anthropocentric world. In other words, the novel figures the panda as the center of a contemporary version of animal worship.

This worship, however, is clearly compromised by condescending benevolence, the belief that "only man can save the giant panda."[45] This point becomes clear in the coda of *Panda Diaries*, where a poem titled "Animal Grammar" offers a list of common English idioms that use animals as metaphors for qualities considered to be subhuman. The panda is the only animal in "Animal Grammar" that is not part of everyday English idioms involving animals. It, instead, appears as part of "Panda-monium," a silly instance of wordplay. The absence of the word *panda* in common English expressions can be seen as a linguistic corollary of the exoticized, exalted place that the panda occupies in Western culture, but the idle wordplay reveals the ironic tension between the panda's semisacred status in the contemporary Western and world imagination and its easy slide into an object of ridicule. Kuo is suggesting here that the logic of contemporary forms of animal worship, as one sees in the rush to save and love giant pandas, is haunted by the irreversible loss of a premodern world where humans and animals worked in close proximity with each other as interdependent parties, if not equal partners. The social position that the panda occupies in our times is a far cry from the position accorded to the mythical bear in traditional tribal cultures. As Richard Tapper explains, the modern urban-industrial society is characterized by the marginalization of animals, which impinge on human lives only as pets or zoo animals or symbolically as animal toys and characters in children's literature.[46] This marginalization reflects the decreased reliance on animals in the relations of production prevalent in urban-industrial societies, which has led conceptually to the anthropocentric belief that humans should reign over animals and their environments.

More important, in *Panda Diaries*, the anthropocentric approach to animal rights and nature conservation is closely associated with the policies and political attitudes affecting ethno-racial minorities in the United States and China. As the Panda mailman is paired up with the disaffected Chinese intellectual Ge, one might read Panda as an animal counterpart of the figure of the Chinese dissident, be it Wei Jingsheng, Harry Wu, or the Dalai Lama, that is often embraced and championed in the West. We can thus project the doubleness—exalted and yet vulnerable—ascribed to pandas onto the Chinese dissidents. In the beginning of *Panda Diaries*, the Panda mailman visits Ge at his apartment and reminisces about his visit to the National Zoo in Washington, D.C. While many visitors were busy taking photos of the pandas inside the cage, they ignored Panda because he was "not where he was supposed to be."[47] The pandas, in other words, are turned into a media spectacle rather than integrated into the fabric of everyday American life. This situation can be read as an implicit critique of the kind of role that Chinese dissidents play in U.S. culture. Like the pandas in the cage, they are often staged in the U.S. media as adorable novelties, objects of paternalistic love and pity, or an endangered species in need of Western protection. The protective impulse they elicit, however, does not quite extend to the raced and ethnicized bodies outside the limits of the staged spectacles. Arguably, Kuo is making a point about the contradiction between the United States' claim to a liberal empire, a benign world power advocating for the rights of racial, ethnic, and other minorities at home and around the world, and the persistence of political and economic inequalities in the country. Kuo's critique, of course, is not confined to the United States. It also concerns itself with the state-centered approach toward the rights of minority and indigenous populations practiced in contemporary China.

Early on in *Panda Diaries*, we see a scene from the Cultural Revolution, when the twelve-year-old Ge is forced to live with the Oroqens after his parents are sent to a separate place for political reeducation. The scene shows that, during the Cultural Revolution, the Oroqens' habitat is irrevocably reduced by the government policy of assimilating them into an agricultural mode of production, coupled with the dwindling of reindeer herds as a result of environmental degradation.[48] At one point, the author intrudes upon the narrative and offers two conflicting accounts of the current population of the Oroqens. One version sets the number at five hundred, and the other, apparently culled from an official history prepared by the Communist government, offers the figure ten thousand and credits the government for great social process achieved among the Oroqens.[49] It is likely that Kuo invokes this official figure to suggest, aside from baseless exaggeration on the part of the government, the fact that a large number of Han Chinese have married Oroqens since the end of Mao's era to gain the preferential treatment benefits that come with minority status. The larger figure clearly serves to bolster the claim that Chinese multiculturalism preserves ethnic cultures, when in fact increased intermarriage has further dissipated the already endangered Oroqen culture.[50] Kuo's comment on the fate of the Oroqens complements his critique of the pattern of the "metaphorical twinning" of humans and animals in the nineteenth-century United States by showing how it is mirrored in post-1949 China.

In exploring the histories of different indigenous communities, Kuo is, of course, consciously turning them into metaphors for each other. Although he spends much energy in *Panda Diaries* analyzing how metaphors function to establish a hierarchy between different species and races, or at least reinforce the established power structure, Kuo also shows that a deliberate use of this conceptual tool can help us bring together disparate political and historical contexts, thus allowing us to break down artificial, ideologically determined boundaries, including the distinction between liberal democracies and authoritarian systems in this particular case. Kuo's accentuation of the deterritorializing power of metaphor recalls Jahan Ramazani's theorization of the figure. For Ramazani, metaphor can operate as a "rhetorical site of resemblance and 'double vision'," and a "linguistic and conceptual 'contact zone' and 'third space'."[51] It has been employed in the postcolonial poetry of Indian diasporic poet A. K. Ramanujan, for instance, as a way of "mediating postcoloniality," a condition that also pivots on displacement and movement.[52] Kuo, likewise, demonstrates that metaphor can be a powerful conceptual and rhetorical apparatus that oscillates between fixing and disrupting power relations. Throughout *Panda Diaries*, he presents as mutually metaphorical the different symptoms of modernity, including speciesism and racism, while at the same time projecting a Utopian vision of harnessing the violent force of metaphor for a comparative mode of cultural critique.

The Two Wests

Panda Diaries is emblematic of Kuo's literary projects in general, which often suggest a kind of imprecise congruence between the processes of national expansion and integration in the United States and China, both of which have involved a form of colonization. In one of his poems from the 1980s, "Andrew Jackson and the Red Guards," for example, Kuo compares the fanaticism of the Red Guards in China, whose "cucumber legs" are "churning up power / As far as Tibet," with Jacksonian democracy implicated ironically in the removal of Indians.[53] Kuo is not the only one drawing this parallel, but he approaches it differently from most others. The significance of Kuo's comparative vision can be illustrated more clearly when we place him alongside other cultural voices that engage in similar U.S.-China comparisons. Written largely in the early 1990s (though not published until more than a decade later), *Panda Diaries* foreshadowed the surge, since the turn of the twenty-first century, of academic writings in China that compare China's development of its western regions, home to many ethnic minorities, with the westward expansion of the United States.[54] In the early 2000s, the Chinese government launched the West China Development Program so as to close the developmental gap between the inland western provinces and the rest of China.[55] For many contemporary Chinese intellectuals, the history of U.S. expansion (1803–1898) from the purchase of Louisiana to the annexation of Hawai'i provides a mixed model for China's development of its own west. Despite the temporal gap between the opening of the American West and the ongoing project of West China Development, such academics find it useful to discuss what may or may not be transferable from the American experience. The comparisons between the "two wests," tend to cast the United States as a flawed but useful precedent that legitimizes China's own enterprise. Most of the scholars taking on this comparative project demonstrate an awareness of the implications of national expansion for the environments and the cultural integrity of ethnic minorities. However, they largely focus on what government policies and initiatives it might take to achieve the goal of environmental and cultural conservation in the process of developing China's west, making little effort to discover or advocate for minority perspectives on this issue. In contrast to Kuo's writings, the emerging intellectual discourse on the "two wests" largely refrains from questioning the imperialist logic of national expansion.

He Chansheng, a professor in the Department of Geography at the University of Michigan, has collaborated with Niu Shuwen and Cheng Shengkui, scholars based in China, on an article titled "Lessons from the Development of the American West for China's Campaign to Develop Its Western Region."[56] The article points out in particular the practice of abusing natural resources during America's westward movement, including the destruction of forests in the Five Lakes region, the erosion of topsoil as a result of excessive mining, and the extinction of animal species (passenger pigeons, bison, and seals, among others). They refer to the Dust Bowl phenomenon, which stemmed from this environmental deterioration and exacerbated the Great Depression, as a warning against irresponsible development in China.[57] Another article, penned by Shao Fen, professor of law at Yunnan University, echoes this view by pointing out that the U.S. government neglected environmental issues associated with the development of the West until the 1930s, when a series of environmental laws started to be instituted.[58]

Shao Fen also observes that, partially as a result of an awareness of historical precedents, like the U.S. example, the Chinese government started paying attention to environmental issues at the very beginning of the West China Development Project. The government integrated environmental protection into its basic policies in 1983 and ratified a number of international treaties on environmental protection, including the Declaration of the United Nations Conference on the Human Environment. A series of laws and regulations regarding natural resources and the environment were created during the 1980s as well. However, many years of irresponsible development in the west prior to the West China Development Project had already severely destroyed the region's ecosystem, leading to desertification and the loss of soil, and the new environmental policies were, for a long time, poorly implemented. It remains a serious question whether, despite the increased environmental awareness among the Chinese leadership, China can avoid the "destruction first, conservation afterwards" pitfall.[59] By being equally critical of the environmental record of both the United States and China, Shao is suggesting a point that has become a common understanding among many environmentalists, namely, that the two countries have a joint responsibility to conserve resources and improve the global environment. China should not use the historical model of the U.S. westward expansion as an excuse for pursuing a high rate of development at the expense of the environment, nor should the U.S. begrudge a commitment to joining global environmental efforts because developing countries like China and India are purportedly obdurate about their wasteful ways. Until recently, the two countries, the top two polluters in the world, had engaged in a kind of blame game over the environment. In a *New York Times* special column in August 2007, renowned China-hand Orville Schell described the situation as one in which, "while the U.S. [hid] behind China, China [hid] behind the U.S.," both "sitting the game out."[60]

Closely related to the problem of the environment is the issue of protecting the lifeworlds of indigenous groups and ethnic minorities. He Changsheng and his collaborators mention in their article the killing of Indians and the destruction of their culture as the cost of U.S. westward expansion.[61] Shao Fen uses the example of Native Americans to argue against dismissing and destroying the cultural heritage of ethnic minorities living in China's west. The minority population in western regions accounts for 87 percent of the country's entire minority population. Most of the minorities in these regions, as Shao points out, are *shiju*, which translates roughly as "indigenous" (in the sense that they had established their habitats there long before the Han presence).

Implicit in this argument is the centrality of the issue of ethnic minorities to China's development of its western region. Indeed, the Chinese government's policy toward its western frontiers has long been shaped by its concerns with national security and the unity of the Han Chinese and various ethnic groups on the frontiers. Changes in the Chinese government's policy toward Tibet during the Mao era, for example, reflected its considerations of how best to minimize the resistance of Tibet's religious and aristocratic elites to the central Communist government.[62] As Robert Bedeski points out, the urgency of developing western regions in the new millennium follows largely from the sense that regional equality will be crucial not only for keeping up a high level of economic growth in China, but also for maintaining the central government's authority over the many ethnic groups in the western regions in a post–cold war world where the United States has become the "dominant power" in Central Asia.[63]

While minority interests occupy a prominent position in the ongoing intellectual discussion around the western region development, this concern remains largely subordinated to national interests, which are often equated with those of the ethnic majority, the Han Chinese. In urging the Chinese state to assume a central role in conserving natural and cultural landscapes in western areas, some choose to emphasize the meaning that this project of conservation holds for the Han Chinese. Indeed, in a sleight of hand dictated by the logic of Chinese nationalism, Shao believes that protecting important cultural sites in the west is about "preserving the roots of the Han Chinese,"[64] who first originated amid ceaseless interactions among the various peoples of the region. In offering a list of these sites, Shao mentions the burial site of Emperor Qin (the first Han Chinese emperor) and the Potala Palace of Tibet in one breath.

The privileging of the national (Han) interest entails the more severe blind spot of disregarding the potential incongruities between state conservation policies and the material and cultural needs of minority peoples. This point is raised, for example, in an essay by Gu Jun and Wan Li, professor of history and researcher in ethnology, respectively, on the history of environmental and cultural conservation in the U.S. West as a model for comparable policies in China. Gu and Wan discuss in particular the idea of establishing U.S. national parks, traditionally credited to George Catlin's appeal for government-enforced measures to protect indigenous cultures and wildlife on the Plains. The two authors applaud the creation of the Yellowstone National Park in 1872, the establishment of National Park Service in 1916, and the appearance of many similar national parks between 1933 and World War II.[65] They neglect to point out, however, that Catlin's original proposal was actually not adopted by the planners of Yellowstone. The troubling legacy of Yellowstone is specifically addressed in the edited collection *Conservation through Cultural Survival.* Editor Stan Stevens points out that Catlin advocated the establishment of a park across a vast area of the Rocky Mountains "in effect to make most of the Great Plains a sanctuary where the scores of different Native American peoples could continue to live their traditional ways of life and the vast herds of buffalo, elk, and antelope could continue with their seasonal migration."[66] However, Native American tribes had been completely excluded from Yellowstone by the mid-1880s, due to the "government policies concerning the confinement of Native Americans on reservations" as well as to "national park policies."[67] Stevens identifies the "Yellowstone model" as one in which strict nature protection is the main goal, to the exclusion of indigenous settlement and land use, a model that was not questioned or revised until the second half of the twentieth-century.[68] Much international effort has been made to promote conservation policies that establish governments and indigenous communities as co-owners and co-managers of protected areas.[69] The nature reserves policies in China, especially the western regions, have been subjected to critical scrutiny for their impact on local minority communities. It has been noted that the Chinese government has since the 1990s introduced a set of initiatives in nature conservation that consciously emphasize the economic needs of minority communities with a historical presence in the conserved areas, thus departing from the Yellowstone model from the very beginning.[70] The Chinese model, however, remains quite limited. The ecological values and knowledge of the indigenous and ethnic communities in western China have hardly been incorporated into the government's approaches to conservation and development.[71] While the government recognizes the economic needs and historical rights of indigenous communities, making allowances for limited use of agricultural and forest lands within protected areas, the local villagers are almost never involved in the management of these areas.[72] Intellectual discussions on the relationship between conservation and minority interests that are currently taking place in China, as we can see, do not push the limits of government policies on conservation. They in fact tend to mirror these limits, by neglecting the importance of employing minority perspectives and experiences in conservation policy-making. Endorsing the Yellowstone legacy reflects a certain intellectual complacency that can preclude efforts to thoroughly critique and transform deeply flawed models of conservation and state-minority relations. This complacency, no doubt, results in a large part from the current intellectual climate in China, that is, the increased but still highly limited intellectual freedom available to Chinese intellectuals, but it also illustrates the unstable and ambiguous politics of cultural translation and cross-national comparisons.

The U.S.-China comparative discourse introduced here offers a hint at the ways in which China's intellectuals and policy-makers scour U.S. political and cultural history for what can provide rationale as well as momentum for China's modernization, even as the United States perceives China as increasingly relevant to its own economic and security priorities. Though Chinese scholars have also shown interest in borrowing from development programs in other nations, they seem to find the U.S. case particularly pertinent.[73] As we have seen, U.S. westward expansion figures in this comparative discourse as an instrument of legitimization, offering a largely effective model that the Chinese government can comfortably follow and improve on in pursuing its own development goals, without fundamentally reconsidering its approach to minority and environmental issues. Kuo's *Panda Diaries* engages in a similar comparison as the policy discussions studied above, but Kuo is far more critical of the histories of national expansion and integration in both countries. He is by no means sanguine that the state can preempt or correct the problems that this process entails for minority and indigenous populations. Instead of relying on the government to assume the responsibility to preserve local cultures and natural ecosystems, he presents the process of state-sponsored economic development and national expansion as an inevitable threat to both. *Panda Diaries*, as we have seen, offers a comparative critique of development projects that entail the elimination of certain species, habitats, and races from a modernized national space. In particular, Kuo's critique of the Chinese state's treatment of the Oroqens, though situated in the earlier moment of the Cultural Revolution, provides a useful rebuttal to the view that state control can eliminate the negative implications of China's current effort to develop minority areas in the west. Extrapolating from Kuo's portrayal of the government's policy toward the Oroqens both during the Cultural Revolution and in more recent years, we can argue that this misguided view is not too far from U.S. exceptionalism, which celebrates the westward expansion as a Puritan errand into wilderness that, as Amy Kaplan puts it, proved "antithetical to the historical experience of imperialism," rather than an encroachment on the world of indigenous peoples.[74]

Kuo's Land Bridge

To sum up, *Panda Diaries* proceeds metaphorically, even as it invokes various instances of the "metaphorical twinning" of animals and humans on both sides of the Pacific. The history of Native Americans and that of minority nationalities in China figure as metaphors for each other, both of which are also linked, metaphorically, to other kinds of political and cultural injustices on both sides of the Pacific. The continuous proliferation and layering of metaphors, a pattern that one might describe as a kind of metaphorical diffusion, suggests that Native Americans do not exactly constitute a U.S. equivalent of the Oroqens in China or exist in a dyad with the latter, just as animals and humans do not constitute a closed circuit even though they can be productively compared. By allowing his metaphors to be destabilized by other metaphors, Kuo demonstrates the usefulness of metaphorical logic for revealing obscured connections between different histories while curbing its power to conceptually fix the world into symmetries. He uses comparisons as a basis for a simultaneous critique of the two nations without erasing their differences. Moreover, Kuo's comparative critique sets itself apart from a powerful intellectual discourse in contemporary China that juxtaposes U.S. westward expansion and China's development of its own west in a way that justifies both.

Panda Diaries has few peers in literary or critical discourses. About the only similar project we can find is a recent critical essay by Steven J. Venturino titled "Signifying on China: African-American Literary Theory and Tibetan Discourse." Venturino argues that African American literary theory, especially Henry Louis Gates's theory of signification, offers a viable framework for discussing narrative tactics in Tibetan literature produced both within and outside China, which has to contend not only with the "multicultural power politics of the contemporary Chinese nation-state" that conceals Han domination, but with "censorship, punishment, or academic reprisal" as well.[75] Just as Venturino compares Tibetan literature with contemporary African American literature to find shared or related patterns of subversion, Kuo emphasizes the parallels between the Oroqens and the Plains Indians as a way of studying the relationship between indigenous rights and the construction of national frontiers in both the United States and China. Both investigate, to use Venturino's words, "the interrelated discursive and political aspects" of the dynamics between state power and minority rights.[76] *Panda Diaries*, therefore, can be seen as a conceptual counterpart of the land bridge that the mythical Oroqen tribe in the novel is said to have crossed. It may well become one of the first passages between Chinese and U.S. indigenous studies.

Notes

Thanks to Rachel Adams, Russ Posnock, Brandon Reuben, Bruce Robbins, Donna Richardson, and the reviewers for insightful and encouraging feedback.

1. Alex Kuo, *Panda Diaries* (Indianapolis: University of Indianapolis Press, 2006), 19.
2. Andrew Jacobs, "Migrants in China's West Bask in Prosperity," *New York Times*, August 6, 2009. The Han Chinese are the ethnic majority in China.
3. S. James Anaya, *Indigenous People in International Law* (New York: Oxford University Press, 2004), 3.
4. Will Kymlicka, *Politics in the Vernacular: Nationalism, Multiculturalism, and Citizenship* (New York: Oxford University Press 2001), 122. In Kymlicka, this is a rule-of-thumb distinction between indigenous populations and stateless nations, both of which can fall under the category of national minorities. For more details, see chapter 6 in Kymlicka.
5. For surveys of the history of the PRC's policy toward minority nationalities and its prehistory in imperial and Republican China, see Colin Mackerras, *China's Minorities: Integration and Modernization in the Twentieth Century* (New York: Oxford University Press, 1994); June T. Dreyer, *China's Forty Millions: Minority Nationalities and National Integration in the People's Republic of China* (Cambridge, Mass.: Harvard University Press, 1976).
6. Mackerras, *China's Minorities*, 21, 2.
7. Other examples include the Ewenki and the Hezhe, also living in northeast China.
8. Arif Dirlik, "Globalization, Indigenism, and the Politics of Place," *Ariel* 34.1 (2003): 16.
9. Ibid., 20.
10. Ibid.
11. Ibid., 19.
12. Shari Huhndorf, "Literature and Politics of Native American Studies," *PMLA* 20.5 (October 2005): 1624, 1625. The concept of "nationalism" is still extremely valuable to Native studies, but, as some critics have argued, it should be understood not as a separatist politics, but as a commitment to "the explication of specific Native values, readings, and knowledges, and their relevance to our contemporary lives." See Jace Weaver, Craig S. Womack, and Robert Warrior, *American Indian Literary Nationalism* (Albuquerque: University of New Mexico Press, 2006), 6.
13. For discussions of the normalization of indigenous rights, see Kymlicka and Anaya. For comparative indigenous studies, see Stan Stevens, ed., *Conservation through Cultural Survival: Indigenous Peoples and Protected Areas* (Washington, D.C.: Island Press, 1997); George J. Sefa Dei, Budd L. Hall, and Dorothy Goldin Rosenberg, *Indigenous Knowledges in Global Contexts: Multiple Readings of Our World* (Toronto: University of Toronto Press, 2000); Roger Maaka and Chris Anderson, *Indigenous Experience: Global Perspectives* (Canadian Scholar Press, 2006).
14. U.S. multiculturalism can be considered to be a circumscribed version of liberal multiculturalism, which prescribes certain minority-specific rights without rejecting classical liberalism's tenet of the state's neutrality in ethnocultural affairs. Its history resides in civil rights legislation and popular mobilizations dating from at least the 1950s. Chinese multiculturalism consists of a system of regional autonomy for ethnic minorities, a severely limited version of the Soviet multinational federation, which in itself fell short of liberal definitions of a federation by concentrating all decision-making power in the center.
15. On the flip side, the two governments allied with each other on the "War on Terror" after 9/11, both tightening state control over ethnoreligious communities, especially Muslims.
16. David Alan Nibert, *Animal Rights/Human Rights: Entanglements of Oppression and Liberation* (Lanham, Md.: Rowman and Littlefield, 2002), xiii.
17. Alex Kuo, *This Fierce Geography: Poems*, 1st ed. (Boise, Idaho: Limberlost Press, 1999); *Changing the River* (Berkeley: I. Reed Books, 1986); *New Letters from Hiroshima and Other Poems* (Greenfield, N.Y.: Greenfield Review Press, 1974); *The Window Tree* (Peterborough, N.H.: Windy Row Press, 1971).
18. Alex Kuo, *Chinese Opera* (Hong Kong: Asia 2000 Ltd., 1998).
19. Interview with Alex Kuo, April 28, 2005. Alex Kuo, *Lipstick and Other Stories* (Hong Kong: Asia 2000 Ltd., 2001).
20. Alex Kuo, *White Jade and Other Stories* (La Grande, Oregon: Wordcraft of Oregon, 2008).
21. Frank Chin et al., *Aiiieeeee! An Anthology of Asian-American Writers* (Washington, D.C.: Howard University Press, 1974).
22. Frank Chin et al., *The Big Aiiieeeee! An Anthology of Chinese American and Japanese American Literature* (New York: Meridian, 1991).

23. Interview with Alex Kuo, April 28, 2005. Kuo also related that misunderstanding played a part in his exclusion as well. During the late 1960s, Kuo was writing for an anti–Vietnam War newspaper, so he took the pseudonym Spike Mulligan to protect his identity. Without understanding the context, Frank Chin saw Kuo's use of a white name as a form of racial betrayal.
24. See Guiyou Huang, ed., *Greenwood Encyclopedia of Asian American Literature* (Westport, Conn.: Greenwood Press, 2009); Zhang Tong, ed., *An Anthology of Chinese American Literature* (Nankai, China: Nankai University Press, 2004).
25. For the term *suspension,* see David Eng, *Racial Castration: Managing Masculinity in Asian America* (Durham, N.C.: Duke University Press, 2001), 211.
26. Gerald Vizenor, *Griever: American Monkey King in China* (Boulder: Fiction Collective; Normal: Illinois State University Press, 1987), 18.
27. Ibid., 30.
28. Ibid., 31, 2.
29. Ibid., 32.
30. Metaphor has been studied intensely in cognitive linguistic theory as a conceptual model constitutive of how humans think and speak. Elaborating on and refining the theory of conceptual metaphor that originated from Mark Johnson and George Lakoff, Zoltán Kövecses explains that metaphor consists in a kind of cognitive mapping that parallels abstract ideas with embodied experiences. See Zoltán Kövecses, *Metaphor in Culture: Universality and Variation* (Cambridge: Cambridge University Press, 2005), 199.
31. Kuo, *Panda Diaries,* 32.
32. Cary Wolfe, *Animal Rites: American Culture, the Discourse of Species, and Posthumanist Theory* (Chicago: University of Chicago Press, 2003), 43.
33. While the naturalists of the eighteenth century believed largely that a great gulf existed between humans and animals, nineteenth-century science was "drawn to the notion of human society constrained by natural laws" and saw "the origins of all human faculties in animal life." See Kenan Malik, *The Meaning of Race: Race, History, and Culture in Western Society* (Washington Square: New York University Press, 1996), 87. Despite this difference, both outlooks enabled the construction of a naturalized hierarchy of life that entails both speciesism and racism.
34. Kuo, *Panda Diaries,* 31.
35. Ibid., 31.
36. Nibert, *Animal Rights,* 36.
37. Kuo, *Panda Diaries,* 96.
38. David Rockwell, *Give Voice to Bear: North American Indian Myths, Rituals, and Images of the Bear* (Niwot, Colo.: Roberts Rinehart, 1991), 7.
39. Ibid., 19–23.
40. Lydia T. Black, "Bear in Human Imagination and in Ritual," *Ursus* 10 (1998): 344.
41. Ibid.
42. Joseph Epes Brown, *The Spiritual Legacy of the American Indian* (Wallingford, Pa.: Pendle Hill, 1964), 38.
43. Anthropocentrism and speciesism do not mean the same thing but are rather two sides of the same coin. Anthropocentrism assumes that animals are valuable only if they serve human interests, thus indirectly denigrating animals, while speciesism denotes negative attitudes toward animals based on their membership in a biological species other than *homo sapiens.*
44. Kuo, *Panda Diaries,* 2.
45. Ibid., 35.
46. Richard Tapper, "Animality, Humanity, Morality, Society," in *What Is an Animal?* ed. T. Ingold (London: Unwin Hyman, 1988), 56–57.
47. Kuo, *Panda Diaries,* 25.
48. English-language sources on the history of the Oroqens are few and far between, and most of them focus on the grammar of the disappearing Oroqen language. However, see Lindsay Whaley, "The Growing Shadow of the Oroqen Language and Culture," *Cultural Survival Quarterly* 25.2 (Summer 2001).
49. Kuo, *Panda Diaries,* 69–70.
50. Wayley discusses the issue of Han-Oroqen intermarriage in his article, explaining that, in the post-Mao era, the government offered the Oroqens "special dispensations," including exempting them from the "one child policy," thus providing a strong incentive for intermarriage.

51. Jahan Ramazani, *The Hybrid Muse: Postcolonial Poetry in English* (Chicago: University of Chicago Press, 2001), 72.
52. Ibid., 78.
53. Kuo, *Changing the River*, 31.
54. Between 2000 and 2009, at least seven or eight book-length studies were published on specific aspects of the history of the U.S. westward expansion, with an eye on providing useful lessons for China's development of its own west. Hundreds of journal articles and academic theses, as well as a number of international conferences, were devoted to comparative studies of the two processes.
55. Ding Lu and William V. W. Neilson, eds., *China's West Region Development: Domestic Strategies and Global Implications* (Singapore: World Scientific Publishing, 2004), 1–24.
56. He Chansheng, Niu Shuwen, and Cheng Shenkui, "Meiguo xibu fazhan dui zhongguo xibu dakaifa de qishi" ["Lessons from Development of the U.S. West to China's West Development Program"], *Ziyuan kexue*, 27.6 (2005): 188–93.
57. Ibid., 191.
58. Shao Fen, "Meiguo xibu kaifa lifa jiyi jingyan jiaoxun" ["Development of the West in the U.S. and Its Lessons"], *Faxuejia* 5 (2002): 119–24.
59. Ibid., 124.
60. Orville Schell, "Expert Roundtable," *New York Times*, Aug. 29, 2007, http://china.blogs.nytimes.com/2007/08/29/answers-from-orville-schell/ (accessed May 1, 2008).
61. He, Niu, and Cheng, "Meiguo xibo," 191.
62. Melvin C. Goldstein, "Tibet and China in the Twentieth Century," in Morris Rossabi, ed., *Governing China's Multiethnic Frontiers* (Seattle: University of Washington Press, 2004), 192–99.
63. Robert Bedeski, "Western China: Human Security and National Security," in Ding Lu and William W. Neilson, eds., *China's West Region Development* (Singapore: World Scientific Publishing, 2004), 43.
64. Shao, "Meiguo xibu," 124.
65. Gu Jun and Wan Li, "Meiguo wenhua ji ziran yichan baohu de lishi yu jingyan" ["History of the Protection of Cultural and Natural Heritage"], *Xibei minzu yanjiu* 3 (2005): 168.
66. Stan Stevens, *Conservation through Cultural Survival: Indigenous Peoples Are Protected Areas* (Washington, D.C.: Island Press, 1997), 29, 30.
67. Ibid., 29.
68. Ibid., 28–32.
69. See Sanjay K. Nepal, "Involving Indigenous Peoples in Protected Area Management: Comparative Perspectives from Nepal, Thailand, and China," *Environmental Management* 30.6 (December 2002): 749–51. Also see the various case studies from both developed and developing countries around the world in Stevens, *Conservation.*
70. See Clem Tisdell and Zhu Xiang, "Reconciling Economic Development, Nature Conservation, and Local Communities: Strategies for Biodiversity Conservation in Xishuangbanna, China," *The Environmentalist* 16.3 (September 1996): 203–11. Tisdell and Zhu point out that, as is the case with other developing countries, China's strategies for easing pressures on biodiversity conservation, which can be traced back to Agenda 21 in 1994, has placed a special focus on improving economic opportunities in the neighborhood of protected areas in a way that benefits local communities. Also see Trevor Sofield and F. M. S. Li, "Processes in Formulating an Ecotourism Policy for Nature Reserves in Yunnan Province, China," in *Ecotourism Policy and Planning*, ed. David A. Fennell and Ross K. Dowling, 141–68 (Cambridge, Mass.: CABI, 2003). They offer a study of the process of formulating an ecotourism strategy for five newly designated reserves in the Yunnan Province in China, and find that it involves much negotiation of the "Western paradigms of environmental conservation, wilderness, and sustainability, upon which ecotourism is based" (142). China's policy toward minority nationalities is cited as an important factor in the government's insistence that the ecotourism policy must benefit first and foremost the minority communities that inhabited the areas within the reserves in the past.
71. See Xu et al., "Integrating Sacred Knowledge for Conservation: Cultures and Landscapes in Southwest China," *Ecology and Society* 10.2 (2005): 7, http://www.ecologyandsociety.org/vol10/iss2/art7/ (accessed August 2, 2009). Using the southwestern province of Yunnan as an example, the authors call for a drive toward "pluralism" in conservation (under "Indigenous Knowledge and Pluralism in Conservation"). They acknowledge the efforts on the part of the various levels of government to heed customary

wisdom, as in the case of moving away from the push to sedentary livestock management, but note that there needs to be more extensive interaction between indigenous specialists and environmental scientists, as well as between indigenous communities and local governments.

72. See Nepal, "Involving Indigenous Peoples," 759.
73. See Gao Guoli, "Guowai qianfada diqu duiyu woguo xibu dakaifa de jidian qishi" ["Lessons from Underdeveloped Areas in Other Countries"], *Jingji yanjiu cankao*, 34 (2000): 32–36. His article cites the development of Hokkaido in Japan and southern Italy, along with that of the American West, as historical precedents that China can learn from.
74. Amy Kaplan, "'Left alone with America': The Absence of Empire in the Study of American Culture," In *Cultures of United States Imperialism*, ed. Amy Kaplan and Donald Pease (Durham, N.C.: Duke University Press, 1993), 4.
75. Steven J. Venturino, "Signifying on China: African-American Literary Theory and Tibetan Discourse," in *Sinographies: Writing China*, ed. Haun Saussy, Eric Hayot, and Steven G. Yao, 280–89 (Minneapolis: University of Minnesota Press, 2008).
76. Ibid., 272.

"Sowing Death in Our Women's Wombs": Modernization and Indigenous Nationalism in the 1960s Peace Corps and Jorge Sanjinés' *Yawar Mallku*

Molly Geidel

In late 1968, director Jorge Sanjinés and the Ukamau film collective traveled to the Quechua community of Kaata, Bolivia, a village accessible only on foot, with the script for their second feature film, *Yawar Mallku* (*Blood of the Condor*). The community leader, Marcelino Yanahuaya, had met them at a screening of their first movie and encouraged them to film in his village, but upon their arrival in Kaata, the Bolivian mestizo filmmakers encountered hostility and suspicion. They offered the villagers high wages and free medical care, but nobody showed up for the filming, and Yanahuaya, though he seemed sympathetic, did not explain the community's absence. After a few frustrating days, the filmmakers discovered that an official from a neighboring town was spreading rumors that they were dangerous communists out to rob and kill the townspeople. Sanjinés recalls that "the initial apathy had turned into open hostility, especially on the part of the women, who were more taken in by the official's self-serving intrigues." The film crew persuaded the Quechua priest, the *yatiri*, to perform a ceremonial reading of the coca leaves to determine their fate. As Sanjinés later recalls, the reading helped the crew understand the differences between their worldview and that of their subjects and to develop relationships that would profoundly influence their filmmaking style:

> Basically, what had happened was that we had judged the community by the same standards we would have used to analyze people and groups within bourgeois society. We had thought that by mobilizing one man who was powerful and influential, we could mobilize the rest of the group, whom we assumed to be vertically dependent on their leader. We had not understood, until that moment, that the indigenous people gave priority to collective over individual interests. We had failed to understand that for them, as for their ancestors, what was not good for all of them could not be good for a single one. That night, after six hours of enormous tension . . . the *yatiri* examined the coca leaves and declared emphatically that our presence was inspired by good, not evil. Our group was accepted and we soon felt the

> old barriers to communication disappearing in embraces and genuine signs of cordiality . . . In light of this and other experiences, we began to question all the films we had made and were planning to make. We began to understand the ways in which our cinematic style was and is impregnated by the concepts of life and reality inherent to our own social class. . . Some time later, when we were discussing how to create a vital and authentic revolutionary cinema, free of fictions and melodramatic characters, with the people as the protagonists in acts of creative participation, so that we might achieve films that would be passed from town to town, we decided that there in Kaata, at that unique moment, we should have thrown away the prepared script and shot a movie about that experience instead.[1]

Despite Sanjinés' regret at having retained bourgeois cinema conventions, *Yawar Mallku* is a movie of "that experience," a story of the alienated modern subject's reabsorption into a revolutionary indigenous community. Intercutting flashbacks of a rural anticolonial detective story with the tale of a desperate quest for life-saving medical care in the urban narrative present, the film depicts Western modernity as relentlessly violent and alienating, arguing that the modernization of its Quechua subjects will lead to their annihilation.

A key text of Latin American radical cinema, *Yawar Mallku* enacts a devastating indictment of foreign and domestic modernizing forces but fails to break completely with the discourse of development, particularly in the gender politics it espouses. Even as it condemns modernization, the film reiterates modernization theory's imperative to transform populations from feminized passive indigeneity to masculine nationalist subjecthood. The film's "impregnation" by the gendered ideologies of modernization and modernity is evident in its portrayal of Quechua women, who, like those in Kaata whom Sanjinés asserts were "more taken in" by self-serving officials, represent the tradition and passivity that revolutionary indigenous nationalists must reject.

By dramatizing the struggle between U.S. modernizing forces and indigenous nationalism as a contest for control over indigenous women's bodies, *Yawar Mallku* demonstrates the centrality of gender and sexual politics to both modernization discourses and anti-imperialist cultural nationalist ideologies. Based on indigenous women's claims that they were forcibly sterilized by the Peace Corps, the film depicts an inept yet powerful group of Americans called the Progress Corps, who, aided by local officials, sterilize unwitting Quechua women. The film, completed in 1969, was eventually seen by more Bolivians than any film before, domestic or foreign. In 1971, faced with evidence of Peace Corps participation in mass IUD-insertion projects in indigenous communities and pressured by an increasingly radical anti-imperialist movement, General Juan José Torres's short-lived leftist government expelled the Peace Corps.

Yawar Mallku articulates the militant anti-imperialism and incipient indigenous nationalism that swept Bolivia in the late 1960s and coalesced in anti–Peace Corps sentiment. James Siekmeier has argued persuasively that the Bolivian government used the Peace Corps as a "sacrificial llama," expelling the volunteers to appease the Bolivian left and indigenous communities without substantively renegotiating its relationship with the United States.[2] My essay takes up the question of why these groups targeted the Peace Corps in the first place, arguing that Bolivian leftist and indigenous communities responded explicitly to the agency's symbolic power as the embodiment of the heroic development ideologies that shaped and justified both Bolivian domestic policy and U.S. intervention there. The article outlines the liberal-developmentalist ideologies that explicitly guided both the Peace Corps and the Revolutionary Nationalist Movement (MNR) government of Bolivia; explores the relationship of the Peace Corps and the Alliance for Progress to the Bolivian radical and indigenous movements of the late 1960s; reads Sanjinés's 1969 film in the context of those movements to arrive at an understanding of how cultural nationalism in Bolivia became directed toward development discourse's ideal of a masculine utopia whose construction would entail controlling women's bodies; and finally, attempts to understand how indigenous Bolivian women have articulated radical political visions within and in response to these discourses.

In my attempt to explain the gendered and sexualized character of U.S. imperialism, modernization theories, and cultural nationalism in the 1960s, I draw on Michel Foucault's theories of sexuality and empire, particularly as elaborated by Ann Laura Stoler, who teases out Foucault's insights about race and colonialism to argue that discourses of nation and nationalism have always been articulated through discourses of race and sexuality.[3] Of course, Foucauldian analysis of U.S. imperial projects and "the link between nationalism and desire" is not new to American studies. Gail Bederman, Shelley Streeby, Amy Kaplan, and Laura Wexler have documented nineteenth-century epistemic shifts that produced new kinds of state and imperial power through and alongside new kinds of gendered, raced, and sexualized bodies.[4] While these scholars have helped establish an important framework for understanding hegemonic discourses of body, race, nation, and empire in the nineteenth century, American studies scholars have been less interested in taking up Foucauldian frameworks to understand twentieth-century epistemic shifts, particularly as they connect to U.S. imperialism. Jasbir Puar has recently written of post-9/11 discourses "that lasso sexuality in the deployment of U.S. nationalism, patriotism, and, increasingly, empire," but her sense that that lassoing was less frequent in earlier moments points to the paucity of works that connect twentieth-century U.S. empire to the production and regulation of sexuality.[5]

Building on María Josefina Saldaña-Portillo's brilliant work, I argue that American studies can serve as an important site for considering an earlier moment of lassoing, namely, the epistemic shift of the postwar era—the rise to hegemony of cold war developmentalist discourses of nationhood, bodies, race, gender, and sexuality—that bolstered and accompanied the United States' rise to superpower status and shaped the revolutionary and anticolonial movements that attempted to oppose U.S. power. In *The Revolutionary Imagination in the Americas and the Age of Development* Saldaña-Portillo elaborates Arturo Escobar's Foucauldian understanding of postwar development discourse to explore the gendered dimensions of both the 1960s and '70s modernization regime and the revolutionary nationalist movements that arose to challenge it, arguing that those revolutionary movements assimilated modernization theory's key principles of individual transformation to modernity and fully realized masculinity.[6]

While conceding that anticolonial and indigenous nationalism have often adopted the patriarchal and violent tendencies of their oppressors, Andrea Smith argues for indigenous nationalist movements as the only solution to the problem of sexual violence in indigenous communities. In her history of sexual violence against Native Americans, *Conquest*, Smith argues that all kinds of violence, including the appropriation by non-native people of native spirituality, constitute sexual violence against a community, contending "if sexual violence is not simply a tool of patriarchy but also a tool of colonialism and racism, then entire communities of color are the victims of sexual violence."[7] Because this violence is rooted in totalizing culture based on conquest and rape, Smith argues that a nationalist vision is the most appropriate feminist response to sexual violence against native women and communities:

> Native women activists have begun articulating spiritually based visions of nation and sovereignty that are separate from nation-states. Whereas nation-states are governed through domination and coercion, indigenous sovereignty and nationhood are predicated on interrelatedness and responsibility. In opposition to nation-states, which are based on control over territory, these visions of indigenous nationhood are based on care and responsibility for land that all can share. These models of sovereignty are not based on a narrow definition of nation that would entail a closely bounded community and ethnic cleansing. So, these articulations pose an alternative to theories that assume that the endpoint to a national struggle is a nation-state and that assume the givenness of the nation-state system.[8]

As Smith suggests in *Conquest,* understanding movements' attempts to realize these visions "predicated on interrelatedness and responsibility" might help those of us within the United States to articulate alternative nationalisms. Under the leadership of Evo Morales, Bolivia is currently pursuing a "spiritually based" nationalist agenda whose stated priorities are "pluricultural" values and an ethic of care and responsibility for land. Morales and his Movimiento a Socialismo (MAS) political philosophy grew out of the Katarista movement of the 1970s and '80s, an anti-imperialist cultural nationalism that *Yawar Mallku* both prefigured and helped to incite. Examining *Yawar Mallku* as an artistic and revolutionary response to the Peace Corps' population control efforts that understood sexual violence much in the way Smith suggests indigenous communities should, alongside Bolivian women's elaborations and critiques of this nationalist vision, may provide important clues as to the nature and limitations of communitarian nationalist visions more generally.

Modernity, Masculinity, Rape: Producing Developmentalist Desires

In the era of decolonization, the development work of agencies like the Peace Corps helped obscure the contradiction between the United States' tradition of anticolonial rhetoric and its drive to secure global hegemony. To win the allegiance of newly independent nations and curb the threat they posed to cold war capitalism, U.S. intellectuals and policymakers formulated and deployed modernization theory, a discursive regime that provided both a rationale and a strategy for broad anticommunist action in the third world. Formulated and propagated by the postwar liberal intellectuals who congregated at Cambridge universities and around John F. Kennedy, modernization theory began to congeal as a framework for U.S. cold war policy in the immediate postwar years, with its definitive works appearing in the late 1950s and early 1960s. Directed at Latin America as well as decolonizing African and Asian nations, modernization theory elaborated and instantiated Enlightenment discourses of rational progress, drawing on U.S. and European history to sketch a universal trajectory of national economic growth and integration into the world economy while prescribing military and economic intervention by wealthy countries in order to assure the third world's adherence to that trajectory. As many critics would later point out, modernization theorists contradictorily framed development as both inexorable and requiring aggressive intervention by "developed" nations.

The aggressive intervention modernization theory prescribed took the form of yet another contradiction. Development required a nation to massively disrupt its economic system while placing equal value on preserving basic socioeconomic hierarchies. To accomplish economic upheaval while maintaining social stability, modernization discourses required a certain level of consent, and even desire, from the workers they would incorporate into the system. Theorists attempted to create this desire for economic upheaval and class-structure stability by emphasizing the necessity and appeal of *individual* transformation to modernity: before a nation would be able to integrate fully into the global economy, its indigenous rural population would have to undergo a spiritual shift, transforming from passive, tradition-and-community-bound villagers into rootless, individuated laborers.

In his modernization classic *Stages of Economic Growth: A Non-Communist Manifesto*, self-described "economist-biologist" and Kennedy advisor Walt Whitman Rostow outlined the transformation that modernity required, arguing that "in rural as in urban areas—the horizon of expectations must lift, and men must become prepared for a life of change and specialized function."[9] Rostow, who wielded tremendous influence in the early days of the New Frontier—he coined the term "New Frontier" and persuaded Kennedy to term the 1960s "the development decade"—and again during Johnson's escalation of the Vietnam War, formulated his theory of universal "stages" of history in an attempt to do battle intellectually with Marx.[10] Inverting Marx's prediction that the globalization of industrial capitalism would create the conditions for widespread worker revolution, Rostow argued that all underdeveloped societies would undergo a "take-off period" in which they were especially vulnerable to the "disease of communism" and that intervention from developed nations was necessary to accelerate this take-off period.

Equating the uprooting and alienation of entire populations with freedom presented a challenge in the 1960s, when socialism and regional economic integration seemed like viable paths for third-world nations, and many of those nations suffered the violent consequences of refusing to accept the vision of modernity the United States offered. But military intervention was not the only tactic by which modernization was implemented; equally important was the powerful vision the United States offered of both itself and of third-world populations. Modernization doctrines and projects appealed to third-world leaders by equating integration into the global economy with freedom, masculinity, and brotherhood; underdevelopment with passive femininity; and modernization with seduction and (or as) rape. Characterizing populations outside of the capitalist order as deviantly gendered and equating the threat of communism with the threats of homosexuality and excessive female power, theorists promised to initiate third-world men into an exclusive, correctly masculine brotherhood.

In *Stages*, Rostow elaborates this violently eroticized logic of modernity, explicitly framing phallic/imperial and state penetration as a necessary step toward capitalist integration. As Saldaña-Portillo observes, Rostow's justification for U.S. intervention figures imperialism as eroticized homosexual rape and underdevelopment as aggrieved masculinity:

> As a matter of historical fact a reactive nationalism—reacting against intrusion from more advanced nations—has been a most important and powerful motive force in the transition from traditional to modern societies, at least as important as the profit motive. Men holding effective authority or influence have been willing to uproot traditional societies not, primarily, to make more money but because the traditional society failed—or threatened to fail—to protect them from humiliation by foreigners.[11]

This passage is remarkable in the degree to which Rostow consciously invokes the threat of rape and sexual humilation in the service of state power. By mobilizing the discourse of invasion-as-rape/humiliation (and, therefore, national sovereignty as intact masculinity), Rostow attempts to produce a "reactive nationalism" in which "men holding effective authority" would avoid this humiliation by following the implicit modernizing course prescribed for them by foreign would-be invaders, violently uprooting "traditional societies" in order to retain their own manhood and nationhood.

Founding Peace Corps director Sargent Shriver's 1964 book of essays, *Point of the Lance*, adopts Rostow's violently homoerotic (yet insistently homophobic) modernizing discourse to explain the agency's mission. In a section of the book devoted to "our unfinished revolution," Shriver argues that "the American Revolution, now in strange forms and shapes and going by other names, is rolling along among the world's people" and that the Peace Corps can "recapture that leadership and assure that the basic ideas of our revolution are neither misunderstood nor misused."[12] Offering the Peace Corps as a remedy for decolonizing nations' misappropriation of revolutionary desire to foment class struggle, Shriver claims to have borrowed his title metaphor from "revolutionary-minded Bolivian official" Alfonso Gumucio Reyes. Shriver's choice to appropriate and elaborate the metaphor of the lance to explain Peace Corps ideology and policy suggests that the agency made use of the gendered strategies of modernization theory, attempting to harness and redirect revolutionary impulses by framing national self-determination as an intermediate step in the journey to modernity and masculinity.

Punta de lanza translates simply as *vanguard* or *forefront*, and Gumucio seems to have used the phrase this way in the conversation Shriver cites directly after returning from Bolivia in 1961.[13] By the time of book's publication, however, Shriver had embellished Gumucio's figure considerably, attributing to the Bolivian official the Rostovian logic of eroticized homosexual rape as rite of passage on the road to development:

> [Gumucio] saw the Peace Corps as the human, cutting edge of the *Alianza para el Progreso*, as the sharpest thrust of the United States policy of supporting democratic change in Latin America. Our Volunteers, he said, are penetrating through all the barriers of protocol, bureaucracy, language, culture, and national frontiers to the people themselves. "They are reaching the minds and hearts of the people." The point of the lance is lean, hard, focused. It reaches its target . . . Since "there is no alternative to peace," this is the most effective power we have.[14]

Imagining "traditional" communities as impediments to progress, Shriver's scenario characterizes the penetration and destruction of those communities as the only path to both modern democracy and transnational affective ties. His attribution to Gumucio of the idea that the Peace Corps must eviscerate everything around the people it serves—including "language, culture, and nation"—in order for development to occur, suggests the extent to which Shriver and the Peace Corps were invested in creating desires for violent modernization in third-world elite men.

Bolivia: Revolution, Assimilation, Intervention

Modernization in Bolivia, as in much of the world, helped contain and redirect indigenous calls for self-determination toward a narrative of nationalism and assimilation. In the 1940s, an organized, radical indigenous movement challenged the established neo-feudal order, producing a series of decrees abolishing slave labor and regulating the landowner-tenant farmer relationship. In her groundbreaking history of Bolivian indigenous resistance, sociologist Silvia Rivera Cusicanqui explains that after the conference, indigenous communities met with extremely violent state repression but formed alliances in prison and elsewhere with striking miners, urban students, and dissidents, building the coalition that would support the Movimiento Nacional Revolucionario (MNR) government in its 1952 revolution.[15]

After seizing power in 1952, the MNR attempted to implement a centrist platform that would grant indigenous laborers a degree of freedom while maintaining enough distance from domestic and foreign communists to receive development aid from the United States. Revolutionary leader Víctor Paz Estenssoro and his MNR government implemented limited land reforms to break up the largest feudal empires and nationalized the mines while negotiating mineral agreements with the United States, accepting direct investment from U.S. companies, and making clear to the United States that they were actively keeping Bolivia from falling into communist hands. In the first ten years of the revolutionary government, Bolivia's balancing act secured it more U.S. aid than any other Latin American country.[16] In his 1992 history of Bolivia, Herbert Klein explains that the United States and the International Monetary Fund (IMF) forced Bolivia to allow U.S. corporate encroachment and end food subsidies for miners, but argues that the modernization measures the aid and loans made possible "undoubtedly gave the government the equanimity to deal with the peasants that it might otherwise not have had if there was real starvation in the cities."[17]

The modernization measures Klein mentions targeted indigenous populations, attempting to bring them out of the feudal order and bestow upon them nationalist, capitalist, and assimilationist identities. The MNR attempted to banish the word *Indio* from the Bolivian vocabulary, designating indigenous people *campesinos* instead. As Rivera explains, the MNR government attempted to convert the entire population into urbanized "gente decente" (mestizos), suppressing not only the indigenous radicalism that had driven the rebellions leading up to the 1952 revolution but all vestiges of indigenous culture.[18] The government communicated its vision through the Instituto Cinematográfico Boliviano, which from 1953 to 1968 sponsored director Jorge Ruiz's triumphalist development-themed films and mandated their showing in all Bolivian cinemas. In accordance with the films and coerced by the MNR's explicit decrees and modernization programs, indigenous Bolivians were pressured to eschew their cultural and communal identities in exchange for national citizenship and a chance to enter the extraction-based global capitalist order.[19]

The Kennedy administration attempted to implement an even more ambitious modernization platform in Latin America than had Eisenhower. The hundreds of millions of dollars of Alliance for Progress money that the United States poured into Bolivia in the 1960s went mostly to military and explicitly anticommunist projects. Not only did Kennedy make Bolivia's receipt of Alliance money dependent upon the jailing and expulsion of leftists and the suppression of striking workers, he also increased military aid to Bolivia by 800 percent, inaugurating a program called Civic Action that gave the Bolivian military new functions building roads and airstrips, conducting literacy campaigns, clearing land, and providing medical services.[20] Civic Action strengthened the military to the point that it seized power in a 1964 coup d'etat, and emboldened it to massacre at least eighty-seven miners during a June 1967 conference at which they had gathered to declare their support for Che Guevara.[21] When Bolivian forces killed Guevara that October, Rostow trumpeted the success of the military modernization strategy in a letter to Lyndon Johnson, writing that the revolutionary's capture and assassination "shows the soundness of our 'preventive medicine' assistance to countries facing incipient insurgency."[22]

The Peace Corps embodied and enacted the more seductive side of anticommunist modernization doctrines in Bolivia, attempting, following Rostow and Shriver's model of desire-production through penetration, to induce Bolivians to want to "help themselves" out of poverty. Volunteer-turned Peace Corps evaluator James Frits echoed modernization theory's attribution of poverty to culture and personality, arguing that in Bolivia "most people expect the government to do everything for them. They have almost no tradition of solving their own problems."[23] The Peace Corps' second director, former professional boxer Jack Vaughn, constructed indigenous Bolivians as similarly passive, but by 1966 could imagine a moment in which development initiatives had worked their magic. In a flowery recounting, Vaughn declares his love for "Latins" and celebrates the triumph of development work in subduing radical indigenous movements, describing indigenous Bolivians' transformation from petulance to hero worship:

> I've been a Latin Lover since 1938, and I've seen a lot of strange things. But I've never seen anything like what I saw in Bolivia a few days ago. I had been stationed in Bolivia a couple of times and left there last in mid-1958. The last six months I was in Bolivia with Warren Wiggins, I reached the point where I was reluctant to go up on the high plains near Lake Titicaca to hunt and fish because of the menacing hostile attitude of the Indians. They were all armed, they seemed resentful, didn't speak Spanish and didn't change. That was seven or eight years ago.
>
> I visited five villages in that very same area in 1965. In all five I was carried into town on the backs of the Indians who wanted to show me that they were in the human race. They had all built a new school, the first school in a thousand years. They all had a clinic for child deliveries, the first clinic in a thousand years. They all had potable water piped in, and they had done it themselves. They had made more physical progress in a couple of years than they had made in the previous thousand.[24]

Vaughn's story depicts the ideal endpoint of the modernization doctrines that the Peace Corps sought to embody. Modernization theory allows him to characterize the premodern indigenous Bolivians as simultaneously violent and stagnant, hostile and passive, prehistoric and inhuman. In order to demonstrate their entry into the human race, they carry Vaughn on their backs, their physical closeness to the boxer-turned-development-hero making palatable their new role as laborers in the global capitalist system. They also show Vaughn their "physical progress" in the form of "a clinic for child deliveries," their ability to regulate reproduction and women's bodies in their communities proving their modernity, masculinity, and humanity.

Bolivia volunteer Chad Bardone evinced similar anticipatory zeal about the inevitable destruction of native cultures, writing in a letter home that the lowland Indians he had just visited were "very poor, from a material standpoint, but very rich in their religious life." However, he injects a bit of melancholy into his premature account of their impending demise:

> They have a belief in a promised land of milk and honey that they will someday encounter. Each year a group of men are sent on an expedition to find the promised land. Because of this hope, these Indians have led a nomadic life for some years. They set up their villages, plant mandioca, sugar cane, bananas, corn, and rice. When the hunting and fishing become too scarce to sustain the village, they move on. In the years to come they will have more and more contact with the world. It will be sad for the older people who cannot accept a more modern world, but the young people will benefit. I'm just glad that I was able to spend a few days with them as they are now. An experience worth remembering.[25]

In his observations about the millenarian Guaraní community in which he spent only a few days, Bardone constructs a narrative of aggrieved masculinity whose only remedy is the forcible imposition of "a more modern world."[26] In recounting the men's futile search for the promised land, he reiterates the developmentalist argument that immersion in the "hopes" and "beliefs" of "traditional society"—in this case a society that sends them on fruitless quests—denies them the masculinity and national stability they can achieve only through the transition to modernity.

Bolivia Peace Corps director Gerold Baumann reiterated the violently gendered nature of the agency's mission in a 1970 article in *Community Development Journal.* In the article he touts the Peace Corps' community development work, using for his epigraph the proverb that "Bolivia is a beggar on a throne of gold." Baumann outlines the National Community Development Programme (NCDP), a Bolivian government program whose purpose "is the integration of the alienated *campesino* into the mainstream of the social and economic process of development." The NCDP employed more than four hundred "Village Level Workers," who were "selected from young men who speak the local language and live in rural areas and have at least a sixth grade education" and were trained in "a variety of basic skills" and "the theory and practice of the principles of community development." Baumann suggests that the Village Level Worker's task was also one of seduction, writing that "his is the job of stimulating, organizing, and teaching the people to discharge from within themselves and their community the powers for action." Boasting that Peace Corps volunteers had been "intimately involved" with the NCDP since 1964, Baumann explains that in Bolivia "the typical jealousies and mutual fears of an inbred peasant society exist abundantly" and thus "constant prodding is needed to get village tasks done." With this prodding, however, Baumann concludes that "this programme might yet get that beggar off his throne of gold and make him a truly free and economically viable man with dignity and pride in his own country."

In the above passage, Baumann echoes Rostow and Shriver's seduction/rape metaphors by characterizing the Peace Corps and their Village-Level counterparts as "constantly prodding" Bolivian villagers in order to "stimulate" them to "discharge" modern capitalist and nationalistic desires. But if the new "economically viable man" must rise from his "throne of gold" in order to reinvest the gold in capitalist and nationalist enterprises, the economically viable woman's role is more circumscribed. Baumann mentions that in addition to the (implicitly male) counterparts of Village-Level Workers, the Peace Corps deployed "home economics women who give courses in hygiene; cooking; sewing, child care." He is particularly excited about the twenty-two-couple "model *campesino*" program, writing that "model *campesino* couples are a unique attempt to provide much of the above in a compact package, i.e., sheep=agriculture through the male, home economics–homemaking-arts and crafts through the female . . . Some emulation has taken place in many areas all over Bolivia."[27] Baumann's focus on Bolivian "emulation" of *campesino* couple behavior suggests that the Peace Corps attempted to pressure Bolivian indigenous societies into adopting "modern" gender roles, making the men into nationalists and laborers in the global economy while constructing women as narrowly concerned with "home economics" and other properly domestic pursuits.

Yawar Mallku: Context, Film, and Aftermath

Baumann's enthusiasm about the Peace Corps' abilities to model and induce correct *campesino* behavior quickly dissipated the following year, when the Peace Corps was expelled from Bolivia. Volunteer Terry West recalls bitterly that "the Bolivian government expelled the Peace Corps in a display of nationalism. A few years earlier, the Bolivian left had made an anti–Peace Corps movie titled *Yawar Mallku*, which purported to show volunteers sterilizing peasant women.

This supposed crime was added to our list of sins."[28] While not itself evidence of sterilizations, West's designation of sterilization as a "supposed crime" suggests that he would not have been particularly alarmed if it had been taking place. His offhandedness reflects the conventional wisdom of the 1960s that third-world populations needed to be controlled, coercively if necessary, in order for nations to modernize. If third-world men could appear in modernization discourse as potential desiring capitalist subjects, women appeared mostly as bodies whose sexuality and fertility posed a threat to development by creating excessive poverty and backwardness.

Historian Matthew Connelly identifies the 1960s as the decade when a "new population establishment" rose to power and succeeded in forging a global consensus, at least among elite policymakers, that population control was an urgent and worthy goal. Influenced by modernization theory, the population establishment framed their project not in terms of women's rights but in terms of mass population regulation in the service of capitalist development.[29] Kennedy advisor Arthur Schlesinger Jr. took a trip to Bolivia in 1961, returning in early March to write the president a "memo on dilemmas of modernization in the hemisphere" whose first point was: "Because population has been growing faster than output in recent years, Latin America has begun to lose ground in the struggle for development."[30] Kennedy, previously ambivalent about publicly endorsing population control, was convinced, and on March 22 delivered a special message to Congress on foreign aid, in which he inaugurated the sixties as the "development decade" and warned that "the magnitude of the problems is staggering. In Latin America, for example, population growth is already threatening to outpace economic growth . . . and the problems are no less serious or demanding in other developing areas of the world."[31] Later the same year, Kennedy privately suggested to the Ford Foundation that it "concentrate all its resources on the population problem around the world."[32]

Like Schlesinger and Kennedy, Johnson understood the fight to stem global population as an integral part of the modernization project, as when he urged in a July 1965 speech: "Let us in all our lands—including this land—face forthrightly the multiplying problems of our multiplying populations and seek the answers to this most profound challenge to the future of the world. Let us act on the fact that less than five dollars invested in population control is worth a hundred dollars invested in economic growth."[33] The Peace Corps, too, explicitly linked population control to development. For example, a 1966 country evaluation of El Salvador argues that "overpopulation and unchecked population growth are the principal obstacles lying in the path of El Salvador's march to modernity . . . Among all health problems facing the

Salvadorean people, over-population and the high rate of population increase are of outstanding importance. Whenever the government is prepared to support a program of population control and/or family planning, Peace Corps El Salvador will offer assistance."[34]

Peace Corps population control policy in 1960s Bolivia was similar to its policy in El Salvador, and Peace Corps and Bolivian authorities alike endorsed population control measures.[35] In April 1966, volunteer Janet Pitts Brome wrote in her journal, "The mothers asked me how they could stop having babies. They said they were embarrassed to talk to a doctor about it. I'll see what can be done." In July of the same year, Brome wrote, "Tomorrow we have a meeting on birth control. The local *sanitario* will speak in Aymara. Next month Dr. Thompson from the hospital in La Paz comes to insert Lippes' Loops. Any woman who has been to one of these meetings WITH her husband is eligible." That December, Brome reported that "people are blaming women who got IUDs. One group of men wanted to get the local *sanitario* to get a list of the women with the loop so they could punish them," suggesting that perhaps the pre-*Yawar Mallku* horror at population control was directed primarily at indigenous women. But the project continued undeterred: in April, Brome reported that "the IUD program has been successful. Collana is the Lippes' loop capital of the altiplano."[36]

The story of the IUD illuminates the way modernization discourses shaped attempts to control the bodies of women in the third world. The plastic-molded IUD, introduced in 1958 at Mount Sinai Hospital, quickly became the method of choice for the population control movement in the 1960s. Throughout the early 1960s, studies of IUDs showed high rates of infection and bleeding, but USAID and private entities like the Ford Foundation continued to fund their mass implantation. Population experts like Guttmacher, while aware of these findings, made no recommendations as to follow-up examinations, arguing, "We dare not lose sight of our goal—to apply this method to large populations." At a population control conference in 1964, Guttmacher reassured drug companies that IUDs would not cut into the market for oral contraceptives:

> As I see it, the IUDs have special application to underdeveloped areas where two things are lacking: one, money and the other sustained motivation. No contraceptive could be cheaper, and also, once the damn thing is in the patient cannot change her mind. In fact, we can hope she will forget it's there and perhaps in several months wonder why she has not conceived.[37]

Guttmacher's assertion that third-world women lack sustained motivation denotes modernization theory's gender split: development workers must cultivate the passivity of "underdeveloped" women in order for the men in the population to become modern. Part of the nation's transition to modernity entails its eschewal of alleged matriarchy and the assertion by the male subject—perhaps in reaction to humiliation—of his dynamic capitalist character. Understood within this history, Brome's journal entries provide another clue as to how modernization discourses produced third-world and indigenous female desire: in her account, a few women's requests for birth control are transformed into desires for containment and control that their insufficiently masculine husbands are unable to fulfill, validating development workers' euphoric quest for suppression and competition over who can best regulate his or her unruly population.

The discovery of population control programs in Bolivia occurred in the increasingly militant political climate of the late 1960s. The radical Katarista movement, according to Rivera, developed in largely indigenous peasant *sindicatos* in the late 1960s, as they faced increasing state repression. Much as they had in the 1940s, students, artists, miners, and urban workers united with the peasants.[38] Katarismo reflected several historical horizons and ideological issues: "the assertion of Indian culture and history, the awareness of the new conditions of exploitation endured by the peasants, its powerlessness to influence State agricultural policies, its rejection of its decadent union organizations, and so forth."[39] Rivera argues that Katarismo "succeeded to a large extent in crystallizing demands for political self-determination by the popular movement, as well as its rejection of left-wing elites' usual methods of political action."[40] The movement's 1973 Tiwanaku manifesto responded to the assimilationist discourse and policies of the 1952 revolution while outlining its own independent development program:

> Bolivia is entering a new stage in its political life, one characteristic of which is the awakening of peasant awareness . . .
>
> We peasants want economic development, but it must spring from our own values. We do not want to give up our noble inherited integrity in favour of a pseudo development. We fear the false "developmentalism" imported from abroad because it is not genuine and does not respect the depth of our values. We want an end to state paternalism and we no longer wish to be considered second class citizens. We are foreigners in our own country.
>
> We do not suggest that this situation can be overcome by paternalist government intervention or by well meaning people . . .
>
> The peasantry has always been a passive force because that was always what was expected of them. The peasantry is what politicians have always wanted it to be: simply a support for their ambitions. The peasantry will be dynamic only when it is allowed to act as an autonomous and original force.[41]

While it affirms the importance of culture and the "depth of [indigenous] values," the Tiwanaku manifesto remains somewhat trapped in the rhetoric and trajectory of development and nationalism, rewriting Bolivia's long history of indigenous militancy to argue that "the peasantry has always been a passive force," "foreigners in [their] own country," whose awareness is finally "awakening." This confluence, which Saldaña-Portillo identifies as the "discursive collaboration between revolutionary and development discourses," appears in the works of Guevara and other revolutionaries. *Yawar Mallku,* like the texts Saldaña Portillo reads, tracks its indigenous subject as he moves from passivity to modernity and finally attains a revolutionary consciousness and returns to lead his people. The film dramatizes the particular bind this trajectory poses for indigenous women, primarily through the character of Paulina, a young Quechua woman whose subject position must be evacuated to make way for the male characters' development and reabsorption.[42]

The film begins as if it intends to tell Paulina's story, opening on a scene of domestic chaos and violence. Her husband, Ignacio, laments his childlessness and blames her, shouting, "My babies. Paulina, you are cursed, you lost them . . . I told you not to go there, not to trust . . . now I will die alone!" Paulina responds first meekly, "I'm not bad luck. It's not my fault"—then angrily, calling him a drunk. The next morning, her face visibly bruised, she silently accepts his apology and they go together to a sacred mountain to bury the dolls representing their children who have died. The film here attributes to Paulina both a spiritual and intellectual/emotional weakness (she is both intrinsically cursed and too trusting of the foreigners) but also positions itself as an exploration of the way imperialist and domestic violence reinforce one another, converging on the bodies of indigenous women. By starting the film with this scene and ending it with revolution, Sanjinés attempts to bring viewers to the conclusion that an indigenous nationalist vision is the most appropriate response to both imperialist and domestic violence.

Subsequent scenes retain their investment in Paulina's perspective. After the local police shoot Ignacio, the camera follows her as she rides into the city with his wounded body, tracking the urban landscape through her increasingly fearful, alienated perspective. But despite casting her as the early protagonist, the film soon makes clear that its most important story is not Paulina's. Sixto, Ignacio's assimilated brother to whom Paulina brings her wounded husband, articulates his (and the film's) stance toward women in his first scene, a scuffle depicted as a routine brush with racism. "Indian? Do you know me? Did you see me being born?" he asks his antagonist. "I'm not an Indian, Goddammit."[43]

Sixto not only rejects his indigenous blood here, signaling the internalized racism reinforced by the MNR's assimilationist modernization doctrines, but also figures it as carried and transmitted entirely by mothers. The film's portrayal of women as vessels for cultural preservation, carriers of indigenous identity and tradition, rather than subjects who can create knowledge or history, is equally evident when Paulina speaks: she tells her story not as an individual but in the collective voice, alternately speaking on behalf of her family and her whole community. "We had three children," she recalls. "We were happy. People liked us. My children were fine. They helped us, until an epidemic came. And they died. Time passed. Ignacio was chosen as head of the community. We all celebrated. Who would have suspected what would threaten us next?"

The threat appears first in flashback, when two of the volunteers accost Paulina on the path into town and demand to buy the eggs in the basket she is carrying to a community festival. Paulina offers to sell them a few, but the female volunteer demands all the eggs in the basket. The male volunteer repeatedly offers her "a good price," but Paulina refuses, repeating that they are for her community. The scene none too subtly allegorizes the secret task the volunteers perform inside their shining white health center, the forced sterilization of Bolivian women in the service of cultural eradication, modernization, and global capital. In a final attempt to get all the eggs "for the center" by interpellating Paulina into the modern order, the male volunteer hails her in slow Spanish—"You are Paulina. Paulina Yanahuaya"—offering her the opportunity to exchange her eggs for differentiated individual subjectivity. "You know us, right?" the volunteer continues. "Why don't you sell us your eggs? We want them for our center. Sell them to us, Paulina." This is the only choice Paulina makes in the film, and she refuses to give in to the logic of capitalist accumulation, steadfastly choosing her community over the "good price" the volunteers offer.

After the first few flashbacks, the film leaves Paulina's perspective behind and splits into its two principal narratives, interlacing Ignacio's earlier attempts to determine why the women in the community are not having children with the story of the narrative present, in which Sixto embarks on a search for blood to save his wounded brother. Because Sixto has rejected his own indigenous blood, the correctly indigenous Ignacio rejects it too, and of course the "cursed" Paulina is not a match either. Desperate and broke, Sixto embarks on a quest to beg for money or blood from whiter, wealthier friends and doctors. The flashback structure reiterates the trajectory of development in its move from the rural-communal past to an urban narrative present, mirroring and mocking the journey to modernization in its depictions of Ignacio's horror and Sixto's despair, which increase as each travels alone along the prescribed course from superstitious rural subjection to assimilated urban citizenship.

By allowing the narrative to slip away from Paulina, the film dramatizes the gendered personal transformation modernization discourse prescribes, the spiritual shift away from a feminized communal identity to a masculine subject position that must take place before a nation is able to insert itself fully into the global economy. The indigenous women's failure at ensuring cultural survival paves the way for this shift from indigenous passivity to masculine agency, providing both the central tragedy of the film and the impetus for the men's heroic drive to revolution. The *yatiri*'s prayers "that fertility makes our women blossom," go unanswered, because like the women of Kaata, the village women are "more taken in"—corralled, swindled, manhandled, folded into the "self-serving intrigues" of global capital. Although Paulina refuses to sell them "all the eggs," the foreigners obtain them anyway and transform her against her will. She ceases to function for the good of her community, so the men must take over as both modern revolutionaries and preservers of indigenous life; the women's failure allows them to both destroy the old nation and give birth to a new one.

The men's usurpation of the female subject position allows a utopian melding of modern and indigenous knowledge. Ignacio, though he has seen the sterilizations through the window of the health center, must confirm his suspicions with the community, just as Sanjinés knew the effects of his film crew's presence would be benign but submitted to the coca leaves anyway. In the film's climactic scene, the *yatiri*, surrounded by men, reads the coca leaves. "Mother Coca, give us the answer," he says, and the good mother speaks in Paulina's stead, confirming the truth of Ignacio's deductions when "the leaf of the foreigners shows up beside death." In both narratives, a lone male adventurer arrives at empirical conclusions and submits them to the collective will; all that remains is to expel the foreign elements and their contaminated local cells. The last scene begins when Sixto, in Quechua clothing, returns to lead his people, having given birth to himself as a newly revolutionary actor, no longer in need of a mother to tell him who he is. Ignacio's death has restored Sixto, transfusing him once again with indigenous blood. Paulina, a small and shadowy presence, begins alongside him but soon walks entirely out of the frame, leaving the close-up to Sixto and reiterating the numerous evacuations the film performs. The final frame shows guns raised in the air, imagining and inciting indigenous nationalist revolution.

Though it did not quite inspire a revolution, the film did spur violent revolts and garner attention throughout the hemisphere. Sanjinés writes that in Bolivia, "as an immediate result of the film's distribution, the North Americans suspended their mass distribution of contraceptives, recalled all the members of the organization who had been working in the three sterilization centers, and received several staff members' resignations. They never took the trouble to deny the accusations made against them by even such conservative publications as *Presencia.*"[44] Sanjinés' equation of the distribution of any birth control with genocidal population control programs makes sense, given the population establishment and the Peace Corps' rhetoric and policies that frame third-world contraception similarly. But the conflation obscures the specific acts of violence against indigenous women from which the film draws its symbolic power, foreclosing questions of what might be owed them by the state and the development establishment and what they might want to do with their bodies.

Postnationalist Indigenous Feminisms

There is one moment in the film in which Paulina's subjectivity unsettles the men's all-encompassing revolutionary desire. In a flashback, the *yatiri* reads Paulina's fortune in the coca leaves and tells her it "seems to come out right," despite "an impediment" to having more children. The fortune upsets Ignacio, but the *yatiri* and Paulina seem unfazed, if sympathetic. In making these seemingly contradictory predictions, the *yatiri* seems to imply that what "comes out right" for Paulina would not necessarily be coterminous with indigenous cultural nationalism, or at least any of the pronatalist versions that exist in her community. But the pronouncement perhaps more immediately alludes to the revolution just beyond the final frame, whose resulting utopian community will come out right for everyone in ways that, as Smith writes, we cannot quite imagine until they happen.

Militant women thinkers and activists in Bolivia, while often rejecting feminism as an imperialist project that can accommodate neither radical racial and class politics nor communitarian values, have preoccupied themselves with questions of how development and nationalism have been imbricated, and how things might still "come out right" for indigenous women.[45] In her 1978 memoir *Let me Speak!* radical indigenous organizer and leader of the Housewives Committee (a radical group of women in mining communities) Domitila Barrios de Chungara describes her frustration when, at the 1974

International Women's Day conference, U.S. and European women wanted to make prostitution and birth control central agenda items. "For us they were real problems, but not the main ones," she explains, before recounting both the population control rhetoric with which the elite women attempted to make their case and her own nationalist response. Chungara makes an argument focused on resources and land rather than race or rights:

> For example, when they spoke of birth control, they said that we shouldn't have so many children living in poverty, because we didn't even have enough to feed them. And they wanted to see birth control as something which would solve all the problems of humanity and malnutrition.
>
> But, in reality, birth control, as those women presented it, can't be applied in my country. There are so few Bolivians by now that if we limited birth even more, Bolivia would end up without people. And then the wealth of our country would remain as a gift for those who want to control us completely, no?
>
> All that could be different, because Bolivia's a country with lots of natural resources. But our government prefers to see things their way, to justify the low level of life of the Bolivian people and the very low wages it pays the workers. And that's why they resort to indiscriminate birth control.[46]

Recognizing the racism and elitism of population control discourse, Chungara counters dominant modernization arguments with similarly resource-centered and territory-based nationalist ones. However, as her use of the collective voice shows—"if we limited birth even more"—it remains the work of women to hand over their bodies to populate the country so that their children might live to extract and fight for its natural resources.

Chungara's nationalist redistributive politics have become more or less the politics of the Morales government, as it pursues what Escobar calls an "alternative modernization project."[47] Escobar contrasts this leftist statist project with the "post-liberal, postdevelopmentalist alternative to modernity" formulated by "intellectuals and activists working with organized peasant, indigenous, and poor urban communities,"[48] whose key elements are "first, territory, the defense of the territory as site of production and the place of culture; second, autonomy, that is, the right over a measure of autonomy and self-determination over the decisions that affect them, for instance, around the control and use of natural resources."[49] In her analysis of population control and leftist and communitarian responses, Aymara radical feminist Julieta Paredes reappropriates this language of autonomy:

> This ideology of control over women's wombs existed then and exists now, both in North America and Bolivia. White and indigenous men don't differ much in their ideas about

> women's bodies, particularly indigenous women's bodies: the gringos want to exterminate us, while the indigenous men want to make us breed without restriction. As a community of feminists we denounce this patriarchal logic that subordinates our bodies to masculine conceptions of the world and of life.
>
> Sadly, leftist women in the 1960s and '70s were also beholden to this patriarchal logic that constructed women as breeders. They made themselves complicit in leftist patriarchies. We want the right to decide, free and voluntary motherhood, decriminalization of abortion, and bodily autonomy within our communities.[50]

While Paredes brings to the forefront the danger for women, particularly indigenous ones, of both imperialist and nationalist ideologies, her vision of autonomy and choice seems somewhat compatible with a (neo)liberal feminist politic.[51] Escobar recognizes this compatibility, writing, "a key question for the states is whether they can maintain their redistributive and anti-neoliberal policies while opening up more decidedly to the autonomous views and demands of social movements." Noting the difficulty of discursive interventions like Paredes's in this "politics of difference," Escobar cautions that "the dangers of essentializing differences are real; these dangers are perhaps felt most acutely by feminists from, or working with, ethnic groups and movements."[52]

Rivera, whom Escobar identifies as a key figure in Bolivian post-statist politics, argues that one of the consequences of government and movement use of both nationalist and land-based rhetorics is that female indigenous domestic workers, who must migrate to cities, are excluded from their territorially focused vision of indigenous rights. She further argues that the lack of attention to these severely undercompensated migrant women makes possible "the postponement of the debate over paternal and male domestic co-responsibilities" and over "the representation of domestic labor as 'naturally' belonging to the feminine sex" in even radical feminist circles in Bolivia. Attempting to value labor, gender equality, and indigenous tradition, Rivera calls for an anti-essentialist feminist politics alongside a communitarian ethos that still retains a "politics of difference," rejecting outright nationalism while valorizing lived indigenous customs:

> As long as ethnic organizations are not capable of facing the phenomena of gendered oppression . . . the notion of human rights will remain empty rhetoric. If this is the case, we will have contributed to the prolongation of the State's aspiration to transform the consciousness of a Bolivian indigenous majority held in the 1980s into a consciousness of a minority that lives only off the crumbs of "development" and the unequal ecological and economic transactions within the *mestizo*-dominated power structure that has not substantially changed with the recent electoral events leading to the ascent of the first indigenous president. The implicit corollary to this entire argument points to the need for a simultaneous decolonization of

> both gender and indigeneity, of the quotidian and the political, by way of a theory and a practice that links alternative and pluralist notions of citizenship rights with rights inhering in traditional indigenous laws and customs, as much in legislation as in the everyday and private practices of the people.[53]

The strategy Rivera sketches to make things "come out right" for women is both more radical and more specific than "spiritually based nationalism." It is not enough, she suggests, to embrace indigenous nationalism; indigenous movements must be decolonized, freed entirely from development ideology, the reactive nationalism it provoked, and the gender binaries it so violently enforced in already unequal societies.

Notes

Agradezco mucho a Nila Heredia, Felipa Huanca Llupanqui, Julieta Paredes, Silvia Rivera Cusicanqui y Mercedes Bernabé Colqué. Thanks very much also to Elora Chowdhury and especially Patricia Stuelke.

1. Jorge Sanjinés, "Revolutionary Cinema: The Bolivian Experience," in *Cinema and Social Change in Latin America*, ed. Julianne Burton, (Austin: University of Texas Press, 1986), 45–47.
2. James Siekmeier, "Sacrificial Llama? The Expulsion of the Peace Corps from Bolivia in 1971," *Pacific Historical Review* 69.1 (February 2000): 65–87.
3. Ann Laura Stoler, *Race and the Education of Desire: Foucault and the Colonial Order of Things* (Durham, N.C.: Duke University Press, 1995), 136; Michel Foucault, *History of Sexuality*, vol. 1, *Introduction* (New York: Vintage, 1990).
4. See Gail Bederman, *Manliness and Civilization: A Cultural History of Gender and Race in the United States, 1880–1917* (Chicago: University of Chicago Press, 1996); Amy Kaplan, *The Anarchy of Empire in the Making of U.S. Culture* (Cambridge, Mass.: Harvard University Press, 2005); Shelley Streeby, *American Sensations: Class, Empire, and the Production of Popular Culture* (Berkeley: University of California Press, 2002); Laura Wexler, *Tender Violence: Domestic Visions in an Age of U.S. Imperialism* (Chapel Hill: University of North Carolina Press, 2000).
5. Jasbir Puar, *Terrorist Assemblages: Homonationalism in Queer Times* (Durham, N.C.: Duke University Press, 2007), 112–13. Mary Renda and Laura Briggs have provocatively traced early twentieth-century moments of U.S. imperialist production of sexualized and racialized bodies, but focus more on reconstructing untold historical narratives than on tracing epistemic shifts. See Renda, *Taking Haiti* (Chapel Hill: University of North Carolina Press, 2000); and Briggs, *Reproducing Empire* (Berkeley: University of California Press, 2002).
6. María Josefina Saldaña-Portillo, *The Revolutionary Imagination in the Americas and the Age of Development* (Durham, N.C.: Duke University Press, 2003).
7. Andrea Smith, *Conquest: Sexual Violence and American Indian Genocide* (Boston: South End Press, 2005), 8.
8. Andrea Smith, "American Studies without America: Native Feminisms and the Nation-State," *American Quarterly* 60.2 (June 2008): 312.
9. Walt Rostow, *Stages of Economic Growth: A Non-Communist Manifesto* (Cambridge: Cambridge University Press, 1960), 26.
10. David Milne, *America's Rasputin: Walt Rostow and the Vietnam War* (New York: Hill and Wang, 2008), 38.
11. Rostow, *Stages of Economic Growth*, 26–27.
12. Sargent Shriver, *Point of the Lance* (New York: Harper & Row, 1964), 35.

13. Shriver, Press Conference, November 18, 1961, JFK Library, Boston, Shriver Papers, box 28, folder 12.
14. Shriver, *Point of the Lance*, 1.
15. Silvia Rivera Cusicanqui, *Oppressed But Not Defeated: Peasant Struggles Among the Aymara and the Qhechwa in Bolivia, 1900–1980* (Geneva: United Nations Research Institute for Social Development, 1987), 53.
16. Herbert Klein, *Bolivia: The Evolution of a Multi-Ethnic Society* (Oxford: Oxford University Press, 1992), 238.
17. Ibid., 239.
18. Rivera, *Oppressed But Not Defeated*, 60.
19. See Marco Arnez, "Las Montañas sí cambian: Apuntes sobre cambio climático, colonialismo y cine boliviano," *El Colectivo* (Marzo 2009): 8–9.
20. Thomas Field (Ph.D. diss., London School of Economics, unpublished).
21. James Dunkerley, *Rebellion in the Veins: Political Struggle in Bolivia, 1952–1982* (London: Verso, 1984), 149.
22. Odd Arne Westad, *The Global Cold War: Third World Interventions and the Making of Our Times* (Cambridge: Cambridge University Press, 2005), 178.
23. James Frits, "The Peace Corps in Bolivia," JFKL RPCV Collection, box 36, folder 7.
24. In Michael Latham, *Modernization as Ideology: American Social Science and "Nation Building" in the Cold War Era* (Chapel Hill: University of North Carolina Press, 2000), 129.
25. Chad Bardone, letter to friends, June 25, 1965, Peace Corps Volunteer Papers, National Anthropological Archives, Box 10 Folder 30, Suitland, Md.
26. See Helene Clastres, *La Tierra Sin Mal: El Profetismo Tupí-Guarani* (Buenos Aires: Del Sol, 1975).
27. Baumann, "The National Community Development Programme in Bolivia and the Utilization of Peace Corps Volunteers," *Community Development Journal* 5.4 (October 1970): 194–95.
28. Terry West, "Anthropology: My Unrequited Love," in *Anthropology and the Peace Corps: Case Studies in Career Preparation*, Brian E. Schwimmer and D. Michael Warren, eds. (Ames: Iowa State University Press, 1993), 201.
29. Matthew Connolly, *Fatal Misconception: The Struggle to Control World Population* (Cambridge, Mass.: Harvard University Press, 2008), 194.
30. Arthur Schlesinger Jr., *A Thousand Days: John F. Kennedy in the White House* (1965; New York: Greenwich House, 1983), 188.
31. John F. Kennedy, "Special Message to the Congress on Foreign Aid," March 22, 1961, http://www.presidency.ucsb.edu/ws/index.php?pid=8545 (accessed May 24, 2010).
32. Connolly, *Fatal Misconception*, 199.
33. Ibid., 212.
34. "El Salvador Country Report," 1966, Office Files of the Latin America Regional Director, box 2, folder 1, National Archives, College Park, Maryland.
35. Baumann, letter to Dr. J. Fine, July 20, 1967, and Baumann, letter to Gary Peterson, August 29, 1967, in Baumann Papers, box 1, folder 2, LBJ Library, Austin, Texas.
36. Janet Pitts Brome, "Bolivia Journal, 1965–67," JFKL RPCV Collection, box 2, folder 12.
37. Connolly, *Fatal Misconception*, 205.
38. Rural *sindicatos* formed to implement the MNR's 1953 land reforms and subsequently became bodies of community and regional governance.
39. Rivera, *Oppressed But Not Defeated*, 117.
40. Ibid., 145.
41. "Tiwanaku Manifesto," 1973, in Rivera, *Oppressed But Not Defeated*, 169–77.
42. A preliminary reading of *Yawar Mallku* appears in my "At the Point of the Lance: Gender, Development, and the 1960s Peace Corps," in *New World Coming: The Sixties and the Shaping of Global Consciousness*, ed. Karin Dubinsky et al. (Toronto: Between the Lines, 2009), 326–329.
43. *Yawar Mallku* (*Sangre del condor*), VHS, directed by Jorge Sanjinés (1969, Argentina). My translations.
44. Sanjinés, "Revolutionary Cinema," 43.
45. Former MAS minister of health Nila Heredia, interview with author, December 10, 2009; Felipa Huanca Llupanqui, La Paz executive secretary of Confederación Nacional de Mujeres Campesinas Indígenas Bartolina Sisa, interview with author, January 23, 2010.

46. Domitila Barrios de Chungara, *Let Me Speak: Testimony of Domitila, a Woman of the Bolivian Mines* (New York: Monthly Review Press, 1978), 199–200.
47. Arturo Escobar, "Latin America at a Crossroads: Alternative Modernizations, Postliberalism, or Post-development?" (revised version of paper presented at "Violence and Reconciliation in Latin America: Human Rights, Memory, and Democracy" at University of Oregon, Eugene, January 31–February 2, 2008), 5.
48. Ibid., 44.
49. Ibid., 10–11.
50. Julieta Paredes, personal correspondence with the author, December 17, 2009. My translation.
51. See Inderpal Grewal, *Transnational America: Feminisms, Diasporas, Neoliberalisms* (Durham, N.C.: Duke University Press, 2005).
52. Escobar, "Latin America at a Crossroads."
53. Silvia Rivera Cusicanqui, "The Notion of 'Rights' and the Paradoxes of Postcolonial Modernity: Indigenous Peoples and Women in Bolivia," *Qui Parle* 18.2 (Spring/Summer 2010): 50–51.

Contributors

Hokulani K. Aikau

Hokulani K. Aikau is assistant professor of indigenous studies in the Department of Political Science at the University of Hawai'i at Mānoa. She writes and teaches in the fields of indigenous politics, contemporary Native Hawaiian politics, qualitative research methods, and feminist theory. She is working on a manuscript tentatively titled *Negotiations of Faith: Mormonism, Identity, and Native Hawaiian Struggles for Self-Determination.*

Ryan E. Burt

Ryan E. Burt is a lecturer in the Comparative History of Ideas Department and the Department of English at the University of Washington. His current book project examines early twentieth-century Lakota and Dakota autobiography in relation to the Dawes Act, the Indian New Deal, and the literary, ethnographic, and performative discourses producing "Indian expectations" in this era.

James H. Cox

James H. Cox is associate professor of English and the director of the Indigenous Studies Graduate Portfolio at the University of Texas at Austin and the coeditor of *SAIL* (*Studies in American Indian Literatures*). He is the author of *Muting White Noise: Native American and European American Novel Traditions* (2006, 2009) and is at work on a book titled *Literary Revolutions: American Indian Writers and Indigenous Mexico.*

Molly Geidel

Molly Geidel is a doctoral candidate in American studies at Boston University. She has published in the *Journal of Popular Music Studies,* the anthology *New World Coming: The Sixties and the Shaping of Global Consciousness,* and a translation in *Qui Parle: Critical Humanities and Social Sciences.* Her dissertation, *Point of the Lance: Gender and Development in the 1960s Peace Corps,* analyzes the Peace Corps and the discourses of modernization and heroic masculinity that the agency embodied and promoted in its iconic decade.

Wen Jin

Wen Jin is an assistant professor of English at Columbia University. Her research fields include Asian American literature, twentieth-century American literature, transpacific writings, and critical race and ethnicity theories. She has completed a book manuscript titled *Bridging the Chasm: An Asian Americanist Critique of U.S. and Chinese Multiculturalisms*, which studies fictional writings concerned with the racial and ethnic politics of the United States and China in the post–cold war era.

Jean J. Kim

Jean J. Kim is an assistant professor of history at Dartmouth College. Her research interests include colonial and domestic intersections of race and empire, U.S. imperial medicine, and Asian American history. She is completing a book manuscript on U.S. imperialism and health care on Hawai'i's sugar plantations, with a concentration on the territorial period, titled *Empire at the Crossroads of Modernity: Plantation Medicine and Hygienic Assimilation in Hawai'i, 1898–1948*.

Paul Lai

Paul Lai teaches classes on Asian American literature, American imprisonment writing, and American literatures outside the continental United States. His current research project focuses on the sounds that articulate Asian American identities to political claims of racial difference and national belonging. His next project considers visual technologies of Native and Asian bodies in North America.

Danika Medak-Saltzman

Danika Medak-Saltzman is an assistant professor in the Department of Ethnic Studies at the University of Colorado, Boulder. Her work seeks to illuminate Native peoples' roles as equal actors in unequal histories and to nuance and complicate our understandings of Indigenous Studies, "America," and colonial interactions. Her current book project is tentatively titled *Trading Colonial Knowledge, Reclaiming Indigenous Experience: Native Peoples, Visual Culture, and Colonial Projects in Japan and the United States, 1860–1904*.

Glen M. Mimura

Glen M. Mimura is an associate professor of film and media studies and Asian American studies, as well as associate dean of graduate study and research,

School of Humanities, at the University of California, Irvine. He is the author of *Ghostlife of Third Cinema: Asian American Film and Video* (2009).

JoAnna Poblete-Cross

JoAnna Poblete-Cross is an assistant professor of history at the University of Wyoming. Her research focuses on issues of U.S. empire in locations including Hawai'i, the Philippines, Puerto Rico, and American Sāmoa. She studies the impact of government structures and policies on the daily labor and migration experiences of people who have come under U.S. authority. Her first book manuscript is *Neither Citizens nor Foreigners: Filipino and Puerto Rican Labor Recruits to Hawai'i, 1900–1940.* She is also working on a book on immigration, tuna canneries, and U.S. authority in American Sāmoa.

Judy Rohrer

Judy Rohrer grew up in Hawai'i and received her PhD from the University of Hawai'i's political science department in 2005. She has written previously about Hawai'i in *Ethnic and Racial Studies* and *The Contemporary Pacific.* Her book *Haoles in Hawai'i* is forthcoming from the University of Hawai'i Press.

Dean Itsuji Saranillio

Dean Itsuji Saranillio is a University of California President's Postdoctoral Fellow in the Department of Ethnic Studies at the University of California, Riverside. He received his PhD from the Program in American Culture at the University of Michigan and has been published in two anthologies, *Positively No Filipinos Allowed* and *Asian Settler Colonialism,* and in the *Journal of Asian American Studies.* He is working on a book titled *The Theatricality of the Settler State: Hawai'i Statehood and the Liberal Politics of Empire Making.*

Andrea Smith

Andrea Smith is the author of *Native Americans and the Christian Right: The Gendered Politics of Unlikely Alliances* (2008). She is associate professor of media and cultural studies at UC Riverside.

Lindsey Claire Smith

Lindsey Claire Smith is an assistant professor of English and affiliate of American studies and women's studies at Oklahoma State University. She teaches courses in Native American, Global Indigenous, African American, and American literatures and recently taught a short course on urban Indigenous literatures at the University of Paderborn in Germany. She is working on a book project on urban Indigenous literatures. Her first book, *Indians, Environment, and Identity on the Borders of American Literature*, was published in 2008.

Jeanne Sokolowski

Jeanne Sokolowski, a former Fulbright junior researcher in South Korea, lived for three years in the Kansai region of Japan and is now a PhD candidate in English at Indiana University Bloomington, where she is working on a dissertation that puts contemporary Native American and Asian American literature in dialogue. Her work on citizenship and the Japanese American internment has appeared in the journal *Multi-Ethnic Literature of the United States* (*MELUS*), and she has a piece forthcoming in *Seeds of Change: Critical Essays on Barbara Kingsolver.*

Stephen Hong Sohn

Stephen Hong Sohn is an assistant professor of English at Stanford University. He is coeditor of *Transnational Asian American Literature: Sites and Transits* (2006) and has edited or coedited three special journal issues on topics related to Asian American literature and culture. He is at work on a manuscript that examines contemporary Asian American fiction and the politics of narration.

Alice Te Punga Somerville

Alice Te Punga Somerville (Te Ati Awa) is a senior lecturer at Victoria University of Wellington, with specialization in Maori, Pacific, and Indigenous writing in English. Born and raised in Aotearoa, New Zealand, she received her PhD in English and American Indian studies at Cornell University and spent time at the University of Hawai'i at Manoa during her doctoral studies. She is putting the finishing touches on her first book *Once Were Pacific*, which explores Maori articulation of connection with the Pacific, and is working on her second book project, *Kanohi ki te Kanohi: Indigenous-Indigenous Encounters.* She also writes the occasional poem.

Index